EVOLUTION, FEMINISM, AND ROMANTIC FICTION

Romantic fiction has long been dismissed as trivial and denounced for peddling supposedly oppressive patriarchal myths of heterosexual love and marriage. Despite such criticism, the popularity of romantic fiction has only increased in recent decades.

Drawing on research from the evolutionary sciences, Ania Grant proposes that narrative patterns of romantic stories and their enduring appeal reflect the importance of love as a fundamental human drive. She examines two of the most successful and critically scrutinized romantic narratives of the past 200 years, Jane Austen's classic novel *Pride and Prejudice* and the hit television series *Sex and the City*, and argues that such texts simulate the cognitive and emotional complexities of mate choice—one of the most consequential decisions from both a biological and a cultural perspective. Her biocultural analysis aligns the interpretation of romantic fiction with the feminist ideals of female autonomy and gender equality. It also suggests that positive identification with romantic heroines gives audiences the hope and energy to pursue the transformation of gender relations in real life.

The book will be of interest to anyone who ever wondered why so many women (and some men) around the world are enthralled by romantic stories. It will also appeal to anyone who has ever been inspired by romantic happy endings to strive for a world in which men and women love and cooperate with each other—even if it seems like a utopian ideal while the war of the sexes rages on.

Ania Grant is a Professional Teaching Fellow and an Honorary Research Fellow in the Schools of Humanities and Psychological Medicine at the University of Auckland, New Zealand. Her research combines evolutionary and feminist perspectives, as well as qualitative and quantitative methods.

"A triumph of clear thinking, wide knowledge, and astute reading. Darwin rightly called *On the Origin of Species* "one long argument." As a feminist and an evolutionist, Grant begins with one long argument showing the value of romantic love and romantic fiction for feminists and everybody else, before her subtle close readings reveal just how much we can learn from two of the most successful of romantic fictions, *Pride and Prejudice* and *Sex in the City*."

**Brian Boyd, Distinguished Professor Emeritus of English,
University of Auckland, New Zealand**

"*Evolution, Feminism, and Romantic Fiction* cements Ania Grant as the preeminent voice on romantic storytelling. Merging feminist theory with bio-cultural insights, Grant reveals powerful connections between *Pride and Prejudice* and *Sex and the City*, redefining the role of women's agency, individuality, and romance across history. Revolutionary, insightful, and unforgettable—this book will be an essential reference for years to come."

**Maryanne Fisher, Professor of Psychology,
Saint Mary's University, Canada**

EVOLUTION, FEMINISM, AND ROMANTIC FICTION

From Mr. Darcy to Mr. Big

Ania Grant

LONDON AND NEW YORK

Designed cover image: @Getty

First published 2025
by Routledge
4 Park Square, Milton Park, Abingdon, Oxon OX14 4RN

and by Routledge
605 Third Avenue, New York, NY 10158

Routledge is an imprint of the Taylor & Francis Group, an informa business

© 2025 Ania Grant

The right of Ania Grant to be identified as author of this work has been asserted in accordance with sections 77 and 78 of the Copyright, Designs and Patents Act 1988.

All rights reserved. No part of this book may be reprinted or reproduced or utilised in any form or by any electronic, mechanical, or other means, now known or hereafter invented, including photocopying and recording, or in any information storage or retrieval system, without permission in writing from the publishers.

Trademark notice: Product or corporate names may be trademarks or registered trademarks, and are used only for identification and explanation without intent to infringe.

British Library Cataloguing-in-Publication Data
A catalogue record for this book is available from the British Library

ISBN: 9781032342030 (hbk)
ISBN: 9781032342023 (pbk)
ISBN: 9781003320982 (ebk)

DOI: 10.434/9781003320982

Typeset in Galliard
by KnowledgeWorks Global Ltd.

*To Steven, the love of my life and the best choice I ever made.
And to Alex—May the choices you make fill your life with love.*

CONTENTS

List of acronyms and abbreviations   ix
Preface and acknowledgements   x

Introduction   1

PART I: LOVE, CHOICE, AND ROMANTIC FICTION   **17**

1 Love: A fundamental human drive   19

2 Choice: From sexual selection to emotional intelligence   33

3 Romantic fiction: Tales of female mate choice   48

PART II: *PRIDE AND PREJUDICE*   **65**

Introduction to *Pride and Prejudice*: "The lady has no choice?"   67

4 Lydia Bennet: "Tenderly flirting with at least six officers at once"   72

5 Charlotte Lucas: "I am not romantic ... I ask only a comfortable home"   85

6 Jane Bennet: "[Her] feelings, though fervent, were little displayed"   97

7 Elizabeth Bennet: "A union ... to the advantage of both"   110

PART III: *SEX AND THE CITY*   **127**

    Introduction to *Sex and the City*: "Spoiled by choices?"   129

  8 Samantha Jones: "I'm try-sexual, I'll try anything once"   134

  9 Charlotte York: "You fantasize about a man with a Park Avenue apartment and a nice stock portfolio"   145

10 Miranda Hobbes: "Soulmates only exist in the Hallmark aisle of Duane Reade Drugs"   153

11 Carrie Bradshaw: "Tell me I'm the one"   163

12 Mothers and others   174

    Conclusion   183

Index   *188*

LIST OF ACRONYMS AND ABBREVIATIONS

The following abbreviations are used in citations for Jane Austen's texts:

- E   *Emma* (1815/2003)
- LF   *Love and Friendship* (2003)
- LS   *Lady Susan* (1871/1984)
- MP   *Mansfield Park* (1814/1998)
- NA   *Northanger Abbey* (1818/2003)
- P   *Persuasion* (1818/1998)
- PP   *Pride and Prejudice* (1813/2003)
- SS   *Sense and Sensibility* (1811/2003)
- W   *The Watsons* (1871/1985)

Citations for the television show of *Sex and the City* follow the format of Season number: Episode number. The title of each cited episode is included only in the first citation in a chapter.

PREFACE AND ACKNOWLEDGEMENTS

Unlike Elizabeth Bennet, I fell in love with Mr. Darcy the moment I first met him while reading *Pride and Prejudice* for an undergraduate course in English literature almost 30 years ago. A few years later, I was a bit more circumspect about Mr. Big of *Sex and the City* but, like Carrie Bradshaw, I eventually fell for him too. But each chapter of an Austen's novel, each episode of a television series like *Sex and the City* felt like a guilty pleasure. I could not reconcile my thorough enjoyment of these and similar stories with the kind of analyses of them I was exposed to in English and Media Studies departments dominated by poststructuralist and feminist theories: Apparently, together with millions of other fans of such romantic narratives, I was being duped by the oppressive patriarchal myth of romantic love. Worse, by buying into these supposedly regressive, disempowering romantic fantasies, I was being complicit in my own subjugation. Could this really be true? I have always considered myself a feminist—and still do—but I had a nagging feeling that when it came to the question of romantic love and romantic fiction, feminism might have got it wrong.

While searching for other possible answers, I was hired as a Teaching Assistant at the University of Auckland for a course "Literature and Science" taught by Brian Boyd, a pioneer of the evolutionary approach to art and fiction. It was Brian's work that provided the inspiration for my PhD thesis which became the basis for this book. I simply cannot thank him enough for the time, expertise, and encouragement he so generously gave me during every step of this very lengthy process. Without him, this book would not exist.

But adopting the evolutionary approach does not mean abandoning the feminist perspective. In this regard, I have immensely benefitted from the constructive criticism of Annamarie Jagose (a feminist and queer studies scholar) and Joanne Wilkes (an expert on Austen and other nineteenth-century female writers), both of whom co-supervised parts of my thesis and provided vital support at different phases of my academic journey.

So, throughout this book, I consider romantic fiction from a bio-cultural, evolutionary-feminist perspective, striving to combine important insights from both sides. This is a tricky balance to strike. Given the ongoing institutional and ideological divisions between the two camps, it is also not easy to find an academic community equally open to both perspectives. I was very fortunate to find early in my doctoral studies a friendly forum in which to test my ideas: the conferences of the NorthEastern Evolutionary Psychology Society (NEEPS) and its sister organization Feminist Evolutionary Perspectives Society (FEPS). Special thanks go to Maryanne Fisher and Daniel Kruger, evolutionary psychologists with an interest in fiction, for helping me develop my ideas through fruitful collaborations. Indeed, Maryanne's enthusiastic support for my research has been invaluable and her own work inspirational.

At various stages of the project, I was also privileged to share and refine parts of my argument at the conferences of the Human Behavior & Evolution Society (HBES), the Australian Research Council Centre of Excellence for the History of Emotions, and most recently at the workshop "From Evolution to Cognition to Fiction" organized by Nicolas Baumard at the Insitute Jean Nicod, École Normale Supérieure in Paris. I am very grateful for all their support.

I would also like to thank my colleague and friend Severi Luoto for stimulating (occasionally heated) conversations about biology and culture, and for many other (usually anxious) ones about our respective academic futures. And I gratefully acknowledge Joseph Carroll, Mathias Clasen, Rina Kim, Jennifer Kirby, and Heidi Logan for their advice on the book writing and publishing process.

Let me also make this disclaimer: This book is about women, men, and heterosexual relationships—not because I think that this is the only way to be, or to love—but because this is the focus of the texts I analyse and because such focus aligns with my own identity and experience. However, I know that many members of the rainbow community have enjoyed *Pride and Prejudice* and *Sex and the City* (just as I have enjoyed such stories as *The L Word* and *Call Me by Your Name*), and so I hope that they may also find some of my ideas relevant to their interpretations of these texts. Although the personal and social challenges we face can be very different, I believe that regardless of our sexual orientation or gender identity, most people recognize and relate to the passion, intimacy, and commitment of romantic love. Indeed, unlike many previous interpretations of romantic fiction, this book takes seriously into account what we know about not only widespread similarities but also individual variations in human desires, emotions, and behaviours.

For this reason, the book will be of interest to anyone who ever wondered why so many women (and some men) around the world spend so much of their time enthralled by romantic stories. It will be especially appealing to anyone who ever felt that the casual dismissals and condescending critiques of such fiction are patronizing and misconceived. Most importantly, it is for anyone who has ever been inspired by romantic happy endings to continue to strive for a world in which men and women respect each other's differences and use them as the basis for mutually enriching cooperation—even if it seems like a utopian ideal while the war of the sexes rages on.

Finally, my deepest love and gratitude go to my husband, Steven, who prefers to read the news rather than Austen's novels and leaves the room when I watch *Sex and the City*, but who has been invariably supportive throughout the sometimes-tortuous process of writing this book. More importantly, he has been the constant real-life reminder that men can be both strong and kind, decisive and sensitive, sexy and devoted. Without him, this book would not make sense.

INTRODUCTION

Romantic fiction: Not "dope for dupes" but tales of female mate choice

Romantic fiction has long had bad press: From early sentimental novels to the latest chick lit or Hollywood rom-coms, it has usually been dismissed as trite, trivial, and escapist. Although Austen's works are now considered great literature, they were initially treated with the same "patronising condescension" that women's fiction in general has received (Waldron, 2005, p. 84). Since the 1970s, feminist critics have argued against such dismissive attitudes towards women's stories and tried to understand their popularity and cultural significance (e.g., Ang, 1985; Ferriss & Young, 2008, 2006a; Gilbert & Gubar, 1979/2000; Harzewski, 2011; Johnson, 1988; Modleski, 1982/2008; Radway, 1984/1991; Roach, 2016; Weisser, 2013; Whelehan, 2005). Many noted that romantic fiction voices valid concerns about gender relations from a specifically female perspective. Nevertheless, whether analysing canonical novels or so-called supermarket romances, feminists remain very critical of the main aspect of popular women's fiction: the quest for love and Mr. Right.

Their objection is largely based on the view that romantic love is a relatively recent Western ideological invention. This position is not exclusively feminist but one widely held within the humanities and the social sciences, and situated within a broader theoretical framework which sees both emotion and gender as arbitrary social constructions (Bloch, 1991; Lewis, 1936/1948; de Rougemont, 1939/1983). Within this paradigm, feminists interpret romantic love and monogamous heterosexuality as oppressive patriarchal myths imposed on women in order to control them (Firestone, 1979; Greer, 1970; Rich, 1980). They condemn romantic fiction for not only reflecting these myths but actively perpetuating them: By presenting heterosexual love and marriage as women's destiny and greatest fulfilment, romantic fiction reconciles women to oppressive patriarchal institutions; by idealizing heroine's passivity, it encourages such passivity in the readers; and by transforming the hero's arrogance or aloofness into love and devotion, it justifies male sexual aggression and social dominance.

Despite such harsh criticism, consciousness-raising efforts, and increased socio-economic independence, millions of women around the world continue to read, watch, and enjoy romantic stories. Indeed, some feminist scholars have noted, with a degree of incredulity and dismay, that the one area which has been largely immune to the feminist critique is women's appetite for romance (Gill & Walker, 1993, p. 69; see also Snitow, 1979). Some admit that this resistance indicates notable gaps between feminist explanations and women's own aspirations for love, sex, and intimate relationships (Teo, 2020, p. 476; Whelehan, 2005, p. 205).

Drawing on recent research from evolutionary sciences, I propose that narrative patterns of romantic fiction and its enduring appeal reflect a fundamental human concern with romantic love as a universal emotional mechanism for mate choice and pair-bonding, which is the basis for the uniquely human cooperative reproduction and ultra-sociality (Buss, 2018; Chapais, 2013; H. E. Fisher, 2016; Fletcher et al., 2015). In particular, romantic fiction foregrounds the importance of female mate choice and the complexities of female sexual strategies in highly variable cultural and personal circumstances. Thus, I argue that by highlighting female autonomy, individuality, and power, such a biocultural explanation aligns romantic fiction with feminist ideals. Far from promoting passive submission to patriarchal order or male desire, such fiction posits female characters as autonomous, proactive decision-makers navigating the constraints of their biological and cultural realities, challenging male domineering tendencies, and influencing the social world around them. In contrast to the view that romantic fiction is mindlessly escapist, I suggest that it is a site of cognitive and emotional simulation and experimentation. It gives audiences opportunities to consider risks and rewards associated with different kinds of intimate relationships, clarify their own preferences and priorities, and vicariously experience highly positive, as well as problematic, solutions to the mate selection process. This process is vitally important for both biological and cultural reasons, on both an individual and a collective level. For most people, being able to attract and retain an appropriate partner is crucial to their personal happiness, social standing, and reproductive success. And the cumulative force of such choices affects the shape of our communities and the evolutionary direction of the physical, psychological, and social characteristics of our species.

To illustrate these points, I examine two of the most successful and critically scrutinized romantic narratives of the past 200 years: Jane Austen's classic novel *Pride and Prejudice* and the hit television series *Sex and the City* (alongside a range of examples from other Austen's novels and modern chick lit or TV). Although created two centuries apart on different continents and in different media, both texts present a compelling and strikingly similar picture of female sociosexuality. While the female characters of the two stories live in quite different cultural, political, and economic environments, they face very similar social, psychological, and moral conflicts: between physical and emotional needs, between short-term and long-term goals, between desires for autonomy and connection, between individual aspirations and collective norms. Humans have faced such dilemmas throughout our evolutionary history, and modern research suggests that the emotional and cognitive mechanisms we use to solve them have deep evolutionary roots but are also exquisitely sensitive to the ever-changing contexts. Moreover, it seems that storytelling has played a crucial role in helping us think through these dilemmas, simulate potential outcomes, and promote those solutions that over generations and across cultures have proven most successful (Boyd, 2009, 2018; Carroll, 2004; Dutton, 2009; Mar & Oatley, 2008; Pinker, 1997).

Incorporating current knowledge from such fields as evolutionary, developmental, and personality psychology, biological anthropology, attachment theory, sexuality studies, and research on emotions, I compare four key female characters from *Pride and Prejudice* with the four protagonists of *Sex and the City*. Each character represents a distinct response to the recurring dilemmas outlined above, a different way of balancing the conflicting motivations. At the same time, however, each character reveals key psychological, cognitive, and behavioural patterns that underscore female psychosexual priorities, some of which may not be fully within our conscious control. These include the force of female sexual desire, the necessity to secure resources, the need to assess a man's commitment, and the utmost importance of kindness, intelligence, and cooperation in intimate relationships.

My biocultural analysis not only makes the study of romantic fiction more consistent with and more relevant to current knowledge in other disciplines but also reveals its alignment with the feminist ideals of female autonomy and gender equality. Romantic heroines, regardless of personal or cultural circumstances, have the strength of character to resist antagonistic or exploitative male tactics and valorize those male traits that are conducive to cooperative, equitable relations both within the romantic pair and outside of it. Positive identification with such characters appears to increase audience members' sense of control and hope for the future (Gregson & Lois, 2020; Radway, 1984/1991; Span, 2022; Thurston, 1987; van Monsjou & Mar, 2019)—and psychologists agree that both of these are important for our emotional well-being and our willingness to act in pursuit of our goals. Thus, the increased popularity of romantic fiction in recent decades is likely not a backlash against feminism but both a symptom of and a further inspiration for change in gender relations.

Evolutionary sciences and feminist politics: Irreconcilable differences or friends with benefits?

The feminist and evolutionary paradigms may seem incompatible, even irreconcilable. Both sides have been dismissive and at times openly hostile to each other, but each has also offered valid critiques and identified points of common interest (e.g., Buss & Schmitt, 2011; Davis, 2021; Eagly, 2018; Fausto-Sterling, 1992, 2001; M. L. Fisher et al., 2020; Garcia & Heywood, 2016; Haraway, 1989, 1991; Hubbard, 1990; O'Neill, 2015; Smith & Konik, 2011; Vandermassen, 2005).

Biology vs. culture

The main schism is often conceived of as the dichotomy between culture and biology, where culture is seen as highly localized and malleable and biology as universal and fixed. But both sides point out that this dichotomy is an oversimplification. Feminists (like most social constructivists) have been deeply suspicious of any biologically based explanations of human behaviour. And for good reasons: In the past, references to nature were used to justify women's subordinate social position, and even modern science is still plagued by entrenched androcentric biases (Saini, 2017). Therefore, feminists emphasize instead the role of social structures and culturally specific discourses in shaping our reality. Evolutionists, meanwhile, are concerned that feminism's disregard for biology and reliance on outdated models of human psychosocial development (such as Freudian psychoanalysis) paint an inaccurate picture of human behaviour and motives and are actually counter-productive to feminist goals (Buss & Schmitt, 2011; Vandermassen, 2005). Indeed, as the feminist philosopher Elizabeth Grosz points out, "there is a certain absurdity in objecting to the notion of nature or biology itself if this is (even in part) what we are and will always be" (2005, p. 13). However, far from ignoring biology, feminism has always been concerned with how the biological, material body functions within its socio-cultural context and how this affects female existence (Fausto-Sterling, 1992; Firestone, 1979; Haraway, 1991; Hubbard, 1990; Price & Shildrick, 1999; Radtke, 2017; Wilson, 2004). And far from ignoring culture, many evolutionists see it as a crucial force in human evolution (Henrich, 2016; Jablonka & Lamb, 2014; Richerson & Boyd, 2005): Genes and culture co-evolve, each exerting selective pressure on the other.

Feminists criticize biological explanations as essentialist and reductionist; evolutionists retaliate by saying that feminism's insistence on plurality renders it incoherent. Once again, the opposition between pluralism and essentialism is too simplistic and unfair to both sides. Feminism's very existence depends on identifying the category "woman" and testifies to the need for generalizing both within and outside of this category, even if one of feminism's main contributions to modern knowledge is the continuing challenge to the limits and validity of these categories and generalizations (Jagose, 2009). These feminist challenges have had a significant impact on the scientific understanding of the variations in women's psychosexuality and their role in human evolution, not least by stoking scientific interest in female-related issues thus far neglected, such as female sexual variability, assertiveness, and competitiveness (Diamond, 2008; M. L. Fisher, 2014; Hrdy, 1981/1999; Roughgarden, 2004). But regardless of feminist influences, the very essence of evolutionary logic is based on continuous modification, diversification, and flexibility of all life forms, even while evolutionary research also seeks to understand species-typical traits and broadly applicable biological patterns. Thus, in both evolution and feminism, there is a tension between individuation and generalization, whether at the level of species or societies.

Another frequent source of misunderstanding is the idea that culture is flexible and dynamic while genes are fixed or at least extremely slow to change. It is true that some of our genes have not changed for millions of years, and we share many of them with other primates and mammals, but others can be modified within a few generations or be switched on or off within one lifetime. And while genes exert control over our behaviour, the opposite is also true: Our behavioural choices create new environmental niches which in turn exert new selection pressures and alter our genes (Jablonka & Lamb, 2014; Odling-Smee et al., 2003).[1] Evolution is much faster and nimbler than we first believed it to be as organisms, genes, and environments are locked in a constant feedback loop (Bonnet, 2022). On the other hand, culture can be very stubborn. Some concepts—such as the subordination of women and gendered division of labour—have survived for millennia across many human societies even though socio-political arrangements have undergone radical transformations, from foraging to feudal, to liberal democratic or communist (Richards, 1994, p. 420).

If we accept that nature is not "the polarized opposite of culture but … its underlying condition" (Grosz, 2005, p. 7), we can analyse patriarchy not as an arbitrary cultural construct but as the human expression of a long-standing biological conflict between the sexes (Smuts, 1995). This is far from saying that women's subordination is natural and permanent; just as sexual conflict manifests in varying degrees across different species, gender inequality exists at different levels within human societies (Saini, 2023). Humans are supremely creative and flexible, so the future of our gender relations does not need to be determined by either biology or history, but in order to transform gender relations, we need to understand all factors that shape them, including their evolutionary roots.

Politics vs. science

This brings me to another important antagonism between feminist and evolutionary approaches. Feminists are explicitly oriented towards social change and accuse evolutionists (especially evolutionary psychologists) of preventing such a change by perpetuating sexist stereotypes as biological truths and reinforcing the political status quo as the "natural" order of things (Fausto-Sterling, 1992; Fine, 2010; Hubbard, 1990). Evolutionists defend their work saying that it is descriptive and agenda-free; it does not aim to prescribe correct behaviour or pass judgement. But given the well-established human inclination to see "natural" as "good", as it "ought to be", scientists must never forget their ethical and moral responsibilities. Nor can they ignore the fact that even ground-breaking science is situated within the ideological context of its time.

The evolutionary view of women is a good example of this: When Darwin proposed his theory of sexual selection, highlighting the importance of female sexual agency, it was vehemently rejected and for the next 100 years evolutionists generally dismissed or ignored it, largely because of the prevailing view of women as passive and inferior (Cronin, 1991). As Anne Fausto-Sterling (2001) points out, generations of male scientists were "'unable' to see what today seems obvious". Even in modern evolutionary psychology, the picture of women is still incomplete and distorted in its overemphasis on female beauty and sexual reticence on the one hand and its relative neglect of female intelligence, resourcefulness, and competitiveness on the other (Burch, 2020). Research correcting these omissions and distortions has been facilitated by the social changes prompted by feminism (e.g., by allowing more female primatologists and anthropologists to conduct field research focusing on female behaviours). In turn, this continually improving scientific understanding can be used to solidify and further women's rights; indeed, it provides some of the strongest arguments for gender equality (Hrdy, 1981/1999, 2024; Konner, 2015).

More and more important research combines the evolutionary and feminist perspectives and recognizes that both disciplines have much to offer to each other (e.g., Campbell, 2002; M. L. Fisher et al., 2013; Gowaty, 2003; Hrdy, 1981/1999, 2024; Konner, 2015; Smuts, 1995; Vandermassen, 2005). This work challenges the hitherto accepted assumptions about female passivity, coyness, and dependence. It uncovers strong evidence of female sexual assertiveness and social competitiveness, of the evolutionary impact of female resource gathering (as opposed to male hunting), and the crucial role of post-menopausal women. It also stresses that human psychology and behaviour are highly variable between individuals and heavily dependent on environmental conditions, which are partially constituted by culture.

Some of the deep epistemological differences between feminist and evolutionary paradigms may never be fully resolved, but those interested in a productive dialogue have suggested ways in which progress can be made; for example, by treating the two approaches as not competing but complimentary levels of analysis within the so-called "extended synthesis" which sees nature and culture as inextricably connected (Garcia & Heywood, 2016; see also Davis, 2021). Importantly, as Grosz argues, the fundamental concepts of evolution—natural and sexual selection driven by individual variation—provide a mode of modification "which may prove helpful in feminist struggles to transform existing social relations and their concomitant value systems" (2005, p. 15).

At the heart of evolutionary and sexual selection theories are questions about the relation between sex and power, about female choice and agency, about the conflict and cooperation between the sexes. Obviously, these considerations are also central to feminist thought. Both feminists and evolutionists note that our individual lives, and our societies, are shaped by arrangements around sexual and family relations: In what circumstances and with whom we can have sex, establish a formal relationship (such as marriage), or have children—and who will be responsible for rearing those children. Both sides agree that for most of the human history, men have used their physical, economic, and political power to control female sexuality, while women have used various strategies to maintain as much sexual and social autonomy as possible. Finally, both sides recognize that humans use stories—from fairy tales to ideology—to help us understand and give meaning to our existence, and that the stories we construct have the power to shape our perception of the world and our own identity.

Overview of Part I

The significant, if imperfect, overlaps between feminist and evolutionary perspectives in relation to romantic love, the notion of choice, and romantic fiction are explored in Chapters 1, 2, and 3, respectively, forming the first, theoretical part of this book. Each chapter starts with a summary of the most pertinent feminist arguments and then develops the evolutionary understanding of these concepts. I challenge much of the dominant feminist interpretations of romantic love in life and fiction not because I disagree with feminist ideals but to demonstrate that an evolutionary reading reconciles romantic love with feminist politics.

In Chapter 1, I summarize the feminist arguments about love, heterosexuality, and marriage which have been most detrimental to the understanding of romantic fiction: The idea that romantic love is a recent invention of Western patriarchy, facilitating the subordination of women, and that heterosexual relationships are inevitably oppressive for women. I note that these views are not shared by all feminists: Some see the transformative potential of love as a powerful tool to overcome patriarchy. This more positive view is supported by current understanding of love in evolutionary sciences and related disciplines. Love is a fundamental human drive combining sexual passion, emotional intimacy, and long-term commitment. It can mediate sex differences and alleviate gender conflict. As such, it is both the cornerstone and the pinnacle of human cooperation not only within individual couples but also within and across communities.

In Chapter 2, I underscore the notion of individual choice as a key element for both feminism and evolution, and a prerequisite for change of any kind. Although feminists are critical of neoliberal individualism for ignoring social constraints, they rightly see lack of choice as an obvious sign of oppression and advocate for access to a greater variety of options for women. Similarly, variation and choice are at the heart of evolutionary logic. I focus mostly on the idea of female mate choice as a sign of women's autonomy, individuality, and power. Through their sexual choices, women influence which male traits will be passed on to the next generations, and in this way play a crucial role in shaping the characteristics of the human species. Finally, I describe the role of love as a cognitive and emotional mechanism of mate selection, promoting those mate choices that are most likely to result in equitable and harmonious gender relations.

Chapter 3 considers how feminist and evolutionary approaches to love and choice influence interpretations of romantic fiction and presents the main argument of this book. Since many feminists condemn romantic love, they also condemn romantic fiction as a form of patriarchal propaganda. Although many admit that such fiction highlights female concerns about male-female relationships, the heroine's preoccupation with heterosexual love remains highly problematic, if not contemptible. For biocultural critics, this preoccupation reflects the fundamental importance of love and sex in the human motivational system. Far from being an invention of Western modernity, the romantic plot dominates in all known literary traditions, and the romantic union which culminates such plots is overwhelmingly associated with the idea of happiness, harmony, and hope. Feminine romantic fiction focalizes the issue of gender relations through the female perspective, highlighting female agency in the process of mate choice and the importance of love as the basis for gender cooperation. Finally, it gives audiences hope necessary to seek change in their own lives.

From *Pride and Prejudice* to *Sex and the City*

The understanding of romantic love, female choice, and romantic fiction provides a theoretical basis for my analysis of *Pride and Prejudice* in Part II of the book and *Sex and the City* in Part III. The pairing of Austen's canonical novel with the hit television series may seem surprising, but the enormous and enduring popularity of the two texts, as well as the vast amount of critical attention each has attracted, speak powerfully about their appeal to female imagination and their status as cultural icons.

Austen's prominence does not require much elaboration: Her unprecedented popularity has already been thoroughly examined (Harman, 2009; Johnson, 2012), and an overview of the critical studies of her fiction runs into hundreds of pages (Mazzeno, 2011). *Pride and Prejudice*, the story of how the spirited Elizabeth Bennet comes to marry the rich and reserved Mr. Darcy, is unquestionably Austen's best known and best liked novel. In fact, almost 200 years after its publication, it topped a BBC online survey as England's favourite book ("*Pride and Prejudice* is top read", 2007). It has been frequently adapted to stage and screen and heavily scrutinized by literary critics and scholars (for overviews see Mazzeno, 2012; Wilkes, 2012).

Sex and the City, focused on the friendship of four women, Carrie Bradshaw, Samantha Jones, Miranda Hobbes, and Charlotte York, and their romantic relationships, is not of the same vintage or literary prestige, but its immense impact on contemporary women's fiction and culture in general is widely acknowledged (Akass & McCabe, 2004; Armstrong, 2018; Evelina, 2022; Harzewski, 2011; Jermyn, 2009). It started in 1994 as a series of articles by Candace Bushnell for the *New York Observer* about the social and sexual exploits of rich Manhattanites. A selection of these articles was published as a best-selling book in 1996. But what turned *Sex and the City* into a global phenomenon was the television show, loosely inspired by the book, which aired from 1998 to 2004 on HBO, an American subscription-only channel. It was followed by two blockbuster films bearing the same title in 2008 and 2010, two book prequels, *The Carrie Diaries* and *Summer and the City* (Bushnell, 2010, 2011), also adapted into a television show (2013–2014), and a television sequel *And Just Like That* which premiered in 2021 (its third season is due to be released in 2025). It is the HBO TV series (six seasons, 94 episodes) that is the main focus of my analysis, but I also take into account the first movie which continues the narrative threads of the TV show, leading to the marital conclusion for the main heroine, Carrie Bradshaw.

The original TV series was phenomenally successful, generating record-high ratings, receiving numerous awards, and sparking endless discussions. In academic research, it became a symbol not only of the new "quality television" but also of postfeminism (Akass & McCabe, 2004; Harzewski, 2011; Jermyn, 2009; Whelehan, 2005). In popular discourses, it came to embody modern femininity, with the four protagonists often featuring on the covers of various magazines (most notably *Time* in 2000) and Carrie Bradshaw earning the title of an "icon of the decade" from Naomi Wolf, writing for *The Guardian* (2009). Fans and critics alike still talk about it in terms of "a revolution, a phenomenon, a cataclysm, almost an insurgency" (Baird, 2008, para. 2). As the subtitle of a recent book about it announces, when it comes to modern women, *Sex and the City* "changed the way we think, live, and love" (Armstrong, 2018).

It is worth noting that while both *Pride and Prejudice* and *Sex and the City* are products of Anglo-American culture, they have had an immense international appeal. Austen's works have been translated into dozens of languages, including Chinese, Japanese, Russian, Persian, and Hebrew. Gillian Dow, who studies Austen's international reception, states that "foreign readers' appetites for Austen's work seem unlimited" (2012, p. 170). *Pride and Prejudice* in particular has been adapted to other cultural settings; for example, India in the Bollywood style film *Bride and Prejudice* (2004) and a Muslim immigrant community in the novel *Ayesha at Last* (Jalaluddin, 2019). *Sex and the City* has been broadcast in numerous countries and strongly resonated in such seemingly unlikely locations as Japan (Armstrong, 2018, p. 105). Its Facebook page and other fan sites regularly attract thousands of views, likes, and comments from people of various ethnic backgrounds, and many international visitors still go on *Sex and the City*-themed tours of New York every day.

Although the two texts have been produced in different media and different historical periods, they are both supreme examples of a certain kind of fiction: focused on a search for romantic relationships, filtered through female perspectives, and providing uplifting happy endings. They may be different narrative species, but they belong to the broad genus that includes early sentimental novels, mass-produced romances of the Harlequin or Mills and Boon type, chick lit, and rom-coms. As I will argue in Chapter 3, love stories with happy endings are common in all storytelling traditions, but the more specific modern romantic formula has often been traced to Samuel Richardson's *Pamela* (1740), the tale of a servant girl who resists the advances of her master only to marry him in the end. Austen's *Pride and Prejudice* provides the most successful application of that formula and the main source of inspiration for other feminine genres. Pamela Regis calls it "the best romance novel ever written" (2003, p. 75), and according to the title of Jennifer Crusie's book (2005), it is "the original chick lit masterpiece".

There is, in fact, a direct line of descent from Austen to the chick lit phenomenon which was arguably started by Helen Fielding's 1996 novel *Bridget Jones's Diary*, a modern reinterpretation of *Pride and Prejudice* (Ferriss & Young, 2006b, p. 4). Fielding's romantic plot follows roughly that of Austen, her hero is called Mark Darcy, and Bridget repeatedly watches the hugely successful 1995 BBC adaptation of the novel (which has in no small part contributed to the modern Austen-mania). But even without direct references to Austen, there are clear similarities between the tone and preoccupations of her novels and chick lit texts, as the journalist Kathryn Robinson put it: "Anyone familiar with Jane Austen's oeuvre will immediately recognize in chick lit a kindred wit, the same obsession with choosing a mate, and a shared attention to the dailiness of women's lives" (quoted in Ferriss & Young, 2006b, p. 5).

The status of *Bridget Jones's Diary* as the quintessential chick lit text is surpassed only by *Sex and the City*. Bushnell's book has a cynical tone, barely developed characters, terse rhythm, and fragmented structure; in many ways, it is "the antithesis of romantic fiction" (Harzewski, 2011, p. 95). However, the TV series inspired by the book is the epitome of modern romantic comedy and has had a powerful impact on both the form and content of popular fiction for women, whether in print or on screen (Harzewski, 2011; Whelehan, 2005).

Importantly, *Pride and Prejudice* and *Sex and the City* attract very similar kinds of feminist critique, in line with the predominant views about romantic fiction in general. Austen "has been an awkward subject for feminist criticism to cope with" (Todd, 1991, p. 71) due to her consistent use of marriage not only as the narrative closure but also as a sign of her heroines' maturity. And *Pride and Prejudice* has been particularly vulnerable to cogent feminist critiques" because it "actually celebrates marital felicity as an ideal" (Johnson, 1988, p. 91). Similarly, the prevailing view of chick lit in general, and *Sex and the City* in particular, is that although they raise valid questions about modern female identity, the answers they provide are decidedly conservative: heterosexuality, monogamy, domesticity (Gerhard, 2005; Gill & Herdieckerhoff, 2006; Harzewski, 2011; Hermes, 2006; Mabry, 2006; Rowntree et al., 2012; Whelehan, 2005). While the show has been praised for its focus on female friendship and sexual empowerment, the fact that at the end of the television series, all four protagonists end up in more-or-less stable relationships with men caused many to question the show's feminist credentials. In the chapters that follow, I will argue that measuring the feminism of such stories as *Pride and Prejudice* or *Sex and the City* by the degree to which their heroines manage to live outside of heterosexual bonds is too narrow and unproductive. My focus is on how these texts illuminate the complexities and the power of female choice; how they highlight choices that help maintain their heroines' integrity in the face of various competing demands; and how these choices promote positive changes in the heroes and wider social networks.

Obviously, the two texts vary considerably due to different formats, media, and modes of production. Their authors' creativity and innovation in these areas have undoubtedly contributed to each text's popularity and critical success. And these text-specific features have already been thoroughly analysed. I focus instead on the narrative trajectories and the psychology of the characters. And even in this respect, the two stories vary considerably, as their content inevitably reflects differences in the cultural contexts in which they were created. Austen focuses on a few families in a small village, and their relatively stable kin and social ties. *Sex and the City*'s environment is characterized by social and geographical mobility, with the four main characters almost completely detached from both the security and the obligations of the traditional kinship networks—but replacing them with equally tight friendships. Both texts minimize the effects of social stratification by focusing exclusively on the relatively wealthy: landed gentry in the case of Austen, and upper-middle class in *Sex and the City*. This socio-economic setting means that the female characters are not preoccupied with basic survival or subsistence, enabling them to focus on higher-order needs, such as emotional fulfilment and self-actualization (Maslow, 1943). Nevertheless, this setting affords more varied options and a greater freedom of choice to the women of *Sex and the City*. Unlike Austen's women, modern heroines are legally and financially independent, have opportunities for education and intellectually rewarding work, and can access reliable contraception and fair divorce laws. Thus, in Austen's fiction, the main narrative tension is between the economic dependence and social subordination on the one hand and the desire for personal autonomy and fulfilment on the other. In *Sex and the City*, the tension is between the newly found sexual and financial freedom and the fundamental need for intimacy and connection. In Austen's world, women's options are severely limited, and her heroines must often challenge restrictions imposed on them by social or family expectations in order to exercise their choices—and only a few of those choices are truly endorsed by the author. Women of *Sex and the City* grapple with seemingly endless options; their challenge is to establish which ones are worth pursuing. They all make some wrong decisions along the way, but in the end, all four protagonists achieve satisfactory resolutions meeting their individual priorities.

Overview of Part II and Part III

In Part II of the book, I analyse the romantic and sexual choices of four female characters from *Pride and Prejudice*: Lydia Bennet, Charlotte Lucas, Jane Bennet, and Elizabeth Bennet (with references to Austen's other texts). In Part III, I provide a parallel analysis of the four women of *Sex and the City*: Samantha Jones, Charlotte York, Miranda Hobbes, and Carrie Bradshaw (with additional examples from other chick lit).

Characters such as Lydia Bennet from *Pride and Prejudice* and Samantha Jones from *Sex and the City* show the thrills and pitfalls of a short-term or unrestricted sexuality at two different stages of life and within significantly different socio-cultural environments. Such a strategy has always been relatively risky for women but, as both romantic stories and cross-cultural empirical research demonstrate, some women pursue it even when social norms strongly discourage them from doing so.[2] Through such characters, romantic fiction explores the tension between female sexual drive and social norms which try to suppress it, as well as the difficulty in managing short-term and long-term goals.

Charlotte Lucas and Charlotte York prioritize financial security and social respectability when choosing a life partner. Their decisions reflect one of the best-documented mate selection criteria across many animal species and various human societies: the female preference for mates who seem likely to provide adequate resources. Their differing socio-cultural and personal circumstances show that this is a psychological tendency not necessarily determined by the degree of women's financial independence. At the same time, however, comparisons with other characters reveal just how variable the strength of this preference can be. Through such characters, romantic narratives highlight the complexities of balancing material and emotional needs in the face of different individual aspirations and external pressures.

The demure Jane Bennet and the fiercely independent Miranda Hobbes, though embodying contrasting personalities and cultural ideals, both highlight the benefits and risks of women's reluctance to reveal their feelings before they are assured of their partner's commitment. Such *commitment scepticism* is likely a female evolutionary adaptation: It helps to identify honest and loyal partners. However, being too emotionally guarded can prevent women from seizing suitable relationships—as both Jane and Miranda discover. These characters exemplify romantic fiction's frequent concern with how to best calibrate the level of trust and circumspection.

Finally, Elizabeth Bennet and Carrie Bradshaw personify the quintessential search for the perfect partner: A powerful and handsome man who is also kind and loyal. From an evolutionary perspective, romantic heroes such as Mr. Darcy and Mr. Big possess all the physical, psychological, and social traits which throughout our evolutionary history have contributed to female reproductive success and personal satisfaction. However, as alpha-males, romantic heroes have the potential to be sexual and social bullies, so before romantic heroines can achieve their happy endings, they need to confront male arrogance and suppress male domineering tendencies. The heroines make their men acknowledge the value of female subjectivity and teach them the importance of empathy and affiliation. In doing so, they promote equitable cooperation not only within the romantic couple but also across wider kin and social networks.

I devote a separate chapter to each character and treat them as detailed psychological case studies of the kind that can be found only in fiction, since fiction gives us access to the thoughts, motivations, and even unconscious desires of other "people". Although such an approach is not generally favoured in literary or media studies, it is a crucial part of how and why "ordinary" readers or viewers engage with fictional characters (Mar & Oatley, 2008; Vermeule, 2010). For each character, I show how their romantic, sexual, and marital choices relate to the individual personalities and life experiences invented for them, but I also argue that these characters capture some of the most important—and recurring—aspects of evolved female sexual psychology. In both texts, the multidirectional character contrasts encourage the audience to consider a multitude of potential relationship scenarios from various angles.

In my analysis, romantic fiction emerges not as mindless escapism but an opportunity to explore cognitive, emotional, and social patterns of sexual selection, which is one of the most important evolutionary engines of change. It emerges not as a tool of women's oppression but as the means of imagining a better world, and consequently a source of hope and strength to demand change.

Notes

1 A prime example of this process in humans is cooking: a cultural invention which altered our digestive system and contributed to a uniquely human evolutionary niche (Wrangham, 2009).
2 It is important to note that the term *mating* or *sexual strategy* as it is used in evolutionary psychology does not necessarily denote conscious planning. It refers to psychological mechanisms which, during the course of our evolution, proved helpful in identifying, attracting, and retaining appropriate mates. Mating strategies result from complex interactions between our personality traits, attachment styles, and life experiences. Nevertheless, our mating decisions are also clearly influenced by conscious reasoning and cultural norms.

References

Akass, K., & McCabe, J. (Eds.). (2004). *Reading Sex and the City*. I. B. Tauris.
And just like that. (2021–2023). [Television series]. Star, D. & King, M. P. (Creators). HBO Max.
Ang, I. (1985). *Watching Dallas: Soap opera and the melodramatic imagination*. Methuen.

Armstrong, J. K. (2018). *Sex and the City and us: How four single women changed the way we think, live, and love* (Kindle ed.). Simon & Schuster.

Austen, J. (1813/2003). *Pride and prejudice*. Penguin.

Baird, J. (2008, May 16). Girls gone mild: *Sex and the City* is back. *Newsweek.* http://europe.newsweek.com/girls-gone-mild-sex-and-city-back-90449?rm=eu

Bloch, R. H. (1991). *Medieval misogyny and the invention of Western romantic love.* University of Chicago Press.

Bonnet, T. (2022). Wild animals are evolving faster than anybody thought. *The Conversation.* https://theconversation.com/wild-animals-are-evolving-faster-than-anybody-thought-183633

Boyd, B. (2009). *On the origin of stories: Evolution, cognition, and fiction.* Belknap Press of Harvard University Press.

Boyd, B. (2018). The evolution of stories: From mimesis to language, from fact to fiction. *Wiley Interdisciplinary Reviews: Cognitive Science, 9*(1), 1–16. https://doi.org/10.1002/wcs.1444

Bride and prejudice. (2004). [Motion picture]. Gurinder Chadha (Director/Writer). Miramax Films.

Burch, R. L. (2020). More than just a pretty face: The overlooked contributions of women in evolutionary psychology textbooks. *Evolutionary Behavioral Sciences, 14,* 100–114. https://doi.org/10.1037/ebs0000166

Bushnell, C. (1996). *Sex and the city.* Abacus.

Bushnell, C. (2010). *The Carrie diaries.* Harper Collins.

Bushnell, C. (2011). *Summer and the city.* Harper Collins.

Buss, D. M. (2018). The evolution of love in humans. In K. Sternberg & R. J. Sternberg (Eds.), *The new psychology of love* (2 ed., pp. 42–63). Cambridge University Press.

Buss, D. M., & Schmitt, D. P. (2011). Evolutionary psychology and feminism. *Sex Roles, 64*(9), 768–787. https://doi.org/10.1007/s11199-011-9987-3

Campbell, A. (2002). *A mind of her own: The evolutionary psychology of women.* Oxford University Press.

Carroll, J. (2004). Human nature and literary meaning: A theoretical model illustrated with a critique of *Pride and Prejudice.* In J. Carroll, *Literary Darwinism: Evolution, human nature, and literature* (pp. 185–212). Routledge.

Chapais, B. (2013). Monogamy, strongly bonded groups, and the evolution of human social structure. *Evolutionary Anthropology: Issues, News, and Reviews, 22*(2), 52–65. https://doi.org/10.1002/evan.21345

Cronin, H. (1991). *The ant and the peacock: Altruism and sexual selection from Darwin to today.* Cambridge University Press.

Crusie, J. (Ed.) (2005). *Flirting with Pride and Prejudice: Fresh perspectives on the original chick-lit masterpiece.* BenBella Books.

Davis, A. C. (2021). Resolving the tension between feminism and evolutionary psychology: An epistemological critique. *Evolutionary Behavioral Sciences, 15*(4), 368–388. https://doi.org/https://doi.org/10.1037/ebs0000193

de Rougemont, D. (1939/1983). *Love in the Western world.* Princeton University Press.

Diamond, L. M. (2008). *Sexual fluidity: Understanding women's love and desire.* Harvard University Press.

Dow, G. (2012). Uses of translation: The global Jane Austen. In G. Dow & C. Hanson (Eds.), *Uses of Austen: Jane's afterlives* (pp. 153–172). Palgrave Macmillan.

Dutton, D. (2009). *The art instinct: Beauty, pleasure, & human evolution.* Bloomsbury Press.

Eagly, A. H. (2018). The shaping of science by ideology: How feminism inspired, led, and constrained scientific understanding of sex and gender. *Journal of Social Issues, 74*(4), 871–888. https://doi.org/10.1111/josi.12291

Evelina, N. (2022). *Sex and the City: A cultural history.* Rowman & Littlefield.

Fausto-Sterling, A. (1992). *Myths of gender: Biological theories about women and men* (2nd ed.). BasicBooks.

Fausto-Sterling, A. (2001). Beyond difference: Feminism and evolutionary psychology. In H. Rose & S. Rose (Eds.), *Alas, poor Darwin: Arguments against evolutionary psychology.* Vintage.

Ferriss, S., & Young, M. (Eds.). (2006a). *Chick lit: The new woman's fiction.* Routledge.

Ferriss, S., & Young, M. (2006b). Introduction. In S. Ferriss & M. Young (Eds.), *Chick lit: The new woman's fiction* (pp. 1–13). Routledge.

Ferriss, S., & Young, M. (2008). *Chick flicks: Contemporary women at the movies*. Routledge.
Fielding, H. (1996). *Bridget Jones's diary: A novel*. Picador.
Fine, C. (2010). *Delusions of gender: How our minds, society, and neurosexism create difference*. W. W. Norton.
Firestone, S. (1979). *The dialectic of sex: The case for feminist revolution*. The Women's Press.
Fisher, H. E. (2016). *Anatomy of love: A natural history of mating, marriage, and why we stray* (Rev., Kindle ed.). W. W. Norton & Company.
Fisher, M. L. (Ed.) (2014). *The Oxford handbook of women and competition*. Oxford University Press.
Fisher, M. L., Garcia, J. R., & Chang, R. S. (Eds.). (2013). *Evolution's empress: Darwinian perspectives on the nature of women*. Oxford University Press.
Fisher, M. L., Garcia, J. R., & Burch, R. L. (2020). Evolutionary psychology: Thoughts on integrating feminist perspectives. In J. H. Barkow, L. Workman, & W. Reader (Eds.), *The Cambridge handbook of evolutionary perspectives on human behavior* (pp. 378–392). Cambridge University Press.
Fletcher, G. J. O., Simpson, J. A., Campbell, L., & Overall, N. C. (2015). Pair-bonding, romantic love, and evolution. *Perspectives on Psychological Science*, *10*(1), 20–36. https://doi.org/10.1177/1745691614561683
Garcia, J. R., & Heywood, L. L. (2016). Moving toward integrative feminist evolutionary behavioral sciences. *Feminism & Psychology*, *26*(3), 327–334. https://doi.org/10.1177/0959353516645368
Gerhard, J. (2005). *Sex and the City*: Carrie Bradshaw's queer postfeminism. *Feminist Media Studies*, *5*(1), 37–49. https://doi.org/10.1080/14680770500058173
Gilbert, S. M., & Gubar, S. (1979/2000). *The madwoman in the attic: The woman writer and the nineteenth-century literary imagination* (2nd, Kindle ed.). Yale University Press.
Gill, R., & Herdieckerhoff, E. (2006). Rewriting the romance. *Feminist Media Studies*, *6*(4), 487–504. https://doi.org/10.1080/14680770600989947
Gill, R., & Walker, R. (1993). Heterosexuality, feminism, contradiction: On being young, white, heterosexual feminists in the 1990s. In S. Wilkinson & C. Kitzinger (Eds.), *Heterosexuality: A feminism & psychology reader* (pp. 68–72). Sage Publications.
Gowaty, P. A. (2003). Sexual natures: How feminism changed evolutionary biology. *Signs: Journal of Women in Culture and Society*, *28*(3), 901–921. https://doi.org/10.1086/345324
Greer, G. (1970). *The female eunuch*. McGraw-Hill Book Company.
Gregson, J., & Lois, J. (2020). Social science reads romance. In J. Kamblé, E. M. Selinger, & H.-M. Teo (Eds.), *The Routledge research companion to popular romance fiction* (pp. 335–351). Routledge.
Grosz, E. A. (2005). *Time travels: Feminism, nature, power*. Duke University Press.
Haraway, D. (1989). *Primate visions: Gender, race, and nature in the world of modern science*. Routledge.
Haraway, D. (1991). *Simians, cyborgs, and women: The reinvention of nature*. Routledge.
Harman, C. (2009). *Jane's fame: How Jane Austen conquered the world*. Canongate.
Harzewski, S. (2011). *Chick lit and postfeminism*. University of Virginia Press.
Henrich, J. (2016). *The secret of our success: How culture is driving human evolution, domesticating our species, and making us smarter*. Princeton University Press.
Hermes, J. (2006). *Ally McBeal*, *Sex and the City* and the tragic success of feminism. In J. Hollows & R. Moseley (Eds.), *Feminism in popular culture* (pp. 79–95). Berg.
Hrdy, S. B. (1981/1999). *The woman that never evolved*. Harvard University Press.
Hrdy, S. B. (2024). *Father time: A natural history of men and babies*. Princeton University Press.
Hubbard, R. (1990). *The politics of women's biology*. Rutgers University Press.
Jablonka, E., & Lamb, M. J. (2014). *Evolution in four dimensions: Genetic, epigenetic, behavioral, and symbolic variation in the history of life* (Rev. ed.). MIT Press.
Jagose, A. (2009). Feminism's queer theory. *Feminism & Psychology*, *19*(2), 157–174. https://doi.org/10.1177/0959353509102152
Jalaluddin, U. (2019). *Ayesha at last* (Kindle ed.). Corvus.
Jermyn, D. (2009). *Sex and the City* (TV milestones series). Wayne State University Press.
Johnson, C. L. (1988). *Jane Austen: Women, politics, and the novel*. University of Chicago Press.
Johnson, C. L. (2012). *Jane Austen's cults and cultures*. University of Chicago Press.
Konner, M. (2015). *Women after all: Sex, evolution, and the end of male supremacy*. W.W. Norton & Company.

Lewis, C. S. (1936/1948). *The allegory of love: A study in medieval tradition*. Oxford University Press.
Mabry, A. R. (2006). About a girl: Female subjectivity and sexuality in contemporary 'chick' culture. In S. Ferriss & M. Young (Eds.), *Chick lit: The new woman's fiction* (pp. 191–206). Routledge.
Mar, R. A., & Oatley, K. (2008). The function of fiction is the abstraction and simulation of social experience. *Perspectives on Psychological Science*, 3(3), 173–192. https://doi.org/10.1111/j.1745-6924.2008.00073.x
Maslow, A. H. (1943). A theory of human motivation. *Psychological Review*, 50(4), 370–396.
Mazzeno, L. W. (2011). *Jane Austen: Two centuries of criticism*. Camden House.
Mazzeno, L. W. (2012). On *Pride and Prejudice*. In L. W. Mazzeno (Ed.), *Critical insights: Pride and Prejudice by Jane Austen* (pp. 3–17). Salem Press.
Modleski, T. (1982/2008). *Loving with a vengeance: Mass-produced fantasies for women* (2nd ed.). Routledge.
O'Neill, R. (2015). Feminist encounters with evolutionary psychology. *Australian Feminist Studies*, 30(86), 345–350. https://doi.org/10.1080/08164649.2016.1157909
Odling-Smee, F. J., Laland, K. N., & Feldman, M. W. (2003). *Niche construction: The neglected process in evolution*. Princeton University Press.
Pinker, S. (1997). *How the mind works*. Norton.
Price, J., & Shildrick, M. (Eds.). (1999). *Feminist theory and the body: A reader*. Edinburgh University Press.
Pride and prejudice. (1995). [Television series]. Langton, S. (Director) & Davies, A. (Writer). British Broadcasting Corporation.
Pride and Prejudice is top read. (2007, March 1). *BBC News*. http://news.bbc.co.uk/2/hi/entertainment/6405737.stm
Radtke, H. L. (2017). Feminist theory in feminism & psychology [Part I]: Dealing with differences and negotiating the biological. *Feminism & Psychology*, 27(3), 357–377. https://doi.org/10.1177/0959353517714594
Radway, J. A. (1984/1991). *Reading the romance: Women, patriarchy, and popular literature* (2nd ed.). University of North Carolina Press.
Regis, P. (2003). *A natural history of the romance novel*. University of Pennsylvania Press.
Rich, A. (1980). Compulsory heterosexuality and lesbian existence. *Signs*, 5(4), 631–660.
Richards, J. R. (1994). *The sceptical feminist: A philosophical enquiry* (2nd ed.). Penguin.
Richardson, S. (1740/1985). *Pamela, or Virtue Rewarded*. Penguin.
Richerson, P. J., & Boyd, R. (2005). *Not by genes alone: How culture transformed human evolution*. University of Chicago Press.
Roach, C. M. (2016). *Happily ever after: The romance story in popular culture*. Indiana University Press.
Roughgarden, J. (2004). *Evolution's rainbow: Diversity, gender, and sexuality in nature and people*. University of California Press.
Rowntree, M., Moulding, N., & Bryant, L. (2012). Feminine sexualities in chick lit. *Australian Feminist Studies*, 27(72), 121–137. https://doi.org/10.1080/08164649.2012.648259
Sex and the city. (1998–2004). [Television series]. Star, D. (Creator), & King, M. P. (Producer and Director). HBO.
Sex and the city. (2008). [Motion picture]. King, M. P. (Director/Writer). New Line Cinema.
Sex and the city 2. (2010). [Motion picture]. King, M. P. (Director/Writer). New Line Cinema.
Saini, A. (2017). *Inferior: The true power of women and the science that shows it* (Kindle ed.). 4th Estate.
Saini, A. (2023). *The patriarchs: The origins of inequality* (Kindle ed.). 4th Estate.
Smith, C. A., & Konik, J. (2011). Feminism and evolutionary psychology: Allies, adversaries, or both? An introduction to a special issue. *Sex Roles*, 64(9), 595–602. https://doi.org/10.1007/s11199-011-9985-5
Smuts, B. (1995). The evolutionary origins of patriarchy. *Human Nature*, 6(1), 1–32. https://doi.org/10.1007/bf02734133
Snitow, A. B. (1979). Mass market romance: Pornography for women is different. *Radical History Review*, 1979(20), 141–161. https://doi.org/10.1215/01636545-1979-20-141
Span, M. (2022). Caring for the self. A case-study on sociocultural aspects of reading chick lit. *Journal of Popular Romance Studies*, 11, 1–18.

Teo, H.-M. (2020). Love and romance novels. In J. Kamblé, E. M. Selinger, & H.-M. Teo (Eds.), *The Routledge research companion to popular romance fiction* (pp. 454–484). Routledge.
Thurston, C. (1987). *The romance revolution: Erotic novels for women and the quest for a new sexual identity*. University of Illinois Press.
Todd, J. (1991). Jane Austen, politics, and sensibility. In S. Sellers (Ed.), *Feminist criticism: Theory and practice* (pp. 71–87). University of Toronto Press.
van Monsjou, E., & Mar, R. A. (2019). Interest and investment in fictional romances. *Psychology of Aesthetics, Creativity, and the Arts, 13*, 431–449. https://doi.org/10.1037/aca0000191
Vandermassen, G. (2005). *Who's afraid of Charles Darwin? Debating feminism and evolutionary theory*. Rowman & Littlefield.
Vermeule, B. (2010). *Why do we care about literary characters?* Johns Hopkins University Press.
Waldron, M. (2005). Critical responses, early. In J. M. Todd (Ed.), *Jane Austen in context* (pp. 83–91). Cambridge University Press.
Weisser, S. O. (2013). *The glass slipper: Women and love stories*. Rutgers University Press.
Whelehan, I. (2005). *The feminist bestseller: From Sex and the Single Girl to Sex and the City*. Palgrave Macmillan.
Wilkes, J. (2012). *Pride and Prejudice*: The critical reception. In L. W. Mazzeno (Ed.), *Pride and Prejudice: Critical insights* (pp. 86–105). Salem Press.
Wilson, E. A. (2004). *Psychosomatic: Feminism and the neurological body*. Duke University Press.
Wolf, N. (2009, December 21). Carrie Bradshaw: Icons of the decade. *The Guardian*.
Wrangham, R. (2009). *Catching fire: How cooking made us human*. Basic Books.

PART I
LOVE, CHOICE, AND ROMANTIC FICTION

1
LOVE

A fundamental human drive

"Love … is the pivot of women's oppression today" writes Shulamith Firestone in one of the foundational texts of second-wave feminism, *The Dialectic of Sex* (1970/1979, p. 121). For her and many other feminists, romantic love is a relatively recent, specifically Western cultural myth permeated by the patriarchal ideology of male dominance and female passivity; by idealizing heterosexual desire, monogamy, and marriage, romantic love is a tool of men's psychological and social control over women (Atkinson, 1974; Comer, 1974; Greer, 1970; Millett, 1970; Rich, 1980). As Kate Millett observes, "love is the only circumstance in which the female is (ideologically) pardoned for sexual activity", and therefore, "the concept of romantic love affords a means of emotional manipulation which the male is free to exploit" (1970, p. 37). Since heterosexual male sexuality, most clearly expressed in pornography, is synonymous with degradation and exploitation of women, heterosexual desire is invariably based on the dynamic of domination and submission; not only intercourse but all heterosexual relationships contain elements of rape and abuse (Dworkin, 1981, 1987; Griffin, 1971/1983; Jeffreys, 1990). Ti-Grace Atkinson goes as far as to claim that "love is the victim's response to the rapist" (cited in Greer, 1970, p. 166).

Many other feminists see love as a threat to woman's autonomy. In her seminal work, *The Second Sex*, Simone de Beauvoir (1949/1972) claims that for a woman love is a religion with a man as her god: "She gives up her own transcendence, subordinating it to that of the essential other, to whom she makes herself vassal and slave" (p. 661). A 1969 feminist manifesto calls for the destruction of love because it "promotes vulnerability, dependence, possessiveness, … and prevents the full development of woman by directing all her energies outwards in the interests of others" (reprinted in Koedt et al., 1973, p. 375). According to the same manifesto, heterosexual love also undermines solidarity between women—another way in which it perpetuates the patriarchal system.

These deeply critical opinions have significantly shaped public discourses about love, marriage, and heterosexuality, and have had a decisive impact on feminist interpretations of romantic fiction. However, not all feminists agree with this radically negative view. Indeed, given the self-proclaimed multifaceted nature of feminism, it is impossible to provide a singular definition of romantic love from a feminist perspective.[1] Some of the more recent contributions recognize love as a powerful human need and call for a more comprehensive understanding of both the oppressive and the empowering aspects of love (Brooks, 2021; García-Andrade et al., 2018; Jackson, 1999; Jónasdóttir, 2013). And for a few feminists, love is the key to transforming both intimate and social gender relations (Gilligan, 2002; Hollway, 1993; hooks, 2001a, 2002)—an idea I will come back to at the end of this chapter.

Evolutionary perspectives confirm feminist concerns about the inherent conflict between the sexes, which often places women in a vulnerable position: Men often try to control women's sexuality and reproductive capacities through various means from physical violence and coercion, through religious, political, and economic restrictions, to emotional manipulation. But romantic love is not the "pivot" of this conflict; on the contrary, it is evolution's best solution for reducing this conflict and encouraging mutually beneficial cooperation, both within the intimate couple and across wider kin and social networks (Chapais, 2013; Fletcher et al., 2015).

All currently available evidence shows that romantic love is a universal human drive underpinned by evolutionarily ancient biological processes (Buss, 2018; Fisher, 2016; Fletcher et al., 2015)—even if cultural and individual attitudes to love vary considerably (Jankowiak, 1995; Jankowiak & Nelson, 2021; Karandashev, 2017). Research across many cultures confirms that far from being invariably detrimental for women, committed relationships—especially marriage—contribute significantly to better physical and emotional health, as well as higher levels of happiness and satisfaction with life for both men and women (Argyle, 1999; Diener et al., 2000; Grover & Helliwell, 2019; Waite & Gallagher, 2000; Waldinger & Schulz, 2023). Finally, far from perpetuating patriarchy, positive sociocultural valuation of romantic love is associated with greater female autonomy and more harmonious gender relations, while normative monogamy is statistically linked to more equitable, democratic social organization (De Munck et al., 2016; Henrich, 2020; Henrich et al., 2012).

The evolution of love

From an evolutionary point of view, romantic love is a pan-human, biologically based phenomenon, a fundamental human drive facilitating reproduction and parenting (Buss, 2018; Fisher, 2005, 2016; Fletcher et al., 2015). This is not to say that every person must fall in love, nor that every person who does fall in love wants to have or ends up having children—such claims ignore the crucial distinction between ultimate evolutionary goals and proximate mechanisms evolved to achieve them.[2] But reproduction underpins evolutionary logic: It is the ultimate goal of every living organism because without it, life would cease to exist. Moreover, individuals who successfully reproduce pass their genes on to next generations and in this way not only participate in the continuation of their species but also influence its specific characteristics.

For humans, reproduction is particularly complex not only because we understand, and can to some extent consciously control, our instincts and desires, but also because human children are more dependent on their caregivers and for much longer than the offspring of any other species. Raising them requires close and long-lasting cooperation. Romantic love is an emotional mechanism helping us choose a partner with whom we can sustain such cooperation by sharing sexual passion, emotional attachment, and long-term commitment—three dimensions of romantic love widely recognized in the scientific literature (Sternberg, 1986). There is also considerable evidence that across cultures romantic love generally entails seeing another person as unique, irreplaceable, and of equal worth; having a profound empathy for that person; reorganizing one's priorities to accommodate their needs; and wanting these feelings to be reciprocated and exclusive (Harris, 1995, pp. 102–103; for a recent overview, see De Munck et al., 2016).[3]

Numerous behavioural, neural, and hormonal similarities between romantic and parental love suggest that evolutionary roots of human attachment go as far as the basic survival instinct, which drives offspring to seek comfort and protection from their caregivers (Bowlby, 1969; for a recent overview, see Fletcher et al., 2015). In mammals, including primates, that caregiver is primarily, often exclusively, the mother. But human infants require so much care that they are more likely to survive and thrive if mothers are not left to look after them alone (Hrdy, 2009). Help does not have to come from the father, but no other individual has an equally large evolutionary incentive to protect his genetic investment. It is this high level of fitness interdependence, as evolutionists call it, that is the basis for human pair-bonding: Male and female reproductive interests are so closely linked that cooperation becomes the most likely route to reproductive success (Buss, 2018).[4]

Scientific explanations of love are sometimes seen as reductive, but in fact, they reveal love as one of the most transformatory forces in human evolution. Our tendency to form stable pair bonds has shaped the uniquely human life history with extended childhood and adolescence, a long post-reproductive (but nevertheless very productive) period of life for women, as well as the exceptionally high level of male care and provisioning of women and children (Hrdy, 2024; Kaplan et al., 2000).[5] It also significantly influenced the social organization of our species, because the tight fitness interdependence—and the cooperation it engenders—does not end with the pair-bonded couple; it extends to intergenerational networks of blood relatives, in-laws, and whole communities, enabling such crucial human adaptations as cooperative breeding and communal food sharing (Chapais, 2013; Fletcher et al., 2015; Hrdy, 2009, 2024; Kaplan et al., 2009). Thus, love inextricably intertwines individual choice of a sexual partner with broader social considerations.[6]

Chemistry of love

The evolutionary impact of love starts with the way regular physical proximity and emotional closeness interact with our hormones and neuropsychology. Helen Fisher, a biological anthropologist and the leading expert on romantic love, devoted most of her career to explaining how this powerful drive evolved to coordinate human pair-bonding and parenting. Her extensive research demonstrates that romantic love plays a primary role in a constellation of emotion-motivation systems linking together sex drive, emotional attachment, and long-term commitment (Fisher et al., 2002, 2006). These systems are interconnected but distinct; each has a specific function, and each is associated with specific neural correlates and behavioural repertoire. Sexual drive, mainly linked to testosterone, motivates us to search for potential mates. Romantic attraction helps us choose a specific partner on whom to focus our attention; it is associated with elevated levels of the neurochemicals dopamine and norepinephrine, and low levels of serotonin, a combination which creates the feeling of exhilaration and craving for closeness. Attachment, associated mainly with the neuropeptides oxytocin and vasopressin, motivates us to form stable relationships, to care for and help each other.

Fisher's research clearly disproves the idea that romantic love is a purely cultural or historically recent construct. In fact, its hormonal and neuropsychological features are not even unique to humans: They are also present in birds and mammals, producing similar behaviours to those associated with human love, such as the intense focus on the special other; trying to maintain proximity to them and showing signs of distress when separated; feeding and grooming each other; or sharing parental duties (Fisher, 2005).

However, this neurohormonal circuitry is not a one-fits-all solution: It varies between species, between the sexes, between individuals, and during the life span of each individual (Fisher et al., 2002). To complicate things even further, the interaction between the three systems is not simple or straightforward: They often work together and reinforce each other, but they can also operate independently and have negative effects on each other (Fisher, 2005; Fisher et al., 2002). For example, romantic feelings are usually connected with sexual desire not only in Mills and Boon fiction but also in terms of the brain's chemistry, because dopamine, "the liquor of romance" (Fisher, 2005, p. 83), often stimulates the release of testosterone, the hormone of sexual desire. Sexual desire, when satisfied, can lead to attachment because oxytocin and vasopressin are released during orgasm (Fisher, 2005, p. 195). Behaviours such as face-to-face copulation (common among humans but rare in other animals) also foster emotional intimacy (Fisher, 2016, p. 182). On the other hand, a strong sex drive, connected with high levels of testosterone, can interfere with attachment and commitment. This is probably why men with high baseline levels of testosterone marry less often and divorce more often than those with low levels of testosterone (Booth & Dabbs, 1993). But levels of testosterone are not fixed: A satisfying relationship, especially when combined with fatherhood, can dramatically lower testosterone levels, reducing men's sex drive and promoting stronger attachment (Gettler et al., 2013; Grebe et al., 2019; Kuzawa et al., 2009). In fact, when men are in love, emotional union becomes more important for them than sexual desire (Tennov, 1979). The independence of these three neural systems enables humans to pursue a range of reproductive strategies depending on individual circumstances and environmental—including cultural—conditions; it can also explain why the length of romantic relationships can vary considerably, and why infidelity and divorce are common features of human relationships (Fisher et al., 2002).

Universal love

Second-wave feminists based much of their critique of romantic love on the assumption that it is a specifically Western invention originating in eleventh-century courtly love poetry, reinforced by the eighteenth-century sentimental novel, and continued in the modern "apparatus of romanticism" (Firestone, 1970/1979, p. 139; see also Greer, 1970; Millett, 1970); this assumption continues to underpin much of the current discussions of romantic love within cultural and literary studies (e.g., Brooks, 2021).[7] For most of the second half of the twentieth century, when social constructivism was the dominant paradigm in the social sciences, the commitment to this view was so strong that any suggestion of love's universality was not only unpopular but almost suspect (Brown, 1991). However, when anthropologists William Jankowiak and Edward Fischer (1992) examined ethnographic records from 166 societies, they found clear evidence of romantic love in 147 of them; for the remaining cultures, there was not enough information to make an adequate assessment of love's presence, but there was also no conclusive evidence of its absence. Since then, extensive research has confirmed that romantic love has existed in every known culture: from ancient Greece, Egypt, India, China, and Japan to the tribal societies of Africa, South America, Australia, and Polynesia (Jankowiak, 1995; Jankowiak & Nelson, 2021; Karandashev, 2017).

Indeed, to the extent that cultural artefacts reflect the prominence of ideas and beliefs within a given society, love appears to be one of the most important and prevalent preoccupations across cultures from different time periods and geographical areas. Communities as varied as the Yukaghir of Siberia and the eastern Cherokees have myths and beliefs about how to find or keep love, and produce love charms, amulets, and potions (Fisher, 2016, p. 33). Poetry about love and heartache is common among the nomadic Bedouin tribes and the Khesurs of Georgia's mountain regions, and in southern rural China, 90 per cent of traditional folksongs are about love (see research cited in Nelson & Jankowiak, 2021). Large-scale, cross-cultural studies of world literatures and folk tales confirm that the theme of romantic union is not only universal but is also the most popular literary topic (Gottschall & Nordlund, 2006; Hogan, 2003)—an idea I will come back to in Chapter 3. Furthermore, folk tale collections from regions such as Japan and India contain on average more references to romantic love than those from European societies, which runs counter to claims that romantic passion is more important or more prevalent in European cultures than in other parts of the world (Gottschall & Nordlund, 2006).

Finally, cross-cultural evidence challenges the assertion, still common in the humanities and social sciences, that "love has no essential or unitary identity" (Seidman, 1991, p. 4). As demonstrated by literature, folklore, and personal accounts, people from different historical eras and different geographical locations describe the experience of romantic love in remarkably similar terms despite different cultural rules and restrictions applied to it. For example, a study of love-related attitudes using over 1,100 individuals from multiple countries in Africa, Asia, South America, and Europe showed relatively little cross-cultural variation in responses to items most relevant to romantic love, such as "My partner and I were meant for each other" (Neto et al., 2000). The same key ingredients of romantic love identified by modern psychologists—sexual passion, emotional intimacy, long-term commitment, idealization of the beloved, and reorganizing of life's priorities for the beloved—are present in the words of lovers from Biblical stories, ancient Greek novels written around the second and third centuries AD, the Chinese caizi-jiaren or scholar-beauty stories, typical stories from Arabic, Persian, and Australian Aboriginal traditions, and the personal account of Nisa, a !Kung woman from the Kalahari Desert (Baumard et al., 2022; Gottschall & Nordlund, 2006; Konstan, 1994; Shostak, 1990). They all express the same sense of belonging with each other, the same yearning when apart, and the same elation when reunited.

This cross-cultural research also shows relatively little variation in men's and women's attitudes to love (Neto et al., 2000). Contrary to the feminist assertion that "men can't love" (Firestone, 1970/1979, p. 129), empirical evidence suggests that both men and women generally want romantic relationships, are similarly dedicated to their partners, and equally believe in life-long commitment to one person (Fisher, 2016, pp. 312–314; Garcia & Reiber, 2008; Waite & Gallagher, 2000, p. 169). In MRI studies, the levels of brain activity connected with romantic love are the same for men and women, heterosexuals and homosexuals, American and Chinese (Fisher, 2016, pp. 35, 312). It is true that men sometimes seek intimacy or express their love differently from women (Cancian, 1986) and are more easily able to disassociate sex from emotional attachment (Garcia & Reiber, 2008; Townsend, 1995; Townsend et al., 1995). But in some ways, men are more romantic than women: They fall in love faster and are 2.5 times more likely to commit suicide after a breakup (Fisher, 2016, pp. 312–313).

Love and culture

If love is a human universal rooted in our biology, why is it that different cultures exalt or disparage romantic love, encourage or restrict individual choice of a partner, and to varying degrees try to connect or disconnect it from sex or marriage? There are indisputable differences in the way different cultures conceptualize love (Jankowiak, 1995; Jankowiak & Nelson, 2021; Karandashev, 2017), and these variations have often been used to deny love's evolutionary foundations. However, a variety of forms does not preclude common biological origin. Consider, for example, the differences between a human hand, a bat wing, and a cow hoof. Or think about food: It is absolutely necessary to the survival of every human being, and yet—or perhaps precisely because of that—different groups of people have their own unique recipes, rituals, and prohibitions connected with food. And within each group, individual diets vary considerably too, depending on availability, affordability, and personal tastes.

We are hungry for love just as we are hungry for food. Local variations do not disprove the universality of these human needs. On the contrary, the expression of any disposition depends largely on the environment. As the prominent evolutionary psychologist David Buss puts it: "Context is everything" (2003, p. 15). Since the human environment is in great measure constituted by culture, cultural variation should be regarded as part of human nature (Scalise Sugiyama, 2003/2010). But cultural variations are not completely arbitrary, as social constructivists, including many feminists, would have it; they are a product of, and are therefore constrained by, the workings of human minds and bodies. The question is not whether biology or culture matter in love—they both do; the question is how they influence each other in different circumstances.

Recent research has identified several factors connected with a greater cultural prominence and more positive cultural valuation of romantic love. For example, a comprehensive survey of the literary output of 19 cultural traditions, including Egyptian, Sumerian, Indian, Persian, Arabic, Chinese, Russian, and several European ones, covering the period from 2000 BC to 1800 AD, found that the importance of romantic love increased since the Medieval times not only in European cultures (as generally accepted within the humanities) but also across Asia and the Middle East, and that similar increases occurred much earlier in ancient Greece and India (Baumard et al., 2022). Using a combination of qualitative and quantitative methods, the survey provides convincing evidence that these increases follow a discernible pattern: At different points in human history, cultures have been more likely to promote love as a cultural ideal when resources become more abundant and when the levels of economic development and population density increase (Baumard et al., 2022).

Social organization is another significant factor: Love is more likely to be endorsed and cherished when the nuclear family is the accepted norm and when support from extended kin networks is less necessary or less readily available (De Munck et al., 2016). This may be related to the level of individualism and collectivism of a given culture. Individualistic cultures put a premium on personal satisfaction and self-realization, while in collectivist cultures, individual feelings and desires are expected to be subordinated to the requirements of one or more groups (family, tribe, or state, for instance). So while people in different cultures can usually identify the emotion of romantic love, they may variously associate it with something more or less achievable or positive (Jankowiak, 1995). However, research confirms that such cultural differences are "a matter of degree rather than polar distinctions" (Lewandowska-Tomaszczyk & Wilson, 2021, p. 1083) and that "individual personality differences may be more powerful than cultural differences" (Hatfield & Rapson, 1996, p. 19). Crucially, and contrary to prevalent feminist claims, the cultural idealization of romantic love is generally related to an increase rather than a decrease in women's autonomy and social status (De Munck et al., 2016).

It is worth noting that this cross-cultural, evolutionary perspective is much broader than but in many ways consistent with standard sociological analyses focused exclusively on Western modernity, which also link the increased cultural importance of romantic love to such processes as economic development, geographical mobility, individualization, and the emancipation of women (Beck & Beck-Gernsheim, 1990/1995; Giddens, 1992; Illouz, 2007). In short, what is special about Western culture is not that it invented romantic love but that it has provided increasingly favourable conditions for this emotion to be expressed and valued.

Love and marriage

One of the most serious feminist charges against romantic love is that it lures women into the trap of a patriarchal marriage where their productive, reproductive, and emotional capacities are exploited in the service of men (Chodorow, 1978; Comer, 1974; Friedan, 1963/1997; Greer, 1970; Rubin, 1975). Feminists argue that "the sexual contract" at the heart of marriage is "a slave contract … hidden beneath a veneer of romance" (Jeffreys, 2004, p. 328), a veneer added as recently as the nineteenth century (Greer, 1970).[8] Feminist objections to marriage are understandable: In some parts of the world, marital laws and customs still drastically disadvantage women, and statistics about domestic violence and intimate partner abuse, most of it perpetrated by men against women, continue to be disturbing. But a broad evolutionary perspective as well as abundant ethnographic and sociological research reveal a long-standing connection between love and marriage, and the benefits they bring to individual women and their communities.

Marriage is clearly a cultural institution, but it most likely capitalizes on the human tendency for long-term pair-bonding—the kind of "sex contract" that evolutionists see as a strategic compromise or "a coincidence of interests" between the sexes through which our female ancestors gained the level of paternal investment not seen in any other primate or mammal (Campbell, 2013; Fisher, 1982; Kaplan et al., 2009; Lancaster, 1991). And the more closely marriage is associated with romantic love, the better it is for women. Such an association affords women more freedom when choosing a husband and greater power within marriage—a point emphasized not only by evolutionists (e.g., Coontz, 2005; Evans, 2003; Illouz, 2006).

If romantic love is a psychological universal, marriage appears to be a cultural universal, or at least "near cultural universal" (Fisher, 2016, p. 49). According to the United Nations Statistical Office, in the first decade of this century, an average of around 90 per cent of men and women worldwide married by age 49 (cited in Fisher, 2016, p. 49). And for most people, marriage means monogamy, even if for some it is serial rather than life-long monogamy. Although in the vast majority (about 84–90%) of traditional societies men are allowed to have several wives, only a small minority (5–14%) of men actually do (Fisher, 2016, pp. 52–53; Henrich, 2020, p. 260).[9] For women, it is even more rare to have more than one husband at a time; this form of marriage is practiced only in a few communities in the Himalayas and the South Pacific (but several other societies, such as the Inuit and the Ache, have less formal arrangements allowing women multiple sexual and reproductive partners).

Of course, marriage is not synonymous with love. Across cultures, marriage is conceptualized first of all as a form of social approval for sex and reproduction (Fisher, 2016, p. 351), which also involves an exchange of resources and building of connections between families and other social groups. For many feminists, this institutional character of marriage is incompatible with the ideals of romantic love, but the prominent philosopher of love Irving Singer proposes that marriage "completes the aspirations of romantic love" (1987, p. 6). From an evolutionary perspective, marriage places sex, reproduction, and emotional intimacy in a communal context, uniting sexual selection with social selection.[10]

And there is a strong link between love and marriage even in cultures which try to minimize it. In the biggest study ever conducted about people's preferences in choosing a spouse, the item "love and mutual attraction" was ranked as *the* most important in the vast majority of cultures spanning six continents and five islands, and featured prominently in the remaining few (Buss et al., 1990). This widespread preference for love may not always be easily realized, given the unique level of parental control over mate choice in humans (Apostolou, 2017). Nevertheless, most foraging communities allow individual choice of marital partners (Nelson & Jankowiak, 2021), and a companionate marriage is a normative ideal in such decidedly non-Western communities as the Lahu from Yunnan in China and the Igbo of Nigeria (Jankowiak & Nelson, 2021). Moreover, parental involvement is not antithetical to love: Parents and children agree to a large degree on what traits their marital partners should have; in many communities with arranged marriages, young people are usually involved in selecting their future partners and sometimes force their parents' hands through elopements; and even when the prospective bride and groom do not know each other, they often fall in love after agreeing to the arranged marriage, as has been documented in India, China, and Egypt (Nelson & Jankowiak, 2021). Studies of polygynous marriages and polyamorous relationships also note the existence of preferences, hierarchies, and jealousies among the partners which suggest that such relationships are not free of the expectations of sexual or emotional pre-eminence usually associated with romantic love (Jankowiak & Nelson, 2021).

Our need for love and our tendency to marry for love are undeniable, but the multifaceted nature of both love and marriage means that affairs and divorce are common for men and women across different cultures; for example, about 40 per cent of the !Kung marriages end in divorce and the Ache of Paraguay divorce on average more than 11 times before the age of 40 (Buss, 2003, p. 168; see also Fisher, 2016; Greiling & Buss, 2000; Scelza, 2013). But even divorce follows cross-cultural patterns consistent with the idea that marriage is underpinned by love, reproduction, and cooperation. Across cultures, divorce is most often caused by infidelity and infertility; women also tend to divorce their husbands because of maltreatment or laziness (Betzig, 1989). Divorce usually happens early in life (especially between ages 25 and 29) and early in marriage (within the first 3–4 years), which is when people are still figuring out their relationship priorities and spouses are adjusting to each other (Fisher, 2016, pp. 95–96). The 3- to 4-year period is also significant because this is how long it takes to raise a baby through the most vulnerable stage (Fisher, 2016, pp. 92–94). Considering all this, many agree that serial rather than life-long monogamy is probably the most common human relationship pattern.

Nevertheless, many people stay married and in love for a long time. In America, 89% of people believe that a marriage can last a lifetime, and more than half of marriages do. According to several studies, at least three quarters of people married or in long-term relationships say they are very much in love, are happy, and would marry the same person again, and this is true for both heterosexual and homosexual couples (Fisher, 2016, pp. 145, 300, 306, and 315). Even when married for more than 30 years, close to 40% of both men and women report being "very intensely in love" (O'Leary et al., 2012).

Finally, marriage has significant benefits which apply almost equally to both sexes: As measured by a range of criteria, married people feel happier and more fulfilled, have better physical and mental health, are better-off financially, and have more satisfying sex than single or divorced people (Argyle, 1999; Fletcher et al., 2015; Waite & Gallagher, 2000). Married men and women from many different countries, across different age groups, and at different stages of their marital relationships consistently report greater subjective well-being than those without stable relationships (Diener et al., 2000; Grover & Helliwell, 2019). And while close relationships in general have a positive impact on happiness and well-being (Waldinger & Schulz, 2023), marriage has the strongest effect (Argyle, 1999).

Love and change

At the heart of the overwhelmingly negative feminist interpretations of romantic love lies the conviction that under patriarchy, love inevitably amounts to the "erotic conflict between the powerful and powerless" (hooks, 2002, p. 243). But even one of the fiercest critics of romantic love, Shulamith Firestone, admits that "love between two equals would be an enrichment, each enlarging himself [sic] through the other" (1970/1979, p. 123). Despite much progress in gender relations, many feminists remain rightly worried that the still uneven power distribution both in the public and private spheres constantly undermines the possibility of such egalitarian couple relationships (Evans, 2003; Ferguson, 2013; Jónasdóttir, 1991). At the same time, however, some feminists argue that heterosexual love needs to be understood as more than a constraining delusion suggested by the second-wave analyses and still persisting in public discourses (Jónasdóttir, 2013, p. 12). Some call for a greater recognition of women's agency in their love relationships, despite oppressive social structures (Jackson, 1999). Some note that even under patriarchy, many heterosexual couples are able to achieve "good enough—never perfect—understanding, support, sharing, mutual pleasure and satisfaction of needs" to constitute love (Hollway, 1993, p. 416). Some admit that cultural valorization of romantic love has had a "softening" effect on Western patriarchy (Millet, 1970, p. 36); that it has "allow[ed] women a greater, legitimate part in the negotiation of marriage" (Evans, 2003, p. 7) and has "slowly eroded male supremacy inside the household" (Illouz, 2006, p. 46). Importantly, a few feminists suggest that love is in fact the best way to equality. The feminist scholar and activist bell hooks declares that "the transformative power of love is the foundation of all meaningful social change" (2001b, p. 17), and the feminist ethicist and psychologist Carol Gilligan points out that "if patriarchy is antithetical to love, then love holds the potential to uproot patriarchy" (2002, pp. 210–211).

Indeed, love is the evolutionary mechanism for gender equality and cooperation, transforming humans at the level of individuals, societies, and the species. At the individual level (as mentioned in the section "Chemistry of Love" above), loving relationships lower testosterone, especially in men. This in turn reduces their aggression, competitiveness, and risk taking, and increases their long-term orientation, nurturance, and trust. When such changes are replicated at a group level through long-term pair-bonding and monogamous marriage norms, they decrease rates of many types of violence, crime, and addiction, and at the same time encourage interpersonal and group cooperation (Henrich, 2020; Henrich et al., 2012).[11] Over the course of our evolution, those changes have turned the human male into the most caring of all primates and the human species into the most cooperative one.

Romantic love is neither new nor unique to Western culture; it is a universal human drive inextricably connected with many of the behavioural, neuropsychological, and social characteristics of our species. And for as long as humans reproduce sexually, it will remain one of the strongest motivational forces encoded in our genes, regardless of whether or not it actually results in children. Moreover, across cultures, greater cultural valuation of romantic love goes hand in hand with greater recognition of the individual value and autonomy of each person, and consequently greater social and economic independence for women (De Munck et al., 2016). Thus, while it is true that the prominence of love in modern Western culture is stronger than ever, this is a sign not of women's oppression but of their power: the power to express their sexuality, to have meaningful control over their reproduction, and to freely choose their partners. The importance of choice as a sign of autonomy and power in both feminist and evolutionary perspectives is the subject of the next chapter.

Notes

1. For a more detailed overview of feminist approaches to love, the notion of choice, and romantic fiction, see Grant (2018).
2. Lack of understanding of this distinction often causes confusion evident in some critiques of evolutionary sciences. Proximate explanations focus on mechanisms directly underlying a behaviour or trait, on things that happen within the lifespan of an individual and in specific circumstances. Ultimate explanations focus on the evolutionary significance of a behaviour or trait, on things that occur in populations over many generations. For a helpful explanation of the ultimate-proximate distinction, though not related to love, see Scott-Phillips et al., 2011.
3. Many of the evolutionarily ancient emotional mechanisms underpinning heterosexual relationships also apply to homosexual ones (even though the evolution of homosexuality is still not fully understood). Homosexual love also involves sexual desire, emotional intimacy, and long-term commitment, as well as jealousy, romantic rejection, and heartbreak; when socially permitted, many homosexual people get married and become parents.
4. Fitness interdependence is the degree to which organisms influence each other's survival and reproduction.

5 Relatively early menopause used to be considered a fitness disadvantage, but we now know that although older women can no longer reproduce, they are usually significant contributors to the fitness of their children, grandchildren, and other kin—thus increasing their own reproductive success, albeit less directly (Hawkes & Coxworth, 2013). This is also true for other species experiencing menopause, such as toothed whales (Ellis et al., 2024).
6 In fact, in all complex organisms, sexual selection is connected to social selection; for all of them "sexual behavior is about more than exchanging gametes" (Rosenthal & Ryan, 2022).
7 As already mentioned in the Introduction, the view of love as an invention of Western modernity is not limited to second-wave feminists but is still the dominant view across the humanities (see Bloch, 1991; de Rougemont, 1939/1983; Lewis, 1936/1948).
8 Many sociologists also trace the strong connection between marriage and love in Europe and America to the social transformations of the late eighteenth and early nineteenth centuries, although they do not generally consider it unequivocally detrimental to women (Coontz, 2005; Giddens, 1992). However, they focus exclusively on Western modernity and do not try to account for cross-cultural patterns.
9 The estimates vary depending on the source.
10 The communal value of marriage is also stressed by the historian Stephanie Coontz (2005). She is equally critical about the feminist view of marriage as exploitative and oppressive for women as she is about the evolutionary basis for marriage, but like many evolutionists, she argues that marriage has always "converted strangers into relatives and extended cooperative relations beyond the immediate family" (Coontz, 2005, p. 6).
11 The socially stabilizing and individually beneficial force of long-term monogamous relationships is also noted by several feminist-inflected arguments, from Mary Wollstonecraft's (1792/2004) to some of the most recent ones (e.g., Evans, 2003; Harrington, 2023; Perry, 2022).

References

Apostolou, M. (2017). *Sexual selection in homo sapiens: Parental control over mating and the opportunity cost of free mate choice.* Springer.

Argyle, M. (1999). Causes and correlates of happiness. In D. Kahneman, E. Diener, & N. Schwarz (Eds.), *Well-being: The foundations of hedonic psychology* (pp. 353–373). Russell Sage Foundation.

Atkinson, T.-G. (1974). *Amazon Odyssey.* Links Books.

Baumard, N., Huillery, E., Hyafil, A., & Safra, L. (2022). The cultural evolution of love in literary history. *Nature Human Behaviour*, 6(4), 506–522. https://doi.org/10.1038/s41562-022-01292-z

Beck, U., & Beck-Gernsheim, E. (1990/1995). *The normal chaos of love.* Polity Press.

Betzig, L. (1989). Causes of conjugal dissolution: A cross-cultural study. *Current Anthropology*, 30(5), 654–676. https://doi.org/10.1086/203798

Bloch, R. H. (1991). *Medieval misogyny and the invention of Western romantic love.* University of Chicago Press.

Booth, A., & Dabbs Jr, J. M. (1993). Testosterone and men's marriages. *Social Forces*, 72(2), 463–477.

Bowlby, J. (1969). *Attachment and loss.* Hogarth P.

Brooks, A. (Ed.). (2021). *The Routledge companion to romantic love.* Routledge.

Brown, D. E. (1991). *Human universals.* McGraw-Hill, Inc.

Buss, D. M. (2003). *The evolution of desire: Strategies of human mating* (Rev., Kindle ed.). Basic Books.

Buss, D. M. (2018). The evolution of love in humans. In K. Sternberg & R. J. Sternberg (Eds.), *The new psychology of love* (2nd ed., pp. 42–63). Cambridge University Press. https://doi.org/10.1017/9781108658225.004

Buss, D. M., Abbott, M., Angleitner, A., Asherian, A., Biaggio, A., Blanco-Villasenor, A., Bruchon-Schweitzer, M., Ch'U, H.-Y., Czapinski, J., Deraad, B., Ekehammar, B., Lohamy, N., Fioravanti, M., Georgas, J., Gjerde, P., Guttman, R., Hazan, F., Iwawaki, S., Janakiramaiah, N., ... Yang, K.-S. (1990). International preferences in selecting mates: A study of 37 cultures. *Journal of Cross-Cultural Psychology*, 21(1), 5–47.

Campbell, A. (2013). *A mind of her own: The evolutionary psychology of women* (2nd ed.). Oxford University Press.
Cancian, F. M. (1986). The feminization of love. *Signs, 11*(4), 692–709. http://www.jstor.org/stable/3174139
Chapais, B. (2013). Monogamy, strongly bonded groups, and the evolution of human social structure. *Evolutionary Anthropology: Issues, News, and Reviews, 22*(2), 52–65. https://doi.org/10.1002/evan.21345
Chodorow, N. (1978). *The reproduction of mothering: Psychoanalysis and the sociology of gender*. University of California Press.
Comer, L. (1974). *Wedlocked women*. Feminist Books.
Coontz, S. (2005). *Marriage, a history: From obedience to intimacy or how love conquered marriage*. Viking.
de Beauvoir, S. (1949/1972). *The second sex*. Penguin.
De Munck, V., Korotayev, A., & McGreevey, J. (2016). Romantic love and family organization. *Evolutionary Psychology, 14*(4), 1–13. https://doi.org/10.1177/1474704916674211
de Rougemont, D. (1939/1983). *Love in the Western world*. Princeton University Press.
Diener, E., Gohm, C. L., Suh, E., & Oishi, S. (2000). Similarity of the relations between marital status and subjective well-being across cultures. *Journal of Cross-Cultural Psychology, 31*(4), 419–436. https://doi.org/10.1177/0022022100031004001
Dworkin, A. (1981). *Pornography: Men possessing women*. Women's Press.
Dworkin, A. (1987). *Intercourse*. Free Press.
Ellis, S., Franks, D. W., Nielsen, M. L. K., Weiss, M. N., & Croft, D. P. (2024). The evolution of menopause in toothed whales. *Nature, 627*(8004), 579–585. https://doi.org/10.1038/s41586-024-07159-9
Evans, M. (2003). *Love, an unromantic discussion*. Blackwell Publishers.
Ferguson, A. (2013). Feminist love politics: Romance, care, and solidarity. In A. G. Jónasdóttir & A. Ferguson (Eds.), *Love: A question for feminism in the twenty-first century* (pp. 250–264). Routledge.
Firestone, S. (1970/1979). *The dialectic of sex: The case for feminist revolution*. The Women's Press.
Fisher, H. E. (1982). *The sex contract: The evolution of human behaviour*. Granada.
Fisher, H. E. (2005). *Why we love: The nature and chemistry of romantic love*. Henry Holt and Co.
Fisher, H. E. (2016). *Anatomy of love: A natural history of mating, marriage, and why we stray* (Rev., Kindle ed.). W. W. Norton & Company.
Fisher, H. E., Aron, A., & Brown, L. L. (2006). Romantic love: A mammalian brain system for mate choice. *Philosophical Transactions: Biological Sciences, 361*(1476), 2173–2186. http://www.jstor.org/stable/20209808
Fisher, H. E., Aron, A., Mashek, D., Li, H., & Brown, L. L. (2002). Defining the brain systems of lust, romantic attraction, and attachment. *Archives of Sexual Behavior, 31*(5), 413–419.
Fletcher, G. J. O., Simpson, J. A., Campbell, L., & Overall, N. C. (2015). Pair-bonding, romantic love, and evolution. *Perspectives on Psychological Science, 10*(1), 20–36. https://doi.org/10.1177/1745691614561683
Friedan, B. (1963/1997). *The feminine mystique*. W.W. Norton.
García-Andrade, A., Gunnarsson, L., & Jónasdóttir, A. (Eds.). (2018). *Feminism and the power of love: Interdisciplinary interventions*. Routledge. https://doi.org/10.4324/9781315200798
Garcia, J. R., & Reiber, C. (2008). Hook-up behavior: A biopsychosocial perspective. *Evolutionary Behavioral Sciences, 2*(4), 192–208.
Gettler, L. T., McDade, T. W., Agustin, S. S., Feranil, A. B., & Kuzawa, C. W. (2013). Do testosterone declines during the transition to marriage and fatherhood relate to men's sexual behavior? Evidence from the Philippines. *Hormones and Behavior, 64*(5), 755–763. https://doi.org/10.1016/j.yhbeh.2013.08.019
Giddens, A. (1992). *The transformation of intimacy: Sexuality, love and eroticism in modern societies*. Polity Press.
Gilligan, C. (2002). *The birth of pleasure*. Alfred A. Knopf.
Gottschall, J., & Nordlund, M. (2006). Romantic love: A literary universal? *Philosophy and Literature, 30*(2), 450–470.
Grant, A. (2018). *From Mr Darcy to Mr Big: An evolutionary-feminist account of love and choice in popular romantic fiction* [Doctoral dissertation, University of Auckland]. http://hdl.handle.net/2292/37473

Grebe, N. M., Sarafin, R. E., Strenth, C. R., & Zilioli, S. (2019). Pair-bonding, fatherhood, and the role of testosterone: A meta-analytic review. *Neuroscience & Biobehavioral Reviews, 98*, 221–233.

Greer, G. (1970). *The female eunuch*. McGraw-Hill Book Company.

Greiling, H., & Buss, D. M. (2000). Women's sexual strategies: The hidden dimension of extra-pair mating. *Personality and Individual Differences, 28*(5), 929–963. https://doi.org/10.1016/S0191-8869(99)00151-8

Griffin, S. (1971/1983). The politics of rape. In *Made from this earth: An anthology of writings* (pp. 39–58). Harper & Row.

Grover, S., & Helliwell, J. F. (2019). How's life at home? New evidence on marriage and the set point for happiness. *Journal of Happiness Studies, 20*(2), 373–390.

Harrington, M. (2023). *Feminism against progress*. Simon and Schuster.

Harris, H. (1995). Rethinking Polynesian heterosexual relationships: A case study on Mangaia, Cook Islands. In W. Jankowiak (Ed.), *Romantic passion: A universal experience?* (pp. 95–127). Columbia University Press.

Hatfield, E., & Rapson, R. L. (1996). *Love and sex: Cross-cultural perspectives*. Allyn and Bacon.

Hawkes, K., & Coxworth, J. E. (2013). Grandmothers and the evolution of human longevity: A review of findings and future directions. *Evolutionary Anthropology: Issues, News, and Reviews, 22*(6), 294–302. https://doi.org/10.1002/evan.21382

Henrich, J. (2020). *The WEIRDest people in the world: How the West became psychologically peculiar and particularly prosperous*. Farrar, Straus and Giroux.

Henrich, J., Boyd, R., & Richerson, P. J. (2012). The puzzle of monogamous marriage. *Philosophical Transactions of the Royal Society of London B: Biological Sciences, 367*(1589), 657–669. https://doi.org/10.1098/rstb.2011.0290

Hogan, P. C. (2003). *The mind and its stories: Narrative universals and human emotion*. Cambridge University Press.

Hollway, W. (1993). Theorizing heterosexuality: A response. *Feminism & Psychology, 3*(3), 412–417. https://doi.org/10.1177/0959353593033020

hooks, b. (2001a). *All about love: New visions*. HarperCollins.

hooks, b. (2001b). *Salvation: Black people and love*. William Morrow.

hooks, b. (2002). *Communion: The female search for love*. William Morrow.

Hrdy, S. B. (2009). *Mothers and others: The evolutionary origins of mutual understanding*. Belknap Press of Harvard University Press.

Hrdy, S. B. (2024). *Father time: A natural history of men and babies*. Princeton University Press.

Illouz, E. (2006). Romantic love. In S. Seidman, N. Fischer, & C. Meeks (Eds.), *Handbook of the new sexuality studies* (pp. 40–48). Routledge.

Illouz, E. (2007). *Cold intimacies: The making of emotional capitalism*. Polity Press.

Jackson, S. (1999). Women and heterosexual love: Complicity, resistance and change. In *Heterosexuality in question* (pp. 113–122). Sage Publications.

Jankowiak, W., & Nelson, A. J. (2021). The state of ethnological research on love: A critical review. In C.-H. Mayer & E. Vanderheiden (Eds.), *International handbook of love: Transcultural and transdisciplinary perspectives* (pp. 23–39). Springer International Publishing. https://doi.org/10.1007/978-3-030-45996-3_2

Jankowiak, W. (Ed.). (1995). *Romantic passion: A universal experience?* Columbia University Press.

Jankowiak, W., & Fisher, T. (1992). A cross-cultural perspective on romantic love. *Ethnology, 31*, 149–155. http://www.jstor.org/stable/3773618

Jeffreys, S. (1990). *Anticlimax: A feminist perspective on the sexual revolution*. Women's Press.

Jeffreys, S. (2004). The need to abolish marriage. *Feminism & Psychology, 14*(2), 327–331. https://doi.org/10.1177/0959353504040314

Jónasdóttir, A. G. (2013). Love studies: A (re)new(ed) field of knowledge interests. In A. G. Jónasdóttir & A. Ferguson (Eds.), *Love: A question for feminism in the twenty-first century* (pp. 11–30). Routledge.

Jónasdóttir, A. G. (1991). *Love power and political interests: Towards a theory of patriarchy in contemporary western societies*. University of Örebro.

Kaplan, H., Hill, K., Lancaster, J., & Hurtado, A. M. (2000). A theory of human life history evolution: Diet, intelligence, and longevity. *Evolutionary Anthropology, 9*(4), 156–185. https://doi.org/10.1002/1520-6505(2000)9:4<156::AID-EVAN5>3.0.CO;2-7

Kaplan, H. S., Hooper, P. L., & Gurven, M. (2009). The evolutionary and ecological roots of human social organization. *Philosophical Transactions of the Royal Society B: Biological Sciences, 364*(1533), 3289–3299.

Karandashev, V. (2017). *Romantic love in cultural contexts.* Springer International Publishing. https://doi.org/10.1007/978-3-319-42683-9

Koedt, A., Levine, E., & Rapone, A. (Eds.). (1973). *Radical feminism.* Quadrangle Books.

Konstan, D. (1994). *Sexual symmetry: Love in the ancient novel and related genres.* Princeton University Press.

Kuzawa, C. W., Gettler, L. T., Muller, M. N., McDade, T. W., & Feranil, A. B. (2009). Fatherhood, pairbonding and testosterone in the Philippines. *Hormones and Behavior, 56*(4), 429–435. https://doi.org/10.1016/j.yhbeh.2009.07.010

Lancaster, J. B. (1991). A feminist and evolutionary biologist looks at women. *American Journal of Physical Anthropology, 34*(S13), 1–11. https://doi.org/10.1002/ajpa.1330340603

Lewandowska-Tomaszczyk, B., & Wilson, P. A. (2021). Focus on cross-cultural models of love. In C.-H. Mayer & E. Vanderheiden (Eds.), *International handbook of love: Transcultural and transdisciplinary perspectives* (pp. 1063–1086). Springer International Publishing. https://doi.org/10.1007/978-3-030-45996-3_56

Lewis, C. S. (1936/1948). *The allegory of love: A study in medieval tradition.* Oxford University Press.

Millett, K. (1970). *Sexual politics.* Doubleday.

Nelson, A. J., & Jankowiak, W. (2021). Love's ethnographic record: Beyond the love/arranged marriage dichotomy and other false essentialisms. In C.-H. Mayer & E. Vanderheiden (Eds.), *International handbook of love: Transcultural and transdisciplinary perspectives* (pp. 41–57). Springer International Publishing. https://doi.org/10.1007/978-3-030-45996-3_3

Neto, F., Mullet, E., Deschamps, J.-C., Barros, J., Benvindo, R., Camino, L., Falconi, A., Kagibanga, V., & Machado, M. (2000). Cross-cultural variations in attitudes toward love. *Journal of Cross-Cultural Psychology, 31*(5), 626–635.

O'Leary, K. D., Acevedo, B. P., Aron, A., Huddy, L., & Mashek, D. (2012). Is long-term love more than a rare phenomenon? If so, what are its correlates? *Social Psychological and Personality Science, 3*(2), 241–249.

Perry, L. (2022). *The case against the sexual revolution.* John Wiley & Sons.

Rich, A. (1980). Compulsory heterosexuality and lesbian existence. *Signs, 5*(4), 631–660.

Rosenthal, G. G., & Ryan, M. J. (2022). Sexual selection and the ascent of women: Mate choice research since Darwin. *Science, 375,* eabi6308. https://doi.org/10.1126/science.abi6308

Rubin, G. (1975). The traffic of women: Notes on the 'political economy' of sex. In R. R. Reiter (Ed.), *Toward an anthropology of women.* Monthly Review Press.

Scalise Sugiyama, M. (2003/2010). Cultural variation is part of human nature: Literary universals, context-sensitivity, and "Shakespeare in the bush". In B. Boyd, J. Carroll, & J. Gottschall (Eds.), *Evolution, literature, and film: A reader* (pp. 483–489). Columbia University Press.

Scelza, B. A. (2013). Choosy but not chaste: Multiple mating in human females. *Evolutionary Anthropology: Issues, News, and Reviews, 22*(5), 259–269. https://doi.org/10.1002/evan.21373

Scott-Phillips, T. C., Dickins, T. E., & West, S. A. (2011). Evolutionary theory and the ultimate–proximate distinction in the human behavioral sciences. *Perspectives on Psychological Science, 6*(1), 8–47. https://doi.org/10.1177/1745691610393528

Seidman, S. (1991). *Romantic longings: Love in America, 1830–1980.* Routledge.

Shostak, M. (1990). *Nisa, the life and words of a !Kung woman.* Earthscan Publications.

Singer, I. (1987). *The nature of love* (Vol. 3: The modern world). The University of Chicago Press.

Sternberg, R. J. (1986). A triangular theory of love. *Psychological Review, 93,* 119–135.

Tennov, D. (1979). *Love and limerence: The experience of being in love.* Stein and Day.

Townsend, J. M. (1995). Sex without emotional involvement: An evolutionary interpretation of sex differences. *Archives of Sexual Behavior, 24*(2), 173–206. https://doi.org/10.1007/bf01541580

Townsend, J. M., Kline, J., & Wasserman, T. H. (1995). Low-investment copulation: Sex differences in motivations and emotional reactions. *Ethology and Sociobiology, 16*(1), 25–51.

Waite, L. J., & Gallagher, M. (2000). *The case for marriage: Why married people are happier, healthier, and better off financially.* Doubleday.

Waldinger, R., & Schulz, M. (2023). *The good life: Lessons from the world's longest scientific study of happiness.* Simon and Schuster.

Wollstonecraft, M. (1792/2004). A vindication of the rights of woman. In J. Todd & M. Butler (Eds.), *The works of Mary Wollstonecraft* (Electronic ed., Vol. 5, pp. 63–267). InteLex Corp.

2
CHOICE

From sexual selection to emotional intelligence

In the previous chapter, I argued against the feminist claim that love is a patriarchal myth. It is now time to dispel an evolutionary myth tracing back to Darwin: the myth of a "coy" and "passive" female (1871/2003, p. 222), more caring than man but ultimately inferior (pp. 563–565). This myth, painting women as "naturally" submissive wives and self-sacrificing mothers, justifiably led feminists to be suspicious of biological definitions of womanhood and critical of androcentric biases in the evolutionary sciences. However, Darwin also granted females the power of choice, and modern evolutionary theory—in no small part because of feminist influences—emphasizes both female agency and female variability, gradually acknowledging that the sexuality, sociality, and cognition of women have impacted human evolution as much as those of men.

Females across species, including our own, routinely make active choices and employ a range of sophisticated strategies in different domains of their lives directed at maximizing their reproduction and survival (Hrdy, 1981/1999, 1999; Rosenthal & Ryan, 2022; Small, 1993). These strategies are not always conscious or calculated; many rely on ancient emotional mechanisms. This does not make them any less significant. Although for centuries emotions were disparaged—and often perniciously linked with the feminine—we now know that they are an indispensable component of human rationality, calibrated by evolution to streamline some of the most complex life decisions (Al-Shawaf et al., 2016; Damasio, 1996; Frank, 1988; Goleman, 1995/2005). Female mate choices are some of the most consequential ones: Not only do they influence the life course of the individual female and her offspring, but they also determine which males are reproductively successful, and consequently which male traits—physical, psychological, and social—will be present in future generations. Although this process is affected by numerous factors, there is no doubt that individual female choices shape the evolutionary trajectory of her species.

This emphasis on continuous change driven by individually variable choices in the face of various constraints is an important point of connection between evolutionary and feminist approaches (Grosz, 2005). Although the two camps are still focused more on mutual critique than cooperation, current evolutionary research provides some of the strongest arguments in support of the feminist goals of female autonomy and gender equality. It also rehabilitates love from a tool of oppression to a mechanism of choice—and a reward for making a choice which benefits both individuals and communities.

Feminism and choice

Since lack of choice is the most obvious sign of oppression, the notion of autonomous choice for women has always been fundamental to feminism. However, what exactly counts as a *feminist* choice has been contested, especially when it comes to love. Feminist critiques of love, marriage, monogamy, and motherhood start from the premise that under patriarchy women lack genuine choice in these areas. Heterosexuality itself is viewed by some scholars as an "oppressive socially constructed patriarchal institution" (Kemp & Squires, 1997, p. 316), which has been "forcibly and subliminally imposed on women" (Rich, 1980, p. 653)—not least with the aid of romantic fiction and biological science. Second-wave feminists criticized women in heterosexual relationships for their passive submission to hegemonic ideals and urged women to denounce their intimate relationships with men as "sleeping with the enemy". These sentiments, although usually not as strongly worded, are still evident in many feminist debates about women's situation. And while there continue to be valid reasons to focus on women's subordination, this dogmatic stance has alienated many women who feel that it does not help them achieve greater autonomy, nor does it expand viable options for them, but mostly makes them feel guilty and ashamed about the ones they already have (see several essays in Vance, 1984; and the overview in Snyder-Hall, 2010).

Some feminist scholars agree that this "negative paradigm of subjectification" is too limited, and that to better understand and effect change within gender relations "a broader notion of agency" is needed (McNay, 2000, p. 155). Many see sexual relationships in particular as opportunities for exercising female agency. Stevi Jackson contends that the lived experience of heterosexual intimacy is rarely completely determined by the structures or ideologies of patriarchy; that within their constraints, "there is some room for manoeuvre", including the possibility of resistance and change (1996, p. 34; 1999). Carol Vance argues that although sexuality is "a domain of restriction, repression, and danger", it is equally a domain of pleasure which women have always strived to define in their own terms (1984, p. 1). Lynne Segal (1994) postulates that sex is the equalizing force in gender relations, and Wendy Hollway sees it as "a primary site of women's power and men's resistance" (1984, p. 68).

The notion of female empowerment, especially through sexual liberation, was embraced by the new generation of feminists, the third wave (as perhaps best illustrated by the success of *Sex and the City*). These feminists emphatically reject "victim feminism" and propose to replace it with "power feminism", the key feature of which is "[tolerance] of other women's choices about sexuality and appearance; [and belief] that what every woman does with her body and in her bed is her own business" (Wolf, 1993, p. 150). They emphasize "self-possession, self-determination, and an endless array of non-dichotomous possibilities" (Walker, 1995, p. xxxiv) as an essential part of asserting women's equality: Just as diversity among men has long been accepted, we need to recognize and accept that women have different opinions and desires (Wolf, 1993, p. 151). Feminism should not try to impose a uniform identity onto women but empower them to make better choices. In Gloria Steinem's words, "the greatest gift we can give one another is the power to make a choice. The power to choose is even more important than the choices we make" (1995, p. xxvi).

This position has in turn been criticized for exaggerating the extent of women's newly-won freedoms, for ignoring the coercive structures that still heavily impact women's lives, and for attempting to "reassert the boundary between public and private that many feminists have long contested" (Ferguson, 2010, p. 251; see also Baker, 2008). Critics point out that the enthusiastic rhetoric of choice is naïve, depoliticized, and aligned with neoliberal individualism and consumerism. Consequently, they see the emphasis on choice as a new regime of constraint, leading to new forms of subordination (McRobbie, 2004).

Despite being highly critical of individualism as an ideology, Denise Thompson (2001, pp. 43–50) reminds us that the notion of the individual and her right to choose must remain at the top of the feminist agenda. She invokes Sarah Hoagland's concept of "moral agency" defined as "the ability to choose in limited situations" (1988, p. 231). Hoagland highlights that "It is not because we are free and moral agents that we are able to make moral choices. Rather, it is because we make choices, ... act in the face of limits, that we declare ourselves to be moral beings" (1988, p. 231, emphasis in the original).[1] This account recognizes systemic constraints but also the possibility of creating change through the choices we make. Similarly, evolutionary theory recognizes the constraints of species-typical traits and life histories but also the possibility of modification through not only random mutation but also through deliberate choices. Crucially, it is not uniformity but variability of choices that is the engine of change—and this is equally true for social and evolutionary change.

Evolution and choice

Sexual selection and female choice

Every living thing has two ultimate goals: survival and reproduction. Darwin's theory of natural selection explains how organisms change over time, adapting to their environments to maximize their chances of survival. But many species have physiological or behavioural traits that may in fact hinder their survival: bright colours or loud vocalizations make many insects, fish, frogs, and birds more easily identifiable by predators; large tails in birds or antlers in deer make them less mobile; and the production of such features seemingly wastes a lot of precious nutrients. To account for the existence of such traits, Darwin (1871/2003) proposed the theory of sexual selection directed at maximizing individuals' reproductive success through competition with other members of the same species.[2] To put it simply, in some species, males fight it out, and the biggest, strongest male wins the right to mate with the available females. This is true for the walrus and the gorilla, for example—and has sometimes been true for men as well, as in the case of harem owners. In many other species, the females *choose* to mate with males that most impress them. One of the most spectacular examples of this process is the peacock's tail—and humans have many such advertising displays, from six-packs to sonnets and sports cars.

While Darwin's contemporaries and subsequent generations of (mostly male) scientists readily accepted the part of his theory relating to male competition, the idea of *female choice* was a lot harder to swallow (Cronin, 1991): Not only did it attribute considerable amount of power to females, but it also effectively turned males into sexual objects. Consequently, with a few notable exceptions (Bateman, 1948; R. A. Fisher, 1915; Maynard Smith, 1956), this part of Darwin's theory was either rejected or ignored for nearly 100 years until, partially due to the feminist movement, it started to be taken seriously.

Since the 1970s, extensive research into the sexual behaviours of numerous species, including humans, confirmed that females routinely make complex choices based on different kinds of male displays, from elaborate dances in fruit flies and intricate colouring in fish and birds to the size of territory a male can control (Prum, 2017; Small, 1993, 1995). Some researchers emphasize the aesthetic value of these displays and the female's sense of pleasure derived from them (Miller, 2000; Prum, 2017); others have demonstrated that such displays are fitness indicators giving females reliable clues about the genetic quality of different males (Hamilton & Zuk, 1982; Zahavi, 1975). Either way, these individually motivated female choices determine, at least in part, which males will reproduce and pass their genes onto future offspring. Importantly, the traits resulting from sexual selection are only imprinted in our genes because of past choices and will be maintained in the population only for as long as they continue to be chosen.

Choosy not chaste

But why should males be more competitive and females more selective? According to parental investment theory (Trivers, 1972), whichever sex invests more time, energy, and resources in the offspring is naturally more discerning about sexual partners. In most species, the reproductive load of the females is significantly heavier than that of males.[3] In all mammals, including primates, it necessarily includes internal fertilization, gestation, and lactation, all of which can take up to several years, while the necessary male investment is limited to several seconds or minutes of copulation. Thus, males can potentially increase their reproductive success simply by increasing the quantity of their sexual partners; females are always more limited by their own reproductive capacity and therefore may benefit more from focusing on the quality of their mates (Bateman, 1948).Consequently, early evolutionary psychologists argued that a highly restricted mating strategy (i.e., a long-term, monogamous relationship) is the only logical option for women. According to Donald Symons (1979), sexual eagerness would actually undermine female choice by promoting random matings; it would also jeopardize male investment in children by undermining his paternity certainty. In Symons's view, a sexually assertive, promiscuous woman was a fantasy that existed "primarily if not exclusively, in the ideology of feminism, the hopes of boys and the fears of men" (1979, p. 92). However, it is becoming increasingly clear that Trivers's and Bateman's principles, while widely accepted in evolutionary sciences, do not easily translate into indiscriminately eager men and invariably chaste women passively waiting for their prince to come (Hrdy, 1981/1999; Tang-Martínez, 2016).

There is now abundant evidence that females of various species can be promiscuous, adulterous, and highly competitive. Some female primates actively solicit hundreds, sometimes thousands of copulations from dozens of different males for every offspring they produce (Hrdy, 1999, p. 85; Small, 1993, p. 111). In many seemingly monogamous bird species, large proportions of chicks are not sired by the official "husband" of the female (Ridley, 1993, pp. 213–215), and in primates, sometimes more than half of the young can be fathered by males from outside the group the female belongs to (Hrdy 1999, p. 85). Female primates also compete for access to high-ranking males and harass lower-ranking females in order to suppress their fertility (Small, 1993, p. 179). Some female birds destroy the eggs of their rivals (Zuk, 2002, pp. 37–38), and in many species of so-called cooperative breeders (such as meerkats, tamarins, or hyenas), the alpha female will cannibalize the young of other females (Campbell, 2013, pp. 158–159).

Given these biological patterns, it seems unlikely that human females are, in contrast, chaste and passive. Indeed, the vast majority of traditional societies believe that women's sex drive is similar to men's (H. E. Fisher, 2016, p. 310). It is certainly strong enough that most cultures have tried to restrain it through various methods such as veiling, genital mutilation, biased laws about adultery or divorce, or idealizing female chastity. Despite these sometimes-extreme prohibitions, women around the world do not invariably opt for life-long monogamy but often look for ways to retain their sexual and reproductive autonomy, be it through one-off hook-ups, on-going affairs, or divorce and remarriage (Greiling & Buss, 2000; Hrdy, 1981/1999, 1999; Scelza, 2013).

We now have a robust theoretical understanding and ample empirical evidence for a number of benefits women derive from such short-term or unrestricted strategies (for useful summaries see Greiling & Buss, 2000; Scelza, 2013).[4] Having several sexual partners increases genetic diversity of offspring and provides a fertility back-up (Hrdy, 1981/1999; Jennions & Petrie, 2000). Through affairs which confuse paternity, women can obtain immediate resources or long-term support and protection for themselves and their children from more than one man (Hrdy, 1981/1999; Meston & Buss, 2009). Short-term relationships can be used by women to clarify their own mate preferences, to improve their skills of attracting mates, to evaluate the prospects of a long-term relationship, to manipulate their current mate, or to obtain a better one (Greiling & Buss, 2000).

Biology of choice

Recent research also demonstrates that women's sexual biology is particularly strongly geared towards enabling choice and flexibility, shattering more evolutionary myths about such traits as concealed ovulation, variable orgasm, and the immobile ovum. Although several other primates do not advertise their ovulation, and a few (like our close relatives, the bonobos) use sex for social, rather than reproductive reasons, none can match women's flexibility in this respect (Hrdy, 1981/1999). The loss of oestrus frees women from the biological compulsion to copulate and allows them to more easily choose when to have sex, with whom, and for what reason, and those reasons can vary from reproduction and love to obtaining pleasure, power, resources, or even revenge (H. E. Fisher, 2016, pp. 184–187; Meston & Buss, 2009).

During sex, the fickle female orgasm, once thought to be an imperfect, inconsequential by-product of its male counterpart (Symons, 1979), turns out to be another choice-enabling feature. On the one hand, since women are more likely to achieve orgasm with attentive, committed partners, it helps them maintain long-term relationships. On the other hand, when women have extra-marital affairs, their orgasms tend to be more intense, especially when the lover is more attractive than the husband. Stronger orgasm increases the chances of impregnation, effectively helping the woman choose which man will father her children (for overviews of research see Buss, 2003; H. E. Fisher, 2016).

Finally, the ovum has often been conceptualized as the paragon of female sexual passivity, patiently waiting for the millions of sperm to fight it out amongst themselves until the most vigorous one reaches its trophy. It turns out, however, that the docile-seeming egg rigs the race: As it is released, the egg changes the biochemistry of oviductal fluids in ways that favour the sperm with specific genetic characteristics while blocking others, and thus it chooses the winner (Nadeau, 2017).

Clearly, sexual passivity is not the defining feature of women's nature. Nevertheless, since even casual sex can have long-term consequences for women, they are generally more interested in committed relationships. This is why romantic fiction, while considering many diverse aspects of female sexuality, focuses so strongly on the search for a long-term partner.

Cads and dads

The myth of naturally monogamous, passive women has long been complemented by the myth of naturally polygynous men invariably chasing unencumbered sex with as many women as possible. Indeed, there is a lot of research supporting the idea that, on average, men are more interested in and more positive about casual sex (Buss & Schmitt, 1993; Campbell, 2008; Schmitt, 2005). But there is also evidence that men may exaggerate and women under-report the extent of their sexual experiences or desires in line with social expectations: When the study subjects think that their responses are being verified by a lie detector, such sex differences become minimal (Alexander & Fisher, 2003). One recent study found that in the United States, only the top 5% of men live up to their promiscuous image while many have fewer sexual partners than do women (Harper et al., 2017).

The rewards of an unrestricted, short-term strategy for men might seem obvious: By having sex with a greater number of women, they can theoretically increase their reproductive success. But this is only possible if they can attract multiple fertile partners and if those partners are able to raise the resulting children to maturity. It seems that in practice only some men opt for the unrestricted strategy, and those who do, often do so only during some periods of their lives (Buller 2005, 220–221). It has been suggested that men have two distinct mating strategies: Some are cads, not interested in long-term relationships but focused on maximizing the number of sexual partners, sometimes by faking romantic feelings; others are dads, trying to maximize their reproductive success through long-term commitment and substantial paternal investment (Barash, 2001; Jobling, 2002; Kruger et al., 2005). However, it is probably more accurate to think of these two strategies not as mutually exclusive but as representing different dimensions of a more complex and flexible approach influenced by factors such as levels of testosterone, personality traits, childhood experiences, social pressures, and mating opportunities. In fact, overwhelming majority of men (99% in these two studies: Garcia & Reiber, 2008; Pedersen et al., 2002) state that they do want a committed, monogamous relationship at some point in their life. And when men find a satisfying relationship, their interest in casual sex dramatically diminishes (Geher & Kaufman, 2013, p. 92). Moreover, given human social organization, a short-term strategy is relatively risky even for men: It increases male-male competition and upsets male coalitions. So, sometimes, some men may like to play around, but when they *stick* around not only do they reap all the benefits of committed relationships mentioned in the previous chapter but also their children are more likely to survive and prosper (Fletcher et al., 2015; Hrdy, 2009, 2024).

One of the biggest challenges for women is to distinguish between dads and cads. Mistakes in gauging men's willingness to commit long-term can have lasting and sometimes disastrous consequences for women, from a broken heart to single motherhood and social ostracism. To minimize such mistakes, women evolved an inferential bias, which generally leads them to be very sceptical about men's intentions in the early stages of courtship (Haselton & Buss, 2000). Not surprisingly, romantic fiction is often concerned with how best to calibrate this commitment scepticism and how to separate dads from cads.

Women's preferences

Sexual reproduction requires a high degree of coordination and compromise. Short-term strategy may be more beneficial for men and a long-term strategy may be more optimal for women, but neither sex can practice their strategy in isolation: Men can pursue unrestricted sex only if there are women willing to participate, and equally, women's long-term strategy can be successful only if there are men prepared to commit. Thus, mate choices are always constrained, at the very least, by what the other sex is looking for. So apart from commitment, what else are women looking for? And if their preference for monogamy is not as straightforward as was once assumed, are other preferences equally complex?

Resources

According to the evolutionary psychologist David Buss, "the most ancient and pervasive basis for female choice in the animal kingdom" is the preference for males who can contribute the resources needed to raise offspring (2003, p. 22). It is also one of the best documented preferences of the human female: Across cultures, women, on average, put greater value on the financial prospects of potential mates than do men (Buss, 1989; Walter et al., 2020). But however prevalent this preference is, it is not immune to context: Sex differences in this preference are greater in countries with greater economic inequality (Eagly & Wood, 1999). Moreover, in at least one case, cultural norms lead to a sex reversal in this preference: In an orthodox Jewish Haredi community, where men are expected to devote themselves to religious studies, they rate their spouse's earning capacity as more important than women do (Malovicki-Yaffe et al., 2024). Nevertheless, numerous other studies confirm that women generally look for wealthy men even if their own financial prospects are good (Townsend, 1987, 1989; Wiederman & Allgeier, 1992). In fact, women with more resources value them in a partner more than women with fewer resources (Buss, 1989). In romantic fiction, mercenary fortune hunting—whether by women or men—is always condemned or ridiculed, but material considerations are always part of love and marriage considerations, showing how deeply they are intertwined.

Status

Women also have a clear preference for socially powerful men. High status signals the man's ability to compete with other men, control resources, and protect his partner and children. But there are important nuances in this preference as well. In experiments, when given the choice of a man who controls other men or a man who is easily controlled by others, women overwhelmingly prefer the former, but when given the choice of a third man described in more neutral terms, women find him more sexually attractive and more desirable as a dating prospect than the other two candidates (see Buller, 2005, pp. 231–232). This may be due to the fact that control over other men can often translate into undue control over one's partner. Indeed, excessively dominant alpha males are the most likely to exploit others for selfish advantage (Boehm, 1999). Consequently, women are generally sensitive to the kind of power a man wields over others, as there are two distinct routes to high status connected with different personality profiles: One is *dominance*, achieved through aggression, arrogance, and exploitation, the other is *prestige*, achieved though competence, leadership, and cooperation (Henrich & Gil-White, 2001). Women looking for long-term mates ideally want men who combine high status with a prosocial orientation (Jensen-Campbell et al., 1995). This preference is evident in romantic fiction. The romantic hero is usually a powerful man, but he is often initially rejected by the heroine for his apparent arrogance and tendency to control others.[5] It is only when the heroine has evidence that his power comes from prestige, not dominance, that she accepts him.

Appearance

While women tend to value resources and status in potential mates more than men do, men tend to put more premium on the youth and beauty of their mates (Buss, 1989). This is true even for homosexual relationships: Gay men place greater importance on physical appearance than lesbians do (Buss, 2003, p. 61). But this does not mean that women do not care about looks. Just as females in many animal species choose their mates based on aesthetically pleasing features, heterosexual women too are most attracted to handsome, masculine-looking men (Buss, 2003, pp. 243–244). Physical symmetry is particularly attractive, as it signals high resistance to pathogens and absence of harmful mutations. But such appearance has its downside too: Very handsome men invest less in romantic relationships, are less willing to spend time with their partners, are less honest with them, and are more interested in other women (Thornhill & Gangestad, 2008, p. 178). So, women are more likely to choose very handsome men as short-term lovers but are less concerned about men's appearance when looking for a long-term partner (Gangestad & Simpson, 1990; Gangestad & Thornhill, 1997; Scheib, 2001). Importantly, men also tend to prioritize female beauty in casual encounters more than in committed relationships (Buss & Schmitt, 1993).

Perhaps even more interestingly, assessments of physical beauty, for both men and women, are affected by other social and psychological attributes: People become more or less attractive as we learn about their levels of intelligence, kindness, or wealth (Geher & Kaufman, 2013, p. 75). These tendencies are clearly illustrated in romantic fiction: While protagonists, both male and female, are hardly ever ugly, their appreciation of each other's appearance often increases as the story proceeds; antagonists, on the other hand, are rejected regardless of how strikingly attractive they may initially appear.

Compatibility

Evolutionary researchers so far have put a lot of effort into documenting differences and conflicts between men and women in the mating domain. These differences are particularly pronounced in the context of short-term relationships (Buss & Schmitt, 1993). But the emphasis on differences is myopic and misleading; in fact, the most famous study about them concludes that "species-typical mate preferences may be more potent than sex-linked preferences" (Buss, 1989, p. 13). In other words, men and women are more similar than they are different—a fundamental fact that is sorely neglected in the evolutionary psychological literature.

Not only do men and women of different cultures use similar criteria to evaluate potential partners (Shackelford et al., 2005), but both sexes put characteristics such as dependable character, emotional stability, kindness, and the intelligence of prospective mates ahead of any others (Buss et al., 1990). Both men and women also put a big premium on expressions of commitment (Buss, 1988) and find promiscuity or infidelity extremely undesirable in the context of a long-term relationship (Buss & Schmitt, 1993). Moreover, people have a strong tendency for homogamy: Overwhelmingly, we choose mates who are like us in terms of overall level of attractiveness (or *mate value*), including intelligence and physical appearance, and who also share our sociocultural background and values (Buller, 2005; Nelson & Jankowiak, 2021). Compatibility is in fact a fundamental mate-choice criterion in any sexually reproducing species, more important than "picking the 'best' mate in absolute sense" (Rosenthal & Ryan, 2022). This entails potentially great variability between choosers, because what is best for one individual may not be so good for another. For humans, compatibility is particularly important and encompasses many different traits. For example, several ingenious studies discovered that people are attracted to those whose immune systems best compliment their own (as a way of enhancing genetic diversity and boosting the immune resilience of potential offspring), which demonstrates the importance of genetic compatibility (Wedekind et al., 1995). Psychological and social compatibility is equally important because of our need for sustained cooperation in reproduction.

And this leads me to the factor identified by men and women across cultures as the most important when choosing a mate: love and mutual attraction (Buss et al., 1990). Unlike all the other traits mentioned above, love is not a trait objectively associated with another person (although it does involve an assessment of such traits) but is a sign of our recognition of the other person's uniqueness and our commitment to them. This ability to make a credible commitment based on something beyond the objective evaluation of the other person's strengths and weaknesses is what transformed human mating and human social life (Frank, 1988; Nesse, 2001).

Love as choice

So how do we choose who to love? A common view of love portrays it as an irrational, irresistible force; "love is blind" and we "fall in love" apparently without much ability to control when and with whom. In contrast, in economics and other social sciences, intimate relationships are often discussed as utility-maximizing transactions (e.g., Becker, 1981/1991). Much of the language routinely used in evolutionary psychology similarly suggests such a materialist view of heterosexual relationships: mate value, parental investment, maximizing reproductive success. There is, however, a significant body of evolutionarily-inspired theory and research suggesting that neither of these perspectives is accurate, that love (like many other emotions) helps us make sensible choices without being selfishly calculating, and that love itself is a matter of choice in response to the unique self of another person.

Theoretical models of the "rational" choosing process involve identifying available options, acquiring information about those options and, after impartial appraisal, selecting the best one (see Todd & Miller, 1999, pp. 288–289). But in reality, this process is always constrained by the amount of time and energy we are able to spend on the search, by the often imperfect knowledge we can obtain, and by the computational capacities of our brain (Gigerenzer, 2001, p. 37).[6] The process of mate selection is particularly complex and fraught with difficulties. We do not know how many prospective mates we will meet, or when, or how suitable they will be; we never meet all of them at once, and therefore have to reject or accept some before being able to assess others (Todd & Miller, 1999, p. 290). We have to weigh up various positive and negative characteristics of each candidate and decide what we are prepared to compromise on (Conroy-Beam & Buss, 2020; Li et al., 2002). We also face the problem of mutual choice: There is no guarantee that whoever we choose will also choose us. And finally, any choices we make are often subject to parental and social approval.

To streamline this incredibly complex decision-making process, we evolved love—and all other emotions associated with it. Love is a very effective mate search tool: It highlights or eliminates certain candidates from the outset and helps us make the selection (H. E. Fisher, 2005, p. 124). Even more importantly, love helps ensure that we do not change our mind the moment another potentially attractive option comes along. In other words, it helps us make a credible long-term commitment in a venture which requires unprecedented levels of trust and mutual support: sharing your life and possessions with another person and very likely having children together (Frank, 1988).

This evolutionary view of love shatters another myth which has often been perniciously used to diminish women's priorities and their way of understanding the world: the dichotomy between reason and emotions. While it is true that strong feelings can sometimes interfere with logic, current understanding of human cognition includes emotions as an integral and indispensable part of human rationality (Damasio, 1996; Frank, 1988). Emotions are cognitive mechanisms evolved to coordinate "other information-processing programs, including those of attention, perception, memory, categorization, learning, and energy allocation" and to direct our behaviour accordingly (Al-Shawaf et al., 2016, p. 173). Or, to put it more simply, emotions are the result of an evolutionary learning process: "Each points us in a direction that has worked well to handle the recurring challenges of human life" (Goleman, 1995/2005, p. 4).

Although emotionally driven behaviour may sometimes seem irrational, it can in the long run be more advantageous than purely rational, opportunistic calculations (Frank, 1988; Nesse, 2001). This is because emotions are tuned not only to personal needs but also to moral principles, social norms, and interpersonal dynamics (Damasio, 1996, p. xiv). As such, emotions constitute a unique form of intelligence which is independent from and often more important than intellectual ability, (Goleman, 1995/2005) especially when it comes to those decisions that significantly affect the course of our life, such as choosing a partner.

However, to recognize that emotions constitute a powerful motivational force is not to say that they do the deciding for us. We do not lose our deliberative faculties to automatic reactions imprinted in our psyche, or as the philosopher Robert Solomon (2003) puts it, we are not slaves of our passions. Solomon argues that emotions should be understood "in terms of the choices we make" (p. 195); they are not deliberate actions, but they are "acts of judgement" influenced by our experiences, expectations, and priorities (p. 210).

So, love does not only help us choose but, within Solomon's framework, love itself is a matter of choice:

> Falling in love is not (as the metaphor suggests) a sudden 'fall' but a slow campaign, looking for, finding, and to some extent creating ever new charms and virtues in the beloved ... It is not a matter of 'falling' but of making incremental decisions and commitments and occasional major ones, ... nurturing both the beloved's good feelings and (more to the point) one's own. (2003, p. 202)

Interestingly, the feminist writer Germaine Greer also contends that love should be "not swoon, possession or mania, but 'a cognitive act'" (1970, p. 166), and while in her view romance novels promote the former, I will argue that stories such as *Pride and Prejudice* and *Sex and the City* encourage the latter.

Choice and change

Sexual choice is "a linchpin of evolution" (Rosenthal & Ryan, 2022). For feminists too, the decisions women make about their relationships with men are of utmost importance. Both paradigms acknowledge the constraints on individual choices, whether through sociopolitical limitations or species-typical traits. However, in both frameworks, individual variability and choice are seen as crucial for driving change. Second-wave feminists wanted women to reject heterosexual relationships. But for most women, this is not a viable option, and this will remain the case for as long as humans rely on sexual reproduction. Feminists rightly criticize past evolutionary accounts for portraying women as naturally coy and passive, but current research reveals evolution as the story of women's persistent determination to retain control and exercise agency.

We are only beginning to understand just how complex and dynamic the process of mate selection is—and feminists can help refine this story further—but it seems that the intense emotions and elaborate rituals of romantic love have been shaped by sexual selection to help us choose a mate with whom a lasting, mutually beneficial partnership is possible, even if never guaranteed. Evolutionary perspectives reveal that love is not blind, irrational madness; it is not some mythical nirvana; nor is it a genetically pre-programmed default-mode for human females; but it is an act of choice informed equally by our own priorities and our appreciation of the beloved's individuality.

Sexual selection theory also shows how cumulative individual choices can gradually transform the characteristics of the whole species—and the criteria for future choices. Our preference for love has done precisely that: It has already redirected human mate selection criteria from those driven by mutual exploitation to those enabling long-term cooperation; it has also amplified the importance of social cooperation as a human survival strategy (or as evolutionists would put it, as a strategy for maximizing fitness). But evolution is an ongoing process and the more individual women—and men—make love the basis for mate choice, the more cooperation will pervade interpersonal and social gender relations. In the next chapter, and in the rest of the book, I will show that romantic fiction examines the complexities of female mate choice and highlights love as the most promising criterion for that choice.

Notes

1 Hoagland's focus is on "lesbian existence" and on "separating from heterosexualism", and some feminists have debated whether her ethics can apply beyond lesbian interactions. However, I find her argument about the possibility of agency despite constraints and her challenge to the split between reason and emotion uncannily relevant to my discussion.
2 Reproductive success is measured not simply by the number of offspring an individual produces, but (due to the concept of *inclusive fitness*) by the number of that individual's genes passed on to future generations by their offspring and any other genetic relatives.
3 And in those relatively few species where the male takes on most of the parental duties, such as the seahorse, he is more sexually selective than the female, supporting Trivers's theory.
4 The expressions *short-term* and *unrestricted* are commonly used in evolutionary literature but neither term fully captures the range of motivations and behaviours it can refer to; for example, extra-marital affairs are often discussed as short-term mating, but they can last for years. Similarly, people with unrestricted sociosexuality may have many sexual partners but still have a range of criteria for choosing them; for example, they prioritize physical appearance or extraverted personality. Another term often used in this context is *high sociosexuality* (or high SOI), denoting a tendency to be more open to engaging in flirting and sexual relationships without the need for emotional closeness or long-term commitment.
5 Austen used this pattern only once, in *Pride and Prejudice*, but it has been repeated in countless romance novels.
6 This is the essence of Herbert Simon's concept of *bounded rationality*, fruitfully and famously developed by Daniel Kahneman.

References

Al-Shawaf, L., Conroy-Beam, D., Asao, K., & Buss, D. M. (2016). Human emotions: An evolutionary psychological perspective. *Emotion Review*, *8*(2), 173–186. https://doi.org/10.1177/1754073914565518

Alexander, M. G., & Fisher, T. D. (2003). Truth and consequences: Using the bogus pipeline to examine sex differences in self-reported sexuality. *Journal of Sex Research*, *40*(1), 27–35.

Baker, J. (2008). The ideology of choice. Overstating progress and hiding injustice in the lives of young women: Findings from a study in North Queensland, Australia. *Women's Studies International Forum*, *31*(1), 53–64. https://doi.org/10.1016/j.wsif.2007.11.001

Barash, D. P. (2001). *The myth of monogamy: Fidelity and infidelity in animals and humans*. W. H. Freeman.

Bateman, A. J. (1948). Intra-sexual selection in Drosophila. *Heredity*, *2*(Pt. 3), 349–368.

Becker, G. S. (1981/1991). *A treatise on the family*. Harvard University Press.

Boehm, C. (1999). *Hierarchy in the forest: The evolution of egalitarian behavior*. Harvard University Press.

Buller, D. J. (2005). *Adapting minds: Evolutionary psychology and the persistent quest for human nature*. MIT Press.

Buss, D. M. (1988). Love acts: The evolutionary biology of love. In R. J. Sternberg & M. L. Barnes (Eds.), *The psychology of love* (pp. 100–118). Yale University Press.

Buss, D. M. (1989). Sex differences in human mate preferences: Evolutionary hypotheses tested in 37 cultures. *Behavioral and Brain Sciences*, *12*(01), 1–14. https://doi.org/10.1017/S0140525X00023992

Buss, D. M. (2003). *The evolution of desire: Strategies of human mating* (Rev., Kindle ed.). Basic Books.

Buss, D. M., Abbott, M., Angleitner, A., Asherian, A., Biaggio, A., Blanco-Villasenor, A., Bruchon-Schweitzer, M., Ch'U, H.-Y., Czapinski, J., Deraad, B., Ekehammar, B., Lohamy, N., Fioravanti, M., Georgas, J., Gjerde, P., Guttman, R., Hazan, F., Iwawaki, S., Janakiramaiah, N., ... Yang, K.-S. (1990). International preferences in selecting mates: A study of 37 cultures. *Journal of Cross-Cultural Psychology*, *21*(1), 5–47.

Buss, D. M., & Schmitt, D. P. (1993). Sexual strategies theory: An evolutionary perspective on human mating. *Psychological Review*, *100*(2), 204–232.

Campbell, A. (2008). The morning after the night before. *Human Nature*, *19*(2), 157–173.

Campbell, A. (2013). *A mind of her own: The evolutionary psychology of women* (2nd ed.). Oxford University Press.
Conroy-Beam, D., & Buss, D. M. (2020). Human mate selection: A multidimensional approach. In J. H. Barkow, L. Workman, & W. Reader (Eds.), *The Cambridge handbook of evolutionary perspectives on human behavior* (pp. 353–365). Cambridge University Press. https://doi.org/10.1017/9781108131797.030
Cronin, H. (1991). *The ant and the peacock: Altruism and sexual selection from Darwin to today*. Cambridge University Press.
Damasio, A. R. (1996). *Descartes error: Emotion, reason and the human brain*. Papermac.
Darwin, C. (1871/2003). *The descent of man and selection in relation to sex*. Gibson Square.
Eagly, A. H., & Wood, W. (1999). The origins of sex differences in human behavior: Evolved dispositions versus social roles. *American Psychologist, 54*(6), 408–423.
Ferguson, M. L. (2010). Choice feminism and the fear of politics. *Perspectives on Politics, 8*(01), 247–253. https://doi.org/10.1017/S1537592709992830
Fisher, H. E. (2005). *Why we love: The nature and chemistry of romantic love*. Henry Holt and Co.
Fisher, H. E. (2016). *Anatomy of love: A natural history of mating, marriage, and why we stray* (Rev., Kindle ed.). W. W. Norton & Company. (1992)
Fisher, R. A. (1915). The evolution of sexual preference. *Eugenics Review, 7*(3), 184–192.
Fletcher, G. J. O., Simpson, J. A., Campbell, L., & Overall, N. C. (2015). Pair-bonding, romantic love, and evolution. *Perspectives on Psychological Science, 10*(1), 20–36. https://doi.org/10.1177/1745691614561683
Frank, R. H. (1988). *Passions within reason: The strategic role of the emotions*. Norton.
Gangestad, S. W., & Simpson, J. A. (1990). Toward an evolutionary history of female sociosexual variation. *Journal of Personality, 58*(1), 69–96.
Gangestad, S. W., & Thornhill, R. (1997). The evolutionary psychology of extrapair sex: The role of fluctuating asymmetry. *Evolution and Human Behavior, 18*(2), 69–88. https://doi.org/10.1016/s1090-5138(97)00003-2
Garcia, J. R., & Reiber, C. (2008). Hook-up behavior: A biopsychosocial perspective. *Evolutionary Behavioral Sciences, 2*(4), 192–208.
Geher, G., & Kaufman, S. B. (2013). *Mating intelligence unleashed: The role of the mind in sex, dating, and love* (Kindle ed.). Oxford University Press.
Gigerenzer, G. (2001). The adaptive toolbox. In G. Gigerenzer & R. Selten (Eds.), *Bounded rationality: The adaptive toolbox* (pp. 37–50). MIT Press.
Goleman, D. (1995/2005). *Emotional intelligence* (10th anniversary ed.). Bantam Books.
Greer, G. (1970). *The female eunuch*. McGraw-Hill Book Company.
Greiling, H., & Buss, D. M. (2000). Women's sexual strategies: The hidden dimension of extrapair mating. *Personality and Individual Differences, 28*(5), 929–963. https://doi.org/10.1016/S0191-8869(99)00151-8
Grosz, E. A. (2005). *Time travels: Feminism, nature, power*. Duke University Press.
Hamilton, W. D., & Zuk, M. (1982). Heritable true fitness and bright birds: A role for parasites? *Science, 218*(4570), 384–387. http://www.jstor.org/stable/1688879
Harper, C. R., Dittus, P. J., Leichliter, J. S., & Aral, S. O. (2017). Changes in the distribution of sex partners in the United States: 2002 to 2011–2013. *Sexually transmitted diseases, 44*(2), 96–100. https://doi.org/10.1097/olq.0000000000000554
Haselton, M. G., & Buss, D. M. (2000). Error management theory: A new perspective on biases in cross-sex mind reading. *Journal of Personality and Social Psychology, 78*, 81–91. https://doi.org/10.1037/0022-3514.78.1.81
Henrich, J., & Gil-White, F. J. (2001). The evolution of prestige: Freely conferred deference as a mechanism for enhancing the benefits of cultural transmission. *Evolution and Human Behavior, 22*(3), 165–196.
Hoagland, S. L. (1988). *Lesbian ethics: Toward new value*. Institute of Lesbian Studies.
Hollway, W. (1984). Women's power in heterosexual sex. *Women's Studies International Forum, 7*(1), 63–68. https://doi.org/10.1016/0277-5395(84)90085-2
Hrdy, S. B. (1981/1999). *The woman that never evolved*. Harvard University Press.
Hrdy, S. B. (1999). *Mother nature: A history of mothers, infants, and natural selection*. Pantheon Books.
Hrdy, S. B. (2009). *Mothers and others: The evolutionary origins of mutual understanding*. Belknap Press of Harvard University Press.

Hrdy, S. B. (2024). *Father time: A natural history of men and babies*. Princeton University Press.

Jackson, S. (1996). Heterosexuality and feminist theory. In D. Richardson (Ed.), *Theorising heterosexuality: Telling it straight* (pp. 21–38). Open University Press.

Jackson, S. (1999). Women and heterosexual love: Complicity, resistance and change. In *Heterosexuality in question* (pp. 113–122). Sage Publications.

Jennions, M. D., & Petrie, M. (2000). Why do females mate multiply? A review of the genetic benefits. *Biological Reviews, 75*(01), 21–64. http://dx.doi.org/10.1017/S0006323199005423

Jensen-Campbell, L. A., Graziano, W. G., & West, S. G. (1995). Dominance, prosocial orientation, and female preferences: Do nice guys really finish last? *Journal of Personality and Social Psychology, 68*(3), 427.

Jobling, I. (2002). Byron as cad. *Philosophy and Literature, 26*(2), 269–311.

Kemp, S., & Squires, J. (Eds.). (1997). *Feminisms*. Oxford University Press.

Kruger, D. J., Fisher, M. L., & Jobling, I. (2005). Proper hero dads and dark hero cads: Alternate mating strategies exemplified in British romantic literature. In J. Gottschall & D. S. Wilson (Eds.), *The literary animal: Evolution and the nature of narrative* (pp. 225–243). Northwestern University Press.

Li, N. P., Bailey, J. M., Kenrick, D. T., & Linsenmeier, J. A. W. (2002). The necessities and luxuries of mate preferences: Testing the tradeoffs. *Journal of Personality and Social Psychology, 82*(6), 947–955. https://doi.org/10.1037//0022-3514.82.6.947

Malovicki-Yaffe, N., Tratner, A. E., & McDonald, M. M. (2024). Culture shapes sex differences in mate preferences. *Evolution and Human Behavior, 45*(3), 281–291. https://doi.org/10.1016/j.evolhumbehav.2024.04.002

Maynard Smith, J. (1956). Fertility, mating behaviour and sexual selection in Drosophila Subobscura. *Journal of Genetics, 56*(2), 261–279. https://doi.org/10.1007/bf02715886

McNay, L. (2000). *Gender and agency: Reconfiguring the subject in feminist and social theory*. Polity Press.

McRobbie, A. (2004). Notes on postfeminism and popular culture: Bridget Jones and the new gender regime. In A. Harris (Ed.), *All about the girl: Culture, power, and identity* (pp. 3–14). Routledge.

Meston, C. M., & Buss, D. M. (2009). *Why women have sex: Understanding sexual motivations—from adventure to revenge (and everything in between)*. Times Books.

Miller, G. F. (2000). *The mating mind: How sexual choice shaped the evolution of human nature*. Doubleday.

Nadeau, J. H. (2017). Do gametes woo? Evidence for their nonrandom union at fertilization. *Genetics, 207*(2), 369–387.

Nelson, A. J., & Jankowiak, W. (2021). Love's ethnographic record: Beyond the love/arranged marriage dichotomy and other false essentialisms. In C.-H. Mayer & E. Vanderheiden (Eds.), *International handbook of love: Transcultural and transdisciplinary perspectives* (pp. 41–57). Springer International Publishing. https://doi.org/10.1007/978-3-030-45996-3_3

Nesse, R. M. (2001). Natural selection and the capacity for subjective commitment. In R. M. Nesse (Ed.), *Evolution and the capacity for commitment* (pp. 1–44). Russell Sage Foundation.

Pedersen, W. C., Miller, L. C., Putcha-Bhagavatula, A. D., & Yang, Y. (2002). Evolved sex differences in the number of partners desired? The long and the short of it. *Psychological Science, 13*(2), 157–161. https://doi.org/10.1111/1467-9280.00428

Prum, R. O. (2017). *The evolution of beauty: How Darwin's forgotten theory of mate choice shapes the animal world—and us*. Doubleday.

Rich, A. (1980). Compulsory heterosexuality and lesbian existence. *Signs, 5*(4), 631–660.

Ridley, M. (1993). *The Red Queen: Sex and the evolution of human nature*. Penguin Books.

Rosenthal, G. G., & Ryan, M. J. (2022). Sexual selection and the ascent of women: Mate choice research since Darwin. *Science, 375*. https://doi.org/10.1126/science.abi6308

Scelza, B. A. (2013). Choosy but not chaste: Multiple mating in human females. *Evolutionary Anthropology: Issues, News, and Reviews, 22*(5), 259–269. https://doi.org/10.1002/evan.21373

Scheib, J. E. (2001). Context-specific mate choice criteria: Women's trade-offs in the contexts of long-term and extra-pair mateships. *Personal Relationships, 8*(4), 371–389. https://doi.org/10.1111/j.1475-6811.2001.tb00046.x

Schmitt, D. P. (2005). Sociosexuality from Argentina to Zimbabwe: A 48-nation study of sex, culture, and strategies of human mating. *Behavioral and Brain Sciences, 28*(2), 247.

Segal, L. (1994). *Straight sex: The politics of pleasure*. Virago.
Shackelford, T. K., Schmitt, D. P., & Buss, D. M. (2005). Universal dimensions of human mate preferences. *Personality and Individual Differences*, *39*(2), 447–458.
Small, M. F. (1993). *Female choices: sexual behavior of female primates*. Cornell University Press.
Small, M. F. (1995). *What's love got to do with it? The evolution of human mating*. Anchor Books.
Snyder-Hall, R. C. (2010). Third-wave feminism and the defense of "choice". *Perspectives on Politics*, *8*(01), 255–261. https://doi.org/10.1017/S1537592709992842
Solomon, R. C. (2003). *Not passion's slave: Emotions and choice*. Oxford University Press.
Steinem, G. (1995). Foreword. In R. Walker (Ed.), *To be real: Telling the truth and changing the face of feminism* (pp. i–xxvi). Anchor Books.
Symons, D. (1979). *The evolution of human sexuality*. Oxford University Press.
Tang-Martínez, Z. (2016). Rethinking Bateman's principles: Challenging persistent myths of sexually reluctant females and promiscuous males. *The Journal of Sex Research*, *53*(4–5), 532–559. https://doi.org/10.1080/00224499.2016.1150938
Thompson, D. (2001). *Radical feminism today*. SAGE.
Thornhill, R., & Gangestad, S. W. (2008). *The evolutionary biology of human female sexuality*. Oxford University Press.
Todd, P. M., & Miller, G. F. (1999). From pride and prejudice to persuasion: Satisficing in mate search. In G. Gigerenzer, P. M. Todd, & A. R. Group (Eds.), *Simple heuristics that make us smart* (pp. 287–308). Oxford University Press.
Townsend, J. M. (1987). Sex differences in sexuality among medical students: Effects of increasing socioeconomic status. *Archives of Sexual Behavior*, *16*(5), 425–444. https://doi.org/10.1007/bf01541424
Townsend, J. M. (1989). Mate selection criteria: A pilot study. *Ethology and Sociobiology*, *10*(4), 241–253. https://doi.org/10.1016/0162-3095(89)90002-2
Trivers, R. L. (1972). Parental investment and sexual selection. In B. Campbell (Ed.), *Sexual selection and the descent of man 1871–1971* (pp. 136–179). Aldine Publishing.
Vance, C. S. (Ed.). (1984). *Pleasure and danger: Exploring female sexuality*. Routledge & K. Paul.
Walker, R. (1995). *To be real: Telling the truth and changing the face of feminism*. Anchor Books.
Walter, K. V., Conroy-Beam, D., Buss, D. M., Asao, K., Sorokowska, A., Sorokowski, P., & Zupančič, M. (2020). Sex differences in mate preferences across 45 countries: A large-scale replication. *Psychological Science*, *31*(4), 408–423.
Wedekind, C., Seebeck, T., Bettens, F., & Paepke, A. J. (1995). MHC-dependent mate preferences in humans. *Proceedings of the Royal Society of London. Series B: Biological Sciences*, *260*(1359), 245–249.
Wiederman, M. W., & Allgeier, E. R. (1992). Gender differences in mate selection criteria: Sociobiological or socioeconomic explanation? *Ethology and Sociobiology*, *13*(2), 115–124.
Wolf, N. (1993). *Fire with fire: The new female power and how it will change the 21st century*. Chatto & Windus.
Zahavi, A. (1975). Mate selection—A selection for a handicap. *Journal of Theoretical Biology*, *53*(1), 205–214. https://doi.org/10.1016/0022-5193(75)90111-3
Zuk, M. (2002). *Sexual selections: What we can and can't learn about sex from animals*. University of California Press.

3
ROMANTIC FICTION
Tales of female mate choice

Many within literary and cultural studies accept the notion that "romantic love (and its centrality to the lives of individuals) is arguably a massive literary creation" (Culler, 2000, p. 68). For feminists in particular, romantic love is a Western patriarchal myth, and romantic fiction is the most effective propaganda in service of this dangerous ideology (Firestone, 1970/1979; Greer, 1970; Modleski, 1982/2008; Radway, 1984/1991). Evolutionists agree that the stories we tell have power, that they shape our perception of the world and of ourselves. But while stories reflect our culture, they are underpinned by our deep-rooted cognitive, psychological, and social preoccupations (Boyd, 2018; Carroll, 2018; Hogan, 2003). So, an evolutionary perspective reverses the relationship between literature and love: It is not literature that produces the experience or emotion, but the emotion that provokes its various expressions in literature—in the same way that various culinary traditions do not create but satisfy our need for food and our habit of sharing it with others. Thus, for as long as love itself is treated as just a narrative, its true importance and its hold on our imaginations cannot be fully explained.

Stories of desire, courtship, love, and marriage have been told for millennia, and across cultures, they highlight the features consistent with the modern understanding of romantic love: physical attraction, emotional attachment, and long-term commitment to one special person. The romantic plot is in fact the most common plot in all known literary traditions (Hogan, 2003), and finding a suitable spouse is the main goal of many male and female protagonists (Gottschall, 2005). Furthermore, the fact that so many stories, from traditional folk tales to modern blockbusters, focus on how women choose their sexual, romantic, and marital partners suggests that female choice has been psychologically and socially significant, even in those cultures where women have had relatively little political or economic power (Gottschall, 2008; Nordlund, 2007; Saunders, 2009, 2018).

Although the romantic plot is not specifically feminine, women should—and clearly are—more interested in it, because (as I outlined in Chapter 2) women must be more discerning when making mate choices; the consequences of making bad ones are more serious for them—both biology and culture are less forgiving. Hence, I argue firstly that romantic stories, from Austen's literary classics to modern chick TV, are tales of female

DOI: 10.4324/9781003320982-5

mate choice, of the multifaceted and dynamic way in which women weigh up various needs and sometimes conflicting desires, and the strategies they employ to achieve their goals. Secondly, romantic fiction highlights love as a mate choice guide because love is the best, although never perfect, predictor of long-term commitment and interpersonal cooperation; it also shows that the equitable partnership established within the romantic couple encourages broader social cooperation. Finally, although the vision of harmonious gender relations in romantic fiction is idealized, it nevertheless gives audiences hope and a sense of control which, according to psychologists, are necessary for implementing any personal or social change in real life.

But before I delve into these arguments, I will first review the most serious charges against romantic fiction and then explain how an evolutionary approach differs from the cultural constructivist approach still dominating the study of fiction.

Silly novels

A common view of romantic fiction is that it is trivial, mindless escapism. The very labels used for its genres—chick lit, chick flicks, soap operas, mass-market romances—are designed to be belittling. Even Austen's novels, now considered among some of the most accomplished texts in the English language, were initially described by (male) reviewers as "trifles" and "harmless amusement" (reprinted in Southam, 1968, pp. 70, 72) and continue to have the reputation of "silly romantic fairy tales" (Deresiewicz, 2011).[1] Some prominent female writers share this sentiment: Just as George Eliot wanted to disassociate herself from the "silly novels by lady novelists" (1856), award-winning contemporary authors, such as Dame Beryl Bainbridge and Doris Lessing, denounce modern chick lit as "instantly forgettable", "a froth sort of thing" and bemoan the fact that women do not read something "more profound" (Ezard, 2001, para. 3).

Austen famously defends feminine fiction in *Northanger Abbey*, saying that

> Although our productions have afforded more extensive and unaffected pleasure than those of any other literary corporation in the world, no species of composition has been so much decried. From pride, ignorance, or fashion, our foes are almost as many as our readers. (1818/2003, p. 36)

More than a century later, Virginia Woolf is more pointed about the sexist hierarchy in the evaluation of literature: "This is an important book, the critic assumes, because it deals with war. This is an insignificant book because it deals with the feelings of women in a drawing-room" (1928/2004, p. 86). Indeed, it is women's feelings, especially their *sexual* feelings, that have always been of utmost concern to the critics. For example, James Fordyce, whose sermons Mr. Collins chooses to read to the Bennet ladies in *Pride and Prejudice*, strongly discourages young women from reading novels by preaching that they are filled with such "lewdness" that "she who can bear to peruse them must in her soul be a prostitute" (as cited in Austen, 1813/2003, p. 424, n. 5). In one of the most influential feminist analyses of romance novels, Janice Radway correctly identifies what is at stake in such critiques when she contends that "the struggle over the romance is itself part of the larger struggle for the right to define and to control female sexuality" (1984/1991, p. 17).

Dope for dupes

Unfortunately, according to most feminists, romantic fiction, from classic Austen's novels to Harlequins and the latest chick lit, is a patriarchal weapon used *against* women in this struggle. This assessment is an inevitable consequence of the assumption that romantic love itself is a recently invented Western patriarchal myth. According to feminists, romantic fiction naturalizes and perpetuates patriarchal gender relations by eroticizing female passivity and dependence, justifying male domination, and presenting marriage as the only desirable end of the story. All these elements are inherent to the often ridiculed romantic formula: The young and spirited heroine meets the handsome hero who is older, richer, and more powerful but also "mocking, cynical, contemptuous, [and] often hostile" (Modleski, 1982/2008, p. 28). She initially dislikes him but eventually submits to his desire and authority as his wife.[2]

Within the "totally anti-feminist world" of popular romance, the feminine is marked by passivity and masochism (Douglas, 1980, pp. 26–27). The heroine is not just a "damsel in distress", needing a man to rescue and guide her; despite her liveliness and pluck—traits that make her attractive to both the hero and the audience—when faced with the hero's overwhelming masculinity, she becomes "utterly ineffectual" (Greer, 1970, p. 173), a passive, receptive "slave to her man's desire" (Assiter, 1988, p. 105). Women's fascination with romance is "the product of male conditioning" designed to normalize the masculine "psychology of the conqueror" and "the pervasive male ideology of rape" (Brownmiller, 1976, p. 360). Men in these stories "are using sexuality to punish and humiliate women", although this punishment "miraculously turns into reward" (Modleski, 1982/2008, p. 34). In the more recent chick lit and popular television (the criticism goes), pernicious romantic myths have been updated through the rhetoric of empowerment and individual choice, seductively repackaging regressive pre-feminist ideals as post-feminist freedoms (Gill, 2003; McRobbie, 2004; Whelehan, 2005). The equality and liberation they offer their female characters and audiences is an illusion: It amounts to the "freedom" to knowingly turn themselves into sexual objects and "choose" traditional heterosexual monogamy and domesticity (Gill, 2003, 2008). Thus, such texts effectively work as a backlash against feminism.

Many critics do note positive elements in romantic fiction. They acknowledge the heroine's efforts to be recognized as a unique individual (Modleski, 1982/2008; Rabine, 1985; Radway, 1984/1991; Thurston, 1987). They see romantic narratives as a forum to discuss women's anxieties around love, relationships, and heterosexuality, sometimes contesting rigid gender categories, breaking sexual taboos, and suggesting alternatives to patriarchal models of relationships (Ferriss & Young, 2006; Hunting, 2012; Mabry, 2006; Rowntree et al., 2012). They also consider the possibility that the act of writing and reading romantic fiction may be a form of covert resistance or protest against patriarchy (Gilbert & Gubar, 1979/2000; Johnson, 1988; Modleski, 1982/2008; Radway, 1984/1991). But these endorsements are rarely straightforward. Those writing from a specifically feminist point of view usually agree with Radway that "romantic fiction must be an active agent in the maintenance of the ideological status quo because it ultimately reconciles women to patriarchal society and reintegrates them with its institutions" (p. 217).[3] Just as Austen apparently "perpetuates ... the myth of romantic love" (Poovey, 1984, p. 237) and reinforces "the necessity of female submission" (Gilbert & Gubar, 1979/2000, p. 154), in chick lit, the "constraints of the genre usually coerce the novels back into complicity" (Mißler, 2017, p. 161).

Nevertheless, just as some feminist psychologists and activists see love as the most effective way to dismantle patriarchy (see Chapter 1), some analyses of romantic fiction argue for its productive role in this process because it "not only challenge[s] the traditional power relationships between men and women but depict[s] a more balanced power alignment as natural and expected" (Thurston, 1987, p. 8). Some suggest that the fact that romantic heroines want "emotionally and sexually satisfying ... monogamous heterosexual partnerships" is not in itself anti-feminist and may actually reflect many women's true desires (Rowntree et al., 2012, p. 134). Others admit that "stories about love are some of the most important that we tell" (Roach, 2016, p. 194). An evolutionary perspective on romantic love and romantic fiction provides a powerful explanation for why this is the case.

The evolution of stories

Storytelling is a uniquely human cultural activity. But all stories are produced by human minds, which, like our hearts and lungs, are the products of the evolutionary and developmental processes all living things are subject to. Therefore, an up-to-date scientific understanding of human cognition, emotions, and behaviour should be integral to the study of fiction, and any explanations of fictional texts need to be consistent with that understanding if they are to be treated as credible contributions to our knowledge of the human condition (Boyd, 2009; Carroll, 2004). Importantly, for humans, evolutionary processes are not limited to biology but consist of significant two-way interactions between biological and cultural elements (Henrich, 2016; Jablonka & Lamb, 2014; Richerson & Boyd, 2005). Imagination, creativity, and ideology are not only a part of our evolutionary make-up but have also influenced it (Boyd, 2018; Carroll et al., 2020). Hence, the biocultural approach to fiction is equally sensitive to the universal, species-typical features of human nature, to how these features are expressed in variable, culturally-specific conditions, and to how they are imaginatively interpreted by individual authors and readers (for recent overviews see Carroll, 2018; Grant, forthcoming; Jonsson, 2020).

Although various explanations have been proposed for the origin and function of art in general, and fiction in particular (Boyd, 2009; Dissanayake, 2000; Dutton, 2009; Miller, 2000; Scalise Sugiyama, 2001), most evolutionary theorists agree that the arts "affect cognitive and emotional organization, influence motives, and thus help regulate behavior" (Carroll, 2018, p. 431). Nowhere is it clearer and more emphatic than in the case of storytelling; as Brian Boyd puts it, "we invented stories and then they changed us" (Boyd 2009, 2018).[4] Stories not only mimic human experience but also amplify and extend it far beyond what we can experience first-hand, or even beyond what is currently possible. They are a form of cognitive and emotional play allowing us to vicariously test multiple scenarios with relatively little expenditure of time and energy, and at minimal physical or social risk (Boyd, 2018; Dutton, 2009). Crucially, since humans are an ultra-social species, our survival and reproduction depend on our capacity to understand other people's thoughts, feelings, and intentions—what psychologists call Theory of Mind (ToM). Storytelling refines this capacity by imitating social situations and engaging the same neural mechanisms involved in interactions with real people (Mar & Oatley, 2008; Oatley, 2016; Vermeule, 2010). And there are few social interactions that test our ToM as much as looking for a suitable partner (Boyd, 1998).

Love: A literary universal

Stories can be about anything, but those that gain popularity and endure are about a limited number of concerns; love and sex are at the top of that list because finding a suitable mate is a fundamental motivation for all sexually reproducing organisms, including humans (Saunders, 2014). The feminist assertion that the importance of romantic love has increased in European fiction since medieval times is correct. However, as discussed in Chapter 1, a broad evolutionary perspective reveals that similar increases occurred in Asia and the Middle East, and at several other times in history; that references to romantic love are in fact more abundant in folk tales from some non-European traditions; and that the key features of romantic love—passion, intimacy, and commitment—are found across many cultures from ancient Greece and China, to Aboriginal and African traditions (Baumard et al., 2022; Gottschall & Nordlund, 2006; Konstan, 1994; Shostak, 1990).

Patrick Colm Hogan (2003), who studies the connections between narrative patterns and human emotion systems, and who draws extensively on non-European literary traditions, makes a compelling argument that a romantic plot, specifically romantic tragi-comedy—the story of love which encounters obstacles but overcomes them to produce a happy ending—is a literary universal, and the theme of romantic union is the most popular literary topic across many literary traditions. Marriage is also a dominant theme across cultures, as confirmed by a large-scale analysis of traditional folk tales from around the world (Gottschall, 2005). Moreover, finding a marriage partner is not presented in these stories as a specifically female goal, as bemoaned by feminists, but "the primary motive of a great proportion of protagonists of both sexes" (Gottschall, 2005, p. 216). This is not some giant coincidence of arbitrary cultural conventions but a reflection of human nature. As Hogan explains, citing several psychological studies, the achievement of a romantic union is one of the two conditions people overwhelmingly associate with happiness; the other one is gaining social or political power (Hogan, 2003, pp. 94–97).[5] As I will argue later, romantic heroines usually achieve both of these goals, as their marriages offer emotionally fulfilling love but also an elevated socioeconomic status.

There are of course variations in individual lives and individual stories: Real people and literary characters may or may not have sex, fall in love, get married, or have children. The universal tendencies of human nature also have different opportunities for expression depending on different physical and cultural environments. And their fictional representations are further differentiated by the different perspectives and purposes of the storytellers, some of whom extoll the ideals of their culture, while others question, ignore, or rebel against them. Still, love, sex, and partner choice are of perennial importance across cultures and are therefore some of the most frequent and prominent themes in many types of fiction. But as Austen observes in the conversation about love between Anne Elliot and Captain Wentworth in *Persuasion*, "Men have had every advantage of us in telling their own story ... the pen has been in their hands" (P, p. 220). In the rest of this chapter, and in the rest of this book, I will argue that Austen's own fiction and the kind of romantic fiction following in her footsteps privileges the female perspective and celebrates the constructive power of love.

Romantic fiction

Romantic fiction and female choice

One of the main feminist charges against romantic fiction is that it perpetuates patriarchy by presenting the romantic heroine as passive and thus encouraging such passivity in the audience. Like many fans and writers of romantic fiction (see Krentz, 1992), I take issue with such claims. In Chapter 2, I showed how new research in the evolutionary sciences disputes the idea of female social and sexual passivity. At the same time, evolutionary literary scholars have been re-examining its fictional representations emphasizing the impact of female choice and the strength of female desire even in cultural environments which restricted female autonomy, such as Homeric Greece, Shakespeare's England, or early twentieth-century America (Boyd, 2009; Gottschall, 2008; Nordlund, 2007; Saunders, 2009, 2018). Several previous evolutionary analyses have demonstrated that Austen is particularly perceptive in representing female sexual and social psychology, vividly depicting a variety of mating and competitive strategies, which remain readily identifiable and relatable to modern audiences (Boyd, 1998; Grant, 2020; Grant & Kruger, 2023; Kruger et al., 2014; Stasio & Duncan, 2007). Evolutionary psychologists have also argued that products of contemporary popular culture, such as mass-produced romances and fanfiction, reflect the most important female mate preferences, such as male physical strength, ability to provide material resources, and willingness to make a long-term commitment (Cox & Fisher, 2009; Salmon, 2005, 2016; Salmon & Symons, 2001).

I combine these previous insights, made separately about classic literature on the one hand and so-called lowbrow entertainment on the other, to argue that regardless of its specific format and intellectual or aesthetic refinement—which can vary dramatically from one text to another—romantic fiction employs similar psychological patterns and fulfils similar cognitive and emotional functions for the audience.

First of all, I argue that romantic fiction positions the heroine, and consequently the reader, as an *active* chooser, highlighting female agency in one of the most complex and consequential decisions made by any sexually reproducing organism. As I explained in Chapter 2, mate choice is a cognitively demanding process with extremely high stakes. It requires assessing other people's personalities, motivations, and intentions to a degree rarely necessary in any other social interaction. Mate choice is of particular consequence for women, both biologically and culturally: Their reproductive load is unavoidably heavier (with pregnancy and lactation), and social repercussions of poor mate choices are much more serious. At the same time, compared with other species, women have exceptional flexibility and cognitive control over their reproductive decisions but relatively few opportunities to get them right, especially in cultures championing lifelong monogamy. That is why romantic fiction is so appealing and useful: It provides opportunities to practice vital cognitive skills and test emotional mechanisms involved in mate selection, simulating real-life dilemmas but without real-life risks or consequences.

Just as the female gamete does not simply wait for the winning sperm, the romantic heroine does not simply wait to be swept off her feet by a paragon of masculinity. In most romantic narratives, the heroine comes across at least two or three potential partners, each with different levels of various desirable or undesirable characteristics. Some candidates she will unequivocally discard (as Elizabeth Bennet does with Mr. Collins), others might discard her (as Col. Fitzwilliam does with Elizabeth), some she will be instantly attracted to but later see as deficient (as Elizabeth does with Mr. Wickham), until she finds that one who seems most likely to match her needs, desires, and moral principles, even if he is not completely flawless (as is the case with Mr. Darcy). The options she has and the choices she makes are often compared with those of her relatives, neighbours, friends, and rivals. And each of the female characters within a story illustrates different priorities and preferences, different solutions to the recurring mate choice conundrums and trade-offs: Is it more important that her partner is sexy or smart, rich or kind, romantic or reliable? Should she seize an opportunity for a passionate dalliance or persist in searching for long-term security? Can she build an intimate attachment without compromising her individuality or surrendering her autonomy? To what extent do her personal hopes and ambitions correspond to family expectations or cultural ideals, and what could be the consequences of submitting to or challenging these expectations? The answers to such questions are rarely straightforward. While facing these numerous biological and cultural constraints, the romantic heroine does everything in her power to maintain the autonomy of her choices, to stay in control of her social, economic, and reproductive destiny. And while working through different options and gathering both positive and negative experiences, she grows in self-awareness and emotional maturity. She may not be routinely slaying dragons (or zombies, as in the 2009 retelling of *Pride and Prejudice* by Seth Grahame-Smith), but she is certainly not passive—and as I will show later, neither is the reader. Moreover, the romantic heroine is active not only in the act of choosing her mate, but through her choices she brings about change in him and the community.

Romantic fiction and gender cooperation

While romantic fiction provides opportunities for considering different mating options, it overwhelmingly endorses one: a long-term loving relationship with a powerful man. According to feminists, the romantic hero is the personification of patriarchal power: "The traits invented for him have been invented by women cherishing the chains of their bondage" (Greer, 1970, p. 176), and the marriage (or a monogamous commitment) at the end of the story is interpreted as the heroine's ultimate capitulation, even humiliation, in the war of the sexes (Fraiman, 1989; Modleski, 1982/2008; Rabine, 1985; Radway, 1984/1991). Romance writers also see the hero as "the most dangerous creature on earth" but claim that it is him, not the heroine, who is tamed and conquered, brought to his knees and forced to acknowledge her power over him (Krentz, 1992, p. 12). Similarly, evolutionary psychologists argue that the plot of mass-produced romances "must vanquish" male sexuality (Salmon & Symons, 2001, p. 91). All these perspectives emphasize the difference and the resulting conflict between the sexes; whether it is the hero or the heroine who ends up on top, the assumed dynamic is that of dominance and submission, a struggle between opposing forces in which only one can prevail. While I cannot categorically rule out that such a dynamic is present in some romantic stories (E. M. Hull's infamous 1919 novel *The Sheik* comes to mind), my own reading suggests that romantic fiction generally aims for more than a power reversal.

Stories are, indeed, usually driven by some form of conflict; however, empirical research reveals that the primary conflict is not based on gender. An analysis of 435 characters from 134 British novels of the nineteenth and early twentieth centuries, including those by Jane Austen, concluded that while these novels have an agonistic structure, the main conflict is between social cooperators and selfish exploiters regardless of their sex. While antagonists, both male and female, are mostly interested in competing for wealth and status, protagonists subordinate the conflict between the sexes to their "shared and complementary interests", and this means that "among the good characters … romantic love is possible" (Carroll et al., 2012, pp. 73–74, 80). This finding is deeply relevant to the way romantic fiction imagines gender power dynamics and resolves sexual conflict. Female success in these stories lies not in defeating a male opponent but in instigating a cooperative relationship with a male partner and extending this cooperation across the families and communities.

The romantic hero is usually an alpha male. This makes him attractive: As suggested by the anthropologist Barbara Smuts (1992, 1995), throughout human evolutionary history, women have consistently preferred powerful men for the simple reason that such men were better able to protect them and their children from other—often aggressive—men. But it is a dangerous attraction: According to another anthropologist, Christopher Boehm (1999, 2012), alpha males are the most serious threat to equitable relations, as they are in the best position to exploit others. And women are particularly vulnerable to both social and sexual exploitation. Moreover, very masculine men tend to opt for a short-term mating strategy (Thornhill & Gangestad, 2008, p. 178), which is generally not optimal for women. As I explained in Chapter 2, the evolutionary solution to this complex dilemma is a strong female preference for a relationship based on love with a man who derives his high status not from aggressive dominance but from cooperative prestige. Unfortunately, the difference between dominance and prestige may not be immediately obvious, as many of the physical cues (e.g., wide, confident stance) and social cues (such as the ability to command others' attention and influence their actions) are very similar (Henrich & Gil-White, 2001).

Romantic fiction warns against the potentially dangerous appeal of the alpha male and the necessity to carefully examine his character by making the hero initially appear aloof and arrogant. It is worth noting that chick lit usually follows the model of Austen's Mr. Darcy, whose main flaws are his haughtiness and detachment; heroes of popular romance novels more often share the traits of Charlotte Brontë's Mr. Rochester's darker, more troubled character. In any case, aware of his power and advantage, the hero often initially treats the heroine simply as a sexual object or "a reproductive resource" (Easterlin, 2013) and expects that any woman he chooses will gratefully accept him. Feminists have rightly pointed out that such an attitude may betray "the rapist mentality" (Modleski, 1982/2008, p. 35). Indeed, in Samuel Richardson's *Pamela* (often identified as the source of the modern romance formula) Mr B. tries to rape the titular heroine, and the Sheik (whose eponymous novel spawned a whole sub-genre of the so-called "desert romances") easily succeeds at abducting and raping the heroine, Lady Diana Mayo. Since both these heroines eventually willingly marry their abusers, feminists have taken this pattern of turning "rape into lovemaking" (Snitow, 1979, p. 153) as characteristic of romantic fiction, but a recent overview of romance novels notes that its prevalence has been "overstated" (Teo, 2020, p. 470). Undoubtedly, the possibility of rape casts a dark shadow over male-female relationships, and sexual abuse statistics remain disturbing. Some romantic narratives may indeed try to help women work through the anxieties associated with this state of affairs. However, part of the constructive vision of gender relations in romantic fiction is a reminder that even though some men may be inconsiderate or insistent, and many may have the physical and social means to impose themselves on women, most men are not rapists.[6] And even the brutal Sheik realizes that more than Diana's submission, he wants her willing consent and reciprocity.

The other part of that vision is that the heroine is able to challenge male hegemony: She refuses the sexual advances or marriage proposals of any man who fails to recognize her as not only equal but unique. Thus, Elizabeth Bennet rejects Mr. Collins's and Mr. Darcy's equally patronising marriage proposals; Fanny Price and Catherine Morland reject their overbearing suitors, Henry Crawford and John Thorpe, respectively;[7] Jane Eyre runs away from the dishonest Mr. Rochester and from the stern St. John Rivers; Anastasia Steel declines to be Christian Grey's "submissive"; and Carrie Bradshaw refuses to continue her relationship with Mr. Big as "just another girlfriend" not special enough to be introduced to his mother (SATC, 1:12 "Oh Come All Ye Faithful"). This unexpected rejection effectively suppresses status differences and attempts at undue domination. It prompts the hero to examine his attitude and behaviour and to reconsider the source of his romantic appeal. He is accepted only after he sufficiently demonstrates to the heroine that he respects her agency and values her individuality and that he will not use his power to supress them—and as I argued in Chapters 1 and 2, love is the psychological mechanism that makes this possible because it changes our attitude towards the beloved and our life priorities.

But it is not enough for the hero to prove his love and loyalty to one woman. He needs to show that he can maintain respectful, positive relationships with his own relatives, friends, and subordinates; that others defer to him not out of fear but out of regard for his judgement and leadership; and that he can extend this respect to the heroine's social circle and beyond to the wider community. Thus, Mr. Darcy is gradually revealed to be a loving brother, loyal friend, and benevolent master, in addition to becoming hospitable to Elizabeth's relatives and saving her family from disgrace. Similarly, Christian Grey, despite his traumatic childhood, has affectionate relationships with his adopted family; his employees call him "a good man"; he invests a lot of money in ventures aiming to "help eradicate hunger and poverty across the globe"; and he "charms the pants off" Anastasia's dad (James, 2012).[8] In Jayne Ann Krentz's best-selling romance novel *The Vanishing* (2020), Slater Arganbright risks his life not only to save the heroine, Catalina Lark, and her close friend, Olivia LeClair, but to defend Catalina and Olivia's whole village. Even Hull's Sheik genuinely cares for his childhood friend and his long-time valet, and is a beloved, if uncompromising, leader of his tribe, willing to sacrifice anything for them.

However, no romantic union can eliminate the possibility of a future conflict: The alignment is never perfect. This is particularly clear in television shows such as *Sex and the City*, with its episodic structure across several seasons and sequels, or in trilogies such as *Fifty Shades of Grey*—each new instalment reveals a new misalignment which needs to be negotiated before commitment to the relationship can be renewed.

Hence, while the relationship with the hero becomes the main one for the heroine, it is hardly ever her only valuable bond; she preserves her safety net. In fact, contrary to the feminist accusation that romantic love separates women from each other, in romantic fiction, the heroine's marriage usually reinforces her existing female ties or creates important new ones. This careful maintenance of kin and social support networks, or what has been termed a "tend-and-befriend" strategy, is an important element of female social psychology highlighted by both feminists and evolutionists (Gilligan, 1982; Taylor et al., 2000; Whissell, 1996). Thus, Elizabeth and Jane Bennet remain emotionally close and live in close proximity, as do Elinor and Marianne Dashwood; Fanny Price's sister moves in with her; Elizabeth Bennet quickly establishes a friendship with her sister-in-law, as do Catherine Morland and Anne Elliot; Emma Woodhouse retains her friendship with Mrs. Weston and mends her relationship with Jane Fairfax. In *Sex and the City* and numerous chick lit novels, an important factor in the heroine's relationship is the mutual acceptance between her social circle and her man.

Finally, the threat of a future conflict is not limited to the romantic couple. No matter how idyllic their symbolic Pemberley may be, beyond its walls not everyone shares their egalitarian ethos and moral principles. The heroine needs to be convinced that her man will not use his power against her, but it would not be to her benefit to diminish this power. As long as the average man remains physically stronger than the average woman, women will need powerful male allies, making the dynamics of sexual choice both a matter of personal agency and social necessity. So, the romantic hero retains his power and authority to keep deterring antagonists, to keep in check those who may want to selfishly exploit or threaten social cooperation. For example, Darcy's authority allows him to occasionally help Wickham with his career, "for Elizabeth's sake" (PP, p. 366), but prevents Wickham and Lydia from exploiting this generosity as they sometimes do with the more accommodating Bingleys.

Romantic fiction and change

In its broad contours, my claim that romantic fiction contains a vision of more egalitarian gender relations is not new. Many analyses of romantic fiction note that it addresses important female concerns and imagines a better world. But most claim that even though this fantasy provides some respite from or compensation for the troubling reality, it is just that: a fantasy, "the quintessential escapist fare" (Krentz, 1992, p. 98). In fact, according to feminists, this "temporary, imaginative consolation" (Poovey, 1984, p. 237) is the most dangerous aspect of romantic narratives because it confines the expression of protest and the possibility of change to the realm of fantasy (Radway, 1984/1991, p. 212); it "doesn't fundamentally challenge man's world" (Roach, 2016, p. 27) but reconciles women to it. Moreover, following Freudian psychoanalytic models, feminists claim that the contradictory nature of romantic plots induces a state of hysteria in both the heroine and the female reader (Modleski, 1982/2008), which is harmful to their psychological and emotional wellbeing.

However, current understanding of the cognitive and emotional effects of fiction as well as empirical research about romance reading do not support such bleak conclusions. Romantic stories certainly are "wish-fulfilling fantasies, well designed to pick the locks of the pleasure circuits" of female brains (Salmon & Symons, 2001, p. 4). They may even be "superstimuli" exaggerating the pleasures of romantic relationships in order to maximize women's evolved interest in long-term pair bonds (Baumard et al., 2022, pp. 506–507). But pleasure and utility are not easily separated in evolution. Indeed, pleasurable feelings likely evolved to motivate behaviours which in the past proved beneficial—just as unpleasant emotions, such as shame or disgust, are designed to deter us from doing things which in the long run have been detrimental (Al-Shawaf et al., 2016). Hence, we crave sugary and fatty foods because they were essential to our ancestors' survival; the intense pleasure of orgasm encourages sex, without which our own genes, and the whole species, would die out; juvenile animals and human children find physical play so compulsively rewarding because it provides practice for skills vital later in life; and humans delight in playing with social patterns through narrative because successfully navigating social interactions is essential to us (Boyd, 2009).

Reading romantic fiction provides a lot of pleasure to its audience, but it is not mindless escapism encouraging female passivity: The reader is cognitively and emotionally, albeit vicariously, engaged in the biologically and culturally significant process of mate selection. Neither is romance reading a compensatory mechanism: As research shows, readers' interest in fictional relationships is primarily motivated not by lack of intimacy or relationship satisfaction in real life but by "how much thought participants put into what they want out of romantic relationships" (van Monsjou & Mar, 2019, p. 446). Romance and chick lit readers report that they put themselves in the heroine's shoes, evaluating her perspectives and considering what they would do in her situation (Gregson & Lois, 2020; Span, 2022). This helps them to clarify their own mate preferences, consider costs and benefits of different relationship options, and vicariously test-run potential solutions.

Furthermore, readers of romantic fiction insist on its positive psychological effects: It "creates a feeling of hope, provides emotional sustenance, and produces a fully visceral sense of well-being" (Radway, 1984/1991, p. 12). Some call these uplifting feelings "a useful illusion" (Vanderbeke & Cooke, 2019), but their effects are far from illusory. In fact, psychologists stress that hope and a sense of control—even if not entirely warranted—are essential to our emotional wellbeing and success of any kind, including the success of our romantic relationships (Goleman, 1995/2005). Perception of control over a situation and optimism about future outcomes not only make us generally happier but also mean that we are more likely to take positive action in pursuit of our goals. It should be noted that this sense of control can be achieved in two ways: either by changing the environment according to one's wishes (called primary or personal control), or by changing oneself to fit with the environment (secondary or compensatory control; Rothbaum et al., 1982). Depending on circumstances, both mechanisms can be beneficial. But while feminists have at best allowed romantic fiction to provide the compensatory type of control for heroines and readers by helping them to accept female subordination, I argue for primary control: Heroines challenge male hegemony and insist on equitable loving relationships—and this inspires readers to do the same in real life. To paraphrase Gilligan's argument about the power of love against patriarchy: We need to see a path before following it can become an option (Gilligan, 2002). Fiction is particularly effective in showing a path: It can "model and motivate personal values like courage, resilience, resourcefulness, circumspection, and social values like generosity, sensitivity, [and] respect for others"; moreover, it "appears able to induce changes of social attitude more readily than nonfictional narrative" (Boyd, 2018 and research cited within).

Feedback from readers confirms that romantic fiction helps them "face and solve real-life problems" (Palmer, 1992, p. 156) and spurs them "to seek change in their own lives" (Thurston, 1987, p. 217). For example, sex therapists Dr. Jennifer Berman and Dr. Laura Berman believe that *Sex and the City* helped women feel more positive about their bodies and "take control of their sexuality" (quoted in Stillion Southard, 2008, p. 150). Many romance writers consider their writing as feminist and claim it is conducive to their own and their readers' feminist efforts (Krentz, 1992). Consuming romantic fiction is conceptualized as a form of self-care and "cultural resistance" in some communities (Gregson & Lois, 2020; Span, 2022). Furthermore, just as the romantic heroine is not separated from her female networks, neither is the reader. She is surrounded by women: imaginatively by the fictional characters, and literally by various fan clubs and reader communities for which women's fiction is famous. They create a sense of connection and solidarity which has been compared to feminist consciousness-raising meetings (Gerhard, 2005, p. 45; Hunting, 2012, p. 196). The women not only share the pleasures of the stories but also support each other in following the path to change.

The change imagined by romantic fiction is not about rejecting or defeating men but about inducing them to love and cooperate. It may not be a radical feminist revolution, but it is a female-led evolution underpinned by the cumulative power of individual choices, creating new gender relations "from the play of repetition and difference within the old" (Grosz, 2005). And the romantic vision is not as unrealistic as some have argued: For much of our evolutionary history, love has been transforming human males and human gender relations, making cooperation the defining feature of our species.

Notes

1 For an insightful analysis of the early criticism of Austen by female reviewers, see Wilkes (2010).
2 For a more comprehensive—and more positive—description of the romantic formula, see Regis (2003).
3 Interestingly, Radway concedes that her ethnographic study does not provide enough evidence to support this claim definitively. In later reflections, she admits that her final conclusions were guided more by her own assumptions than by readers' responses.
4 Boyd extends here Daniel Dor's (2015) argument about the invention of language and its subsequent effects on our communication, cognition, and sociality.
5 Correspondingly, people usually associate the feeling of sorrow with the two opposite situations: separation from the beloved (e.g., due to rejection or death) and loss of social or political power.
6 For example, in a study investigating the self-reported likelihood of "raping" or "forcing a female to do something sexual she does not want to" provided that "nobody would ever know and there wouldn't be any consequences", 13.6% of the male participants answered "yes" to the first option and 31.7% answered "yes" to the second option (Edwards et al., 2014). While ideally the number of men answering "yes" to either option would be zero, the study shows that even in this consequence-free scenario, the vast majority of men in this sample would not rape a woman. Presumably, the possibility of detection or punishment would deter even more men in a real-life situation.
7 For an insightful discussion of John Thorpe's domineering tendencies and Catherine Morland's resistance, see Anderson (2018).
8 All quotes taken from the Kindle edition; no page numbers available.

References

Al-Shawaf, L., Conroy-Beam, D., Asao, K., & Buss, D. M. (2016). Human emotions: An evolutionary psychological perspective. *Emotion Review*, *8*(2), 173–186. https://doi.org/10.1177/1754073914565518
Anderson, K. (2018). *Jane Austen's women: An introduction*. State University of New York Press.
Assiter, A. (1988). Romance fiction: Porn for women? In G. Day & C. Bloom (Eds.), *Perspectives on pornography: Sexuality in film and literature* (pp. 101–109). St. Martin's Press.
Austen, J. (1811/2003). *Sense and sensibility*. Penguin.
Austen, J. (1813/2003). *Pride and prejudice*. Penguin.
Austen, J. (1814/1998). *Mansfield Park*. W. W. Norton & Company.
Austen, J. (1815/2003). *Emma*. Oxford University Press.
Austen, J. (1818/1998). *Persuasion*. Oxford University Press.
Austen, J. (1818/2003). *Northanger Abbey*. Penguin Books.

Baumard, N., Huillery, E., Hyafil, A., & Safra, L. (2022). The cultural evolution of love in literary history. *Nature Human Behaviour*, *6*(4), 506–522. https://doi.org/10.1038/s41562-022-01292-z

Boehm, C. (1999). *Hierarchy in the forest: The evolution of egalitarian behavior*. Harvard University Press.

Boehm, C. (2012). *Moral origins: The evolution of virtue, altruism, and shame* (Kindle ed.). Basic Books.

Boyd, B. (1998). Jane, meet Charles: Literature, evolution, and human nature. *Philosophy and Literature*, *22*(1), 1–30.

Boyd, B. (2009). *On the origin of stories: Evolution, cognition, and fiction*. Belknap Press of Harvard University Press.

Boyd, B. (2018). The evolution of stories: From mimesis to language, from fact to fiction. *Wiley Interdisciplinary Reviews Cognitive Science*, *9*(1), 1–16. https://doi.org/10.1002/wcs.1444

Brontë, C. (1847/2010). *Jane Eyre*. HarperCollins.

Brownmiller, S. (1976). *Against our will: Men, women and rape*. Bantam Books.

Carroll, J. (2004). *Literary Darwinism: Evolution, human nature, and literature*. Routledge.

Carroll, J. (2018). Evolutionary literary theory. In D. H. Richter (Ed.), *A companion to literary theory* (pp. 423–438). John Wiley & Sons.

Carroll, J., Clasen, M., & Jonsson, E. (Eds.). (2020). *Evolutionary perspectives on imaginative culture*. Springer.

Carroll, J., Gottschall, J., Johnson, J. A., & Kruger, D. J. (2012). *Graphing Jane Austen: The evolutionary basis of literary meaning*. Palgrave Macmillan.

Cox, A., & Fisher, M. L. (2009). The Texas billionaire's pregnant bride: An evolutionary interpretation of romance fiction titles. *Journal of Social, Evolutionary, and Cultural Psychology*, *3*(4), 386.

Culler, J. D. (2000). *Literary theory: A very short introduction*. Oxford University Press.

Deresiewicz, W. (2011). *A Jane Austen education: How six novels taught me about love, friendship, and the things that really matter*. Penguin Press.

Dissanayake, E. (2000). *Art and intimacy: How the arts began*. University of Washington Press.

Dor, D. (2015). *The instruction of imagination: Language as a social communication technology*. Oxford University Press. https://doi.org/10.1093/acprof:oso/9780190256623.001.0001

Douglas, A. (1980). Soft-porn culture: Punishing the liberated woman. *The New Republic*, *183*(009), 25–29.

Dutton, D. (2009). *The art instinct: Beauty, pleasure, & human evolution*. Bloomsbury Press.

Easterlin, N. (2013). From reproductive resource to autonomous individuality? Charlotte Brontë's Jane Eyre. In M. L. Fisher, J. R. Garcia, & R. S. Chang (Eds.), *Evolution's empress: Darwinian perspectives on the nature of women* (pp. 390–405). Oxford University Press.

Edwards, S. R., Bradshaw, K. A., & Hinsz, V. B. (2014). Denying rape but endorsing forceful intercourse: Exploring differences among responders. *Violence and Gender*, *1*(4), 188–193. https://doi.org/10.1089/vio.2014.0022

Eliot, G. (1856). Silly novels by lady novelists. *Westminster Review*.

Ezard, J. (2001, August 24). Bainbridge tilts at 'chick lit' cult. *The Guardian*. https://www.theguardian.com/uk/2001/aug/24/books.generalfiction

Ferriss, S., & Young, M. (2006). Introduction. In S. Ferriss & M. Young (Eds.), *Chick lit: The new woman's fiction* (pp. 1–13). Routledge.

Firestone, S. (1970/1979). *The dialectic of sex: The case for feminist revolution*. The Women's Press. (1970).

Fraiman, S. (1989). The humiliation of Elizabeth Bennet. In P. Yeager & B. Kowaleski-Wallace (Eds.), *Refiguring the father: New feminist readings of patriarchy* (pp. 168–187). Southern Illinois University Press.

Gerhard, J. (2005). Sex and the City: Carrie Bradshaw's queer postfeminism. *Feminist Media Studies*, *5*(1), 37–49. https://doi.org/10.1080/14680770500058173

Gilbert, S. M., & Gubar, S. (1979/2000). *The madwoman in the attic: The woman writer and the nineteenth-century literary imagination* (2nd, Kindle ed.). Yale University Press.

Gill, R. (2003). From sexual objectification to sexual subjectification: The resexualisation of women's bodies in the media. *Feminist Media Studies*, *3*(1), 100–106.

Gill, R. (2008). Empowerment/Sexism: Figuring female sexual agency in contemporary advertising. *Feminism & Psychology*, *18*(1), 35–60. https://doi.org/10.1177/0959353507084950

Gilligan, C. (1982). *In a different voice: Psychological theory and women's development*. Harvard University Press.

Gilligan, C. (2002). *The birth of pleasure*. Alfred A. Knopf.

Goleman, D. (1995/2005). *Emotional intelligence* (10th anniversary ed.). Bantam Books. (1995)

Gottschall, J. (2005). Quantitative literary study: A modest manifesto and testing the hypotheses of feminist fairy tale studies. In J. Gottschall & D. S. Wilson (Eds.), *The literary animal: Evolution and the nature of narrative* (pp. 199–224). Northwestern University Press.

Gottschall, J. (2008). *The rape of Troy: Evolution, violence, and the world of Homer*. Cambridge University Press.

Gottschall, J., & Nordlund, M. (2006). Romantic love: A literary universal? *Philosophy and Literature, 30*(2), 450–470.

Grahame-Smith, S. (2009). *Pride and Prejudice and zombies*. Penguin.

Grant, A. (2020). "Sneering civility": Female intrasexual competition for mates in Jane Austen's novels. *EvoS Journal: The Journal of the Evolutionary Studies Consortium, 11*(1), 15–33. https://doi.org/10.59077/QSHP9625

Grant, A. (forthcoming). Literary studies. In M. L. Fisher (Ed.), *The American Psychological Association handbook of evolutionary psychology*. APA Press.

Grant, A., & Kruger, D. J. (2023). "Such an alternative as this had not occurred to her": The transformation of Jane Austen's Emma as understood from an evolutionary perspective. *Evolutionary Behavioral Sciences, 17*(1), 43–60. https://doi.org/10.1037/ebs0000271

Greer, G. (1970). *The female eunuch*. McGraw-Hill Book Company.

Gregson, J., & Lois, J. (2020). Social science reads romance. In J. Kamblé, E. M. Selinger, & H.-M. Teo (Eds.), *The Routledge research companion to popular romance fiction* (pp. 335–351). Routledge.

Grosz, E. A. (2005). *Time travels: Feminism, nature, power*. Duke University Press.

Henrich, J. (2016). *The secret of our success: How culture is driving human evolution, domesticating our species, and making us smarter*. Princeton University Press.

Henrich, J., & Gil-White, F. J. (2001). The evolution of prestige: Freely conferred deference as a mechanism for enhancing the benefits of cultural transmission. *Evolution and Human Behavior, 22*(3), 165–196.

Hogan, P. C. (2003). *The mind and its stories: Narrative universals and human emotion*. Cambridge University Press.

Hull, E. M. (1919/2020). *The Sheik* (Kindle ed.). e-artnow.

Hunting, K. (2012). Women talk: Chick lit TV and the dialogues of feminism. *The Communication Review, 15*(3), 187–203. https://doi.org/10.1080/10714421.2012.702002

Jablonka, E., & Lamb, M. J. (2014). *Evolution in four dimensions: Genetic, epigenetic, behavioral, and symbolic variation in the history of life* (Rev. ed.). MIT Press.

James, E. L. (2012). *Fifty shades trilogy: Fifty shades of Grey, Fifty shades darker, Fifty shades freed* (Kindle ed.). Random House.

Johnson, C. L. (1988). *Jane Austen: Women, politics, and the novel*. University of Chicago Press.

Jonsson, E. (2020). Evolutionary literary theory. In T. K. Shackelford (Ed.), *The SAGE handbook of evolutionary psychology: Integration of evolutionary psychology with other disciplines* (Vol. 1, pp. 403–420). Sage Publications.

Konstan, D. (1994). *Sexual symmetry: Love in the ancient novel and related genres*. Princeton University Press.

Krentz, J. A. (Ed.) (1992). *Dangerous men and adventurous women: Romance writers on the appeal of the romance* (Kindle ed.). University of Pennsylvania Press.

Krentz, J. A. (2020). *The Vanishing* (Kindle ed.). Piatkus.

Kruger, D. J., Fisher, M. L., Strout, S. L., Clark, S., Lewis, S., & Wehbe, M. (2014). Pride and prejudice or family and flirtation? Jane Austen's depiction of women's mating strategies. *Philosophy and Literature, 38*(1), A114–A128.

Mabry, A. R. (2006). About a girl: female subjectivity and sexuality in contemporary 'chick' culture. In S. Ferriss & M. Young (Eds.), *Chick lit: the new woman's fiction* (pp. 191–206). Routledge. http://www.loc.gov/catdir/toc/ecip0512/2005013904.html

Mar, R. A., & Oatley, K. (2008). The function of fiction is the abstraction and simulation of social experience. *Perspectives on Psychological Science, 3*(3), 173–192. https://doi.org/10.1111/j.1745-6924.2008.00073.x

McRobbie, A. (2004). Post-feminism and popular culture. *Feminist Media Studies, 4*(3), 255–264.

Miller, G. F. (2000). *The mating mind: How sexual choice shaped the evolution of human nature.* Doubleday.

Mißler, H. (2017). *The cultural politics of chick lit.* Routledge. https://doi.org/10.4324/9781315626536

Modleski, T. (1982/2008). *Loving with a vengeance: Mass-produced fantasies for women* (2nd ed.). Routledge.

Nordlund, M. (2007). *Shakespeare and the nature of love: Literature, culture, evolution.* Northwestern University Press.

Oatley, K. (2016). Fiction: Simulation of social worlds. *Trends in cognitive sciences, 20*(8), 618–628.

Palmer, D. (1992). Let me tell you about my readers. In J. A. Krentz (Ed.), *Dangerous men and adventurous women: Romance writers on the appeal of the romance* (pp. 155–158). University of Pennsylvania Press.

Poovey, M. (1984). *The proper lady and the woman writer: Ideology as style in the works of Mary Wollstonecraft, Mary Shelley, and Jane Austen.* University of Chicago Press.

Rabine, L. W. (1985). *Reading the romantic heroine: Text, history, ideology.* University of Michigan Press.

Radway, J. A. (1984/1991). *Reading the romance: Women, patriarchy, and popular literature* (2nd ed.). University of North Carolina Press.

Regis, P. (2003). *A natural history of the romance novel.* University of Pennsylvania Press.

Richardson, S. (1740/1985). *Pamela, or virtue rewarded.* Penguin.

Richerson, P. J., & Boyd, R. (2005). *Not by genes alone: How culture transformed human evolution.* University of Chicago Press. http://www.loc.gov/catdir/description/uchi052/2004006601.html

Roach, C. M. (2016). *Happily ever after: The romance story in popular culture.* Indiana University Press.

Rothbaum, F., Weisz, J. R., & Snyder, S. S. (1982). Changing the world and changing the self: A two-process model of perceived control. *Journal of Personality and Social Psychology, 42*(1), 5–37.

Rowntree, M., Moulding, N., & Bryant, L. (2012). Feminine sexualities in chick lit. *Australian Feminist Studies, 27*(72), 121–137. https://doi.org/10.1080/08164649.2012.648259

Salmon, C. (2005). Crossing the abyss: Erotica and the intersection of evolutionary psychology and literary studies. In J. Gottschall & D. S. Wilson (Eds.), *The literary animal: Evolution and the nature of narrative* (pp. 244–255). Northwestern University Press.

Salmon, C. (2016). What do romance novels, pro wrestling, and Mack Bolan have in common? Consilience and the pop culture of storytelling. In J. Carroll, D. P. McAdams, & E. O. Wilson (Eds.), *Darwin's bridge: Uniting the humanities and sciences* (pp. 167–182). Oxford University Press.

Salmon, C., & Symons, D. (2001). *Warrior lovers: Erotic fiction, evolution and female sexuality.* Weidenfeld & Nicolson.

Saunders, J. P. (2009). *Reading Edith Wharton through a Darwinian lens: Evolutionary biological issues in her fiction.* McFarland & Co.

Saunders, J. P. (2014). Darwinian literary analysis of sexuality. In T. K. Shackelford & R. D. Hansen (Eds.), *The evolution of sexuality* (pp. 29–55). Springer International Publishing. https://doi.org/10.1007/978-3-319-09384-0_2

Saunders, J. P. (2018). *American classics: Evolutionary perspectives.* Academic Studies Press. http://www.jstor.org/stable/10.2307/j.ctv4v3226

Scalise Sugiyama, M. (2001). Food, foragers, and folklore: The role of narrative in human subsistence. *Evolution and Human Behavior, 22*(4), 221–240.

Shostak, M. (1990). *Nisa, the life and words of a !Kung woman.* Earthscan Publications.

Smuts, B. (1992). Male aggression against women. *Human Nature, 3*(1), 1–44. https://doi.org/10.1007/bf02692265

Smuts, B. (1995). The evolutionary origins of patriarchy. *Human Nature, 6*(1), 1–32. https://doi.org/10.1007/bf02734133

Snitow, A. B. (1979). Mass market romance: Pornography for women is different. *Radical History Review, 1979*(20), 141–161. https://doi.org/10.1215/01636545-1979-20-141

Southam, B. C. (Ed.). (1968). *Jane Austen: The critical heritage.* Routledge & Kegan Paul.

Span, M. (2022). Caring for the self. A case-study on sociocultural aspects of reading chick lit. *Journal of Popular Romance Studies, 11*, 1–18.

Stasio, M. J., & Duncan, K. (2007). An evolutionary approach to Jane Austen: Prehistoric preferences in *Pride and Prejudice*. *Studies in the Novel, 39*(2), 133–146. https://www.jstor.org/stable/20831911

Stillion Southard, B. A. (2008). Beyond the backlash: *Sex and the City* and three feminist struggles. *Communication Quarterly, 56*(2), 149–167.

Taylor, S. E., Klein, L. C., Lewis, B. P., Gruenewald, T. L., Gurung, R. A. R., & Updegraff, J. A. (2000). Biobehavioral responses to stress in females: Tend-and-befriend, not fight-or-flight. *Psychological Review, 107*(3), pg. 411–429.

Teo, H.-M. (2020). Love and romance novels. In J. Kamblé, E. M. Selinger, & H.-M. Teo (Eds.), *The Routledge research companion to popular romance fiction* (pp. 454–484). Routledge.

Thornhill, R., & Gangestad, S. W. (2008). *The evolutionary biology of human female sexuality*. Oxford University Press.

Thurston, C. (1987). *The romance revolution: Erotic novels for women and the quest for a new sexual identity*. University of Illinois Press.

van Monsjou, E., & Mar, R. A. (2019). Interest and investment in fictional romances. *Psychology of Aesthetics, Creativity, and the Arts, 13*, 431–449. https://doi.org/10.1037/aca0000191

Vanderbeke, D., & Cooke, B. (2019). *Evolution and popular narrative*. Brill.

Vermeule, B. (2010). *Why do we care about literary characters?* Johns Hopkins University Press.

Whelehan, I. (2005). *The feminist bestseller: From Sex and the Single Girl to Sex and the City*. Palgrave Macmillan.

Whissell, C. (1996). Mate selection in popular women's fiction. *Human Nature, 7*(4), 427–447. https://doi.org/10.1007/bf02732902

Wilkes, J. (2010). *Women reviewing women in nineteenth-century Britain: The critical reception of Jane Austen, Charlotte Brontë and George Eliot*. Ashgate Publishing Company.

Woolf, V. (1928/2004). *A room of one's own*. Penguin Books.

PART II
PRIDE AND PREJUDICE

INTRODUCTION TO *PRIDE AND PREJUDICE*

"The lady has no choice?"[1]

In *Northanger Abbey*, Henry Tilney tells Catherine Morland that in both matrimony and dancing, "man has the advantage of choice, woman only the power of refusal" (NA, p. 71). Modern critics have noted that even this power was often "no power at all" given pressure from family, economic circumstances, and social standards (Jones, 2009, p. 30). Indeed, as Ivor Morris rightly observes, the fact that "a woman should have feelings which determine choice, and the right as a human being to exercise it, is by no means undisputed in the world Jane Austen sets before us" (1987, p. 115). Austen's position in that dispute has been interpreted in various, sometimes contradictory ways.

In a comprehensive overview of Austen scholarship, Laurence Mazzeno notes that "Since the nineteenth century, feminists seem to have had a love-hate relationship with Austen" (2011, p. 107). Two great British female novelists of the nineteenth century with strong feminist sensibilities, Charlotte Brontë and George Eliot, did not like Austen's work, finding it too restrained and quotidian. However, many other nineteenth and early twentieth-century female writers and critics, most notably Virginia Woolf (1928/2004), praised Austen for her ability to capture human nature and turn the minutiae of women's daily lives into art; they also defended her portrayal of women's ideas about and experiences of love as her particular contribution to literature (Wilkes, 2010).

The feminist movement of the 1970s brought detailed attention to Austen's position as a female novelist writing about women's lives, but there is no consensus about the nature and strength of Austen's politics. Some see her writing as conservative, reflecting the views of the Christian moralists (Butler, 1975), with her insistence on love seen as the most regrettable sign of that conservatism (Poovey, 1984). Others note Austen's affiliation with progressive ideas, such as those of Mary Wollstonecraft (Brown, 1973b; Johnson, 1988; Kirkham, 1983; Sulloway, 1989). Claudia Johnson emphasizes that historical circumstances, especially the anti-feminist controversy after the publication of Wollstonecraft's memoirs, meant that "to write novels of social criticism authors had to develop strategies of subversion and indirection" which would allow them "to advance reformist positions about women through the back door" (1988, pp. 19–20). Consequently, Johnson argues that the abundant "orthodox pronouncements" in Austen's novels should be seen not

DOI: 10.4324/9781003320982-7

as "definitive and incontestable truths ... but as propositions that [her] novels test and turn inside out" (1988, p. 23). Many interpretations are ambivalent, even contradictory. For example, Sandra Gilbert and Susan Gubar note that "Austen is rigorous in her revolt against the conventions she inherited", but at the same time, they maintain that "Austen's cover story of the necessity for silence and submission reinforces women's subordinate position in patriarchal culture" (1979/2000, pp. 119, 154). Their book *The Madwoman in the Attic* is recognized as "a standard of feminist criticism" (Brown, 1990, p. 303) with a significant impact on the direction of feminist analysis of Austen throughout the 1980s and 1990s, even though its interpretations have been acknowledged as "distorting" and "overreaching" (Marshall, 1992, p. 41), and its feminism as "hopelessly confused" (Brown, 1990, p. 304).

The feminist ambivalence is perhaps most obvious in the way the critics oscillate between praising Austen's independent, intelligent, self-aware heroines who "live powerfully" despite cultural constraints (Newman, 1983, p. 705) and lamenting the fact that they all end up married. In fact, even the power of Austen's heroines has been repeatedly seen as "equivocal" (Auerbach, 1976, p. 14), "illusory" (Poovey, 1984, p. 237), "nominal" (Gilbert & Gubar, 1979/2000, p. 136), or "manipulative and indirect" (Newton, 1981, p. 69). Some critics applaud the quality of female bonds (Kaplan, 1992; Knuth, 1989), but there is no consensus on that issue either, especially with regards to *Pride and Prejudice*: Auerbach claims that the Bennet sisters are "separate and hierarchical" (1976, p. 9), and Johnson (although more positive on the subject) thinks that "Austen does not extensively consider female friendship as an important alternative or even supplement to the marital relationship" (1988, p. 91). Some try to justify Austen's marital endings as a formal requirement of the genre rather than a sign of her endorsement of marriage as a woman's ultimate reward (Yeazell, 1974). Others insist that the credibility of Austen's romantic conclusions is undercut by their irony (Brown, 1973a). Those who have attempted to positively re-evaluate Austen's marriage plots remind us what a difficult task it is because for many feminists "marriage, after all, is just a less dramatic form than rape of terminating a heroine's original identity" (Morgan, 1989, p. 35). Thus, Austen's marital happy endings are "false", and "as critics and feminists, we must refuse [their] *effect*" (Newman, 1983, pp. 699, 694, emphasis in the original). *Pride and Prejudice* is particularly liable to such feminist objections.

Nevertheless, several critics not only praise Austen for putting female consciousness at the centre (Anderson, 2018) but also defend Austen's vision of love and marriage as compatible with feminist ideals: Austen constructs marriage as a reconciliation between the individual self and the wider world, a means of moral growth for both the heroine and the hero, and a promise of a social reform (Bromberg, 1993; Brown, 1979; Tauchert, 2005)—an interpretation in line with the argument of this book.

Austen has also been the subject of pioneering work in biocultural and cognitive studies of literature (Boyd, 1998; Carroll, 2004; Zunshine, 2007). Several studies using a combination of qualitative and quantitative methods have established that Austen is particularly insightful in portraying female sexual psychology and highlighting traits conducive to harmonious interpersonal relationships (Grant, 2020; Grant & Kruger, 2023; Kruger et al., 2014; Stasio & Duncan, 2007); her work has been called "a tutorial in romantic relationships that precedes the confirmatory research" (Kruger et al., 2014, p. A115). Austen is also supremely gifted at representing and engaging our Theory of Mind and social intelligence (Boyd, 1998; Jones, 2017; Lau, 2018; Zunshine, 2007), both of which are integral to the mate selection process. And she underscores the value of fiction when she makes her own heroines clarify their life and relationship priorities by using imaginative, hypothetical scenarios, as is most evident in the case of Emma Woodhouse (Grant & Kruger, 2023).

In a perceptive analysis of Austen informed by cognitive science, Patrick Colm Hogan argues that Austen overstates the importance of personality over circumstances as determinants of human behaviour (Hogan, 2018, p. 182). I argue instead that Austen focuses on individual disposition so much in order to show the variety of possible responses to similar circumstances. She fully acknowledges all the limitations her cultural context imposes on women's lives; however, she highlights how individual differences in personality affect some of the most important life decisions. She also presents those decisions as made by autonomous agents often defying family wishes or cultural conventions. Her heroines do not passively wait for men to choose them but are proactive in their desires: The exuberant Marianne Dashwood, Emma Woodhouse, and Elizabeth Bennet assert their right to flirt with men they find attractive (even if they turn out to be rogues); the reserved Elinor Dashwood and the timid Fanny Price fall in love before their chosen men do; Catherine Morland's love for Henry Tilney is so obvious that he gratefully returns it; and Anne Elliot declares her love, albeit indirectly, before Captain Wentworth does. Austen's women know what they want, and what they do not want, and are prepared to fight for it: Elizabeth Bennet, Anne Elliot, and Fanny Price reject very eligible suitors approved by their families; all three of them, as well as Elinor Dashwood, compete and win with other women who are younger (Louisa Musgrove), more elegant (Caroline Bingley), more confident (Mary Crawford), or downright manipulative (Lucy Steele); and finally, Catherine Morland, Elinor Dashwood, and Elizabeth Bennet marry against the wishes of their husbands' families. In all of Austen's fiction, the issue of female choice is a central concern, and *Pride and Prejudice* is the most salient example.

In the following four chapters, I analyse the romantic and sexual choices of four female characters from *Pride and Prejudice*: Lydia Bennet, Charlotte Lucas, Jane Bennet, and Elizabeth Bennet. Three of them are sisters with the same upbringing and circumstances; the fourth, although not biologically related, is in a very similar social and financial position. And yet, each of them responds to this shared reality in a unique way due to her individual personality and priorities. Each of them illustrates a different balancing out of the most important female mate choice criteria: physical attractiveness and sexual desire, material resources and social status, intelligence and emotional stability, long-term commitment and cooperative attitude. Each is contrasted with the other three, and with other females in the story, such as the insincere and competitive Caroline Bingley, the rich but insipid Anne de Bourgh, and the immature but well-meaning Georgiana Darcy.

Moreover, the four women share many of their traits with the men they choose: Lydia Bennet and Mr. Wickham are similarly reckless; both Charlotte Lucas and Mr. Collins approach marriage as an unemotional transaction; Jane Bennet and Mr. Bingley are both so accommodating and modest that they almost miss out on a good relationship; while neither Elizabeth Bennet nor Mr. Darcy are prepared to compromise in mate choice until they find a partner who not only meets their high expectations but also inspires personal growth. With her symmetrical pairings, Austen illustrates human tendency for homogamy and highlights similarities, rather than differences, between the sexes.

I start with Lydia, the youngest of the Bennet sisters who simply cannot wait to get married and is the first one of the five sisters to do so. Her path to marriage is the most controversial one, as she is the only one to prioritize short-term, instead of long-term, goals. I then turn to Charlotte Lucas who beats even Lydia to the altar by following the most conventional path: marrying for financial security. Neither Lydia's not Charlotte's choice has authorial approval. The next chapter is about Jane Bennet whose marriage promises happiness but whose high *Agreeableness*—a personality trait essential for good interpersonal and social relationships—has often been misinterpreted as passivity. And finally, I consider Elizabeth Bennet who, as the heroine, is faced with the most complex decision-making process and secures a marriage which promises personal happiness and improvement in social relations.

Note

1 SS, p. 278.

References

Anderson, K. (2018). *Jane Austen's women: An introduction*. State University of New York Press.
Auerbach, N. (1976). Austen and Alcott on matriarchy: New women or new wives? *Novel, 10*, 6–26.
Austen, J. (1811/2003). *Sense and sensibility*. Penguin.
Austen, J. (1818/2003). *Northanger Abbey*. Penguin Books.
Boyd, B. (1998). Jane, meet Charles: Literature, evolution, and human nature. *Philosophy and Literature, 22*(1), 1–30.
Bromberg, P. (1993). Teaching about the marriage plot. In M. McClintock Folsom (Ed.), *Approaches to teaching Austen's Pride and Prejudice* (pp. 126–133). Modern Language Association of America.
Brown, J. P. (1979). *Jane Austen's novels: Social change and literary form*. Harvard University Press.
Brown, J. P. (1990). The feminist depreciation of Austen: A polemical reading. *NOVEL: A Forum on Fiction, 23*(3), 303–313. https://doi.org/10.2307/1345955
Brown, L. W. (1973a). *Bits of ivory: Narrative techniques in Jane Austin's fiction*. Louisiana State University Press.
Brown, L. W. (1973b). Jane Austen and the feminist tradition. *Nineteenth-Century Fiction, 28*(3), 321–338. https://doi.org/10.2307/2933003
Butler, M. (1975). *Jane Austen and the war of ideas*. Clarendon Press.
Carroll, J. (2004). Human nature and literary meaning: A theoretical model illustrated with a critique of *Pride and Prejudice*. In J. Carroll, *Literary Darwinism: Evolution, human nature, and literature* (pp. 185–212). Routledge.
Gilbert, S. M., & Gubar, S. (1979/2000). *The madwoman in the attic: The woman writer and the nineteenth-century literary imagination* (2nd, Kindle ed.). Yale University Press.
Grant, A. (2020). "Sneering civility": Female intrasexual competition for mates in Jane Austen's novels. *EvoS Journal: The Journal of the Evolutionary Studies Consortium, 11*(1), 15–33. https://doi.org/10.59077/QSHP9625
Grant, A., & Kruger, D. J. (2023). "Such an alternative as this had not occurred to her": The transformation of Jane Austen's Emma as understood from an evolutionary perspective. *Evolutionary Behavioral Sciences, 17*(1), 43–60. https://psycnet.apa.org/doi/10.1037/ebs0000271
Hogan, P. C. (2018). Persuasion: Lessons in sociocognitive understanding. In B. Lau (Ed.), *Jane Austen and sciences of the mind* (pp. 180–199). Routledge. https://doi.org/10.4324/9780203732526-10
Johnson, C. L. (1988). *Jane Austen: Women, politics, and the novel*. University of Chicago Press.
Jones, H. (2009). *Jane Austen and marriage*. Continuum.
Jones, W. (2017). *Jane on the brain: Exploring the science of social intelligence with Jane Austen*. Simon and Schuster.
Kaplan, D. (1992). *Jane Austen among women*. Johns Hopkins University Press.

Kirkham, M. (1983). *Jane Austen, feminism and fiction*. Harvester Press.

Knuth, D. J. (1989). Sisterhood and friendship in *Pride and Prejudice*: Need happiness be "entirely a matter of chance"? *Persuasions Online, 11*, 99–109.

Kruger, D. J., Fisher, M., Strout, S. L., Clark, S., Lewis, S., & Wehbe, M. (2014). Pride and prejudice or family and flirtation? Jane Austen's depiction of women's mating strategies. *Philosophy and Literature, 38*(1), A114–A128.

Lau, B. (2018). *Jane Austen and sciences of the mind*. Routledge. https://doi.org/10.4324/9780203732526

Marshall, C. (1992). "Dull Elves" and feminists: A summary of feminist criticism of Jane Austen. *Persuasions, 14*, 39–45.

Mazzeno, L. W. (2011). *Jane Austen: Two centuries of criticism*. Camden House.

Morgan, S. (1989). *Sisters in time: Imagining gender in nineteenth-century British fiction*. Oxford University Press.

Morris, I. (1987). *Mr. Collins considered: Approaches to Jane Austen*. Routledge & Kegan Paul.

Newman, K. (1983). Can this marriage be saved: Jane Austen makes sense of an ending. *ELH, 50*(4), 693–710.

Newton, J. L. (1981). *Women, power, and subversion*. University of Georgia Press.

Poovey, M. (1984). *The proper lady and the woman writer: Ideology as style in the works of Mary Wollstonecraft, Mary Shelley, and Jane Austen*. University of Chicago Press.

Stasio, M. J., & Duncan, K. (2007). An evolutionary approach to Jane Austen: Prehistoric preferences in *Pride and Prejudice*. *Studies in the Novel, 39*(2), 133–146. https://www.jstor.org/stable/20831911

Sulloway, A. G. (1989). *Jane Austen and the province of womanhood*. University of Pennsylvania Press.

Tauchert, A. (2005). *Romancing Jane Austen: Narrative, realism, and the possibility of a happy ending*. Palgrave Macmillan.

Wilkes, J. (2010). *Women reviewing women in nineteenth-century Britain: The critical reception of Jane Austen, Charlotte Brontë and George Eliot*. Ashgate Publishing Company.

Woolf, V. (1928/2004). *A room of one's own*. Penguin Books.

Yeazell, R. (1974). Fictional heroines and feminist critics. *NOVEL: A Forum on Fiction, 8*(1), 29–38.

Zunshine, L. (2007). Why Jane Austen was different, and why we may need cognitive science to see it. *Style, 41*(3), 275–298.

4

LYDIA BENNET

"Tenderly flirting with at least six officers at once"[1]

Lydia, the youngest of the five Bennet sisters, is a frivolous, immature girl, with a seemingly irrepressible appetite for flirting, no respect for social rules, and very little self-control. She falls for and runs away with George Wickham, a handsome and charming but selfish and manipulative seducer. In Austen's world, such a move was almost fatal for a woman: Not only her own reputation, but the reputation of her whole family was tarnished. Lydia's future, as well as the future of her sisters, is saved only when Darcy, the hero of the story, bribes Wickham into marrying her.

Lydia is often seen as a double victim: Not only is she very immature and therefore easily "duped by Wickham" (Stasio & Duncan, 2007, p. 193), but more importantly, she is "obviously ... the victim of the double standard" (Dabundo, 2012, p. 46), punished for her unrepressed desire (Allen, 1985). Some modern readers even applaud her defiance and self-assertion. In a highly influential feminist analysis, Claudia Johnson claims that Lydia is a "decoy" whose blatant transgressions distract from Elizabeth's more subtle nonconformity, thus enabling Austen to introduce a feminist agenda covertly (1988, p. 20). Many others blame Lydia's narrative trajectory on the oppressive patriarchal culture, emphasizing that the lack of education and productive employment left women with few aspirations beyond romantic fantasies (Fraiman, 1993; Perry, 1980). Gilbert and Gubar state emphatically that the imaginations of young women like Lydia are "tainted by romantic notions which fuel their excessive materialism or sexuality" and, "provided with only the naive clichés of sentimental literature", these women "insist on acting out" the degrading sensationalist plots of romance novels (1979/2000, p. 123).

Clearly, Lydia's elopement is crucial to Austen's plot development: It is one of the most serious obstacles in the main romantic plot between Elizabeth and Darcy and the most severe test of Darcy's love. It is equally evident that Austen is acutely critical of the many limitations placed on women in her time. Through her handling of Lydia's subplot, she denounces both the sexual double standard and the conventions of sentimental fiction. But in doing so, Austen never loses her focus on how individual differences affect her characters' responses to a common reality. Catherine Morland and Isabella Thorpe shut themselves together to read novels, and yet while Isabella constantly imagines herself a heroine of a passionate romance, Catherine is completely baffled by her behaviour. The Bertram sisters wonder at Fanny's ignorance, but their formal education does not save them from failing the test of emotional intelligence and moral integrity. Elizabeth Bennet assures Lady Catherine that those among her sisters who "wished to learn never wanted the means" (PP, p. 161), but at the same time, Mary's bookishness seems no more admirable than Lydia's empty-headedness.

Austen locates the source of Lydia's fall—fall in love and fall from grace—in her pursuit of instant gratification without much consideration for long-term consequences of her actions. In other words, Lydia's story is an uncannily accurate portrayal of a woman with short-term or unrestricted mating strategy in a cultural environment which strongly discourages such a strategy, especially for women.[2] Although Lydia does not get a chance to be promiscuous, her temperament, her upbringing, her fantasies and desires, and finally the nature of her attraction to Wickham, capture all the elements consistently associated with high sociosexuality (see Simpson & Gangestad, 1991). Lydia's lack of restraint contrasts sharply with Jane's reserve, Mary's social ineptitude, and Charlotte Lucas's unsentimental calculation. It also contrasts with Georgiana Darcy's innocence: Georgiana is a genuine victim of Wickham's scheming and is later ashamed of her naivety, while Lydia actively contributes to her own seduction and is proud of its result. And finally, there is a telling contrast between Lydia and Elizabeth: two sisters with some similarities in personality, raised in the same household, and attracted to the same man—but with dramatically different outcomes. By comparing their stories, Austen shows the importance of distinguishing between genuine and dishonest suitors, or dads and cads—a challenge repeatedly present in romantic fiction. She also shows two approaches to female agency: one selfish, thoughtless, and short-sighted, the other self-reflexive and taking into account social and familial responsibilities.

Sense and sensibility

Austen was writing at a time when controlling female sexuality was equally a moral and political issue. Not only was Christian "virtue" synonymous with "chastity" and "vice" with "sexual misconduct" (Kirkham, 1983, p. 16), but as Johnson explains, "With the countryside full of Jacobin riffraff out to ruin English families by seducing women away from fond fathers and rightful husbands, female modesty—that is to say, the extent to which women do not feel, express, and pursue their own desires—[was] no less than a matter of national security" (1988, p. 14). And yet it is clear from historical and literary evidence that despite potentially severe consequences, many women chose to defy cultural and familial expectations of female chastity and obedience. Despite the admonitions of sermons and conduct books, newspapers and drawing rooms were full of gossip about elopements, adultery, and divorce (Jones, 2009, pp. 101–118). Popular fiction may have included numerous cautionary tales, but, as William Deresiewicz puts it, it was also "ripe with lurid sexuality" (2011, p. 231).

Austen's handling of sexual matters sets her apart equally from the politically conservative moralists and the popular sensationalists. Unlike the conservative writers of her time, Austen validates female desire and strongly advocates love—and hence, individual choice—as the most important basis for marriage not only in her fiction but also in real life, as evidenced by her advice to her niece Fanny Knight.[3] She also knew the power of passion first-hand, as suggested by the letters between herself and Cassandra concerning her short-lived romance with Tom Lefroy.[4] And as Juliet McMaster notes, Austen's heroines experience enough "pleasure in proximity and contact with the men they love" for us to know "they are warm and responsive" (1978, p. 71). All of Austen's novels contain stories of dangerous attractions, impulsive desires, and sometimes illicit sex, but unlike many popular novelists, Austen minimizes the sensationalist content of her plots by placing her seductions off-stage and never providing any salacious details. Her aim is not to titillate her readers but to make them ponder the motivation of her characters.

Austen shows that women, like men, vary in their sexual appetites. A few of her women, Lady Susan, Maria Bertram, and Eliza Brandon, do have more than one lover, but Austen associates high sociosexuality not so much with the number of sexual partners as with the ease of falling in love based on superficial reasons. For example, in *Love and Friendship*, Laura thinks the stranger who turns up on her doorstep is "the most beauteous and amiable youth" she had ever seen, declares instant attachment and marries him the same night (LF, Letter 5th, p. 7). In this early piece, Austen mainly ridicules the conventions of sentimental fiction, but in her later works, she closely examines the psychology and consequences of such instant infatuations and hasty matches. There is Georgiana Darcy's near elopement and Lydia's actual elopement; Maria Bertram's adultery and Julia Bertram's rushed marriage; Eliza Brandon's string of lovers, Marianne Dashwood's disastrous love for Willoughby and his seduction of Eliza Williams; and Isabella Thorpe's shameless flirtation with Captain Tilney. Elizabeth Bennet and Emma Woodhouse also temporarily fall under the spell of charming seducers but manage to recover, and Louisa Musgrove, who falls in love twice almost as quickly as Marianne or Lydia, is lucky enough that neither Captain Wentworth nor Captain Benwick has any dishonest intentions. All the other men connected with these impulsive and short-lived romances are typical cads: George Wickham, Henry Crawford, John Willoughby, Captain Tilney, and even Frank Churchill are selfish and manipulative narcissists, as reckless with women's feelings as they are with money. In only one case, the Crofts in *Persuasion*, love at first sight leads to a happy relationship.

Austen clearly understands the stirrings of desire: The passion that Lydia or Marianne display reveals the myth of women's coyness and passivity as false. However, through all the above scenarios, Austen argues that in her world, indiscriminately giving in to sexual impulse is hardly ever a good idea: Your heart is broken, your reputation is ruined, or you end up in a miserable marriage. For Austen, short-term passion is simply short-sighted. However, she objects to it not in the name of female chastity and filial obedience, but because she sees behaviour such as Lydia's as not conducive to personal growth and happiness or more equitable gender relations. Like modern psychologists, Austen links such quick romances with youthful naivety, a good dose of vanity, and a certain type of exuberant, irreverent personality.

"The most determined flirt"[5]

Personality is so closely related to sociosexuality that the behavioural scientist Daniel Nettle posits that personality variations reflect the trade-offs between costs and benefits of different survival and mating strategies (Nettle, 2006). And while there is no universally optimal personality, some traits are better suited to certain environments. Lydia is described as having a "good-humoured countenance", "high animal spirits", and "natural self-consequence" (PP, p. 45). She is, in many ways, similar to her mother—unsurprisingly, since personality is partly heritable. And she shares this cheerful confidence with Elizabeth, but, unlike her older sister, she is also "always unguarded and often uncivil", "self-willed and careless", "vain, ignorant, idle, and absolutely uncontrouled [*sic*]"

(PP, pp. 124, 206, 223). As Elizabeth predicts, it is Lydia's "disdain of all restraint" that has dire consequences for her and the rest of the family (PP, p. 223). Psychologists associate this kind of adventurous personality, marked by extraversion, social assertiveness, lack of self-control, and risk taking, with unrestricted sexuality (Fisher, 2011, pp. 42–61; Gangestad & Simpson, 1990, p. 71; Meston & Buss, 2009, pp. 164–166). And so do ordinary people: In studies examining female mating strategies in Austen's fiction, participants given only short descriptions of Lydia's personality and social behaviour, overwhelmingly link her with promiscuous sexuality (Kruger et al., 2014; Strout et al., 2010).

Of course, as a gentleman's daughter growing up in a small community, Lydia would not have had many opportunities to engage in any sexual activities, but her compulsive flirting as well as her fantasies testify to the strength of her sexual appetite. Together with shopping and dancing, flirting is Lydia's favourite occupation. And while it may seem innocent enough to the modern reader, in Austen's lexicon, being called a flirt is rather damning. When Elizabeth desperately tries to convince Mr. Bennet not to let Lydia go to Brighton, her strongest warning is: "she will, at sixteen, be *the most determined flirt* that ever made herself and her family ridiculous. A flirt too, *in the worst and meanest degree of flirtation*" (PP, p. 223, emphasis added).

Lydia's vision of Brighton reveals the extent of her desires:
> In Lydia's imagination, a visit to Brighton comprised every possibility of earthly happiness. She saw, with the creative eye of fancy, the streets of that gay bathing place covered with officers. *She saw herself the object of attention, to tens and to scores of them at present unknown.* She saw all the glories of the camp … crowded with the young and the gay, and dazzling with scarlet; and to complete the view, she saw herself seated beneath a tent, *tenderly flirting with at least six officers at once.* (PP, p. 224, emphasis added)

Lydia does not dream of one Prince Charming. Instead, as Robert Polhemus argues, this passage reveals Lydia's "pornographic imagination, which seeks for the self a sensually realized, beautiful, but undifferentiated and impersonal *more*. Lydia typically wants an endless supply of lovers" (1990, p. 44, emphasis in the original). Even as she is eloping with Wickham, she regrets missing the opportunity to dance with Pratt (PP, pp. 276–277). Lydia's erotic appetite, her "rage for admiration" (PP, p. 223), would have certainly been condemned in Austen's time, but it was not entirely fictional: Austen's cousin Eliza de Feuillide, when asked about her intentions after her first husband's death, wrote in a letter: "The Lady is so well pleased with her present situation that She cannot find it in her Heart to change it, and says in her giddy way that independence and the homage of half a dozen are preferable to subjection and the attachment of a single individual" (as cited in Jones, 2009, p. 34).

Clearly, Lydia's *nature* does not comply with, nor is it entirely suppressed by, the ideals of her *culture*. Let's consider how it was shaped by *nurture*.

"Disadvantages which must attend the children of so unsuitable a marriage"[6]

Developmental factors can have a profound effect on women's mating strategies, and evolutionists often emphasize that human children need a lot of multi-generational support (Hrdy, 2009; Sterelny, 2012). Evolutionary theory of socialization and interpersonal development posits that "children develop psychological and behavioural orientations consistent with the life-course experiences for which parents 'prepare' them" through their rearing (Belsky et al., 1991, p. 655). For example, a childhood environment marked by the absence of the father, marital discord, and insensitive or inconsistent parenting, signals to the growing child that the world is uncaring and relationships unreliable (Belsky et al., 1991, p. 655). Such affectively negative or unstable childhood experience often leads to earlier sexual maturation, more promiscuous sexual behaviour, and less stable relationships in adulthood (Del Giudice, 2009).

Austen certainly places much of the blame for Lydia's transgressions on her parents. There is no doubt that Mrs. Bennet is "the person to whose ill-judging indulgence the errors of her daughter must principally be owing" (PP, p. 273). But Mr. Bennet is equally at fault, for as Elizabeth suggests, had he taken his fatherly obligations more seriously, he "might at least have preserved the respectability of his daughters, even if incapable of enlarging the mind of his wife" (PP, p. 229). The Bennet household is not "a very pleasing picture of conjugal felicity or domestic comfort" (PP, p. 228). Although Mr. Bennet has not literally abandoned his family, he is physically absent, withdrawing to his library whenever possible, and emotionally unavailable, even somewhat abusive to his wife and his younger daughters. He has no "real affection" or respect for his wife, treats her ignorance as a source of his amusement, and exposes her "to the contempt of her own children" (PP, p. 228). Even Elizabeth, who loves and respects her father, considers this behaviour "highly reprehensible" and a "continual breach of conjugal obligation and decorum" (PP, p. 228). Mr. Bennet is as contemptuous of his youngest daughters as he is of his wife, and repeatedly calls Kitty and Lydia "two of the silliest girls in the country" (PP, p. 30). Although the reader may tend to agree with his opinion, we must also admit that this kind of treatment would not be likely to contribute to a healthy psychological and emotional development of any child.

Research shows that such disruptions to parent-child attachment, especially with regards to the father, "whose parental investment is far more discretionary than that of the mother" (Campbell, 2013, p. 300; see also Ellis et al., 2012), often have a significant impact on intimate relationships in later life. The Bennet girls are, of course, fictional characters without any real childhood, but Austen accurately captures different ways in which such unsupportive parenting can affect people. Mary and Lydia exhibit characteristics of what psychologists have identified as avoidant and preoccupied attachment styles (Bartholomew & Horowitz, 1991; Del Giudice, 2009). Avoidant individuals tend to shun emotional connection and struggle with intimacy.[7] Mary fits this description as she seems to be incapable of any genuine expression of feelings or emotional engagement with any of her sisters, resorting instead to a seemingly cool detachment, a sense of superiority and constant moralizing. Individuals with a preoccupied attachment style, on the other hand, are extremely needy of relationships and often try to establish them on very insubstantial grounds. Lydia fits this category as her threshold for affection and intimacy, both emotional and physical, and equally in friendship and in romance, is clearly very low. Austen signals this in her dismissive description of Lydia's "invaluable" friendship with Mrs. Forster: "A resemblance in good humour and good spirits had recommended her and Lydia to each other, and out of their *three* months' acquaintance they had been intimate *two*" (PP, p. 222, emphasis in the original). It is even more obvious in Elizabeth's reflections about her sister: "Lydia had wanted only encouragement to attach herself to any body.

Sometimes one officer, sometimes another had been her favourite, as their attentions raised them in her opinion. Her affections had been continually fluctuating, but never without an object" (PP, p. 266). Lydia also displays other characteristics usually associated with preoccupied attachment style: earlier sexual maturation and intercourse, as well as impulsive partner choice (Del Giudice, 2009).

In all Austen's novels, whenever young people stray, parental absence and mismanagement is always implicated. Georgiana Darcy, who lost both her parents at a young age, is an easy prey for Wickham. Another orphan, Eliza Brandon, becomes promiscuous after her inconsiderate guardian forces her to marry the older Brandon brother while she is in love with the younger, and her daughter's disastrous seduction by Willoughby is partially attributed to the conduct of the mother. Mrs Dashwood, a widow, admits that it was her irresponsible encouragement of a passionate romance that caused Marianne's pain and unhappiness. Maria Bertram's adultery is blamed on the indolence of her mother, the indulgence of her aunt, and on her father's encouragement of a loveless marriage to Mr. Rushworth. Henry and Mary Crawford's lax attitude to marital fidelity follows the bad example of their uncle and guardian who has a mistress.

Given the importance of parental influence, how is it possible that Elizabeth and Jane Bennet, raised in the same house by the same parents, have grown into sensible, well-adjusted women, with a dramatically different outlook on life and relationships from Lydia's? Of course, part of the explanation is Austen's creative motivation: Since character contrast is an important element of almost any narrative, Austen needs characters significantly different from one another. But in fulfilling this narrative goal, Austen does not sacrifice any of the psychological plausibility: Siblings often differ significantly in both psychological and physical traits. For various reasons, even because of the birth order, parents may treat siblings differently, which can in turn amplify innate differences. This is certainly the case in the Bennet family: Elizabeth is her father's favourite but her mother's "least dear" daughter (PP, p. 101); the reverse is true for Lydia; Jane enjoys the approval of both parents, while Mary is not liked by either. Importantly, differential parental treatment, especially by the father, can influence sexual behaviour among siblings (Ellis et al., 2012). Even identical twins brought up in the same family can develop different personalities, interests, and abilities. Variation is evolution's most powerful tool and one of literature's greatest pleasures.

Wickham: Appearance of goodness[8]

Lydia's high sociosexuality and her short-term orientation is also evident in her choice of partner. George Wickham is handsome and charming but dishonest and reckless. Soon after his departure from Meryton, "he was declared to be in debt to every tradesman in the place, and his intrigues, all honoured with the title of seduction, had been extended into every tradesman's family. Every body declared that he was the wickedest young man in the world" (PP p. 279–280).[9] In short, Wickham is a typical cad—the kind of man modern women consistently choose for casual sex but not for committed relationships (Kruger & Jonsson, 2019; Kruger et al., 2005). In romantic literature, as in life, cads are usually cast as antagonists (Jonason et al., 2012; Kruger et al., 2005) not only because their mating strategy does not align with women's preferred strategy, but also because they undermine social cooperation (see Chapter 2). Their exploitative social and sexual tactics are facilitated by several personality traits such as narcissism, Machiavellianism, and psychopathy, often referred to as the Dark Triad (Geher & Kaufman, 2013, pp. 172–176). Austen rogues—Wickham, Willoughby, Henry Crawford, Mr. Elliot, and Captain Tilney—are not murderous villains, but they all display aspects of the Dark Triad: They are narcissistic, cleverly manipulative, and emotionally shallow and disingenuous. Crucially, what they also have is superficial charm which enables them to quickly endear themselves to new acquaintances, something Austen was clearly warning against when she chose *First Impressions* as the initial title for *Pride and Prejudice*.

Despite the importance and complexity of the mate selection process, the evolutionary psychologists Glenn Geher and Scott Barry Kaufman note that "mate choice often happens fast, with men and women (often unconsciously) deciding whether a person is an appropriate long-term partner within the first few minutes of meeting him or her" (2013, p. 66). And experiments show that we can often accurately perceive certain personality traits even after meeting someone for only a few seconds (Geher & Kaufman, 2013, p. 66). Furthermore, whether we like to admit it or not, one of the main things that contributes to our initial assessment is physical attractiveness. It is particularly important in the mating domain because it serves as a fitness indicator: Facial and bodily symmetry indicate low levels of harmful genetic mutations and high pathogen resistance. This makes handsome men appealing as short-term sexual partners, even if their willingness to invest long-term is not certain (Buss & Schmitt, 1993). In some circumstances, women may prioritize handsome physique over commitment (as is the case with *Sex and the City*'s Samantha Jones), but in Austen times, such a strategy was very risky.

Austen's male antagonists not only have good looks but also a pleasant, friendly demeanour—a winning combination for a cad. When we first meet Wickham, we are told that "his appearance was greatly in his favour; he had all the best part of beauty, a fine countenance, a good figure, and very pleasing address" (PP, p. 71)—in short, "every charm of person and address that [could] captivate a woman" (PP, p. 270). No wonder "every girl in or near Meryton, was out of her senses about him for the first two months" (PP, p. 271). Even Elizabeth, after spending an evening in Wickham's company, "went away with her head full of him" (PP, p. 82). Willoughby, another cad, has "a manner so frank and so graceful that his person, which was uncommonly handsome, received additional charms from his voice and expression" (SS, p. 44). On meeting Frank Churchill, Emma "felt immediately that she should like him" based on the fact that "he was a *very* good looking young man; height, air, address ... he looked quick and sensible" (E, p. 149, emphasis in the original). Henry Crawford is the only seducer who is not obviously handsome, but the combination of his "pleasing address" and the Bertram sisters' susceptibility to it very quickly makes him "the most agreeable young man the sisters had ever known" (MP, p. 33).

Austen's repetitive insistence on the "pleasing address" is not due to lack of imagination but a sign of her perceptiveness. Research shows that when trying to attract women, men "act more polite than they really are, appear to be more considerate than they really are, and seem more vulnerable than they really are" (Buss, 2003, p. 103). This is clearly the case with Wickham, as Elizabeth comments: "There is such an expression of goodness in his countenance! Such an openness and gentleness in his manner" (PP, p. 217); and on another occasion: "There was a solicitude, an interest which she felt must ever attach her to him with a most sincere regard" (PP, p. 150). But in true cad style, Austen's rogues show interest in women's feelings only to further their own interests. Thus, Wickham quickly realizes Elizabeth's antipathy for Darcy and by presenting himself as Darcy's victim, exploits it to increase her sympathy for himself. Willoughby ostensibly shares Marianne's likes and dislikes, and both him and Frank Churchill cast themselves as victims of their wealthy relatives who control their financial circumstances. And Henry Crawford soon figures out that he can use Fanny's love for her brother to his own advantage.

All Austen cads are great pretenders, with the ability to be "every thing to every body" (MP, p. 209), always "acting a part or making a parade of insincere professions" (E, p. 155). In other words, they are cheats or *dishonest signallers*. By focusing on their selfishness and deception, Austen identifies the most serious problem not only for romantic relationships but also for human sociality and cooperation in general (Boehm, 2012; Frank, 1988). Cheater detection is, in fact, a crucial element in many stories, so much so that William Flesch argues that "our capacity for narrative developed as a way for us to keep track of cooperators, defectors [and] punishers" (2007, p. 67). Indeed, the harsh judgement of Wickham by the Meryton community quoted earlier proves how swift people are to punish social cheaters, and the most easily available punishment is to give them a bad reputation. This is also why Wickham spreads gossip about Darcy's alleged mistreatment of him: It is the most powerful weapon the former can employ against the latter. And it is a false signal of Wickham's integrity and benevolence: He wants to appear prepared to make his misfortunes public to warn others against Darcy's character (something that Darcy is not prepared to do in relation to Georgiana's near elopement, which he later admits was a mistake when Wickham runs away with Lydia).

Of course, as Geher and Kaufman make abundantly clear, "deception permeates all facets of the human mating domain", and therefore "being able to tease apart a false courtship display from a genuine courtship display is a central component of mating intelligence" (2013, pp. 148, 179–180).

Austen's cads are particularly good at faking their level of affection and attachment. This *principle of least interest* (Geher & Kaufman, 2013, p. 165) facilitates their licentiousness. Wickham dupes Georgiana Darcy into loving him, flirts with Elizabeth while dallying with many other women in Meryton, courts Miss King, and runs away with Lydia, which is "brought on by the strength of her love, rather than by his" (PP, p. 301). Willoughby admits that he tried to make Marianne fall in love with him without getting too involved himself (SS, pp. 298–299), gets Miss Williams pregnant but refuses to marry her, and then marries Miss Grey while still professing his feelings for Marianne. Henry Crawford allows himself "great latitude" (MP, p. 45) on the points of love, thus enjoying the attentions of both Bertram sisters and having an affair with the already married Maria while pursuing Fanny. Captain Tilney fakes interest in Isabella Thorpe (although she is equally disingenuous) but soon gets bored and starts flirting with a Charlotte Davis, while his brother doubts that he will ever commit to one woman in marriage. Mr. Elliot makes everyone believe he loves Anne while secretly romancing Mrs. Clay—in both cases with less than honest intentions. And Frank Churchill flirts with Emma, fuelling her romantic fantasies and the local gossip mill, only to deflect attention from his secret engagement to Jane Fairfax. Although he may seem less culpable than other cads because he does not think Emma likely to fall for him, she rightly condemns his behaviour: "How could he tell what mischief he might be doing?—How could he tell that he might not be making me in love with him?—very wrong, very wrong indeed" (E, p. 312). So how do you detect a cheat? What you need is patience and time—and Lydia is unwilling to use either.

"The temptation of immediate relief"[10]

Both Lydia and Elizabeth are attracted to Wickham, but they handle this attraction very differently. Austen does not blame either for desiring him, but she judges them based on what other desires and responsibilities they take into account. When Aunt Gardiner warns Elizabeth against falling for Wickham, Elizabeth admits that "he is, beyond all comparison, the most agreeable man [she] ever saw" (PP, p. 142), but she also acknowledges "the imprudence" of the match. Weighing up these two considerations, she comes down on the side of affection:

> Since we see every day that where there is affection, young people are seldom withheld by immediate want of fortune, from entering into engagements with each other, how can I promise to be wiser than so many of my fellow-creatures if I am tempted, or how am I even to know that it would be wisdom to resist? (PP, p. 143)

She does, however, promise her aunt "I will not be in a hurry to believe myself his first object. When I am in company with him, I will not be wishing" (PP, p. 143). And when Wickham starts courting Miss King, Elizabeth congratulates herself: "My watchfulness has been effectual" (PP, p. 147).

Patience, Austen correctly suggests, is the best defence against cads because they cannot keep up appearances for long and they lack the self-control required to persevere. But the women who really fall for cads, Lydia, Marianne Dashwood, Maria Bertram, similarly lack self-restraint and prioritize instant gratification (Georgiana Darcy is the exception as she is genuinely duped by Wickham). While Elizabeth endeavours to have some control over her own feelings to give herself time to test Wickham's character, Lydia thinks of nothing but "love, flirtation, and officers" and does "every thing in her power by thinking and talking on the subject, to give *greater... susceptibility to her feelings*, which are naturally lively enough" (PP, pp. 269–270, emphasis added). Marianne is similarly prone to "indulgence of feeling" (SS, p. 83). It is this lack of emotional moderation that Austen criticizes. And rightly so, because as modern psychologists argue, "emotional self-control—delaying gratification and stifling impulsiveness—underlies accomplishment of every sort" (Goleman, 1995/2005, p. 43). It makes us better partners, parents, friends, and community members.

Unfortunately, neither Lydia nor Wickham can resist "the temptation of immediate relief" (PP, p. 306), and this lack of impulse control manifests itself both in compulsive spending and in sexually permissive attitudes. Lydia justifies the purchase of a bonnet she does not even like by saying "I might as well buy it as not" (PP, p. 211), and her impulsive purchase is not dissimilar to her decision to run away with Wickham mainly because the opportunity presents itself. Wickham is even more reckless: He quickly gambles away his inheritance, leaves a trail of debts and seductions in Meryton (PP, pp. 279–280), and is forced to leave Brighton because of "debts of honour" at which point he "was not the young man to resist an opportunity of having a companion" such as Lydia (PP, pp. 305, 301).

Of course, prioritizing short-term rewards, or *future discounting*, is a hallmark of short-term mating strategy. And it is not always bad. In fact, in many situations it is essential: "When selection pressures are intense, current payoffs are often the *only* ones that matter" (Frank, 1988, p. 89) emphasis in the original. Such short-term rewards can also give us a lot of pleasure, which evolved to motivate us to seek more similar experiences. However, pleasure is not the only impulse for action, and we have evolved an array of other feelings to guide our behaviour, such as fear, disgust, shame, guilt, and loyalty (Frank, 1988; Sznycer, 2019). Such emotions act as self-control devices, and while they have been sometimes used against women, a complete lack of them would make interpersonal commitments and social life impossible. For example, Georgiana is so embarrassed by her planned elopement that at the mere mention of Wickham's militia unit by Miss Bingley, she is "overcome with confusion, and unable to lift up her eyes" (PP, p. 257). But neither Lydia nor Wickham has such feelings: At the news of their marriage, "[Elizabeth] blushed, and Jane blushed; but the cheeks of the two who caused their confusion, suffered no variation of colour" (PP, p. 299).

"The indignities of stupidity, and the disappointments of selfish passion"[11]

As the married Lydia arrives back in Longbourn, she does so with a sense of having achieved her goals: She satisfied her sexual desire, won the marriage race with her sisters, acquired a handsome husband who will be the object of envy of other women (albeit only those who do not know him too well), and became rich (at Darcy's expense, and only for a short while). But of course, these are not the goals that Austen wants her readers to aspire to. Lydia's married life turns out to be far from her own romantic fantasy, let alone her author's vision of rational happiness. Her success is as short-lived as her motivation was short-sighted. The passion soon dissipates, and the money is squandered: The Wickhams' "manner of living ... was unsettled in the extreme. They were always moving from place to place in quest of a cheap situation, and always spending more than they ought. His affection for her soon sunk into indifference; her's [*sic*] lasted a little longer" (PP, p. 366).

Lydia and Wickham are removed to Newcastle, but they are not banished forever. They both make frequent and long visits at the Bingleys' new home, and although Wickham is never admitted to Pemberley, Lydia does "occasionally" stay there. Both Jane and Elizabeth often help them financially and even Darcy, "for Elizabeth's sake" helps to further Wickham's career (PP, p. 366). Such a punishment might seem light, but it is not so in Austen's moral economy. Lydia and Wickham's financial survival depends not only on her family's forgiveness but also on their continuing kindness and charity. In other words, Lydia and Wickham depend on, and exploit, the fact that other people are not as selfish and reckless as they are. Furthermore, as in *Mansfield Park*, where Henry Crawford and Maria Bertram, embroiled in their affair, are for a while "each other's punishment" (MP, p. 314), Lydia and Wickham must live with each other, and that for Austen is no small price to pay. Most importantly, they never learn, never grow, "their characters [suffer] no revolution" (PP, p. 365). They remain at the mercy of their impulses. The same shallowness and lack of introspection that prevented Lydia's blushing about her wedding will save her from realizing the full extent of her marital failure, but Austen hopes that her readers are not such "dull elves".[12]

"Heedless of the future"[13]

In *Pride and Prejudice*, as in other Austen's novels, the seduction/deception plot is a test of social, emotional, and mating intelligence, and Lydia fails this test quite spectacularly. For some of Austen's heroines, like Elizabeth Bennet and Emma Woodhouse, a misguided infatuation is a chance for moral growth, even if occasionally it takes them to the brink of disaster, as is the case with Marianne Dashwood. Others, like Maria Bertram or Isabella Thorpe, are too naïve, too impulsive, and too self-indulgent to recognize false courtship and resist a charming seducer. They fall in love, and sometimes have sex, without sufficiently testing the man's commitment. Their decision-making processes are more appropriate for short-term, less committed relationships—which in some circumstances may be both pleasurable and beneficial for women (see Chapter 3). However, they are out of sync with Austen's cultural environment, which requires women to choose one man "till death do us part", not only as the exclusive sexual partner but also as someone who will control their economic, legal, and social identity. Austen is clearly critical of this state of affairs, but given that this is her reality, she stresses how important it is for a woman to choose carefully.

In all her novels, Austen recognizes the power and legitimacy of female desire, but she remains very clear-headed about all the potential physical, emotional, and social consequences of following it indiscriminately. She advocates for women's right to choose their marital and sexual partners (an argument I develop further in Chapters 6 and 7) but also urges that these choices should be made judiciously. In questioning the idea of love at first sight and in undermining the attractions of charming, mysterious strangers who sweep young women off their feet, she simultaneously criticizes the formulas of sentimental literature and articulates a more constructive vision of romantic love. Austen advocates passion which is not blind and desire which is not pornographic. But, as Claudia Johnson rightly points out, Austen is not interested in "portentous moralizing on female virtue" (1988, p. 3). She distances herself from the brutal remarks of Mr. Collins and Mr. Price about Lydia and Maria Bertram, respectively, from Mary Bennet's "moral extractions", and from the gossip of "the spiteful old ladies" (PP, pp. 275, 293). She is, however, deeply interested in the nature of human morality, sociality, and cooperation, and through the contrast between her long-term and short-term oriented characters, she shows that at the basis of all these phenomena is the ability to curb our selfish impulses. In the 1940 film adaptation of *Pride and Prejudice*, when Lydia comes back to Longbourn, she asks: "Don't you envy me Lizzy?" and Elizabeth replies: "Ask me that question again five years from now." Lydia's reaction is: "Who cares what happens in five years!" This line is not in the novel, but it perfectly captures Lydia's personality, the nature of her relationship with Wickham, as well as Austen's objections to it.

Lydia's story undoubtedly shows the operation of the sexual double standard, and her elopement is, on one level, a rebellion against it—insofar as she completely disregards the expected standards of conduct. But any defence of her behaviour in the name of freedom of choice is misguided. Lydia does not consider the impact of her choices on others; she does not even consider their long-term impact on herself. She exercises her female choice in a way that aligns with her own priorities, but in the process, she inflicts significant costs on her sisters, potentially preventing them from being able to choose at all. Her actions lack any political or moral consciousness and do not result in any constructive social outcome, nor do they promise any long-term personal happiness. In fact, attaching herself to a man who treats women as easily replaceable pawns in his pursuit of sexual pleasure and social advancement is counterproductive to any feminist ideals.

Notes

1 PP, p. 224.
2 It is worth restating that the term "strategy", as it is used in evolutionary psychology, refers not only to conscious reasoning but mostly to how our decision-making processes are affected by underlying psychological mechanisms, including personality, attachment styles, upbringing, etc.
3 See for example, Austen's letters to Fanny dated 18 and 30 November 1814 (Le Faye, 1995). I quote short excerpts from these letters in the last section of Chapter 5.
4 For example, in a letter dated 9 January 1796, Austen writes: "You scold me so much … that I am almost afraid to tell you how my Irish friend and I behaved. Imagine to yourself everything most profligate and shocking in the way of dancing and sitting down together. I *can* expose myself, however, only *once more*, because he leaves the country soon after next Friday" (Le Faye, 1995, p. 1, emphasis in the original). Austen uses similar language to describe Lydia and Wickham.
5 PP, p. 223.
6 PP, pp. 228–229.
7 Avoidant attachment is further differentiated into fearful and dismissing, something I will come back to in more detail when discussing Miranda Hobbes in Part III of the book.
8 See PP, p. 217.
9 Of course, there is some irony in this description, showing the fickleness of Meryton's public opinion, but it also shows a cad's modus operandi.
10 PP, p. 306.
11 This quote comes from *Mansfield Park* (p. 315), but Austen's views on mate choice are very consistent across all her novels, and the line is as applicable to Lydia as it is to Maria Bertram.
12 Austen used this expression when writing about *Pride and Prejudice* in a letter to Cassandra dated 29 January 1813 (Le Faye, 1995).
13 PP, p. 366.

References

Allen, D. W. (1985). No love for Lydia: The fate of desire in *Pride and Prejudice*. *Texas Studies in Literature and Language*, 27(4), 425–443.
Austen, J. (1811/2003). *Sense and sensibility*. Penguin.
Austen, J. (1813/2003). *Pride and prejudice*. Penguin.
Austen, J. (1814/1998). *Mansfield Park*. W. W. Norton & Company.
Austen, J. (1815/2003). *Emma*. Oxford University Press.
Austen, J. (2003). *Love and friendship*. Hesperus.
Bartholomew, K., & Horowitz, L. M. (1991). Attachment styles among young adults: A test of a four-category model. *Journal of Personality and Social Psychology*, 61(2), 226–244.
Belsky, J., Steinberg, L., & Draper, P. (1991). Childhood experience, interpersonal development, and reproductive strategy: An evolutionary theory of socialization. *Child Development*, 62(4), 647–670. https://doi.org/10.2307/1131166
Boehm, C. (2012). *Moral origins: The evolution of virtue, altruism, and shame* (Kindle ed.). Basic Books.
Buss, D. M. (2003). *The evolution of desire: Strategies of human mating* (Rev., Kindle ed.). Basic Books.
Buss, D. M., & Schmitt, D. P. (1993). Sexual strategies theory: An evolutionary perspective on human mating. *Psychological Review*, 100(2), 204–232.
Campbell, A. (2013). *A mind of her own: The evolutionary psychology of women* (2nd ed.). Oxford University Press.
Dabundo, L. (2012). The feminist critique and five styles of women's roles in *Pride and Prejudice*. In L. W. Mazzeno (Ed.), *Pride and Prejudice: Critical insights* (pp. 39–53). Salem Press.
Del Giudice, M. (2009). Sex, attachment, and the development of reproductive strategies. *Behavioral and Brain Sciences*, 32(1), 1–21. https://doi.org/10.1017/S0140525X09000016
Deresiewicz, W. (2011). *A Jane Austen education: How six novels taught me about love, friendship, and the things that really matter*. Penguin Press.

Ellis, B. J., Schlomer, G. L., Tilley, E. H., & Butler, E. A. (2012). Impact of fathers on risky sexual behavior in daughters: A genetically and environmentally controlled sibling study. *Development and Psychopathology, 24*(1), 317–332.
Fisher, H. E. (2011). *Why him? Why her? How to find and keep lasting love.* Oneworld.
Flesch, W. (2007). *Comeuppance: Costly signaling, altruistic punishment, and other biological components of fiction.* Harvard University Press.
Fraiman, S. (1993). *Unbecoming women: British women writers and the novel of development.* Columbia University Press.
Frank, R. H. (1988). *Passions within reason: The strategic role of the emotions.* Norton.
Gangestad, S. W., & Simpson, J. A. (1990). Toward an evolutionary history of female sociosexual variation. *Journal of Personality, 58*(1), 69–96.
Geher, G., & Kaufman, S. B. (2013). *Mating intelligence unleashed: The role of the mind in sex, dating, and love* (Kindle ed.). Oxford University Press.
Gilbert, S. M., & Gubar, S. (1979/2000). *The madwoman in the attic: The woman writer and the nineteenth-century literary imagination* (2nd, Kindle ed.). Yale University Press.
Goleman, D. (1995/2005). *Emotional intelligence* (10th anniversary ed.). Bantam Books.
Hrdy, S. B. (2009). *Mothers and others: The evolutionary origins of mutual understanding.* Belknap Press of Harvard University Press.
Johnson, C. L. (1988). *Jane Austen: Women, politics, and the novel.* University of Chicago Press.
Jonason, P. K., Webster, G. D., Schmitt, D. P., Li, N. P., & Crysel, L. (2012). The antihero in popular culture: Life history theory and the Dark Triad personality traits. *Review of General Psychology, 16*(2), 192–199.
Jones, H. (2009). *Jane Austen and marriage.* Continuum.
Kirkham, M. (1983). *Jane Austen, feminism and fiction.* Harvester Press.
Kruger, D. J., Fisher, M. L., & Jobling, I. (2005). Proper hero dads and dark hero cads: Alternate mating strategies exemplified in British romantic literature. In J. Gottschall & D. S. Wilson (Eds.), *The literary animal: Evolution and the nature of narrative* (pp. 225–243). Northwestern University Press.
Kruger, D. J., Fisher, M. L., Strout, S. L., Clark, S., Lewis, S., & Wehbe, M. (2014). Pride and prejudice or family and flirtation? Jane Austen's depiction of women's mating strategies. *Philosophy and Literature, 38*(1), A114–A128.
Kruger, D. J., & Jonsson, E. (2019). The Viking and the farmer: Alternative male life histories portrayed in the Romantic poetry of Erik Gustaf Geijer. *Evolutionary Studies in Imaginative Culture, 3*(2), 17–38.
Le Faye, D. (Ed.). (1995). *Jane Austen's letters* (3rd ed.). Oxford University Press.
McMaster, J. (1978). *Jane Austen on love.* University of Victoria.
Meston, C. M., & Buss, D. M. (2009). *Why women have sex: Understanding sexual motivations—from adventure to revenge (and everything in between).* Times Books.
Nettle, D. (2006). The evolution of personality variation in humans and other animals. *American Psychologist, 61*(6), 622–631. https://doi.org/10.1037/0003-066X.61.6.622
Perry, R. (1980). *Women, letters, and the novel.* AMS Press.
Polhemus, R. M. (1990). *Erotic faith: Being in love from Jane Austen to D. H. Lawrence.* University of Chicago Press.
Simpson, J. A., & Gangestad, S. W. (1991). Individual differences in sociosexuality: Evidence for convergent and discriminant validity. *Journal of Personality and Social Psychology, 60*(6), 870–883. https://doi.org/10.1037/0022-3514.60.6.870
Stasio, M. J., & Duncan, K. (2007). An evolutionary approach to Jane Austen: Prehistoric preferences in *Pride and Prejudice*. *Studies in the Novel, 39*(2), 133–146. https://www.jstor.org/stable/20831911
Sterelny, K. (2012). *The evolved apprentice.* MIT Press.
Strout, S. L., Fisher, M. L., Kruger, D. J., & Steeleworthy, L.-A. (2010). Pride and prejudice or children and cheating? Jane Austen's representations of female mating strategies. *Journal of Social, Evolutionary, and Cultural Psychology, 4*(4), 317–331.
Sznycer, D. (2019). Forms and functions of the self-conscious emotions. *Trends in Cognitive Sciences, 23*(2), 143–157.

5
CHARLOTTE LUCAS

"I am not romantic ... I ask only a comfortable home"[1]

Charlotte Lucas, a neighbour and friend of Elizabeth Bennet, is a "sensible, intelligent young woman" (PP, p. 19). She marries the pompous and obsequious Mr. Collins, a cousin and heir of the Bennets, despite realizing that he is "neither sensible nor agreeable" (PP, p. 120). She does it "from a pure and disinterested desire of an establishment" (PP, p. 120). From a feminist point of view, Charlotte's decision is an act of desperation dictated by the patriarchal system which compels women into marriage by severely limiting other means of supporting themselves and by stigmatizing spinsterhood. Undoubtedly, these factors would have had a profound impact on Charlotte's decision, but there are others suggesting that she is not a passive victim of a misogynist system. While her options are limited by the realities of a patriarchal society, they are also sharply delineated by her own priorities and attitudes. She views marriage solely in terms of maintaining financial security: "Without thinking highly either of men or of matrimony, marriage had always been her object; it was the only honourable provision for well-educated young women of small fortune, and however uncertain of giving happiness, must be their pleasantest preservative from want" (PP, p. 120). It could be argued that such an attitude was an inevitable response to the oppressive reality and that if Charlotte had other ways of supporting herself—in the lifestyle she was accustomed to, we might add—she would have made a different choice. Very likely. But our choices are always limited in one way or another, and as I argued in Chapter 2, it is the choices we make in the face of limitations that reveal our priorities and character. By contrasting Charlotte's pursuit of Mr. Collins with Elizabeth's emphatic rejection of him, Austen clearly shows that the former's choice was not inevitable. Austen provides an even more powerful proof of this with her own refusal of a financially attractive but emotionally dubious proposal. She shows that Charlotte's marriage was indeed *a choice*.

In their evolutionary analysis of *Pride and Prejudice*, Michael Stasio and Kathryn Duncan see Charlotte's decision as a result of a "cost-benefit trade-off" which "increases her chances at reproduction" (2007, p. 139). Certainly, through Charlotte's story, Austen highlights an ancient and pervasive female preference for resource-rich mates, which has been extensively documented across human cultures and in many animal species (Buss, 2003). She also demonstrates the workings of female choice: Charlotte analyses

DOI: 10.4324/9781003320982-9

her own, relatively low, mate value and her rather limited options, and then exercises a considerable level of agency in pursuing a mate selected according to her own, although somewhat narrow, criteria. While Charlotte's choice appears more rational and less risky than Lydia's, it has its own considerable downside, given that human relationships are about more than just reproduction and given that reproductive success is about more than just producing *any* offspring. Austen has a good deal of sympathy for Charlotte's situation, but the choice Charlotte makes is not one that Austen wants her heroines or her readers to emulate.

"Pure and disinterested desire of an establishment"[2]

Charlotte is undoubtedly the active agent who makes her marriage happen. She does not quietly wait for some man—who may or may not be a more attractive prospect than Mr. Collins—to notice her despite her plain looks, her advancing age, and her lack of fortune. Instead, after Elizabeth refuses Mr. Collins, Charlotte spots an opportunity and takes the initiative. She meets Mr. Collins at the Netherfield ball where she gets a full report from Elizabeth about his quirks and can observe him. Perceiving his intentions and knowing her friend's temperament and attitude to marriage, she is well equipped to anticipate Elizabeth's rejection of him. When it happens, Charlotte puts her "scheme" into action: She draws Mr. Collins's attention to herself, devotes her time to him, and "keeps him in good humour" (PP, p. 119). While Elizabeth sees it as an act of friendship, Charlotte's behaviour is deliberate and strategic: "Charlotte's kindness extended farther than Elizabeth had any conception of; its object was nothing else than to secure her from any return of Mr. Collins's addresses, by engaging them towards herself" (PP, p. 119). After being rejected by Elizabeth, Mr. Collins is "comparatively diffident", but Charlotte is "tolerably encouraging" (PP, p. 119). Within days, she gives him a perfect, discreet opportunity to propose: "Miss Lucas perceived him from an upper window as he walked towards the house, and instantly set out to meet him accidentally in the lane" (PP, p. 119).

Elizabeth is appalled: "She had always felt that Charlotte's opinion of matrimony was not exactly like her own, but she could not have supposed it possible that when called into action, she would have sacrificed every better feeling to worldly advantage" (PP, p. 123). Elizabeth considers the prospective marriage "a most humiliating picture" (PP, p. 123). In contrast, Charlotte's "reflections" on the subject are "in general satisfactory" (PP, p. 120). Jane puts it down to the "difference of situation and temper" (PP, p. 133). Indeed, Charlotte's mating strategy is clearly meant to serve as a contrast to Elizabeth's: two close friends in a similar financial position making dramatically different personal choices.

Charlotte is considered "plain" and is six years older than Elizabeth, which gives her less bargaining power in the competitive marriage market and less time left to find a partner. At 27, Charlotte is relatively old to be still unmarried, given that for women in the late eighteenth century, the average age for marriage was 24 (Jones, 2009, p. 173). In fact, her younger siblings half-expect her to become an old maid (PP, p. 120), and with some justification: It was the fate of about 25% of gentlemen's daughters during Austen's lifetime. The most likely reason was a shortage of men: Not only did women significantly outnumber men in England during that period but also a quarter of younger sons never married, which diminished the pool even further (Jones, 2009, pp. 8, 173). Given all this, Charlotte is probably aware that the odds of finding a good husband are stacked against her. Hers is a situation Mr. Collins warns Elizabeth against when she rejects his proposal. It is also one Anne Elliot, aged 27, is in when we meet her in *Persuasion*.

Neither Elizabeth nor Charlotte has much money. But Charlotte's situation is arguably better because her father's property will be inherited by her brothers whose generosity she should be able to count on if unmarried, in the same way that Austen and her sister Cassandra relied on their brothers for support. Elizabeth has no such back-up option as the Bennet estate is entailed to an estranged cousin Mr. Collins (this is similar to Anne Elliot's circumstances). Still, the actual amount of money is less important than the attitude to it, as Austen clearly shows in *Sense and Sensibility*, when Marianne and Elinor argue about the connection between wealth and happiness in life. While the sensible Elinor says wealth is important, the passionate Marianne claims that "money can only give happiness where there is nothing else to give it" (SS, p. 90). However, it soon transpires that Marianne considers an income of 2000 pounds a year to be the bare minimum, while Elinor would consider herself rich with half the amount. In Austen's unfinished novel, *The Watsons*, a pair of sisters, reveal a similar divergence of priorities in relation to money and marriage. Emma Watson proclaims: "I would rather be Teacher at a school (and I can think of nothing worse) than marry a man I did not like", to which her eldest sister replies: "I would rather do any thing than be Teacher at a school" (W, p. 10).

Charlotte's upbringing also likely contributed to her attitude. She comes from a family of social climbers, and her upbringing has taught her to rate upward social mobility highly. We learn at the beginning of the novel that her father, who used to be "in trade", was recently knighted and that "the distinction had perhaps been felt too strongly" (PP, p. 19). Subsequently, he not only "think[s] with pleasure of his own importance" (PP, p. 19) but has similar ambitions for his children. After Charlotte's engagement, both he and his wife "[begin] directly to calculate" (PP, p. 120) the advantages of the Bennet entail for their daughter.

In addition to their circumstances and upbringing, Elizabeth's and Charlotte's temperaments and personal priorities play an equally important role in their different mating strategies. Early in the novel, Charlotte reveals her pragmatic approach to love and matrimony in a conversation about Jane and Bingley, when she insists that Jane should show more affection in order not to lose him (PP, p. 24). Her philosophy is that "happiness in marriage is entirely a matter of chance" and that "it is better to know as little as possible of the defects of the person with whom you are to pass your life" (PP, p. 24). Elizabeth criticizes this approach as too calculated: "Your plan is a good one ... where nothing is in question but the desire of being well married; and if I were determined to get a rich husband, or any husband, I dare say I should adopt it" (PP, p. 24). She rejects Charlotte's approach as "not sound" and is convinced that her friend "would never act in this way" (PP, p. 24). To Elizabeth's shock, this is exactly how Charlotte acts. Moreover, while Charlotte's view of matrimony differs from Elizabeth's, it is very similar to that of Mr. Collins.

"Remarkable resemblance of character and ideas"[3]

Like Elizabeth, the reader may be initially reluctant to admit it, but the more we learn about Charlotte, the more we should notice that there is a level of compatibility between Mr. and Mrs. Collins. When Elizabeth is leaving Hunsford, after visiting the newlyweds, Mr. Collins declares: "My dear Charlotte and I have but one mind and one way of thinking. There is in everything a most remarkable resemblance of character and ideas between us. We seem to have been designed for each other" (PP, p. 209). Of course, the statement is full of Austen's signature irony, but as in many other cases, Austen uses irony to reveal the truth.

For Charlotte and Mr. Collins, marriage is a practical consideration not based on romantic feelings, and they both approach their choice of marriage partners in a very impersonal way: He is looking for *a wife*, and she for *a husband*, without too much consideration for the individuality of their partners. Because of that, Charlotte does not mind being Mr. Collins's third choice, in the same way that Mr. Collins does not object to changing his mind and making two proposals (or even three if we count his expressed plan to propose to Jane) within the space of a few days. Michael Suk-Young Chwe, who uses game theory to analyse Austen's novels, claims that Mr. Collins's actions suggest an order of preference and "are consistent with liking Jane best, Elizabeth second, and Charlotte third" (2013, p. 163). But Mr. Collins's criteria for a wife are so devoid of any emotions that it is hardly appropriate to talk about *preferences*. Although he assures Elizabeth of "the violence of [his] affection", within a few days, he professes the same with regards to Charlotte, and each woman is equally convinced that "his regard for her was quite imaginary" (PP, pp. 104, 110, 120).

In all his choices, Mr. Collins is guided not by his own feelings towards the three women but by external factors. His decision to get married is largely prompted by the urging of his patroness, Lady Catherine de Bourgh, and he comes to look for a wife in Longbourn because that is the easiest option: The Bennet girls have a strong incentive to accept him as he will inherit their family home—although he flatters himself that his plan is "excessively generous and disinterested on his own part" (PP, p. 69). He wants to propose to Jane because the eldest daughter is expected to marry first, and he is helped in his resolve by the happy coincidence that she is the prettiest: "Miss Bennet's lovely face confirmed his views, and established all his strictest notions of what was due to seniority" (PP, pp. 69–70). He switches to Elizabeth, "equally next to Jane in birth and beauty" (PP, p. 70), as soon as Mrs. Bennet hints that Jane is already spoken for. But going for the most obvious option of next in line backfires for both Mr. Collins and Mrs. Bennet. Had they skipped Elizabeth and gone for Mary, the third oldest sister and the only one with a positive opinion of their cousin, both would have achieved their goals: Mr. Collins would have spared himself the embarrassment of a refused proposal and Mrs. Bennet would have had a daughter married to the heir of their estate. Finally, after all this unsuccessful "choosing", Mr. Collins does not even consider "liking" Charlotte until she very deliberately encourages it.

Charlotte's mate choice criteria are similarly impersonal: She only asks for "a comfortable home" (PP, p. 123), and her scrutiny of the owner is limited to his ability to provide it. Her preferences coincide with Mr. Collins's assessment that "a good house and very sufficient income" (PP, p. 69) make him an eligible candidate. Their shared focus on resources and status is also demonstrated by the fact that they are equally impressed by Lady Catherine's fortune. In fact, Charlotte's father and sister also share this attitude: On their first visit to Rosings, Sir William is "completely awed" and follows his son-in-law's lead in complimenting everything and bowing excessively, and Maria is "frightened almost out of her senses" (PP, pp. 159–163). And it soon becomes clear that Charlotte is as eager to flatter and be servile to her husband's patroness as he is, although Charlotte may be doing it a bit more elegantly.

What is more, Charlotte's modest-sounding wish for a "comfortable home" is not fully satisfied by the Hunsford parsonage and the prospect of inheriting Longbourn. As Elizabeth quickly realizes, the Collinses' frequent visits to Rosings are likely motivated by the fact that "there may be other family livings to be disposed of" (PP, p. 165). Charlotte's mating strategy extends even to how she assesses Elizabeth's marriage prospects when she compares Colonel Fitzwilliam and Mr. Darcy:

> In her kind schemes for Elizabeth, she sometimes planned her marrying Colonel Fitzwilliam. He was beyond comparison the pleasantest man; he certainly admired her, and his situation in life was most eligible; but to counter balance these advantages, Mr. Darcy had considerable patronage in the church, and his cousin could have none at all. (PP, p. 177)

In other words, Charlotte rates Elizabeth's potential husbands according to how the match would affect Mr. Collins's employment opportunities. Even in this purely hypothetical analysis, Charlotte prioritizes her own material benefits over all other considerations.

The same motivation and temperament that led her to pursue Mr. Collins allow Charlotte to create a tolerable existence for herself. In fact, her "successful adjustment" to her marital life despite the company she has to keep is a further indication of her priorities (Johnson, 1988, p. 81). Although Elizabeth is convinced that "it was impossible for [Charlotte] to be tolerably happy in the lot she had chosen" (PP, p. 123), her letters from Hunsford show no distress or disappointment:

> She wrote cheerfully, seemed surrounded with comforts, and mentioned nothing which she could not praise. The house, furniture, neighbourhood, and roads, were all to her taste, and Lady Catherine's behaviour was most friendly and obliging. *It was Mr. Collins's picture of Hunsford and Rosings rationally softened.* (PP, p. 144, emphasis added)

Indeed, when Elizabeth comes to visit the newly-weds, she notes that her friend "seems perfectly happy" (PP, p. 174). She also notes that this happiness is enabled by Charlotte's strategic management of her husband. Charlotte keeps Mr. Collins out of her way by encouraging his interest in gardening and spends most of her time in a room at the back of the house. Elizabeth is at first surprised at that since there is a much nicer parlour at the front of the house, adjacent to Mr. Collins's book room, but she soon realizes that in this way, Charlotte can avoid the company of her husband, and "she gave Charlotte credit for the arrangement" (PP, p. 164). Chwe thinks that Elizabeth reads too much "strategicness" into the situation: "Elizabeth has no reason to believe … that any difference in pleasantness [of the room] even registers with Mr. Collins, who is hardly an aesthete" (2013, p. 177). But Chwe misses the hints of the narrator which are as subtle as Charlotte's manoeuvring. It is not the "pleasanter aspect" that Mr. Collins is after but the ability to observe the traffic on the road, not least in case Lady Catherine's carriage should stop in front of his gate. Charlotte is well aware of his strong motivation to stay at the front of the house and capitalizes on it. Just as she cleverly manoeuvred Mr. Collins into marrying her, she cleverly manoeuvres him out of her way as much as possible, so that she can maximize the enjoyment of what really attracted her to him: his property.

A "woman's good opinion"[4]

During her stay in Hunsford, Elizabeth admits that "when Mr. Collins could be forgotten, there was really an air of great comfort throughout, and by Charlotte's evident enjoyment of it, Elizabeth supposed he must be often forgotten" (PP, p. 155). For Elizabeth, such enjoyment would not be possible as she remains scathing in her assessment of Mr. Collins: "a conceited, pompous, narrow-minded, silly man" (PP, p. 133). Charlotte, however, pointedly reminds her about the possibility of individual differences in taste: "Do you think it incredible that Mr. Collins should be able to procure any woman's good opinion, because he was not so happy as to succeed with you?" (PP, p. 122). And as a husband, Mr. Collins cannot be forgotten all the time, since before the end of the novel, Charlotte is expecting a child. Although this is only mentioned briefly, it inevitably provokes questions about the intimate side of Charlotte's clearly loveless marriage. Is it possible that her "good opinion" of Mr. Collins extends into the bedroom?

In her article "Sleeping with Mr. Collins", Ruth Perry (2003) observes that Austen in no way registers any aversion to the idea. According to Perry,

> The reason that Austen is able to imagine Charlotte's sleeping with Mr. Collins with equanimity is because sex had less psychological significance in eighteenth-century England than in our own post-Freudian era; it was less tied to individual identity, and more understood as an uncomplicated, straightforward physical appetite. *Sexual disgust*—the feeling that sex with the "wrong" person could be viscerally disturbing—*was an invention of the eighteenth century.* (p. 217, emphasis added)

Following Michel Foucault, Perry suggests that this apparently new somatic reaction is a product of cultural conditioning, part of the regulatory mechanisms of the sexual double standard and female sexual repression. While men's libido is not expected to be inhibited in this way, "for a woman, sexual disgust … is supposed to operate as a restraint on her desire for inappropriate men, to confine her sexual activity to intercourse with a single partner from the right social class in a legitimate marriage" (p. 219). Perry's explanation is indicative of the extreme social constructivist approach to sexuality adopted by many feminist and literary scholars but is implausible in light of overwhelming scientific, historical, and literary evidence.

Perry is right in saying that "sexual disgust … evolved to condition women's sexual choices" (2003, p. 219), but it evolved a lot earlier than the eighteenth century. It is as evolutionarily old, and as fundamental to our motivational system, as sexual desire. As much as sexual desire motivates us to have sex with partners we—consciously and unconsciously—evaluate as suitable, sexual disgust motivates us to avoid sex with those we deem unsuitable (Al-Shawaf et al., 2015; Crosby et al., 2020). Sexual disgust is indeed stronger in women because the costs of having sex with a wrong man are much higher for them. Hence, like females of numerous other species, women vigorously resist approaches by unwanted males (Brennan et al., 2010; Muller & Wrangham, 2009).

While Austen does not elaborate on the physical aspects of the relationships she creates, there is more than a hint of repulsion from one woman who considers Mr. Collins a wholly unsuitable mate. For Elizabeth, the two dances she is obliged to have with her cousin at Netherfield are a source of "distress", "mortification", "shame", and "misery", and "the moment of her release from him was exstacy [sic]" (PP, p. 89). Elizabeth's relationship with Mr. Collins never gets more physical than those two dreaded dances, but the proposal scene once again shows her vehement resistance to his unwanted advances.[5] Hence, if Charlotte does not display sexual disgust at the idea of sleeping with Mr. Collins, it is not because the sensation did not exist but because her emotional and physical response to Mr. Collins is very different from Elizabeth's, and while she is obviously not in love with her husband, she does not give any indication that she finds him repulsive. And we have no reason to believe that he is physically repulsive. Austen's descriptions of physical appearance are minimal, but we usually know who is "handsome" and who "plain". Mr. Collins is simply described as "a tall, heavy looking young man of five and twenty" (PP, p. 63)—not very flattering but not offensive either. So, Elizabeth's physical aversion to Mr. Collins is due to her overall negative assessment of Mr. Collins and the fact that she is at the time strongly attracted to a completely different man—George Wickham.

From an evolutionary point of view, such variability in tastes is to be expected. As I explained in Chapter 2, compatibility is a fundamental consideration in mate choice, and people usually choose mates who are similar to themselves in terms of overall mate value. For example, research shows that dating and married couples usually match each other's physical attractiveness (Meston & Buss, 2009, p. 25). One reason for this is simple economy of exchange: We can only get what we can give in return. Another is fear of rejection and the high cost of retaining a mate much more desirable than ourselves (Meston & Buss, 2009, pp. 25–26). Mr. Collins initially overestimates his desirability, but two unsuccessful mate choices (Jane and Elizabeth) are a good enough reason for him to adjust his expectations and settle for a woman who pursues him. Charlotte, as a woman who is consistently described as "plain", probably never aimed very high but still failed to attract a husband—and is not allowed to forget it. She is therefore strongly motivated to capitalize on an opportunity where she can see good odds of success.

The marriage of Charlotte and Mr. Collins is a good example of trade-offs on *both* sides but is a particularly vivid illustration of how much the preference for males with resources, common among females of many species, may affect women's feelings about prospective mates. Cross-cultural research shows that women look for mates with resources even when they have plenty of their own (see Chapter 2), but in a culture where women were almost entirely dependent on their husbands, this factor would have been especially significant.[6] Importantly, the evolved drive to secure resources affects women's emotional responses and assessments of men's overall attractiveness. For example, in several experiments, women were asked to rate photographs of men dressed either in expensive clothes indicating well-paid professions, such as a white shirt and tie, or in clothes indicating low-paid occupations, such as a Burger King uniform (Townsend & Levy, 1990; Townsend & Wasserman, 1998). The same men were rated as more handsome and better prospects for dating, sex, and marriage when dressed in professional attire.

Charlotte's focus on resources, combined with her temperament and circumstances, inclines her to give Mr. Collins a lot of credit for his financial and social position, resulting in her overall "good opinion", even if Elizabeth, with her different personality, priorities, and strong feelings for Mr. Wickham, is not prepared to allow Mr. Collins any redeeming features. But Charlotte is not alone: Elizabeth's sister Mary is sufficiently impressed by their cousin to consider accepting him as "a very agreeable companion" (PP, p. 122). And Jane, who always looks for the best in people, wants to believe that Charlotte "may feel something like regard and esteem" (PP, p. 133) for her husband. Charlotte's "degree of contentment" (PP, p. 155) with her marriage indicates that Jane may be right.

"She had chosen it with her eyes open"[7]

In her influential feminist analysis, Claudia Johnson sees Charlotte's marriage as "frankly mercenary" but claims that "no specifically authorial moral opprobrium is ever attached to [it]" (1988, p. 81). Laurence Mazzeno asserts that Austen wants her readers "to understand Charlotte's behavior and recognize that, for better or worse, this was the lot to which most women could aspire" (2012, p. 11). Stasio and Duncan's evolutionary reading goes even further, arguing that Austen shows Charlotte's choice as "less than perfect but in some ways desirable" (2007, p. 139). Indeed, Austen generates a great deal of sympathy for Charlotte and presents her mating strategy with *some* understanding. Readers are inclined to like Charlotte because she is a close friend of an extremely likeable heroine, not a rival who would interfere with the heroine's happiness. In fact, in narrative terms, her removal to Hunsford promotes a crucial development in the central relationship between Elizabeth and Mr. Darcy. Moreover, unlike other mercenary fortune hunters (such as Caroline Bingley, Lucy Steele, or Isabella Thorpe), Charlotte is not mean or vain. And even though she acts strategically, she is not devious: She does not lure Mr. Collins under false pretences. On the contrary, she appreciates him for the things that he himself sees as his biggest assets: his income and connections.

Nevertheless, Elizabeth considers Charlotte's decision a lack of "a proper way of thinking" (PP, p. 133). In her conversation with Jane, she exclaims: "You shall not defend her, though it is Charlotte Lucas. You shall not, for the sake of one individual, change the meaning of principle and integrity, nor endeavour to persuade yourself or me, that selfishness is prudence, and insensibility of danger, security of happiness" (PP, p. 133). Her indignation abates somewhat with time, but she remains disappointed *for* and *in* her friend. Marilyn Butler claims that Elizabeth's reflections on the subject, her horror at Charlotte's engagement contrasting with her easy acceptance of Wickham's mercenary pursuit of Miss King, are "pointlessly inconsistent" (1975, p. 214). But Elizabeth's *actions*, her rejections of both Mr. Collins and initially Mr. Darcy, are unequivocal. And when we place them within the context of Austen's life and all her other fiction, a very consistent pattern emerges, as Emma Watson opines: "Poverty is a great Evil; but to a woman of Education & feeling it ought not, it cannot be the greatest" (W, p. 10). Elizabeth, with no financial safety net, would rather face the prospect of poverty than a miserable marriage. For Charlotte, poverty, or rather the prospect of having to be supported by her brothers, is such a great evil that it overshadows Mr. Collins's flaws.

Austen faced a dilemma exactly like Charlotte's. In 1802, as a 26-year-old woman with little money, she received a marriage proposal from Harris Bigg-Wither who could have secured her and her family's financial future. He was a younger brother of Austen's good friends, and by all accounts, she liked him. She initially accepted the proposal but changed her mind overnight. The general consensus is that she did not love Harris enough to marry (Jones, 2009, p. 38). Austen remained single and relatively poor for the rest of her life (as did her sister Cassandra who lost her beloved fiancé to illness). In 1817, Austen famously wrote in a letter to her niece Fanny Knight, who asked for marital advice, that "Single Women have a dreadful propensity for being poor—which is one very strong argument in favour of Matrimony" (Le Faye, 1995, p. 332). This quip has often been quoted as a proof of Austen's pragmatism even though in the very next sentence of the same letter, Austen urges her niece not to be in a hurry to marry, to wait for love. This is consistent with Austen's earlier advice to Fanny: On 18 November 1814, Austen wrote that "Anything is to be preferred or endured rather than marrying without Affection", and on 30 November 1814, that "Nothing can be compared to the misery of being bound *without* Love" (Le Faye, 1995, pp. 280, 286, emphasis in the original).

Austen is well aware of the constraints faced by women, as she explains through Emma Woodhouse with regards to Jane Fairfax's unenviable position: "If a woman can ever be excused for thinking only of herself, it is in a situation like Jane Fairfax's.—Of such, one may almost say, that 'the world is not their's [*sic*], nor the world's law'" (E, p. 315).[8] Austen is also realistic enough to admit that women's feelings and actions are affected by material considerations. Elinor Dashwood, who is thoroughly unselfish and honourable throughout her story, is not "quite enough in love" (SS, p. 343) to marry Edward Ferrars until he has sufficient income to live on. Elizabeth herself half-jokingly tells Jane when asked how long she has loved Darcy: "It has been coming on so gradually, that I hardly know when it began. But I believe I must date it from my first seeing his beautiful grounds at Pemberley" (PP, p. 353). However, Austen is very clear about her moral priorities. Fanny Price is prepared to go back to her very poor and "vulgar" family in Portsmouth, rather than marry Henry Crawford whom she does not trust or respect, and Frederica Vernon in *Lady Susan* announces: "I would rather work for my bread than marry [Sir James]" (LS, Letter 21, pp. 89–90). Austen's heroines do not hesitate to reject materially advantageous proposals when they conflict with their sense of personal dignity and moral principle. And it is their *feelings* that guide them through these difficult dilemmas. In contrast, Charlotte's reasoning is completely devoid of emotions, which is why Austen disapproves of it—as much as she disapproves of Lydia's unbridled passion. Importantly, through her dispassionate mate choice, Charlotte not only validates but willingly reciprocates Mr. Collins's purely instrumental attitude to women and to human relations more generally. Elizabeth, in contrast, driven by moral emotions, vigorously challenges this attitude in both Mr. Collins and Mr. Darcy, which only baffles the former but prompts a significant change in the latter.

It should also be noted that Charlotte underestimates the importance of social cooperation and female coalitions. She knows that her marriage will cause some awkwardness in relations between the Lucas and the Bennet families and will put significant strain on her friendship with Elizabeth. Indeed, anticipating Elizabeth's reaction is "the least agreeable circumstance in the business" (PP, pp. 120–121), but she is prepared to risk the friendship to secure her own financial future. Elizabeth, for her part, is so appalled at Charlotte's decision that she expects that "no real confidence could ever subsist between them again" (PP, p. 125), and after the wedding, she notes that in their correspondence, "all the comfort of intimacy was over" (PP, p. 144). Charlotte's loveless mate choice does exactly what many feminists worry about in relation to love: It separates Charlotte from female support networks by distancing her emotionally from Elizabeth and geographically from her female relatives. Instead, Charlotte puts herself at the mercy of the disdainful and capricious Lady Catherine.

And she soon experiences the precariousness of this situation when she needs to leave her own house for a while to escape Lady Catherine's anger at Darcy's engagement to Elizabeth (PP, p. 362).

Stasio and Duncan see Charlotte's decision as an example of "bounded rationality": "not optimal" but "good enough" (2007, p. 139). Indeed, it fits perfectly within Todd and Miller's (1999) model of "satisficing" in mate choice—making a decision as soon as the main criterion is met. But if Frank (1988), Goleman (1995/2005), Damasio (1996), and others are right about the importance of emotions in our reasoning (see Chapter 2), Charlotte's decision falls well short of what might be considered personally and evolutionarily beneficial. Insofar as Charlotte secures a husband and steady resources, she increases her chances of reproduction and, unlike Lydia, does it in a socially sanctioned way. But in individual terms, human relationships are about more than just reproduction—they are emotional and social contracts; and in evolutionary terms, the idea of reproductive success extends beyond simply producing *any* offspring. If Mr. Collins is a product of his "illiterate and miserly father" (PP, p. 69), then the prospects for Charlotte's children are not very bright. Indeed, kindness and intelligence are crucially important in human mate choice, and Mr. Collins does not have much of either. The lack of genuine affection between Charlotte and her husband would also have a detrimental effect on the emotional development of their children. Of course, this is just speculation, but perhaps being dependent on her brothers and becoming a wise and caring aunt would have been a more dignified option for Charlotte. This is what Austen chose for herself. Importantly, such an option is not an evolutionary dead end. The notion of *inclusive fitness* means that contributing to the reproductive success of our close relatives increases our own reproductive success because we share many of the same genes. Moreover, while humans are subject to the biological reproductive imperative, unlike animals, we are able to pass more than just genes onto the future generations, we consciously care about that non-genetic legacy, and such legacy can make a meaningful difference to our kin. Austen referred to her books as her children, and it would not be an overstatement to say that her intellectual offspring have made a lasting impact on the evolution of her own, and increasingly global, culture.

Austen is compassionate enough not to present Charlotte's fate as tragic, just as she does not punish Lydia with prostitution.[9] What she does show is the possible consequences of an interaction between a particular individual, with her unique set of personality traits and life experiences, and the environmental conditions she finds herself in. Charlotte's choice may be "in *some* ways desirable" for *her*, but it is certainly not what Austen wants her heroines, or her readers, to aspire to. After Elizabeth leaves Hunsford, we only hear from Charlotte indirectly in Mr. Collins's letters, a situation which can justifiably be interpreted as an "absorption of Charlotte's opinions and moral identity by her husband" (Bromberg, 1993, p. 130). Indeed, in those letters, willingly or not, Charlotte participates in Mr. Collins's meanness and stupidity, for example, when she apparently joins him in condemning Lydia.[10] Elizabeth sees Charlotte for the last time just after her engagement to Mr. Darcy, and even though she enjoys her friend's company, the presence of Mr. Collins means that "the pleasure [is] dearly bought" (p. 362). Together with Sir William Lucas's vacuity and Mrs. Philips's "vulgarity", it leads Elizabeth to look forward to being "removed from society so little pleasing to either [her or Darcy], to all the comfort and elegance" of Pemberley (PP, p. 363). Once Elizabeth gets there, Charlotte seems to be relegated to the past. Even Lydia, Miss Bingley, and Lady Catherine are occasionally admitted to Pemberley, but Charlotte is simply not mentioned again. To paraphrase Joseph Carroll's (2004) argument about *Pride and Prejudice*: Despite her intelligence, Charlotte fails Elizabeth's (and Austen's) test for integrity and cannot remain in her inner circle.

Notes

1. PP, p. 123.
2. PP, p. 120.
3. PP, p. 209.
4. PP, p. 122
5. Indeed, in the way Mr. Collins insists on "considering her repeated refusals as flattering encouragement" (PP, p. 106), he reveals not only utter disregard for her feelings but also something of a rapist mentality: He simply cannot fathom why a woman like Elizabeth would refuse an eligible man like him. Darcy is equally incredulous at Elizabeth's rejection of his proposal, as is Henry Crawford at Fanny Price's resistance to his courtship.
6. It is important to note this "almost" because as Austen's life and fiction show, there were women who were independently wealthy and others who relied on their relatives rather than husbands for support.
7. PP, p. 209.
8. The law of Austen's world also makes a difference to what Wickham and Charlotte achieve in their pursuit of money: The former will become the master of his wife's fortune, but the latter will be legally subordinate to her husband.
9. Such authorial decisions undoubtedly contribute to the overwhelmingly positive emotional palette of *Pride and Prejudice*, which in turn is one of the reasons for its enduring popularity. Other female novelists have been more candid about the potentially tragic consequences of prioritizing resources in marital decisions. Edith Wharton's Lily Bart, the heroine of *The House of Mirth*, fails to find a husband and eventually commits suicide because she maladaptively overemphasizes material resources as a mate-selection criterion, and also because she overestimates the value of her own beauty (Saunders, 2009). A similar combination of factors is evoked and criticised by George Eliot in *Daniel Deronda*, where the exceptionally beautiful Gwendolen marries the very wealthy but immoral and vicious Mr. Grandcourt.
10. After Lydia's elopement, Mr. Collins writes to Mr. Bennet: "The death of your daughter would have been a blessing in comparison of this. And it is the more to be lamented, because there is reason to suppose *as my dear Charlotte informs me*, that this licentiousness of behaviour in your daughter has proceeded from a faulty degree of indulgence; … Howsoever that may be, you are grievously to be pitied; *in which opinion I am not only joined by Mrs. Collins*, but likewise by Lady Catherine and her daughter, to whom I have related the affair" (PP, pp. 281–282, emphasis added). This may not be an entirely accurate representation of Charlotte's position, but the point is that Charlotte never gets the chance to present it herself.

References

Al-Shawaf, L., Lewis, D. M., & Buss, D. M. (2015). Disgust and mating strategy. *Evolution and Human Behavior*, *36*(3), 199–205.
Austen, J. (1811/2003). *Sense and sensibility*. Penguin.
Austen, J. (1813/2003). *Pride and prejudice*. Penguin.
Austen, J. (1814/1998). *Mansfield Park*. W. W. Norton & Company.
Austen, J. (1815/2003). *Emma*. Oxford University Press.
Austen, J. (1871/1984). *Lady Susan*. The Athlone Press.
Austen, J. (1871/1985). *The Watsons*. The Athlone Press.
Brennan, P. L. R., Clark, C. J., & Prum, R. O. (2010). Explosive eversion and functional morphology of the duck penis supports sexual conflict in waterfowl genitalia. *Proceedings of the Royal Society B*, *277*(1686), 1309–1314. https://doi.org/10.1098/rspb.2009.2139

Bromberg, P. (1993). Teaching about the marriage plot. In M. McClintock Folsom (Ed.), *Approaches to teaching Austen's Pride and Prejudice* (pp. 126–133). Modern Language Association of America.

Buss, D. M. (2003). *The evolution of desire: Strategies of human mating* (Rev., Kindle ed.). Basic Books.

Butler, M. (1975). *Jane Austen and the war of ideas*. Clarendon Press.

Carroll, J. (2004). Human nature and literary meaning: A theoretical model illustrated with a critique of *Pride and Prejudice*. In J. Carroll, *Literary Darwinism: Evolution, human nature, and literature* (pp. 185–212). Routledge.

Chwe, M. S.-Y. (2013). *Jane Austen, game theorist*. Princeton University Press.

Crosby, C. L., Durkee, P. K., Meston, C. M., & Buss, D. M. (2020). Six dimensions of sexual disgust. *Personality and Individual Differences, 156*, 109714. https://doi.org/10.1016/j.paid.2019.109714

Damasio, A. R. (1996). *Descartes error: Emotion, reason and the human brain*. Papermac.

Frank, R. H. (1988). *Passions within reason: The strategic role of the emotions*. Norton.

Goleman, D. (1995/2005). *Emotional intelligence* (10th anniversary ed.). Bantam Books.

Johnson, C. L. (1988). *Jane Austen: Women, politics, and the novel*. University of Chicago Press.

Jones, H. (2009). *Jane Austen and marriage*. Continuum.

Le Faye, D. (Ed.). (1995). *Jane Austen's letters* (3rd ed.). Oxford University Press.

Mazzeno, L. W. (2012). On *Pride and Prejudice*. In L. W. Mazzeno (Ed.), *Critical insights: Pride and Prejudice by Jane Austen* (pp. 3–17). Salem Press.

Meston, C. M., & Buss, D. M. (2009). *Why women have sex: Understanding sexual motivations—from adventure to revenge (and everything in between)*. Times Books.

Muller, M. N., & Wrangham, R. W. (2009). *Sexual coercion in primates and humans: An evolutionary perspective on male aggression against females*. Harvard University Press.

Perry, R. (2003). Sleeping with Mr. Collins. In S. R. Pucci & J. Thompson (Eds.), *Jane Austen and Co.: Remaking the past in contemporary culture* (pp. 213–228). State University of New York Press.

Saunders, J. P. (2009). *Reading Edith Wharton through a Darwinian lens: Evolutionary biological issues in her fiction*. McFarland & Co.

Stasio, M. J., & Duncan, K. (2007). An evolutionary approach to Jane Austen: Prehistoric preferences in *Pride and Prejudice*. *Studies in the Novel, 39*(2), 133–146. https://www.jstor.org/stable/20831911

Todd, P. M., & Miller, G. F. (1999). From pride and prejudice to persuasion: Satisficing in mate search. In G. Gigerenzer, P. M. Todd, & A. R. Group (Eds.), *Simple heuristics that make us smart* (pp. 287–308). Oxford University Press.

Townsend, J. M., & Levy, G. D. (1990). Effects of potential partners' costume and physical attractiveness on sexuality and partner selection. *The Journal of Psychology, 124*(4), 371–389. https://doi.org/10.1080/00223980.1990.10543232

Townsend, J. M., & Wasserman, T. (1998). Sexual attractiveness: Sex differences in assessment and criteria. *Evolution and Human Behavior, 19*(3), 171–191. https://doi.org/10.1016/S1090-5138(98)00008-7

6
JANE BENNET

"[Her] feelings, though fervent, were little displayed"[1]

Jane, the oldest of the Bennet sisters, is serene, nurturing, and unassuming. She is prettier than Elizabeth, and while intelligent, lacks Elizabeth's wit, energy, and confidence. She falls in love with the kind but diffident Mr. Bingley who seems to return her feelings. For a large part of the novel, Jane is separated from Bingley by the scheming of his sisters and his closest friend, Mr. Darcy. Eventually, however, the gentle lovers are reunited, with Darcy's blessing and an authorial promise of happiness.

Feminists generally see Jane's shy, caring character as the embodiment of culturally idealized feminine passivity and weakness (Armstrong, 1987; Brown, 1973; Gilbert & Gubar, 1979/2000; Shaffer, 1992). Evolutionary scholars also routinely refer to Jane as passive (Kruger et al., 2013, 2014; Stasio & Duncan, 2007). Admittedly, Jane is introverted and high in *Agreeableness*, a personality trait associated with being compassionate and non-confrontational. Because of this, she does not pursue her desire as assertively as some of Austen's other women, and risks losing a potential husband, but she never compromises her integrity or dignity. Unlike the truly silent and submissive Anne de Bourgh, Jane actively exercises her female choice; her restraint results in a much more satisfying relationship than Charlotte's instrumentalism or Lydia's lust; and her sincerity is favourably contrasted with Caroline Bingley's flattery and superficial elegance. Her temporary separation from Bingley is not a punishment for her "passivity" but a necessary opportunity for Bingley to prove the strength and stability of his commitment. And by the way Jane copes with the possibility that she may never be united with her beloved, she proves her strength of character and self-reliance. In the story of Jane and Bingley, Austen perfectly captures the benefits and costs of such personality traits as Agreeableness, empathy, and honesty. These traits are necessary for sustained cooperation and satisfaction in all kinds of relationships: intimate, familial, and social. However, they also make Jane and Bingley vulnerable to the machinations of other, more assertive characters.

Furthermore, Austen engages readers' attention not only through the psychological accuracy and complexity of her characterization but also by the way she plays with our expectations: The caring and beautiful Jane as well as the rich and sociable Bingley are both very desirable mates and should both be confident about their marital prospects, and yet

DOI: 10.4324/9781003320982-10

they are both more humble and diffident than any other character in the novel. Through their story, Austen shows that human love relationships are not only complex coordination problems between two individuals but are also deeply embedded in networks of social relations and susceptible to interference from other people.

"Rectitude and delicacy"[2]

Most feminists interpret Jane's character with reference to the ideals of female delicacy and chastity prescribed in James Fordyce's sermons and Samuel Richardson's novels. Consequently, they are deeply critical of what they see as the archetypal damsel in distress: "Jane ... suffers silently throughout the entire plot, until she is finally set free by her Prince Charming" (Gilbert & Gubar, 1979/2000, p. 157); "Jane, the Richardsonian sister, languishes for want of a husband until the very end of the novel" (Armstrong, 1987, p. 58). They also claim that Austen evokes this ideal of femininity in order to undermine it. However, seeing Jane as "Austen's satire on Richardson's illogical notion of modesty" and interpreting her "tenderness" as "merely a damaging result of social conditioning" (Brown, 1973, pp. 336, 327) has produced conclusions which clearly go against Austen's ethos, not only in the case of Jane but also Austen's other shy heroines. For example, Lloyd W. Brown compares Jane to the cruel, manipulative, and promiscuous Lady Susan, suggesting that both women are "prisoners of [the same] repressive image of womanhood" (1973, p. 336). Gilbert and Gubar actually prefer Lady Susan's "energetic ... pursuit of pleasure" to her daughter Frederica (a prototype of characters such as Jane Bennet and Fanny Price), whom they describe as "vapid and weak" and "socialized into passivity" (1979/2000, p. 156). Similarly, when writing about *Sense and Sensibility*, they note the appeal of "Marianne's sincerity and spontaneity" as opposed to "the civil falsehoods and the reserved, polite silences of Elinor" (p. 157). They are also utterly disparaging of Fanny Price, of what they consider as "her invalid deathliness" and "purity that seems prudish and reserve bordering on hypocrisy" (pp. 165–166). Such readings are hard to reconcile with Austen's narrative positioning of these characters. Lady Susan and other characters like her, including Lydia Bennet, Isabella Thorpe, and Lucy Steele, are consistently positioned as antagonists whose stories never achieve a positive resolution. Jane Bennet, on the other hand, even though she plays a supporting role to Elizabeth, is very similar to many of Austen's heroines, like Elinor Dashwood, Fanny Price, and Anne Elliot, who have strong authorial approval and are awarded with happy endings. For this reason, the rare validation of Jane's and Bingley's humility by Marilyn Butler is actually closer to Austen's intention, but it goes too far: Seeing the couple as a crucial formative influence on Elizabeth and Darcy on their way to achieve Austen's ideal of "the truly Christian character" (1975, p. 212) is an overstatement, and Butler's overall thesis about Austen's conservatism has been robustly challenged.

The force of Richardson's ideal of femininity is evident in the way Austen's brother Henry tried to soften the image of the sharp-witted author by portraying her to be as angelic as Jane Bennet: "Faultless herself, as nearly as human nature can be, she always sought, in the faults of others, something to excuse, to forgive or forget. ... She never uttered a hasty, a silly, or a severe expression" (H. Austen, 1817/1968, p. 75).[3] However, I argue that what Austen was aiming for with Jane, and all the other heroines like her, was the ideal of modesty as defined by the pioneering feminist Mary Wollstonecraft

(1792/2004). Wollstonecraft rejects the kind of feminine delicacy which results from a "puerile kind of propriety" and is therefore connected with pretence and "cunning" (p. 88). Modesty is for her a "sacred offspring of sensibility and reason", "a true delicacy of mind" combined with "consciousness of our own dignity" (p. 191). It is as antithetical to self-abasement as it is to vanity. Most importantly, modesty is not a "sexual virtue" but "must be equally cultivated by both sexes" (p. 196). Even Jane Bennet's reserve is in line with Wollstonecraft's assurance that it is "the handmaid of modesty" (p. 198), and the apparent lack of physical passion between Jane and Bingley, disappointing to some feminists (e.g., Johnson, 1988, p. 90), is also in accordance with Wollstonecraft's preference for "the calm tenderness of friendship" over passionate love which she associates with "an animal appetite" (pp. 99, 141).

Jane not only epitomizes Wollstonecraft's ideals but she also illustrates Brown's (1973) claims about Austen's feminism—contrary to his own reading of Jane's character. Brown juxtaposes Jane's supposed compliance with the oppressive feminine ideal to Catherine Morland's liberation from it. As he rightly observes, Catherine's obvious infatuation with Henry Tilney directly challenges Richardson's dictum that a woman should not fall in love until the man's love has been declared. In this way, Austen questions attitudes towards female sexuality and in particular the assumption that female desire is, or should be, "suppressed to a purely responsive level" (Brown, 1973, p. 336). But Catherine Morland is not the only Austen heroine who challenges this assumption. Many of Austen's heroines (except for, ironically, the most confident ones: Elizabeth Bennet, Emma Woodhouse, and Marianne Dashwood) are in love earlier and more securely than the men they marry. Even the most timid ones, Frederica Vernon and Fanny Price, are proactive in their desires. Jane Bennet's love may not be quite as obvious as Catherine Morland's, but it is no less autonomous.

"All loveliness and goodness as she is"[4]

One of the first things we learn about Jane is that she is remarkably beautiful. It is what initially attracts Bingley and what later rekindles his affection. Mrs. Bennet sees it as her daughter's biggest asset and an assurance of marital success. In that respect, she would agree with Emma Woodhouse's pronouncement about Harriet Smith's prospects: "Till it appears that men are much more philosophic on the subject of beauty than they are generally supposed; till they do fall in love with well-informed minds instead of handsome faces, a girl, with such loveliness as Harriet, has a certainty of being admired and sought after, of having the power of choosing from among many" (E, p. 51). However, Emma is wrong, since Harriet's beauty, for a variety of reasons, some of them more noble than others, is not sufficient to attract any men other than Mr. Martin, especially not "a man of sense" such as Mr. Knightley. Jane also does not have a line-up of eager men to choose from: One admirer mentioned by Mrs. Bennet left without making Jane an offer; while Darcy, who acknowledges Jane's beauty, is completely unmoved by it and thinks that "she smile[s] too much" (PP, p. 18). Yes, men do want pretty wives, but Austen's men who choose their wives based on their pretty faces, like Mr. Bennet or Mr. Palmer (in *Sense and Sensibility*), soon live to regret it.

Jane's conspicuous beauty sets her apart from Austen's main heroines and highlights Austen's approach to the subject. For Austen, being pretty is neither a necessary nor sufficient qualification for being a heroine and for achieving a happy ending. She deemphasizes physical appearance in order to underline the importance of character. None of her heroines enjoys Jane's status of being "about five times as pretty as every other woman in the room" (PP, p. 16). Other women in the novels are often more beautiful than the main heroine, for example, Isabella Thorpe or Mary Crawford. In these and other cases (Caroline Bingley, Lady Susan, Maria Bertram, Elizabeth Elliot), obvious beauty is paired with emotional shallowness and lack of moral integrity. And it does not attract quality partners: Many of these beauties remain single at the end of their stories, others get married to selfish or stupid men. As I will argue in the next chapter, Austen's heroines *become* more and more beautiful as the heroes learn to appreciate their other qualities. In short, Austen consistently challenges the focus on female appearance as the basis of women's value, power, and relationship success. And she is right to do so, for while men like pretty women (as evolutionary psychologists stress, sometimes overly so), in long-term relationships, not beauty but kindness, intelligence, and commitment are their priority (Buss et al., 1990).

In addition to being beautiful, Jane is smart: "her understanding excellent, her mind improved" (PP, p. 182). Interestingly, literary scholars often miss this part of her characterization. For example, Butler, who praises Jane's humility, mistakes it for lack of rational intelligence: "As far as the reader knows Jane herself hardly thinks at all" (1975, p. 216). Admittedly, Jane's intelligence is not witty and sparkly like Elizabeth's, but it is there, quiet and reflective like Elinor Dashwood's, Fanny Price's, and Anne Elliot's. Jane also shares with these heroines her two defining personality traits: very high Agreeableness and low Extraversion.[5]

Agreeableness is one of the five main personality dimensions identified by modern psychology. People who are high in Agreeableness are "cooperative, trusting, and empathetic"; they have more harmonious and supportive social relations and relatively little interpersonal conflict; those who are low in Agreeableness are "cold-hearted, hostile, and non-compliant" (Nettle, 2007, pp. 161–162). Agreeableness is, therefore, an index of our orientation towards others and, together with our well-developed Theory of Mind (i.e., our capacity to understand other people's thoughts and intentions), it is crucial for human prosociality (Nettle, 2007).[6] Being able to build supportive networks within the family and wider social group is particularly important for women. Throughout our evolutionary history, female reproductive success has largely depended on the woman's ability to keep her children safe and healthy, and that would have been significantly impacted on by her ability to maintain cooperative relationships not just with a sexual partner but with relatives and other community members (Hrdy, 2009). Secure group membership reduces vulnerability to threats and facilitates sharing of resources and responsibilities. It has been proposed that this greater proclivity for affiliation, or what has been termed a "tend-and-befriend" pattern, is a typically female response to stress (as opposed to more typically male fight-or-flight mechanism), and has been an effective female survival strategy (Taylor et al., 2000; Whissell, 1996).

Some feminists also emphasize empathy and affiliation as particularly important and valuable feminine traits, a foundation of the feminine ethics of care (e.g., Gilligan, 1982). For most, however, such insistence on women's nurturing abilities is another form of inequality and female exploitation: While women are expected to provide emotional support to men and other family members, their efforts are often not reciprocated, or even properly appreciated (Bartky, 1990).[7] It is this second position that usually informs feminist responses to such characters as Jane Bennet and leads them to be critical of narrative events showing female nurturance or sacrifice; for example, when Elizabeth goes travelling with the Gardiners, Jane is left home to look after their children. However, Jane's ability to care for others is not a sign of self-abasement. Rather, it is a sign of her emotional maturity and resilience. Her mothering potential is in line with Wollstonecraft's vision of "the maternal solicitude of a reasonable affectionate woman" who can be expected to "govern a family with judgment" (1792/2004, pp. 213, 276). While both Wollstonecraft and Austen advocate for more options for women, they both realize that motherhood is highly likely for most of them. How they fulfil this role determines their social and personal value. Austen shows enough infantile, self-absorbed, overbearing, and irresponsible mothers for her readers to see the importance of competent caregivers.

Jane's "steady sense and sweetness of temper" (PP, p. 231) are in stark contrast to both Lady Catherine's domineering mothering and Mrs. Bennet's utter inability to provide moral guidance or emotional support to anybody. For example, although Jane is still hurting after Bingley's apparent abandonment, she refuses to be melodramatic about it, unlike Mrs. Bennet, who performs a "parade" of grief after Lydia's elopement (PP, p. 284), making a complete nuisance of herself. Neither Mary nor Kitty, nor even Mr. Bennet, is up to the task of guiding the family through this crisis. Similarly, Austen applauds Elinor Dashwood who can show composure in a distressing situation and compassion for her sister's anguish, while Marianne can only wallow in her own unhappiness without a shred of resilience or regard for the feelings of others around her. When Austen tells us that Anne Elliot was "peculiarly fitted" for the domestic life (P, p. 29), she means it as a recognition rather than a denial of Anne's intelligence and strength: She is a more sensible and affectionate guardian of her little nephews than their self-centred mother, Anne's younger sister. She is also the only woman who can stay calm and be helpful after Louisa Musgrove's dramatic fall. Fanny Price, too, is the source of comfort for the Bertram family in the aftermath of Maria's affair, and to Edmund in his disappointment over Mary Crawford.

These events have often been interpreted as acts of self-abnegation, but in many cases, they inadvertently promote the interests of the woman in question. For example, it is in these situations requiring both empathy and strength of character that Captain Wentworth and Edmund Bertram (as well as his father) realize the true value of Anne and Fanny, respectively. As many evolutionists point out, the ultra-social evolutionary niche of *Homo sapiens* "produces the unusual selection pressure whereby there are strong *self-interest* benefits to being very attentive to the interests of *others*, because that makes you a valued and secure group player" (Nettle, 2007, pp. 173–174, emphasis in the original), not to mention a good intimate partner. What is important, however, is that Austen's heroines show concern and generosity to others *without* a specific goal of self-promotion—unlike Austen's female antagonists, such as Caroline Bingley, Lucy Steele, or Mrs. Elton, and unlike Austen's cads who always have ulterior motives.

"She is not acting by design"[8]

Genuine feeling and honest motivation are particularly important in love. Austen stresses, through Elizabeth, that Jane's attraction to Bingley is not primarily motivated by a plan "to find a rich husband" and that "she is not acting by design" (PP, p. 23). In this respect, Brown's comparison between Jane and Lady Susan quoted earlier is inadvertently very apt, because Lady Susan's philosophy is exactly the opposite of Jane's: She is desperate to find rich husbands for herself and for her daughter, and in her view "artlessness will never do in Love matters" (LS, Letter 19, p. 77). Brown is right that Jane and Lady Susan experience similar social pressures, but their coping strategies are diametrically different, and Austen leaves us in no doubt about where her sympathies lie. While Lady Susan is "Mistress of Deceit" (LS, Letter 23, p. 101), Jane is distressed at a mere suggestion that people like Wickham and Miss Bingley might be dishonest. Jane's genuine affection for Bingley and her reluctance to "fix" him are in stark contrast not only to Lady Susan's ruthless manipulations but also to Caroline Bingley's efforts to attract Mr. Darcy and Charlotte Lucas's determination to secure "any husband" regardless of the absence of affection.

The high value Austen puts on Jane Bennet's sincerity becomes even more apparent when we compare her with Jane Fairfax from *Emma*. The two Janes' characterizations and narrative functions are very similar (and both have been interpreted as "totally passive and quiet, ... paragon[s] of submissive politeness and patience"; Gilbert & Gubar, 1979/2000, p. 158). Both are sensible, gentle, and beautiful, and both play secondary roles to the more exuberant heroines. Both are temporarily disappointed by the men they love but are given happy resolutions shortly before the main, even happier, conclusions of the novels take place. However, while Jane Bennet is Elizabeth's closest ally and confidant, Jane Fairfax, despite all her positive traits, has a somewhat ambivalent relation to Emma. This is partially a consequence of Emma's vanity and immaturity, but we are also alerted to Jane Fairfax's lack of transparency: She must conceal her engagement with Frank Churchill and consequently cannot be open and sincere with those around her. This, as Emma points out once the secret has been revealed, is a violation of the social contract of honesty and trust: "I shall always think it a very abominable sort of proceeding. What has it been but a system of hypocrisy and deceit,—espionage, and treachery?— To come among us with professions of openness and simplicity; and such a league in secret to judge us all!— Here have we been, the whole winter and spring, completely duped, fancying ourselves all on an equal footing of truth and honour" (E, p. 314).

Emma's reaction reveals her own wounded pride, and she can see some extenuating circumstances, but even Miss Fairfax admits that her conduct had been "contrary to all [her] sense of right" (E, p. 329). She is exonerated because her secrecy was motivated by genuine attachment (in contrast to Lucy Steele's manipulative and heartless secret engagement to Edward Ferrars), but it had alienated her from potential friends and deprived her of much needed social support. It was not just Emma who could not warm to Jane. Mr. Knightley also observed, "Jane Fairfax is a very charming young woman—but ... [s]he has a fault. She has not the open temper which a man would wish for in a wife" (E, p. 225). People who are capable of deliberate deception (regardless of what motivates this deception) arouse suspicion as potential partners in all kinds of ventures that require trust, and men are particularly sensitive (sometimes overly so) to any signs of a woman's sexual dishonesty. Austen seems to be well aware of that, and she often juxtaposes authenticity and performance, sincerity and calculation in order to reward the former and condemn the latter, especially when it comes to love and marriage.

Jane Fairfax is not selfishly opportunistic or maliciously manipulative, like Isabella Thorpe or Lucy Steele, but she knowingly puts herself in a position that requires concealment and suppression of true emotions. For Jane Bennet, meanwhile, the relatively subdued expression of emotions stems from her natural introversion. Miss Bennet does not like being the centre of attention, being looked at or talked of. According to Elizabeth, "Jane united, with great strength of feeling, a composure of temper and a uniform cheerfulness of manner" (PP, p. 22) and "[her] feelings, though fervent, were little displayed" (PP, p. 202). Her poise is criticized by Charlotte who claims that it is "a disadvantage to be so very guarded" because Jane "may lose the opportunity of fixing" Bingley (PP, p. 22). Even the reserved Darcy seems to expect Jane to be more expressive: Her serenity convinces him that she is not really in love with Bingley and gives him the strongest argument to persuade his friend to give her up.

Obviously, Jane is much less eager or single-minded than Lydia or Charlotte, but her restraint has an important evolutionary function. When Charlotte urges that Jane should "secure" Bingley as soon as possible, Elizabeth reminds her: "As yet, [Jane] cannot even be certain of the degree of her own regard nor of its reasonableness. She has known him only a fortnight. … This is not quite enough to make her understand his character" (PP, p. 23). Austen insists that her heroines take their time when assessing potential partners; those who do not do that often get into trouble. Usually, it is reproductively advantageous for women to be more discriminating about their mates than men are, and more reluctant to enter into a sexual or romantic partnership. Such behaviour has often been mistakenly interpreted as coyness or passivity, but this circumspection is necessary for a woman to properly assess both her own feelings and the man's suitability: his physical and psychological attributes, his family and future prospects, not to mention his commitment. Austen shows that this is a time-consuming process. It does carry the risk of missing out on a mate, but both in biological and in cultural terms, women have more to lose by being too hasty.

Jane is cautious, but she is neither passive nor weak. Her "sweetness and disinterestedness" may be "really angelic", but "Jane was firm where she felt herself to be right" (PP, pp. 132, 58). Although not as self-assured as Elizabeth, she can stand up to her sister's teasing: "Laugh as much as you chuse [*sic*], but you will not laugh me out of my opinion" (PP, p. 84). She assures Elizabeth: "I speak what I think" (PP, p. 16), unlike Miss Fairfax, who seems "determined to hazard nothing" (E, p. 132). And when it comes to choosing a husband, Jane is like neither Miss de Bourgh, who completely submits to her overbearing mother, nor Harriet Smith, who keeps changing her mind about who to be in love with.

Jane is, in fact, more certain and accurate about her own and Bingley's feelings than Elizabeth is of hers and Wickham's or Darcy's. And while Elizabeth attracts Darcy "unconsciously" (at least to begin with; PP, p. 189), Jane "does help [Bingley] on, as much as her nature will allow" (PP, p. 23). For example, as Juliet McMaster points out, although Jane is "no coquette" she "makes her beauty effective" (1978, p. 64): "On entering the room, [Bingley] seemed to hesitate; but Jane happened to look round, and happened to smile: it was decided. He placed himself by her" (PP, p. 321). She actively pursues Bingley when she follows him to London. She cultivates the friendship with Bingley's sisters, knowing that this brings her closer to him, but only for as long as she believes that friendship to be genuine. And when she realizes the duplicity of Bingley's circle, Jane tells Elizabeth that she would be prepared to marry him against their wishes: "You must know that though I should be exceedingly grieved at their disapprobation, I could not hesitate" (PP, p. 117). Like Fanny Price and Frederica Vernon, who are the meekest of Austen's heroines but who do not hesitate to defy the authoritative Sir Thomas and the scheming Lady Susan respectively, Jane is neither too timid to know her own mind nor too weak to stand by her decision. The fact that she almost misses out on Bingley is due not to *her* weakness but to *his*.[9]

Mr. Bingley: "That easiness of temper, that want of proper resolution"[10]

Bingley is generous and considerate, handsome and rich. Jane's early impression of him is that "he is just what a young man ought to be" (PP, p. 16), but Austen reminds us—once again—not to rely completely on first impressions. To begin with, Bingley's open and friendly manners are explicitly, and favourably, contrasted with Darcy's aloofness and rigidity, but as the novel progresses, we see the feebleness of the former and the steadfastness of the latter.[11] At the same time, Bingley's liveliness and charm initially appear similar to Wickham's, until we realize that one man is genuinely kind and trustworthy, while the other uses his social skills to deceive and exploit.

Bingley perfectly matches Jane's high Agreeableness, but not her patience: He is swift to act, often without much reflection, and he is easily influenced by others. In all these traits, he is set up as "a great opposition of character" with Darcy (PP, p. 18). He declares, not without some satisfaction: "Whatever I do is done in a hurry" (PP, p. 42). For example, he rents Netherfield based on "an accidental recommendation" and a "half-an-hour" inspection (PP, p. 18). When talking about his letter writing skills, Bingley says: "My ideas flow so rapidly that I have not time to express them" (PP, p. 47); in contrast, Darcy writes "rather slowly". This seemingly innocuous comment is an early hint of the relative stability of the two men and is important when we consider how often Austen uses letters to reveal the truth of the characters.[12] For example, Mr. Collins's letters reveal the extent of his meanness and stupidity; Isabella Thorpe's and Lucy Steele's shallowness and insincerity become blatantly obvious in their letters; Elizabeth's view of Darcy changes after he writes to her, and his regular correspondence with Georgiana is an early sign of his capacity for sustained affection; similarly, William Price's regular and warm correspondence with Fanny is contrasted with Henry Crawford's relative neglect of his sister Mary. While Elizabeth interprets Bingley's confessions as signs of his "humility" which "must disarm reproof", Darcy warns her, and us, that they may also signal "carelessness of opinion", "imperfection of the performance", and even "an indirect boast" (PP, pp. 47–48).

Bingley is equally quick and uncritical when judging people. He likes everybody even before he knows anything about them while Darcy dislikes everybody until he knows them well, as demonstrated by the way they react to the Meryton assembly:

> Bingley had never met with pleasanter people or prettier girls in his life; every body had been most kind and attentive to him; ... Darcy, on the contrary, had seen a collection of people in whom there was little beauty and no fashion, for none of whom he had felt the smallest interest, and from none received either attention or pleasure. (PP, p. 18)[13]

Bingley's warmth and affability instantly win him a lot of friends, but his lack of discrimination when it comes to women might not bode well for a relationship requiring exclusive commitment to one. Indeed, Darcy doubts the seriousness of Bingley's attachment to Jane because, as he says, "I had often seen him in love before" (PP, p. 192). In fact, Jane is not the only one to catch Bingley's eye at the Meryton assembly, as he declares, "Upon my honour,

I never met with so many pleasant girls in my life as I have this evening; and there are several of them you see uncommonly pretty" (PP, p. 13). Bingley also thinks all ladies are "accomplished": "They all paint tables, cover skreens and net purses" (PP, pp. 38–39). It is a sign of Bingley's undiscriminating generosity and his readiness to be pleased but should also alert us to the superficiality of his assessment of women. In contrast, Darcy is much more reluctant to bestow praise because he looks for more "substantial" qualities of mind (PP, p. 39).[14]

Jane's excellent understanding, improved mind, and captivating manners (PP, p. 182) meet Darcy's high expectations, as well as Miss Bingley's requirement of elegance. However, since neither his friend nor his sister share Bingley's uncritical disposition, Jane's relatively low social status is a serious impediment for them, and her family's "total want of propriety" (PP, p. 193) only confirms their view. Their insistence on the importance of family connections is snobbish and will be corrected in the course of the novel, but Bingley's complete disregard for it is not wise either, given the ultra-social nature of human mating. Evolutionists emphasize the fact that human reproduction is a cooperative venture, not just between two individuals but between their families, and beyond (Apostolou, 2017; Hrdy, 2009). In the words of the economist Paul Seabright,

> The evolutionary niche occupied by early *Homo sapiens* meant that every pregnancy imposed large costs on fathers, grandparents, neighbors, and siblings, on the whole supporting team that each newborn required for its survival. In a world without contraception and delicately dependent on maintaining the incentives for cooperation, those costs of sex could not be socialized unless the decisions about engaging in sex were socialized too. (2012, pp. 161–162)

This need for cooperation also creates potential conflict because the interests of different members of a family do not align perfectly. Conflict between lovers and their parents is a common literary theme (Boyd, 2014), and parental disapproval is often the obstacle to a romantic union (Hogan, 2003). Austen's fiction is full of parents and guardians who try to control their children's marital choices (although they rarely succeed), as well as other relatives and friends who have vested interests in either promoting or preventing a particular union. In *Pride and Prejudice* alone, Mrs. Bennet shamelessly boasts about the advantages of Jane's marriage to Bingley, including the fact that it would "throw [her sisters] in the way of other rich men" (PP, p. 97); Caroline Bingley, on the other hand, wants her brother to marry Georgiana Darcy because that would further raise the status of the Bingley family and improve Caroline's own marital prospects; and Lady Catherine tries to stop her bloodline being "polluted" (PP, p. 338) by Elizabeth marrying Darcy.

Bingley does not need to contend with parental interference, and it is his own diffidence that leads him to abandon his courtship of Jane. From the moment Bingley is introduced, we know that he relies on Darcy's judgement more than on his own (PP, p. 18). Darcy has, therefore, no trouble persuading his friend that Jane does not really love him. Darcy believes that he is acting in Bingley's best interest, but he also exploits Bingley's accommodating nature. This quality, which is associated with high Agreeableness, is initially presented more favourably than Darcy's uncompromising attitude. At first, Elizabeth prefers Bingley's willingness to allow for "the influence of friendship and affection" (PP, p. 49) to Darcy's assurance that his "feelings are not puffed about with every attempt to move them" (PP, p. 56), but she soon comes to think of Bingley's readiness to yield with "utmost contempt" (PP, p. 117). Although she never suspects Bingley of intentional wrongdoing, she accuses him of causing "misery" through "thoughtlessness, want of attention to other people's feelings, and want of resolution" (PP, p. 134). Her anger abates when she learns the full story from Darcy's letter, but even towards the end of the novel, when Darcy tells her how easily he convinced Bingley that Jane *does* love him, Elizabeth still disapproves of Bingley's pliability, as well as Darcy's inclination to direct him.

However, Bingley is exonerated because "his affection was proved to have been sincere" (PP, p. 207). Unlike Willoughby and Wickham who transfer their attention effortlessly from one woman to another, unlike Frank Churchill and Henry Crawford who do not mean what they say when they are flirting with Emma and Fanny, respectively, Bingley is always genuine and turns out to be constant.[15] While he is away from Jane, his love withstands the test of time, the upsetting notion that it was not reciprocated, the distractions of London, and the allure of another attractive woman, Georgiana Darcy. When he comes back to Longbourn, Jane can be sure that his feelings are not just "a common and transient liking" (PP, p. 135).

Through Bingley, Austen not only shows the risks of high Agreeableness but also demonstrates that true autonomy and integrity are a function not of financial freedom or other external circumstances but of strength of character—and that this applies equally to men and women. Unlike many of Austen's men (e.g., Frank Churchill, Edward Ferrars, Henry Tilney, John Willoughby), let alone Austen's women, Bingley is financially independent and in a position to be "his own master" (PP, p. 115). Instead, he turns out to be, at least for a while, "the slave of his designing friends," prepared to "sacrifice of his own happiness to the caprice of their inclination" (PP, p. 131). As Claudia Johnson rightly points out, Bingley fails to adhere to "the principles of dignity and self-respect", which Elizabeth will later insist on in her showdown with Lady Catherine despite being in a much weaker position than Bingley to do so (1988, p. 86). This autonomous stance is characteristic of all Austen's heroines, even those who have consistently been accused of being passive: Despite the circumstances which make them dependent on others and despite timid personalities, they do not allow their marital decisions to be overruled by other people's interests.

"Oh! why is not everybody as happy?"[16]

Elizabeth sees the marriage of Jane and Bingley as "the happiest, wisest, most reasonable end!" (PP, p. 328). Curiously, many feminist assessments of their union (apart from Butler's) are rather lukewarm: "Bingley and Jane—always nice and morally correct, if bland" (Shaffer, 1992, p. 66); "the marriage of Bingley and Jane illustrates the pleasures of wedlock between two people of no particular talents at all" (Chandler, 1975, p. 100). Ironically, such dismissals are very similar to Mrs. Bennet's opinion that compared with Elizabeth's marriage, "Jane's is nothing to it—nothing at all" (PP, p. 357). What is overlooked in these assessments is the high value Austen places on empathy, kindness, and connection, even though she clearly spells out their risks as well.

Austen's conclusion is uncannily consistent with evolutionary psychologists' assessment of the benefits and costs of high Agreeableness (Geher & Kaufman, 2013; Nettle, 2006).

Both Jane and Bingley are selfless, trusting, and non-confrontational. These qualities mean that instead of maximizing their own advantage, they are sometimes taken advantage of. Mr. Bennet may be a bit too cynical about the Bingleys' prospects, but he is not far from the truth when he says: "I have not a doubt of your doing very well together. Your tempers are by no means unlike. You are each of you so complying, that nothing will ever be resolved on; so easy, that every servant will cheat you; and so generous, that you will always exceed your income" (PP, p. 329). And as Austen glimpses into the future of her characters, we see that Lydia, Wickham, and Mrs. Bennet impose on the Bingleys' kindness more than they do on Elizabeth and Darcy's. But even Jane and her husband learn their lesson and quickly move out of Netherfield: "So near a vicinity to her mother and Meryton relations was not desirable even to *his* easy temper, or *her* affectionate heart" (PP, p. 364, emphasis in the original).

At the same time, Jane's and Bingley's kindness puts them in a very good position to form enduring, benevolent partnerships of all kinds: social, familial, and romantic. Indeed, Agreeableness is the personality dimension most directly associated with all three dimensions of consummate love: passion, intimacy, and commitment (Ahmetoglu et al., 2010). Considering this, Elizabeth (like Austen) is right in predicting for Jane and Bingley "all the felicity which a marriage of true affection could bestow" (PP, p. 96). Clearly, Jane's choice of partner is markedly superior to Charlotte's or Lydia's, and her mating strategy is more successful than Caroline Bingley's or Anne de Bourgh's. Bingley is kind, generous, and loyal. He is the antithesis of male sexual aggression and social domination, and his egalitarianism comes from his disposition, while Darcy will have to learn its value from experience. Bingley has earned the goodwill and respect of his neighbours and has built a genuine friendship with Darcy. These positive social relations will be as beneficial for his wife's happiness and reproductive success as his personal qualities.

Still, Bingley is not the man of whom women around the world have been dreaming for the last two centuries (nor is Jane the woman the readers would most like to be). Physically, mentally, and socially, he does not measure up to Darcy, the alpha male. When Elizabeth finally gets her man, she will say "I am happier even than Jane; she only smiles, I laugh" (PP, p. 361).

Notes

1 PP, p. 202.
2 PP, p. 125.
3 This is clearly an idealized picture. One of the things that make Austen such a great writer is her ability to be very pointed about the faults of others, as both her fiction and her letters show. For example, on 20 November 1800, she wrote to Cassandra: "Miss Debary, Susan & Sally … made their appearance, & I was as civil to them as their bad breath would allow me" (Le Faye, 1995, p. 61).
4 PP, p. 182.
5 These personality assessments are based on hundreds of readers' responses collected by Joseph Carroll and his colleagues (2012, p. 113). Although their study does not provide a personality profile of Jane (because she is not the main heroine), it is easy to see that she is very similar to Elinor, Anne, and Fanny who are all low on Extraversion and Openness to Experience, and high on Agreeableness and Conscientiousness.
6 Theory of Mind refers to our *ability* to recognize other people's thoughts, beliefs, and intentions as potentially different from our own; Agreeableness is connected to our *willingness* to attend to them and factor them in our behavioural choices.

7 For a recent discussion of this divergent evaluation and a call for "androgynization" of empathy as "a fundamental human capacity", see Lobb (2013).
8 PP, p. 23.
9 Stasio and Duncan also contend that "the real problem ... is not Jane but Bingley" (2007, p. 142), but our arguments differ to the extent that they claim that Jane *is* passive, in line with the cultural ideal (p. 138).
10 PP, p. 131.
11 Although I do not have space to explore this further, I should like to point out that through the contrast between Bingley and Darcy, Austen explores the difference between two personality dimensions we most readily perceive and most urgently assess in others: warmth (associated with friendliness and trustworthiness) and competence (associated with capability and assertiveness). For the evolutionary significance of this aspect of social cognition, see Fiske et al. (2007).
12 Carroll (2004) aptly demonstrates this with a comparison of Darcy's and Collins's letters.
13 Not incidentally, this contrast in the two men is perfectly mirrored in the women they choose: Jane cannot think ill of anyone, while Elizabeth admits that "there are few people whom I really love, and still fewer of whom I think well" (PP, p. 133).
14 Their discussion of female accomplishments echoes Wollstonecraft's concerns about women's education: "It is acknowledged that they spend many of the first years of their lives in acquiring a smattering of accomplishments; meanwhile strength of body and mind are sacrificed" (1792/2004, p. 76).
15 Frank Churchill is also pardoned for his "inconsideration and thoughtlessness" because "he is, beyond a doubt, really attached to Miss Fairfax" (E, p. 352).
16 PP, p. 327.

References

Ahmetoglu, G., Swami, V., & Chamorro-Premuzic, T. (2010). The relationship between dimensions of love, personality, and relationship length. *Archives of Sexual Behavior, 39*(5), 1181–1190. https://doi.org/10.1007/s10508-009-9515-5

Apostolou, M. (2017). *Sexual selection in Homo sapiens: Parental control over mating and the opportunity cost of free mate choice.* Springer.

Armstrong, N. (1987). *Desire and domestic fiction: A political history of the novel.* Oxford University Press.

Austen, H. (1817/1968). Biographical notice of the author. In B. C. Southam (Ed.), *Jane Austen: The critical heritage* (pp. 73–78). Routledge & Kegan Paul.

Austen, J. (1813/2003). *Pride and prejudice.* Penguin.

Austen, J. (1815/2003). *Emma.* Oxford University Press.

Austen, J. (1818/1998). *Persuasion.* Oxford University Press.

Austen, J. (1871/1984). *Lady Susan.* The Athlone Press.

Bartky, S. L. (1990). *Femininity and domination: Studies in the phenomenology of oppression.* Routledge.

Boyd, B. (2014). Life history into story. *Philosophy and Literature, 38*(1A), A267–A278

Brown, L. W. (1973). Jane Austen and the feminist tradition. *Nineteenth-Century Fiction, 28*(3), 321–338. https://doi.org/10.2307/2933003

Buss, D. M., Abbott, M., Angleitner, A., Asherian, A., Biaggio, A., Blanco-Villasenor, A., Bruchon-Schweitzer, M., Ch'U, H.-Y., Czapinski, J., Deraad, B., Ekehammar, B., Lohamy, N., Fioravanti, M., Georgas, J., Gjerde, P., Guttman, R., Hazan, F., Iwawaki, S., Janakiramaiah, N., ... Yang, K.-S. (1990). International preferences in selecting mates: A study of 37 cultures. *Journal of Cross-Cultural Psychology, 21*(1), 5–47.

Butler, M. (1975). *Jane Austen and the war of ideas.* Clarendon Press.

Carroll, J. (2004). Human nature and literary meaning: A theoretical model illustrated with a critique of *Pride and Prejudice*. In J. Carroll, *Literary Darwinism: Evolution, human nature, and literature* (pp. 185–212). Routledge.

Carroll, J., Gottschall, J., Johnson, J. A., & Kruger, D. J. (2012). *Graphing Jane Austen: The evolutionary basis of literary meaning.* Palgrave Macmillan.

Chandler, A. (1975). "A pair of fine eyes": Jane Austen's treatment of sex. *Studies in the Novel, 7*(1), 88–103. https://doi.org/10.2307/29531706

Fiske, S. T., Cuddy, A. J. C., & Glick, P. (2007). Universal dimensions of social cognition: warmth and competence. *Trends in Cognitive Sciences*, 11(2), 77–83. https://doi.org/10.1016/j.tics.2006.11.005

Geher, G., & Kaufman, S. B. (2013). *Mating intelligence unleashed: The role of the mind in sex, dating, and love* (Kindle ed.). Oxford University Press.

Gilbert, S. M., & Gubar, S. (1979/2000). *The madwoman in the attic: The woman writer and the nineteenth-century literary imagination* (2nd, Kindle ed.). Yale University Press.

Gilligan, C. (1982). *In a different voice: Psychological theory and women's development*. Harvard University Press.

Hogan, P. C. (2003). *The mind and its stories: Narrative universals and human emotion*. Cambridge University Press.

Hrdy, S. B. (2009). *Mothers and others: The evolutionary origins of mutual understanding*. Belknap Press of Harvard University Press.

Johnson, C. L. (1988). *Jane Austen: Women, politics, and the novel*. University of Chicago Press.

Kruger, D. J., Fisher, M. L., Strout, S. L., Clark, S., Lewis, S., & Wehbe, M. (2014). Pride and prejudice or family and flirtation? Jane Austen's depiction of women's mating strategies. *Philosophy and Literature*, 38(1), A114–A128.

Kruger, D. J., Fisher, M. L., Strout, S. L., Wehbe, M., Lewis, S., & Clark, S. (2013). Variation in women's mating strategies depicted in the works and words of Jane Austen. *Journal of Social, Evolutionary, and Cultural Psychology*, 7(3), 197–210.

Le Faye, D. (Ed.). (1995). *Jane Austen's letters* (3rd ed.). Oxford University Press.

Lobb, A. (2013). The agony and the empathy: The ambivalence of empathy in feminist psychology. *Feminism & Psychology*, 23(4), 426–441.

McMaster, J. (1978). *Jane Austen on love*. University of Victoria.

Nettle, D. (2006). The evolution of personality variation in humans and other animals. *American Psychologist*, 61(6), 622–631. https://doi.org/10.1037/0003-066X.61.6.622

Nettle, D. (2007). *Personality: What makes you the way you are* (Kindle ed.). Oxford University Press.

Seabright, P. (2012). *The war of the sexes: How conflict and cooperation have shaped men and women from prehistory to the present* (Kindle ed.). Princeton University Press.

Shaffer, J. (1992). Not subordinate: Empowering women in the marriage plot—the novels of Frances Burney, Maria Edgeworth, and Jane Austen. *Criticism: A quarterly for literature and the arts*, 34(1), 51–73.

Stasio, M. J., & Duncan, K. (2007). An evolutionary approach to Jane Austen: Prehistoric preferences in *Pride and Prejudice*. *Studies in the Novel*, 39(2), 133–146. https://www.jstor.org/stable/20831911

Taylor, S. E., Klein, L. C., Lewis, B. P., Gruenewald, T. L., Gurung, R. A. R., & Updegraff, J. A. (2000). Biobehavioral responses to stress in females: Tend-and-befriend, not fight-or-flight. *Psychological Review*, 107(3), pg. 411–429.

Whissell, C. (1996). Mate selection in popular women's fiction. *Human Nature*, 7(4), 427–447. https://doi.org/10.1007/bf02732902

Wollstonecraft, M. (1792/2004). *A vindication of the rights of woman*. In J. Todd & M. Butler (Eds.), *The works of Mary Wollstonecraft* (Electronic ed., Vol. 5, pp. 63–267). InteLex Corp.

7

ELIZABETH BENNET

"A union ... to the advantage of both"[1]

Writing to her sister Cassandra in January 1813, Austen said of Elizabeth Bennet: "*I* think her as delightful a creature as ever appeared in print, & how I shall be able to tolerate those who do not like *her* at least, I do not know" (Le Faye, 1995, p. 201, emphasis in the original). Indeed, Elizabeth is very much liked and often thought "superior" to other romantic heroines (Jones, 2003, p. xiii), praised for her wit, vivacity, and independence. However, as the protagonist of Austen's most optimistic romance and the beneficiary of her most obviously satisfying marriage, Elizabeth bears the brunt of the feminist critique, as outlined in previous chapters. Gilbert and Gubar summarize feminist objections well when they say, "Dramatizing the necessity of female submission for female survival, Austen's story is especially flattering to male readers because it describes the taming not just of any woman but specifically of a rebellious, imaginative girl who is amorously mastered by a sensible man" (1979/2000, p. 154). Susan Fraiman, whose essay is often reprinted as an example of the feminist critique of *Pride and Prejudice*, takes an even more negative view, comparing Elizabeth to Lydia and claiming that the two sisters "differ more in style than substance ... their fates are similar" (1989, p. 178). The "coercion, capitulation, and lamentation" Fraiman claims underly those fates are consistent with the second-wave feminist assessment of love and heterosexuality (see Chapters 1–3).

My argument is that Elizabeth's story focuses on some of the most important aspects of the mate selection process, taking into account both sexual and social aspects of romantic relationships and demonstrating the transformative power of love for individuals and their social networks. While each of the three female characters discussed in Chapters 4-6 is linked to one man and highlights one criterion of mate choice, Elizabeth assesses several men, illustrating the multidimensional nature of the process. Like Lydia, she is instantly attracted to the handsome and likeable Wickham despite his relatively low income; but unlike Lydia, she realizes that Wickham is dishonest and unreliable. Like Charlotte, she will be poor without a husband, but she is repulsed by the pompous Mr. Collins despite the financial stability he offers to her and the rest of her family. Like Jane, she wants a kind man but is not impressed by Mr. Bingley's diffidence. She likes Colonel Fitzwilliam, who also likes her, but she does not pursue him because he openly discounts her as a serious candidate for a wife due to her lack of fortune. Finally, she is well aware of Mr. Darcy's wealth and status, and comes to appreciate his intelligence and manly appearance, but before she can accept him, she needs to be convinced of his kindness, loyalty, and his willingness to cooperate, not just to dominate.

The three couples discussed in the previous chapters are from the start well aligned in their priorities and attitudes: Lydia and Wickham are both impulsive, Charlotte and Collins instrumental, Jane and Bingley humble. Elizabeth and Darcy similarly match each other's intelligence and integrity but arrive at their relationship from opposite directions: He tries to suppress his feelings and rationalize mate choice so much that he offends the woman he professes to love; she trusts her feelings so much that she initially misses rational evidence against them. However, in the process they correct each other's weaknesses and enhance each other's strengths, achieving the kind of love which is enriching not only for them but also for those around them.

"Tolerable; but not handsome enough"[2]

Evolutionary psychologists often emphasize, perhaps overly so, the contrast in men's desire for female beauty and women's desire for men with resources and status. In *Pride and Prejudice*, Austen notes the importance of these mate selection criteria: Darcy excites marriage ambitions in Meryton because of his fortune, and he initially ignores Elizabeth because she does not meet his high standards of beauty. However, Austen also shows just how similar male and female priorities really are in long-term relationships. She starts by exploring how nuanced our assessments of physical attractiveness are.

We know that Elizabeth is not as beautiful as her older sister Jane, but neither is she considered "plain" like Charlotte Lucas. Beyond that, assessments of her attractiveness vary depending on the motivation of the characters who make them. According to Mrs. Bennet, "she is not half so handsome as Jane" (PP, p. 6), but Mrs. Bennet is upset about her husband's favouring Elizabeth, her least favourite daughter, over their other daughters. Mr. Collins finds her "equally next to Jane in birth and beauty" (PP, p. 70), but he is not very discerning. When Mr. Bingley and Sir William Lucas encourage Darcy to dance with Elizabeth, they both refer to her beauty, with Bingley calling her "very pretty" (PP, p. 13), but Bingley considers many women pretty and Sir William is known for his platitudes. Miss Bingley mocks the idea of Elizabeth as "a reputed beauty" and claims she "never could see any beauty in her" (PP, p. 258), but Miss Bingley is too jealous to be objective, and indeed, her jealousy proves her appreciation of Elizabeth's strength as a rival, since competitor denigration is one of the most common tactics in female intrasexual competition (Grant, 2020).

When Darcy first meets Elizabeth at the Meryton assembly, he famously declares: "She is tolerable; but not handsome enough to tempt *me*" (PP, p. 13:, emphasis in the original). In his assessment of Elizabeth's suitability as a dance partner, not to mention a marriage partner, Darcy reveals his alpha-male attitude: He believes that he deserves the best. Since Bingley has shown a strong preference for Jane, who in Darcy's own words is "the only handsome girl in the room" (PP, p. 13), Darcy declares that "there is not another woman in the room whom it would not be a punishment to me to stand up with" (PP, p. 13). His pickiness is obviously contrasted with Bingley who finds all girls pretty and accomplished and is happy to dance with anyone, starting with the plain Charlotte. But it is also an early indication of Darcy's long-term orientation. Human males, unlike other primates, are highly selective about their long-term mates due to an unusually high level of paternal investment (Ridley, 1993, p. 330). Socially imposed monogamy makes culturally successful men even more selective, as it constrains them to invest their considerable resources in a single woman and her children (Geary et al., 2004, p. 38). Importantly, Darcy's assessment of Elizabeth's physical beauty is affected by his sense of her social inferiority, to which I will come back later. He does not have a chance to attend to her individual qualities but makes a general judgment about the class of the party—"little beauty and no fashion" (PP, p. 18)—and dismisses Elizabeth as a member of that group.

However, as the psychologists Geher and Kaufman point out, our initial gut reactions to appearance "can be overwritten by mental and dispositional fitness indicators" (2013, p. 76). And so Mr. Darcy gradually, and almost in spite of himself, changes his opinion of Elizabeth:

> Mr. Darcy had at first scarcely allowed her to be pretty; he had looked at her without admiration at the ball; and when they next met, he looked at her only to criticise. But no sooner had he made it clear to himself and his friends that she hardly had a good feature in her face, than he began to find it was rendered uncommonly intelligent by the beautiful expression of her dark eyes. To this discovery succeeded some others equally mortifying. Though he had detected with a critical eye more than one failure of perfect symmetry in her form, he was forced to acknowledge her figure to be light and pleasing; and in spite of his asserting that her manners were not those of the fashionable world, he was caught by their easy playfulness. (PP, p. 24)

Towards the end of the end of the novel, Darcy declares Elizabeth to be "one of the handsomest women of [his] acquaintance" (PP, p. 259). His change of heart may seem like an unrealistic romantic cliché, but it is consistent with empirical findings that men's perception of women's beauty is profoundly influenced by mental, dispositional, and behavioural factors (Geher & Kaufman, 2013, p. 75).

This two-way relationship between physical beauty and non-physical traits is usually a prominent part of romantic narratives. Romantic heroines are rarely plain like Charlotte Brontë's Jane Eyre, but neither are they the most beautiful women in the room, like Jane Bennet. Their beauty is rarely the first or the most significant reason why the heroes are attracted to them. Some evolutionary literary analyses claim that this deprioritarization of beauty deviates from "standard models of sexual selection" (Vanderbeke, 2019, p. 94) or feminizes the heroes (Carroll et al., 2012), but in fact it testifies to two well-documented facts: First, that our perception of beauty is affected by the presence or absence of other personal qualities, as well as external circumstances (Geher & Kaufman, 2013, pp. 75–76); and second, that both men and women prioritize beauty more in short-term relationships, but in long-term contexts, they put more value on intelligence, kindness, and reliability (Buss et al., 1990).[3]

"His large estate in Derbyshire"[4]

Just as Austen shows the intricacies of male assessment of female beauty, she shows that a man's desirability is determined by a complex evaluation of not only his resources and status, but also a myriad of other factors. When Darcy first appears on the scene, he seems to have all the external characteristics women want: He is rich and powerful, not to mention handsome. Austen's presentation of him starts off as a cynical comment on the power of money to enhance a man's appearance, a fact confirmed by empirical studies (Townsend & Levy, 1990; Townsend & Wasserman, 1998).[5] But it also shows how quickly the attraction of both wealth and good looks fades if they are not accompanied by other socially desirable traits. We initially see Darcy through the eyes of the Meryton community, but since, as the first sentence of the novel indicates, it is a community on the mission to marry off their daughters, their assessment is very much concerned with his mate value:

> Mr. Darcy soon drew the attention of the room by his fine, tall person, handsome features, noble mien, and the report which was in general circulation within five minutes after his entrance, of his having ten thousand a year. The gentlemen pronounced him to be a fine figure of a man, the ladies declared he was much handsomer than Mr. Bingley, and he was looked at with great admiration for about half the evening, till his manners gave a disgust which turned the tide of his popularity; for he was discovered to be proud; to be above his company, and above being pleased; and not all his large estate in Derbyshire could then save him from having a most forbidding, disagreeable countenance, and being unworthy to be compared with his friend. (PP, p. 12, emphasis added)

It is worth noting that just as with Elizabeth's beauty, assessments of Darcy's appearance are also closely related to how people feel about him, as demonstrated not only by the passage quoted above. His devoted housekeeper, who thinks very highly of him in every respect, claims he is the most handsome man she knows (PP, p. 237). Meanwhile, Mrs. Gardiner, who is unsure how to reconcile the negative reports she had previously heard of Darcy with the politeness and generosity she has experienced at Pemberley, is also wavering in her judgement of his appearance: "He is not so handsome as Wickham; or, rather, he has not Wickham's countenance, for his features are perfectly good" (PP, p. 246). Again, these variable evaluations are consistent with empirical findings: Men who are rated as average looking by strangers can be rated as particularly handsome or particularly ugly by those who know them better (Geher & Kaufman, 2013, pp. 75–76).

"He likes to have his own way very well"[6]

One of the factors often mentioned as influencing women's ratings of men's desirability is their perceived social status. However, as discussed in Chapters 2 and 3, the appeal of dominance is somewhat problematic, both in life and in fiction. The anthropologist Christopher Boehm, whose research concerns the political arrangements of human and nonhuman primate groups, claims that we react negatively to individuals who try to exercise *undue* dominance: "Human groups have been vigilantly egalitarian for tens of thousands of years because we have inherited tendencies from our ape ancestor to resent being dominated and being placed in a disadvantageously unequal position" (2012, p. 69). A study of readers' responses to nineteenth-century novels also shows that the trait of social dominance is most important for antagonists, both male and female, who consistently look for mates with wealth and power (Carroll et al., 2012, pp. 73, 102). Protagonists, on the other hand, prioritize intrinsic qualities, such as intelligence, kindness, and reliability, and while they often have high social status, they derive it not from dominance (connected with aggression and arrogance) but from prestige (connected with competence, leadership, and cooperation) (Henrich & Gil-White, 2001).

The two routes to social status are also connected to two different types of pride: hubristic and authentic (Tracy & Robins, 2007). Hubristic pride is associated with narcissism and low levels of the personality traits Conscientiousness and Agreeableness. Authentic pride is linked to genuine self-esteem, confidence, as well as *high* Conscientiousness and Agreeableness. Women looking for long-term mates are sensitive to these distinctions and what they find most appealing is the combination of high status with a kind disposition (Jensen-Campbell et al., 1995). Austen seems to have been aware of this when she made the issue of pride so central to the relationship between Elizabeth and Darcy.

Darcy's fortune and status make him unquestionably attractive to those women who prioritize resources and power, and who are clearly positioned as antagonists: Miss Bingley and Lady Catherine (who wants Darcy to marry her daughter). Charlotte Lucas, too, judges Darcy on that basis when she warns Elizabeth "not to be a simpleton, and allow her fancy for Wickham to make her appear unpleasant in the eyes of a man ten times his consequence" (PP, p. 89). She also defends Darcy's sense of superiority: "He has a *right* to be proud" (PP, p. 21). Elizabeth recognizes Darcy's status but is not prepared to compromise her own dignity and self-respect: "I could easily forgive *his* pride, if he had not mortified *mine*" (PP, p. 21, emphasis in the original). Others also feel offended by Darcy and are not so willing to overlook his apparent arrogance and bad manners. Even Mrs. Bennet, so determined to find rich sons-in-law, turns against him because she attributes Darcy's behaviour at the Meryton assembly to misguided self-importance: "He is eat up with pride" (PP, p. 20).

Darcy's reluctance to socialize also stands in stark contrast to Bingley's excellent social skills. Bingley may not be as handsome as Darcy, and he is definitely not as rich, but he wins the popularity contest because of his likeable personality and his willingness to participate in social activities:

> Mr. Bingley had soon made himself acquainted with all the principal people in the room; he was lively and unreserved, danced every dance ... What a contrast between him and his friend! Mr. Darcy danced only once with Mrs. Hurst and once with Miss Bingley, declined being introduced to any other lady, and spent the rest of the evening in walking about the room, speaking occasionally to one of his own party. His character was decided. He was the proudest, most disagreeable man in the world, and everybody hoped that he would never come there again. (PP, pp. 12–13)

Of course, this harsh reaction is partly motivated by the fact that Darcy does not seem to be interested in marrying any of the Meryton young ladies, but it is also consistent with evolutionary theories regarding the social organization of our species. We dislike "big-shot" behaviour and are quick to punish it, usually by expulsion from the group (Boehm, 2012). We also look for empathy and prosociality in those who aspire to high status (Geher & Kaufman, 2013, p. 33). Darcy's refusal to participate in social rituals, such as small talk and dancing, is interpreted as a sign not only of bad manners but also of his lack of generosity, his desire to assert his social superiority, and his unwillingness to cooperate.

This assessment is presented as the view of the Meryton community, but Elizabeth shares these feelings. Her initial rejection of Darcy revolves around the issue of pride—his excessive pride and her wounded pride. But soon she has more reasons to discount Darcy as a potential mate. Not only does his personality pale in comparison with Bingley's and Wickham's, but also Wickham's allegations that Darcy unfairly deprived him of an inheritance makes Darcy appear dishonourable, selfish, and spiteful—a classic example of undue dominance. When Elizabeth rejects Darcy's first proposal, she objects equally to Darcy's perceived attitude and to his actions towards Wickham: "You have reduced him to his present state of poverty … and yet you can treat the mention of his misfortunes with contempt and ridicule" (PP, p. 187). To Elizabeth, Darcy's alleged mistreatment of Wickham violates the criteria of *social rationality* which is an integral part of our decision-making process crucial for maintaining social cooperation. As Gerd Gigerenzer explains, social rationality includes

> transparency (i.e., making decisions that are understandable and predictable by the group with which one associates), fairness (i.e., making decisions that do not violate the expectations between people of equal social standing), and accountability (i.e., making decisions that can be justified and defended). (2001, p. 48)

Elizabeth is even more upset about Darcy's involvement in separating Jane and Bingley. She describes it as "unjust and ungenerous" (PP, p. 186). Darcy's ruining "the happiness of a most beloved sister" (PP, p. 186) obviously has a much more personal dimension than ruining Wickham's prospects, but Elizabeth interprets it as yet another example of Darcy's undue dominance, of his desire to "impose upon others" (PP, p. 187). In fact, based on Elizabeth's observations, Darcy holds a dominant position in all his relationships. Bingley is influenced by Darcy's opinion in all serious matters from choosing a house to relinquishing a woman he loves. Miss Bingley constantly flatters Darcy and is described as being "incapable of disappointing [him] in anything" (PP, p. 55). His sister Georgiana would not dare question or contradict him, and Colonel Fitzwilliam is "at [Darcy's] disposal", admitting that Darcy "likes to have his own way very well" (PP, p. 179). Even Mr. Bennet says of Darcy: "He is the kind of man, indeed, to whom I should never dare refuse anything" (PP, p. 356). Based on all these cues, Elizabeth is convinced that Darcy would also try to unduly control his wife, as she remarks to Colonel Fitzwilliam: "I imagine your cousin brought you down with him chiefly for the sake of having someone at his disposal. I wonder he does not marry, to secure a lasting convenience of that kind. But, perhaps, his sister does as well for the present, and, as she is under his sole care, he may do what he likes with her" (PP, p. 180).

"The inferiority of her connections"[7]

In her analysis of Mr. Rochester's relationship with Jane Eyre, Nancy Easterlin suggests that a man's desire for control over others can interfere with his search for a mate with valuable personal attributes, such as kindness, intelligence, or sense of humour (2013,

p. 395). This seems to be precisely the case with Mr. Darcy. Because of his pride in his social superiority and his determination to maintain it, Darcy initially rejects Elizabeth as a dance partner, and when he starts appreciating her intelligence and vitality, he does not welcome those feelings and tries to suppress them. While Elizabeth is staying at Netherfield, we find out that "Darcy had never been so bewitched by any woman as he was by her. He really believed, that were it not for the inferiority of her connections, he should be in some danger" (PP, p. 51).

At the beginning of the novel, Darcy appears as snobbish and superficial as Caroline Bingley. While Mr. Bingley maintains that having "low connections" does not make the Bennet sisters "one jot less agreeable" (PP, pp. 36–37), his own sister and his friend agree that "it must very materially lessen their chance of marrying men of any consideration in the world" (PP, p. 37). This assessment of Elizabeth's position in the marriage market is remarkably similar to Mr. Collins's who warns her that her lack of fortune "will in all likelihood undo the effects of [her] loveliness and amiable qualifications" (PP, p. 106). And as we soon find out, Darcy is not the only man to let Elizabeth's good qualities be outweighed by her circumstances. Wickham, who is clearly attracted to Elizabeth, soon turns his attention to Miss King and her 10,000 pounds. Similarly, Col. Fitzwilliam, a man with much more integrity than Wickham, alludes to his need for a rich bride, despite his appreciation of Elizabeth's "amiable qualifications". Clearly, in many social environments, men too must pay attention to women's resources—and several of Austen's young men (Wickham, Willoughby, Frank Churchill) are in this predicament so often ascribed exclusively to women. Darcy does not need a wealthy wife, but he is so concerned about Elizabeth's social inferiority that he considers his love for her inappropriate. In his first proposal, he even refers to a sense of "degradation" (PP, p. 185). He frames his suit in terms of a struggle between "judgement" and "inclination" but places too much weight on the former without yet understanding that the latter may be just as valuable a guide for choosing a wife.

Mr. Darcy's first proposal is in some respects very similar to Mr. Collins's. Both men focus on their own needs and desires and completely fail to recognize Elizabeth's individual consciousness. It is not that either of them misinterprets the signs—they simply do not bother to read them, as both are too sure of their own eligibility and convinced that women simply wait *to be chosen*.[8] Darcy certainly has "no doubt of a favourable answer" and when Elizabeth rejects him, he shows "no less resentment than surprise" (PP, pp. 185–186). But unlike Mr. Collins, Darcy does not deny Elizabeth the authority to make her own choices, and instead of dismissing her refusal, he tries to understand her position.

Both men also invoke their sense of kin loyalty. Collins claims he proposes because of it; Darcy feels he is violating it. But as I argue in Chapter 5, Collins's professed family loyalty is more an expression of his laziness. In contrast, Darcy proves his capacity for loyalty with his brotherly love for Georgiana and strong friendship with Bingley. This will eventually count in Darcy's favour because it is a sign of his future commitment to his wife and children, and women are very sensitive to such signals and find them attractive (Buss, 2003, pp. 102–106; Geher & Kaufman, 2013, p. 86). In her rejection of Darcy, Elizabeth is also guided by loyalty to her kin, claiming that it is even more important than her own feelings for Darcy: "Had not my feelings decided against you—had they been indifferent, or had they even been favourable, do you think that any consideration would tempt me to accept the man who has been the means of ruining, perhaps for ever, the happiness of a most beloved sister?" (PP, p. 186). From an evolutionary point of view, loyalty to kin is a very important consideration, one of the strongest motivational forces (Carroll, 2004). Austen acknowledges its importance but not unconditionally. Elizabeth prioritizes her personal dignity over her family's security when she rejects first Collins and then Darcy; Darcy proposes to Elizabeth first with a feeling that he diminishes his family's standing and later in spite of his aunt's strong disapproval. Similarly, Fanny Price refuses to marry Henry Crawford despite her uncle's pressure, while Anne Elliot, Edward Ferrars, and Henry Tilney marry against their families' wishes.

"It saved her from something very like regret"[9]

Darcy has many of the characteristics women look for in men. He certainly scores very high for material resources and social status, he is also very intelligent, and has a handsome, masculine appearance. For some women, like Miss Bingley and Charlotte Lucas, these credentials are more than enough. But on the basis of the information Elizabeth has up to the point of his first proposal, Darcy is crucially lacking kindness and warmth. Cross-cultural research shows that when looking for a long-term mate, women rate kind and understanding men more highly than those who have the potential to acquire resources and status but lack those personality traits (Buss, 1989). There is a good evolutionary reason for this. From a woman's point of view, it is not enough that a man has resources—he has to be willing to invest those resources in her and her children for a relatively long period of time. Moreover, long-term relationships are just as much about sharing emotional resources. We look for companionship and intimacy, both of which are highly dependent on the empathy, Agreeableness, and emotional generosity of our partners.

Elizabeth's mating strategy is certainly not about maximizing material resources or social status. She unequivocally rejects two financially advantageous proposals, does not discount Wickham as a potential partner despite his relatively poor financial position, and initially favours Colonel Fitzwilliam over his much richer cousin. It is not that she has no consideration for her own and her family's financial situation, or that she is so idealistic that she does not pay *any* attention to the fortunes of her suitors. In a conversation with her aunt Gardiner, she admits that Wickham would be an "imprudent" choice, and that for this reason, she will be cautious (PP, pp. 142–143). Also, while staying at Netherfield, she abandons her book to attend to a conversation about Darcy's estate (PP, p. 38), and later in the novel, the first-hand experience of that estate contributes to her changing opinion of Darcy. Elizabeth admits to being impressed with its beauty and elegance: "At that moment she felt that to be mistress of Pemberley might be something!", and she later jokes that it was the moment when she started falling in love with its owner (PP, pp. 235, 353). However, Pemberley alone is not enough to convince her that Darcy might be a suitable husband—the recollection of his disdain for her family and the possibility that as his wife she would be forced to cut ties with them "save[s] her from something very like regret" (PP, p. 236).

Throughout the story, Elizabeth demonstrates that she values internal qualities of potential partners more than the external ones—but the latter are much more difficult to assess than the former. Her determination not to compromise on them testifies to her superior mating intelligence and her confidence in her own value as a long-term partner; as William Flesch argues, Elizabeth's valuing of altruism is a costly, and therefore an honest, signal of high mate value (2007, pp. 64–65). Lucy Steele and Isabella Thorpe also claim to value their chosen men for their good characters but reveal themselves to be dishonest in this signalling as soon as the men turn out to be not as rich as expected. As I explained in Chapter 3, the ability to distinguish between honest and dishonest signallers, to *read* other people's motivations and intentions is essential to all humans, but in the mating domain, it is especially important for women because of the higher biological and cultural costs of making a wrong choice. Indeed, Catherine Salmon likens female mate choice adaptations to detective work and points out that in romantic fiction, as in life, a great deal of effort is expanded in determining the hero's qualities and feelings (2012, pp. 157–158).

"Ill-qualified to recommend [himself] to strangers"[10]

Darcy is particularly hard to read, not only because he is naturally introverted but also because he actively hides his feelings for Elizabeth. Towards the end of her stay at Netherfield, "he wisely resolved to be particularly careful that no sign of admiration should now escape him" (PP, p. 59). And Elizabeth is not the only one who cannot accurately interpret his behaviour. Jane is oblivious to Darcy's admiration of Elizabeth, and Charlotte, who notices that he often looks at Elizabeth, cannot decipher his motives: "She watched him whenever they were at Rosings, and whenever he came to Hunsford; but without much success" (PP, p. 176). Miss Bingley, however, who knows Darcy much better and who watches him very closely for her own reasons, very quickly realizes his attraction to—and his reservations about—Elizabeth.

Nina Auerbach calls Darcy "a muddled contradiction" because of the contrasting impressions he makes on people, and because of the seeming inconsistency between his own description of his character and his actions (1976, p. 16). For example, Mrs. Gardiner remembers Darcy "spoken of as a very proud, ill-natured boy" (PP, p. 141), but when she meets him at Pemberley, she comments that "he is perfectly well behaved, polite, and unassuming" (PP, p. 246); she agrees with Darcy's housekeeper that although "some people call him proud" (PP, p.239), she has not seen any evidence of it. Like perceptions of people's appearance, our perceptions of their characters are not entirely objective and may be affected by a number of biases. One such bias in social cognition, called the *fundamental attribution error*, refers to our tendency to interpret other people's actions as resulting more from internal causes, such as people's personality or intelligence level, than from external, situational factors (when it comes to our own behaviour, we tend to do the opposite).[11] Thus, the people of Meryton feel offended by Darcy's reserve, attributing it solely to his snobbery, but his behaviour results just as much from the fact that he does not like dancing and feels uncomfortable when interacting with complete strangers. When Bingley encourages him to dance, Darcy says "You know how I detest it, unless I am particularly acquainted with my partner" (PP, p. 13). In fact, it is not just at the Meryton public hall that he refuses to dance, he does so also at St. James's Royal Palace (PP, p. 26).

Another common bias concerns our conviction that other people are like us, that they have similar thoughts, feelings, and opinions. That is one reason why Elizabeth is so shocked about Charlotte's calm acceptance and evident enjoyment of her marriage. Similarly, as an extravert, Elizabeth finds it hard to relate to Darcy's discomfort in social situations. She cannot understand why "a man of sense and education, and who has lived in the world, is ill qualified to recommend himself to strangers" (PP, p. 171). But Darcy defends himself by saying: "I certainly have not the talent which some people possess … of conversing easily with those I have never seen before. I cannot catch their tone of conversation, or appear interested in their concerns, as I often see done" (PP, p. 171). That is, he does not have the instant charm of Wickham and other cads. Elizabeth suggests that he should practice those skills more, and Colonel Fitzwilliam, another sociable person, believes that Darcy simply "will not give himself the trouble" (PP, p. 171). He is partially right: Darcy's haughtiness is a big factor in his behaviour and, as Lisa Zunshine (2022) argues, socially dominant individuals simply do not need to be very attentive to others. However, while Darcy is reserved among strangers, with "his intimate acquaintances … he is remarkably agreeable" (PP, p. 20). His brotherly devotion and his friendship with Bingley testify to that. Colonel Fitzwilliam also corroborates it (PP, p. 176), and Darcy's reception of Elizabeth and her relatives at Pemberley is a further proof. Unfortunately, Elizabeth (like the reader) does not get much evidence of Darcy's affability until much later in the novel (although the reader does at least know quite early on that Darcy takes notice of Elizabeth because he admires her, not because he is trying to mock her). Instead, she receives numerous cues of his pride and dominance. So, while Elizabeth's extraversion helps Darcy discover her qualities, Elizabeth has a much harder job. Because of Darcy's introversion, people have to exert much more effort if they want to know him better, and for a long time, Elizabeth has no reason to do so because "she like[s] him too little to care" (PP, p. 50).

"Till this moment I never knew myself"[12]

The visits to Rosings go some way towards adjusting Elizabeth's and our assessment of Darcy's pride: By juxtaposing him with the pomposity and condescension of Lady Catherine, Austen is making a distinction similar to that made by modern psychologists between authentic and hubristic pride. But it is Darcy's long letter after his failed proposal that makes Elizabeth realize for the first time that with regard to Wickham and Darcy "she had been blind, partial, prejudiced, absurd … Pleased with the preference of one, and offended by the neglect of the other … [she has] driven reason away, where either were concerned" (PP, pp. 201–202). While Darcy tried to suppress his feelings, she trusted hers too much. This unique moment of self-recognition has been criticized by many feminists as a narrative renunciation of Elizabeth's intelligence and authority (Fraiman, 1989; Newton, 1981, p. 68). But more recent interpretations appreciate Austen's emphasis on self-knowledge as the basis for her heroines' happy endings (Weisser, 2013, p. 28; see also Deresiewicz, 2011). Indeed, for Austen, love is as much about knowing the other person as it is about knowing yourself, and she often pairs her heroines with men who help them achieve better self-knowledge. Elizabeth's reaction to Darcy's letter and her subsequent reappraisal of her feelings is also a good illustration of Robert Solomon's claim that "the most obvious source of freedom and choice regarding our emotions is to be found in reflection, our thoughts about and our taking responsibility for our emotions" (2003, p. 208). Thus, Austen heroines are not swept off their feet by uncontrolled passion (it happens only to Marianne) but closely examine their feelings and cultivate those that *make sense*. This is different from manipulative calculations of Miss Bingley or Lucy Steele; this is emotional intelligence.

Darcy's letter makes Elizabeth see his integrity; crucially, it also provides evidence of Darcy's caring attitude towards his family and friends. His kindness is later confirmed by the glowing testimony of his housekeeper, then by his reception of Elizabeth and the

Gardiners at Pemberley, and finally by his intervention in Lydia's elopement. The praise of the housekeeper is a significant proof of the extent of Darcy's prosociality and benevolence: "He is the best landlord, and the best master ... that ever lived; not like the wild young men nowadays, who think of nothing but themselves" (PP, p. 239). Mrs. Gardiner's friends in Lambton validate this by saying that "he was a liberal man, and did much good among the poor" (PP, p. 252). The housekeeper also notes Darcy's love for Georgiana: "Whatever can give his sister any pleasure is sure to be done in a moment. There is nothing he would not do for her" (PP, p. 239). If Elizabeth thought earlier that Darcy's control of his sister is a sure sign of how he would treat a wife, this testimonial, soon after confirmed by Georgiana herself and by Elizabeth's first-hand experience of Darcy's relationship with his sister, forces her to reconsider her ideas of what it would be like to be Mrs. Darcy (in addition to being the mistress of Pemberley): "She thought of his regard with a deeper sentiment of gratitude than it had ever raised before; she remembered its warmth, and softened its impropriety of expression" (PP, p. 240).

When Darcy finds Elizabeth at Pemberley, he is not only respectful and welcoming to her but also to her relatives, which surprises them all: "Never had he spoken with such gentleness as on this unexpected meeting" (PP, p. 242). Mr. Gardiner is at first suspicious, wondering if Darcy's civility may be "whimsical" (PP, p. 246), but an introduction to Georgiana and invitations to Pemberley soon convince him otherwise. Stasio and Duncan argue that because of the importance of manners in Austen's world, Darcy "must learn to perform—improve his manners" (2007, p. 142). But given Austen's dislike of performers and pretenders (see Chapter 4), I think Austen's argument is more substantial: She makes Darcy face his own prejudice, learn the value of egalitarianism, and show his capacity for empathy.

Darcy's help in Lydia's affair not only proves that he has learned those lessons but also meets the test of social rationality discussed above. He intervenes because he feels guilty that, for reasons of his own family pride, he did not reveal Wickham's character and consequently exposed other families to his scheming (PP, pp. 304–305). Also, Georgiana's near-elopement has made it possible for Darcy to realize that this sort of thing can happen even in the most respectable family. It is possible that without that precedent, Darcy would have considered Lydia's elopement as yet another example of the Bennets' social and moral inferiority. His own family crisis increased his ability to empathize with Elizabeth's and her family's distress. Above all, Darcy's intervention is "the greatest and most intimate service" to Elizabeth and a dramatic display of his commitment to her: "He demonstrates that his preference for her outweighs even the disgrace of a marital association with a sluttish sister married to a reprobate of inferior birth" (Carroll, 2004, p. 208). In other words, he is prepared to risk his own welfare and status to help Elizabeth and gain her trust and respect. Such a reordering of life priorities is not just a romantic fantasy but one of the hallmarks of romantic love identified by modern psychological research (De Munck et al., 2016).

"The liveliness of [her] mind"[13]

But if Darcy's most generous intervention proves his mate value, what does it say about Elizabeth? How should we interpret the fact that she, like so many damsels in distress, needs to be rescued by her knight in shining armour? Does it prove her passivity and prompt her submission? This is how many feminists interpret Elizabeth's marriage: She submits to the benevolent but absolute authority of Darcy (Gilbert & Gubar, 1979/2000, p. 154) and "dwindles" into a wife (Newton, 1981, p. 9). According to Gilbert and Gubar's emblematic analysis, this argument applies to other Austen heroines: Since women are "acceptable to men only when they inhabit the glass coffin of silence, stillness, secondariness" (1979/2000, p. 162), the heroines go through a process of maturation in the course of which they "learn the necessity of curbing their tongues" and "must be initiated into a secondary role of service and silence" (1979/2000, p. 160). However, like several critics before me (Anderson, 2018; Hardy, 1984; Tauchert, 2005), I propose a dramatically different reading. All of Austen's heroines, even those who are relatively subdued, like Fanny Price, Elinor Dashwood, or Anne Elliot, speak up and take action when it really matters (see Chapter 6). Perhaps more than any of them, Elizabeth is anything but silent and still; and it is her speech, her vitality, her lack of artifice, and her independence of mind that draw Darcy to her. Hence, I argue, together with J. P. Hardy, that "the very thing that attracts Darcy to Elizabeth is what gives the lie to the suggestion that she needs to abandon her individual 'consciousness' in order to find happiness with him" (1984, p. 56). The strength of her individuality, and the honesty with which she reveals it are what makes her different from the other two candidates for Darcy's wife, Miss Bingley and Miss de Bourgh. Moreover, her physical and mental vitality not only make her an iconic romantic heroine but are also important in evolutionary terms.

Everything about Elizabeth challenges the ideal of a "still and silent" lady; neither her body nor her mind is passive. Austen shows Elizabeth's physical energy when she has her walk three miles in bad weather, "crossing field after field at a quick pace, jumping over stiles and springing over puddles", so that she arrives in Netherfield "with weary ankles, dirty stockings, and a face glowing with the warmth of exercise" (PP, p. 33). Caroline Bingley opines that Elizabeth's solitary walk from Longbourn to Netherfield is a sign of "an abominable sort of conceited independence, a most country-town indifference to decorum" (PP, p. 36). And she is right, in a sense, because the walk shows Elizabeth's refusal to be constrained, be it by lack of transportation, or social norms. The walk makes a more positive impression on the gentlemen: To Bingley, it makes Elizabeth look "remarkably well", and Darcy finds her eyes "brightened by the exercise" (PP, p. 36). At this point, Darcy agrees with Miss Bingley that he would not want his own sister to "make such an exhibition" (PP, p. 36), but he soon has an opportunity to compare Elizabeth's stamina with Miss Bingley's feeble attempt at exercise and a more calculated "exhibition": Walking around the room to show off her figure (PP, p. 55). Also, despite Darcy's attention to social status and the wishes of his family, he never seems to consider Miss de Bourgh as a possible mate, very likely because she is "pale and sickly" (PP, p. 159). Clearly, Elizabeth's liveliness and vigour are sexually appealing, not least because they make her a viable reproductive partner (I will come back to this idea in Chapter 12).[14]

Elizabeth's physical energy is matched by her mental agility. Critics disagree about how much Elizabeth's conversation and manner is different from the expectations of the time (Parrill, 2002, p. 64), but it is clear that Elizabeth is markedly different from all the other women in the novel. She faces some criticism for her irreverence and non-conformity. Lady Catherine, for example, is shocked at Elizabeth's confidence: "Upon my word … you give your opinion very decidedly for so young a person" (PP, p. 162). Even Mrs. Bennet, not known for her tact or restraint, chastises Elizabeth when she teases Bingley: "Lizzy … remember where you are, and do not run on in the wild manner that you are suffered to do at home'" (PP, p. 42). On the other hand, however, Lydia laughs at Elizabeth's "formality and discretion" (PP, p. 212). But as all this criticism is voiced by characters we do not like or respect, we can safely assume that it is not shared by the author, who highlights the importance of Elizabeth's speaking in several ways.

If the romantic journey is largely about the heroine being heard, as a few critics have argued (McAllister, 2022), then Elizabeth finds an attentive listener very early on. As soon as Darcy notices the sparkle in Elizabeth's dark eyes, he begins to pay attention to her speech: "He began to wish to know more of her, and as a step towards conversing with her himself, attended to her conversation with others" (PP, p. 24). Meanwhile, any such effort on his part in relation to Miss de Bourgh would be futile as she hardly says a word—her mental apathy seems to match her physical lethargy. Miss Bingley, on the other hand, talks a lot but is quite often ignored by Darcy who realizes the vacuity of her remarks. During one evening at Netherfield, she "could not win him ... to any conversation" (PP, p. 54), and soon after, in her desperate attempt to flatter Darcy, she admits that she is unable to match his intellect: "Tease calmness of manner and presence of mind! No, no—I feel he may defy us there" (PP, p. 56). Unlike Miss Bingley, Elizabeth is not intimidated by Darcy's intelligence, and he falls in love with her because of "the liveliness of [her] mind" (PP, p. 359). Carroll and his colleagues note that this is true of Austen's other male protagonists who select their wives "on the basis of their admiration and respect for qualities of character and mind" (2012, p. 103). Importantly, such appreciation is not a romantic fantasy: Across cultures, for many men, the intelligence of a prospective partner is as important as, or more important than, her physical beauty (Buss et al., 1990).

Feminists acknowledge the allure of Elizabeth's liveliness and wit but argue that she "renounces all her pertness the instant she agrees to marry [Darcy]" (Armstrong, 1987, p. 59). But the evidence for this claim is weak. Admittedly, right after Darcy's second proposal, rather than making a sharp comment, Elizabeth "checked herself ... [and] remembered that he had yet to learn to be laughed at, and it was rather too early to begin" (PP, p. 351). But this is only momentary, because the very next time they see each other, she tells Darcy: "It belongs to me to find occasions for teasing and quarrelling with you as often as may be; and I shall begin directly" (PP, p. 360). And her temporary restraint is not different from the beginning of the book: When Mr. Bingley is making fun of Darcy at Netherfield, "Elizabeth thought she could perceive that he was rather offended, and therefore checked her laugh" (PP, p. 49). This proves her emotional intelligence and is favourably contrasted with Miss Bingley's lack of such awareness when she embarrasses Darcy and Georgiana at Pemberley by alluding to Wickham. In fact, it is not Elizabeth's submissiveness but the *boldness* of her speech that attracts Darcy: "You were sick of civility, of deference, of officious attention. You were disgusted with the women who were always speaking, and looking, and thinking for your approbation alone. I roused, and interested you, because I was so unlike them" (PP, p. 359). Moreover, her unrestrained speech becomes a model for other women. Georgiana, for whom Darcy "had always inspired ... a respect which almost overcame her affection, ...at first often listened with an astonishment bordering on alarm at [Elizabeth's] lively, sportive, manner of talking to her brother", but she soon realizes that a woman does not have to be silent and submissive, that she "may take liberties with her husband" (PP, p. 366). It is "by Elizabeth's instructions" that "her mind received knowledge which had never before fallen in her way" (PP, pp. 366).

Most importantly, it is Elizabeth's speech that prompts Darcy's transformation:

> Your reproof, so well applied, I shall never forget: 'had you behaved in a more gentlemanlike manner.' Those were your words. You know not, you can scarcely conceive, how they have tortured me;—though it was some time, I confess, before I was reasonable enough to allow their justice. (PP, p. 347)

Until Elizabeth speaks up, Darcy is quite happy with his character and behaviour (PP, p. 349), but as Hardy argues, "[Elizabeth's] words prevent Darcy from taking refuge in arrogance and force him to engage with real questions about himself" (1984, p. 43). Since childhood, Darcy was "allowed, encouraged, almost taught ... to be selfish and overbearing; to care for none beyond [his] own family circle ... to think meanly of [others'] sense and worth compared with [his] own", but Elizabeth teaches him a lesson about other people's worth. She also makes him reconsider his idea of gender relations: "You showed me how insufficient were all my pretensions to please a woman worthy of being pleased" (PP, p. 349). When he first proposes to Elizabeth, Darcy assumes Elizabeth's complete dependence on him, but through this declaration he acknowledges their interdependence: His moral growth would not have occurred without her. And although earlier in the novel Elizabeth chastised herself for her poor judgement of him, through this declaration, Darcy confirms her authority. Finally, Elizabeth shows Darcy and everyone else the importance of social cooperation by the way she manages a reconciliation with Miss Bingley and Lady Catherine.

Judith Lowder Newton claims that "most readers of *Pride and Prejudice* find the end less satisfactory than the beginning" (1981, p. 84). This is certainly the case with many feminists who see Elizabeth's marriage as a renunciation of her control and relinquishment of her subjectivity, even "humiliation" (Fraiman, 1989). However, some critics recognize the merits of Austen's vision of marriage as a "relationship fostering personal moral growth, self-discovery, and the mutual benefit of individuals, families, and the wider community" (Bromberg, 1993, p. 126; see also Brown, 1979; Tauchert, 2005). The unprecedented and enduring popularity of *Pride and Prejudice* is a strong clue that "ordinary" readers are more likely to agree with the latter interpretation, and so am I. As I argue elsewhere about Emma and Mr. Knightley, Austen's marriages never limit the heroine but are in every way enriching for both her and her partner (Grant & Kruger, 2023). Elizabeth and Austen's other heroines are neither passive during the mate selection process, nor submissive to the men they choose, nor for that matter, to the families or social standards which try to influence their decisions. Instead, these women make active choices which promise marital happiness without compromising their subjectivity. They choose men who value their individuality and autonomy, and who acknowledge their equal status within the relationship. That, in turn, has social consequences not only within their fictive worlds but also in the way it inspires the readers to imagine the possibilities for their real lives.

Notes

1 PP, p. 295.
2 PP, p. 13.
3 For example, as the closing time at bars draws near, people's standards of beauty tend to become more relaxed (Rosenthal & Ryan, 2022).

4 PP, p. 12.
5 As mentioned in Chapter 5, the same men were rated as more handsome when dressed in professional-looking clothes, as opposed to a Burger King uniform.
6 PP, p. 179.
7 PP, p. 51.
8 Alice Chandler even goes as far as to suggest that Darcy's proposal represents "verbal rape" (Chandler, 1975, p. 98).
9 PP, p. 236.
10 PP, p. 171.
11 For a perceptive discussion of this cognitive bias in relation to Austen's *Persuasion*, see Hogan (2018).
12 PP, p. 202.
13 PP, p. 359.
14 Anne de Bourgh's weak constitution has been noted by many critics before me (Fraiman, 1989; Stasio & Duncan, 2007; Wiltshire, 1992) and so has the sexual attraction of Elizabeth's physicality (Chandler, 1975; Saunders, 2014). An evolutionary approach explains why the weakness of the former is unattractive despite its seeming compliance with the cultural ideal of the time.

References

Anderson, K. (2018). *Jane Austen's women: An introduction*. State University of New York Press.
Armstrong, N. (1987). *Desire and domestic fiction: A political history of the novel*. Oxford University Press.
Auerbach, N. (1976). Austen and Alcott on matriarchy: New women or new wives? *Novel, 10,* 6–26.
Austen, J. (1813/2003). *Pride and prejudice*. Penguin.
Boehm, C. (2012). *Moral origins: The evolution of virtue, altruism, and shame* (Kindle ed.). Basic Books.
Bromberg, P. (1993). Teaching about the marriage plot. In M. McClintock Folsom (Ed.), *Approaches to teaching Austen's Pride and Prejudice* (pp. 126–133). Modern Language Association of America.
Brown, J. P. (1979). *Jane Austen's novels: Social change and literary form*. Harvard University Press.
Buss, D. M. (1989). Sex differences in human mate preferences: Evolutionary hypotheses tested in 37 cultures. *Behavioral and Brain Sciences, 12*(01), 1–14. https://doi.org/10.1017/S0140525X00023992
Buss, D. M. (2003). *The evolution of desire: Strategies of human mating* (Rev., Kindle ed.). Basic Books.
Buss, D. M., Abbott, M., Angleitner, A., Asherian, A., Biaggio, A., Blanco-Villasenor, A., Bruchon-Schweitzer, M., Ch'U, H.-Y., Czapinski, J., Deraad, B., Ekehammar, B., Lohamy, N., Fioravanti, M., Georgas, J., Gjerde, P., Guttman, R., Hazan, F., Iwawaki, S., Janakiramaiah, N., ... Yang, K.-S. (1990). International preferences in selecting mates: A study of 37 cultures. *Journal of Cross-Cultural Psychology, 21*(1), 5–47.
Carroll, J. (2004). Human nature and literary meaning: A theoretical model illustrated with a critique of *Pride and Prejudice*. In J. Carroll, *Literary Darwinism: Evolution, human nature, and literature* (pp. 185–212). Routledge.
Carroll, J., Gottschall, J., Johnson, J. A., & Kruger, D. J. (2012). *Graphing Jane Austen: The evolutionary basis of literary meaning*. Palgrave Macmillan.
Chandler, A. (1975). "A pair of fine eyes": Jane Austen's treatment of sex. *Studies in the Novel, 7*(1), 88–103. https://www.jstor.org/stable/29531706
De Munck, V., Korotayev, A., & McGreevey, J. (2016). Romantic love and family organization. *Evolutionary Psychology, 14*(4). https://doi.org/10.1177/1474704916674211
Deresiewicz, W. (2011). *A Jane Austen education: How six novels taught me about love, friendship, and the things that really matter*. Penguin Press.
Easterlin, N. (2013). From reproductive resource to autonomous individuality? Charlotte Brontë's Jane Eyre. In M. L. Fisher, Garcia, J. R., & Chang, R. S. (Eds.), *Evolution's empress: Darwinian perspectives on the nature of women* (pp. 390–405). Oxford University Press.
Flesch, W. (2007). *Comeuppance: Costly signaling, altruistic punishment, and other biological components of fiction*. Harvard University Press.
Fraiman, S. (1989). The humiliation of Elizabeth Bennet. In P. Yeager & B. Kowaleski-Wallace (Eds.), *Refiguring the father: New feminist readings of patriarchy* (pp. 168–187). Southern Illinois University Press.

Geary, D. C., Vigil, J., & Byrd-Craven, J. (2004). Evolution of human mate choice. *The Journal of Sex Research*, *41*(1), 27–42. https://doi.org/10.1080/00224490409552211

Geher, G., & Kaufman, S. B. (2013). *Mating intelligence unleashed: The role of the mind in sex, dating, and love* (Kindle ed.). Oxford University Press.

Gigerenzer, G. (2001). The adaptive toolbox. In G. Gigerenzer & R. Selten (Eds.), *Bounded rationality: The adaptive toolbox* (pp. 37–50). MIT Press.

Gilbert, S. M., & Gubar, S. (1979/2000). *The madwoman in the attic: The woman writer and the nineteenth-century literary imagination* (2nd, Kindle ed.). Yale University Press.

Grant, A. (2020). "Sneering civility": Female intrasexual competition for mates in Jane Austen's novels. *EvoS Journal: The Journal of the Evolutionary Studies Consortium*, *11*(1), 15–33. https://doi.org/10.59077/QSHP9625

Grant, A., & Kruger, D. J. (2023). "Such an alternative as this had not occurred to her": The transformation of Jane Austen's Emma as understood from an evolutionary perspective. *Evolutionary Behavioral Sciences*, *17*(1), 43–60. https://psycnet.apa.org/doi/10.1037/ebs0000271

Hardy, J. P. (1984). *Jane Austen's heroines: Intimacy in human relationships*. Routledge & Kegan Paul.

Henrich, J., & Gil-White, F. J. (2001). The evolution of prestige: Freely conferred deference as a mechanism for enhancing the benefits of cultural transmission. *Evolution and Human Behavior*, *22*(3), 165–196.

Hogan, P. C. (2018). Persuasion: Lessons in sociocognitive understanding. In B. Lau (Ed.), (pp. 180–199). Routledge. https://doi.org/10.4324/9780203732526-10

Jensen-Campbell, L. A., Graziano, W. G., & West, S. G. (1995). Dominance, prosocial orientation, and female preferences: Do nice guys really finish last? *Journal of Personality and Social Psychology*, *68*(3), 427.

Jones, V. (2003). Introduction. In *Pride and Prejudice* (pp. xi–xxxvi). Penguin.

Le Faye, D. (Ed.). (1995). *Jane Austen's letters* (3rd ed.). Oxford University Press.

McAllister, J. (2022). Love and listening: The erotics of talk in the popular romance novel. In A. Brooks (Ed.), *The Routledge companion to romantic love* (pp. 117–127). Routledge. https://doi.org/10.4324/9781003022343-9

Newton, J. L. (1981). *Women, power, and subversion*. University of Georgia Press.

Parrill, S. (2002). *Jane Austen on film and television: A critical study of the adaptations*. McFarland & Co.

Ridley, M. (1993). *The Red Queen: Sex and the evolution of human nature*. Penguin Books.

Rosenthal, G. G., & Ryan, M. J. (2022). Sexual selection and the ascent of women: Mate choice research since Darwin. *Science*, *375*. https://doi.org/10.1126/science.abi6308

Salmon, C. (2012). The pop culture of sex: An evolutionary window on the worlds of pornography and romance. *Review of General Psychology*, *16*(2), 152.

Saunders, J. P. (2014). Darwinian literary analysis of sexuality. In T. K. Shackelford & R. D. Hansen (Eds.), *The evolution of sexuality* (pp. 29–55). Springer International Publishing. https://doi.org/10.1007/978-3-319-09384-0_2

Solomon, R. C. (2003). *Not passion's slave: Emotions and choice*. Oxford University Press.

Stasio, M. J., & Duncan, K. (2007). An evolutionary approach to Jane Austen: Prehistoric preferences in *Pride and Prejudice*. *Studies in the Novel*, *39*(2), 133–146. https://www.jstor.org/stable/20831911

Tauchert, A. (2005). *Romancing Jane Austen: Narrative, realism, and the possibility of a happy ending*. Palgrave Macmillan.

Townsend, J. M., & Levy, G. D. (1990). Effects of potential partners' costume and physical attractiveness on sexuality and partner selection. *The Journal of Psychology*, *124*(4), 371–389. https://doi.org/10.1080/00223980.1990.10543232

Townsend, J. M., & Wasserman, T. (1998). Sexual attractiveness: Sex differences in assessment and criteria. *Evolution and Human Behavior*, *19*(3), 171–191. https://doi.org/10.1016/S1090-5138(98)00008-7

Tracy, J. L., & Robins, R. W. (2007). The psychological structure of pride: A tale of two facets. *Journal of Personality and Social Psychology*, *92*(3), 506–525.

Vanderbeke, D. (2019). On love and marriage in popular genres. In D. Vanderbeke & B. Cooke (Eds.), *Evolution and popular narrative* (pp. 83–105). Brill.

Weisser, S. O. (2013). *The glass slipper: Women and love stories*. Rutgers University Press.

Wiltshire, J. (1992). *Jane Austen and the body: "The picture of health"*. Cambridge University Press.

Zunshine, L. (2022). *The secret life of literature*. MIT Press.

PART III
SEX AND THE CITY

INTRODUCTION TO *SEX AND THE CITY*

"Spoiled by choices?"[1]

Feminist criticism of *Sex and the City* and other chick lit texts is marked by the same ambivalence present in the criticism of Austen's fiction. On the one hand, the show is praised for demonstrating women's empowerment, for its frank portrayal of sexuality, and for its focus on female friendships (Armstrong, 2018; Evelina, 2022; Gerhard, 2005; Henry, 2004; Jermyn, 2009; Mabry, 2006). At the same time, however, the four female protagonists are condemned as personifications of various forms of backlash against feminism (Evelina, 2022; Gerhard, 2005; Hermes, 2006; Mabry, 2006; Weisser, 2013; Whelehan, 2005). Samantha Jones is an obvious example of the sexual liberation gone too far, Charlotte York represents the idealization of traditional domesticity, Miranda Hobbes shows the predicaments of female professional ambitions, and Carrie Bradshaw personifies the regressive attitude to love as the ultimate female goal, with Mr. Big as her god. Importantly, even those who acknowledge many positive elements in the show often see its focus on finding a lasting heterosexual relationship as incompatible with feminism (e.g., Evelina, 2022). And just as Austen's marital conclusions were pronounced to be "false", chick lit happy endings are seen "at the level of gender politics, a bait-and-switch" (Harzewski, 2017, p. 515).

However, as I argued throughout Part I, the persistent search for romantic union in women's fiction likely reflects the prominence of love in human emotional and motivational systems, and the way modern romantic heroines select their partners reflects the long-standing dilemmas of female mate choice. Unquestionably, the external pressures on women have changed significantly. Most of Austen's young heroines *need* to marry in order to secure their financial prosperity, social status, and socially acceptable reproduction. Modern heroines have their own money, careers, and access to modern reproductive technologies that allow them to control their fertility or to have children without having sex. So, while Austen's women exercise their female choice *despite* many restrictions placed on them, for the heroines of *Sex and the City*, it seems like the "choices are endless" (SATC, 3:10 "All or Nothing") and hard to handle because of it. Indeed, critics have noted that *Sex and the City* "was perfectly timed to tap into a zeitgeist consumed by the question of what women want", and the show openly declared "its preoccupation with the politics of women's choice(s) at the start of the new millennium" (Jermyn, 2009, p. 2, 4).

Austen's novels (as well as many other romantic narratives) outline different mating strategies but usually emphasize one as significantly better than others. Even in *Sense and Sensibility*, which has two female protagonists, authorial approval is much stronger for Elinor than for Marianne. In contrast, *Sex and the City* presents four very different but equally important female characters, each with a distinct approach to love and relationships. It is true that Carrie's perspective is foregrounded in several ways, most notably through her voice-over narration, but the perspectives of the other three characters are presented as equally viable alternatives. Fan literature suggests that there was plenty of room for identification with the other three characters. Popular women's magazines offered surveys and quizzes asking "which *Sex and the City* character are you?", and fan feedback shows that many identified more closely with Miranda, Charlotte, or Samantha than with Carrie (Jermyn, 2009, pp. 60–61). And even Carrie's final choice of partner is not idealized in the same way as Elizabeth Bennet's.[2] Many fans still think Carrie should have chosen the down-to-earth Aidan rather than the glamorous Big, and in Season 2 of the sequel *And Just Like That*, when she rekindles her relationship with Aidan after Big's untimely death, Carrie herself wonders if Aidan was always her true love (but Aidan decides to prioritize his children). The emphasis on plurality and inclusiveness is likely at the heart of the show's appeal. It is also a reflection of the significantly different cultural environment in which women's life choices are much less constrained.

Sex and the single girl

One of the most obvious differences between Austen's novels and *Sex and the City* is the overt focus on sexuality in the latter. It reflects the changes in socio-cultural environments and deserves a moment of attention before I move on to the analysis of individual characters in the next four chapters. Another significant difference is the fact that while for Austen's women, motherhood was a more-or-less inevitable consequence of sex, for modern women it is a more deliberate choice—I will come back to this important idea in Chapter 12.

With their frequent dates which almost invariably end in the bedroom, the four women of *Sex and the City* "have been hailed as prototypes for the new sexually empowered woman" (Siegel, 2007, p. 154). Out of the four, Samantha has a particularly high sex drive, which I will discuss in more detail in the next chapter, but her three friends, regardless of their individual differences, do not have too many reservations about sex either. In fact, most modern romantic or chick lit heroines are active sexual players, aware of and acting on their desires (Gill & Herdieckerhoff, 2006, p. 499; Mabry, 2006, p. 192; Rowntree et al., 2012). For example, Bridget Jones, instead of being offended by her boss's comments about her short skirt, welcomes the opportunity to flirt and has sex with him soon after (Fielding, 1996). In modern romantic fiction, the assertive expressions of sexuality are often accompanied by a rhetoric of sexual liberation, empowerment, and the importance of pleasure similar to that of third-wave feminism (see Denfeld, 1995; Roiphe, 1993; Wolf, 1993).

The open attitude to sex is also clear in the way *Sex and the City* characters discuss their sexual experiences with each other.[3] Although some critics see these explicit conversations as nothing more than dirty talk with no political value (Hermes, 2006, p. 81), others believe they do have a liberating, subversive potential similar to the consciousness-raising sessions of the second-wave era (Gerhard, 2005; Hunting, 2012). They create a sense of intimacy and solidarity among women, both inside and outside of the text, and create communities within which to discuss various relationship issues. The debates initiated by the fictional characters are often continued on numerous fan websites and in countless articles in the popular press. Through these conversations, the female characters stake their claim to the pleasures of heterosexual sex for themselves and for other women. Jane Gerhard interprets this as a sign that "these women are the subjects of heterosexual sex, not its objects" (2005, p. 45).

However, feminists have long been sceptical about equating women's liberation with sexual liberation. In her analysis of the iconic, sexually explicit novel *Fear of Flying* (Jong, 1973), Imelda Whelehan notes that many second-wave feminists considered sexual freedom to be "a chimera where women were being sold the idea of sex as liberation but often it cast them in just as strong a thrall to men, with new pressures to perform sexually at every occasion" (2005, p. 109).[4] Many feminist media scholars continue to see popular expressions of female sexual empowerment as "a false freedom" (Kim, 2001, p. 324). As Rosalind Gill points out, "what is novel and striking about contemporary sexualized representations of women in popular culture is that they do not (as in the past) depict women as passive objects but as knowing, active, and desiring sexual subjects" (2003, p. 103). However, this move from "sexual objectification to sexual subjectification" is in Gill's view "a higher or deeper form of exploitation than objectification" because it replaces the "external male judging gaze" with "a self-policing narcissistic gaze" and in this way creates "a new disciplinary regime" (2003, p. 104). This "new kind of tyranny" proclaims itself to be about female sexual desire but is in fact much more about female sexual desirability (Gill, 2008, p. 53).

While chick lit heroines usually have active sex lives, their stories are also marked by certain suspicion about whether unencumbered sex is something that women really desire or "mere posturing or performance" they are "required to enact" in a postfeminist world (Gill & Herdieckerhoff, 2006, p. 494). A good case in point is Ariel Steiner, the heroine of Amy Sohn's novel *Run Catch Kiss* (1999; a sort of tribute, or follow-up, to Bushnell's *Sex and the City*), who has difficulties in reconciling her real sex life (which is rarely satisfactory) with the titillating version of it she is expected to present in the sex column she writes for a local newspaper. There is also a clear disparity between "intention and reception", between the way Ariel would like to act and be perceived and the way her sexual partners and readers of her column respond to her (Kiernan, 2006, p. 213). This tension highlights another problem, namely that although women may be trying to create their own pleasures and experience them on their own terms, this is always "open to patriarchal recuperation" (Moseley & Read, 2002, p. 241). This is evident in a sequence from *Ally McBeal* in which Ally teaches Georgia how to maximize the enjoyment of drinking coffee, but their pleasure is sexualized in a way reminiscent of soft-porn, through extreme close-ups showing the women licking the foam off their lips and through cuts to their bosses Billy and Richard positioned as voyeurs (*Ally McBeal*, 1:8 "Drawing the Lines"). It is also keenly felt in an episode of *Sex and the City* about the launch of Carrie's newspaper column (SATC, 1:6 "Secret Sex"). As part of the advertising campaign, pictures of Carrie in a seductive pose, wearing a flesh-coloured dress, are put on city buses. Carrie and her friends decide to celebrate her success by meeting to watch one of the buses drive by, but when the bus arrives, they are horrified to see that someone drew a penis close to Carrie's mouth. Moreover, in at least three different episodes, Carrie is taken for a prostitute.

From an evolutionary point of view, such instances of the disparity between the "intention and reception" of female sexual confidence are not always ideologically motivated but may signal a basic, but often problematic, misalignment in male and female sexual psychology.

Since men can more easily benefit from casual sex, they are much more sensitive to cues of sexual availability and often overestimate women's sexual interest in them (Abbey, 1982; Haselton & Buss, 2000). More importantly, however, the more assertive expression of female sexuality evident in chick lit is a strategic and expected response to the change in environmental conditions in modern Western democracies. David Schmitt, who conducted a study of sex and culture in 48 diverse countries, found that

> when resources are plentiful, life expectancies are long, and cultures invest heavily in human development and welfare, women adaptively shift toward more promiscuous mating strategies and the natural gap between men's and women's sociosexuality narrows. In this way, the effects of culture on sex differences in sociosexuality may be viewed as a series of environmentally contingent psychological adaptations. (2005, p. 273)

Nevertheless, even for women in the most progressive countries, casual sex still carries potentially significant risks, and the pursuit of sexual satisfaction rarely eliminates the desire for long-term attachment (Garcia & Reiber, 2008). This is true for at least three out of the four main characters of *Sex and the City*, as well as for most other chick lit heroines.

In the next four chapters, I analyse the relationship choices of *Sex and the City*'s protagonists, noting their individual differences but also the parallels between their sexual strategies and those of Austen's characters. Samantha Jones values sexual variety and physical attractiveness of her partners more than relationship stability or emotional intimacy, and unlike Lydia Bennet, she can satisfy her sexual appetite without being socially stigmatized. Charlotte York prioritizes her mate's material resources and social respectability, even though she is not dependent on them in the way Charlotte Lucas was. Miranda Hobbes is more assertive than Jane Bennet but equally emotionally guarded, which means that she almost misses out on a valuable partner. Carrie Bradshaw, like Elizabeth Bennet, selects a physically and socially powerful man but only when he proves his loyalty, kindness, and appreciation for her subjectivity. The final chapter of the book considers the issue of motherhood in both Austen's and modern romantic fiction.

Notes

1 SATC, 3:10 "All or Nothing".
2 This is partly because of the serial narrative structure: Each episode, season, and sequel needs to introduce some instability into the relationship.
3 Interestingly, the circles of friends often cross gender boundaries and include gay men. This is true of both *Sex and the City* and the Bridget Jones stories.
4 For other articulations of a similar sentiment, see Harrington (2023) and Perry (2022).

References

Abbey, A. (1982). Sex differences in attributions for friendly behavior: Do males misperceive females' friendliness? *Journal of Personality and Social Psychology*, *42*(5), 830–838. https://doi.org/10.1037/0022-3514.42.5.830
Ally McBeal. (1997–2002). [Television series]. Kelley, D. E. (Creator). Fox Network.
And just like that. (2021–2023). [Television series]. Star, D. & King, M. P. (Creators). HBO Max.

Armstrong, J. K. (2018). *Sex and the City and us: How four single women changed the way we think, live, and love* (Kindle ed.). Simon & Schuster.

Denfeld, R. (1995). *The new Victorians: A young woman's challenge to the old feminist order*. Warner Books.

Evelina, N. (2022). *Sex and the City: A cultural history*. Rowman & Littlefield.

Fielding, H. (1996). *Bridget Jones's diary: A novel*. Picador.

Garcia, J. R., & Reiber, C. (2008). Hook-up behavior: A biopsychosocial perspective. *Evolutionary Behavioral Sciences*, 2(4), 192–208.

Gerhard, J. (2005). *Sex and the City*: Carrie Bradshaw's queer postfeminism. *Feminist Media Studies*, 5(1), 37–49. https://doi.org/10.1080/14680770500058173

Gill, R. (2003). From sexual objectification to sexual subjectification: The resexualisation of women's bodies in the media. *Feminist Media Studies*, 3(1), 100–106.

Gill, R. (2008). Empowerment/Sexism: Figuring female sexual agency in contemporary advertising. *Feminism & Psychology*, 18(1), 35–60. https://doi.org/10.1177/0959353507084950

Gill, R., & Herdieckerhoff, E. (2006). Rewriting the romance. *Feminist Media Studies*, 6(4), 487–504. https://doi.org/10.1080/14680770600989947

Harrington, M. (2023). *Feminism against progress*. Simon and Schuster.

Harzewski, S. (2017). The cultural politics of chick lit: Popular fiction, postfeminism, and representation by Heike Mißler (review). *Tulsa Studies in Women's Literature*, 36(2), 514–516. https://doi.org/10.1353/tsw.2017.0046

Haselton, M. G., & Buss, D. M. (2000). Error management theory: A new perspective on biases in cross-sex mind reading. *Journal of Personality and Social Psychology*, 78, 81–91. https://doi.org/10.1037/0022-3514.78.1.81

Henry, A. (2004). Orgasms and empowerment: *Sex and the City* and the third-wave feminism. In K. Akass & J. McCabe (Eds.), *Reading Sex and the City* (pp. 65–82). I. B. Tauris.

Hermes, J. (2006). *Ally McBeal, Sex and the City* and the tragic success of feminism. In J. Hollows & R. Moseley (Eds.), *Feminism in popular culture* (pp. 79–95). Berg. http://www.loc.gov/catdir/toc/ecip061/2005028760.html

Hunting, K. (2012). Women talk: Chick lit TV and the dialogues of feminism. *The Communication Review*, 15(3), 187–203. https://doi.org/10.1080/10714421.2012.702002

Jermyn, D. (2009). *Sex and the City* (TV milestones series). Wayne State University Press.

Jong, E. (1973). *Fear of flying: A novel*. Holt.

Kiernan, A. (2006). No satisfaction: *Sex and the City, Run Catch Kiss,* and the conflict of desires in chick lit's new heroines. In S. Ferriss & M. Young (Eds.), *Chick lit: The new woman's fiction* (pp. 207–218). Routledge. http://www.loc.gov/catdir/toc/ecip0512/2005013904.html

Kim, L. S. (2001). "Sex and the Single Girl" in postfeminism: The F word on television. *Television & New Media*, 2(4), 319–334. https://doi.org/10.1177/152747640100200403

Mabry, A. R. (2006). About a girl: Female subjectivity and sexuality in contemporary 'chick' culture. In S. Ferriss & M. Young (Eds.), *Chick lit: The new woman's fiction* (pp. 191–206). Routledge. http://www.loc.gov/catdir/toc/ecip0512/2005013904.html

Moseley, R., & Read, J. (2002). "Having it Ally": Popular television (post-)feminism. *Feminist Media Studies*, 2(2), 231–249. https://doi.org/10.1080/14680770220150881

Perry, L. (2022). *The case against the sexual revolution*. John Wiley & Sons.

Roiphe, K. (1993). *The morning after: Sex, fear and feminism*. Little, Brown.

Rowntree, M., Moulding, N., & Bryant, L. (2012). Feminine sexualities in chick lit. *Australian Feminist Studies*, 27(72), 121–137. https://doi.org/10.1080/08164649.2012.648259

Schmitt, D. P. (2005). Sociosexuality from Argentina to Zimbabwe: A 48-nation study of sex, culture, and strategies of human mating. *Behavioral and Brain Sciences*, 28(2), 247.

Sex and the city. (1998–2004). [Television series]. Star, D. (Creator), & King, M. P. (Producer and Director). HBO.

Siegel, D. (2007). *Sisterhood, interrupted: From radical women to grrls gone wild*. Palgrave Macmillan. https://doi.org/10.1057/9780230605060

Sohn, A. (1999). *Run catch kiss*. Scribner.

Weisser, S. O. (2013). *The glass slipper: Women and love stories*. Rutgers University Press.

Whelehan, I. (2005). *The feminist bestseller: From Sex and the Single Girl to Sex and the City*. Palgrave Macmillan.

Wolf, N. (1993). *Fire with fire: The new female power and how it will change the 21st century*. Chatto & Windus.

8
SAMANTHA JONES
"I'm try-sexual, I'll try anything once"[1]

Many critics and fans agree that the most enduring legacy of *Sex and the City* is its treatment of female sexuality: from the unambiguous title, to frequent depictions of sex, and explicit discussions about it. All four female protagonists are sexually liberated, but the character who deserves this title most is Samantha Jones, the audacious PR specialist. In the pilot episode of the show, Samantha famously sets out her philosophy on love and sex and encourages the other three women to abandon their romantic illusions: "You have two choices: you can bang your head against the wall and try to find a relationship or you can say SCREW 'EM, and just go out and have sex like a man", which for her means "without feeling" (SATC, 1:1 "Sex and the City"). And for the most part, this is exactly what she does.

Providing a strong counterpoint to her friends' determined search for Mr. Right, Samantha is mainly interested in Mr. Right Now. In her view, "the right guy is an illusion; you don't understand that, you can't start living your life" (SATC, 1:1). She actively resists becoming emotionally attached. Any kind of intimacy beyond the sexual makes her uncomfortable. What she craves is not romantic attachment or long-term commitment but sexual satisfaction. Nevertheless, she is not completely immune to romance, especially if her partner is incredibly handsome and very good in bed. She has several relationships that go beyond casual sex, but they all end because of Samantha's irrepressible appetite for sexual variety. Importantly, Samantha is not an evolutionary aberration or a feminist fantasy, as early evolutionary psychologists would have argued (see Chapter 2). Her strategy is not the most common for women, but it falls within the expected range of variability, and is portrayed as such within the narrative of *Sex and the City*.

"That is my life, and I don't have to justify it"[2]

Like Lydia Bennet, Samantha is a short-term strategist with high sociosexuality, justifying her actions in terms of immediate sensual pleasure. However, thanks to changes in cultural attitudes and easy access to reliable contraception, Samantha can pursue her strategy much more easily. While Lydia can only fantasize about "tenderly flirting with at least six officers at once" (PP, p. 224), Samantha is more or less free to pursue sex as a recreational sport and to put into action many of her sexual fantasies. While Lydia has to justify her high libido by falling madly in love and is socially obliged to marry the first man she has sex with, Samantha can openly separate sex from love and marriage. She goes even further: She separates sex from any meaningful emotional connection, claiming that the best sex she has had was with men she did not even know.

Their cultural environments may be significantly different, but the psychology of the two women is very similar. Like Lydia, Samantha is loud-mouthed and assertive, a thrill-seeker and a risk-taker. She describes herself as "demanding, stubborn, self-sufficient, and always right. In bed, at the office, and everywhere else" (SATC, 6:4 "Pick-a-Little, Talk-a-Little"). Her motto is: "That is my life and I don't have to justify it" (SATC, 5:6 "Critical Condition"). In her self-confidence and in her attitude to romance, Samantha stands in stark contrast to many chick lit heroines who are mildly neurotic and self-deprecating. Unlike Bridget Jones, she is not obsessed with her thigh circumference; unlike Ally McBeal, she takes on the world without trying to get married first; and unlike her own friend Carrie Bradshaw, she knows exactly what she wants and is not too shy to ask for it. Most importantly, she is not anxious about being single and—in line with third-wave feminism—is "unapologetically sexual" (Wolf, 1993, p. 149). One of the most frequently quoted lines from the show is Samantha's claim "I'm try-sexual, I'll try anything once" (SATC, 3:4).

Fans have found her self-confidence inspiring. In articles with titles such as "12 Reasons Why Samantha Jones is the Best Character on *Sex and the City*", young female bloggers describe her as "hilarious, out-spoken, and a whole lotta woman" (Varasteh, 2014, para. 1). Others say "Samantha Jones taught us about being confident and independent" and call her "one fierce, inspirational female" (Dye, 2015, para. 3, 11). In many ways, Samantha's attitude reflects feminist politics: She adopts second-wave rejection of romance as disempowering for women and embraces third-wave emphasis on sexual expression and pleasure. Samantha would readily agree with Debbie Stoller, the editor and co-founder of *Bust* magazine who proclaims: "In our quest for total sexual satisfaction, we shall leave no sex toy unturned and no sexual avenue unexplored. Women are trying their hands (and other body parts) at everything from phone sex to cybersex, solo sex to group sex, heterosex to homosex. Lusty feminists of the third wave, we're more than ready to drag-race down sexual roads less traveled" (1999, p. 84). And with Meg Daly who confesses: "I revel in the swaggering pleasure that comes from saying 'I did it this many times, in this many ways, with this many people.' Why shouldn't I?" (as cited in Henry, 2004, p. 78). For Samantha, like for many third-wavers, sexual freedom is her personal right as well as a political stance, an expression of gender equality. Some critics (e.g., Jermyn, 2009) have also linked Samantha's flamboyant language and behaviour with the tradition of the comedic "unruly woman" who "contests the institutions and structures of authority through inversion, mockery and other forms of travesty" (Rowe, 1995, p. 32).

At the same time, however, while romantic heroines are usually criticized for promoting false and damaging ideals of female passivity, Samantha has been criticized for the opposite reasons. In an interview for the *Mirror*, the author Nikki Gemmell complained: "Popular culture, through TV shows such as *Sex and the City*, feeds us the idea that we are all like Samantha Jones and her friends. ... People think women are confident, sexually aggressive, know exactly what they want and demand it of their men. ... In reality, we find it hard to say what we want" (Ridley, 2003, para. 28). Such scepticism about Samantha as a reflection of female sexuality goes beyond the usual feminist suspicion about sexual liberation mentioned in my introduction to Part III of this book. Samantha does not turn herself into a sex object, she apparently turns herself into a man: She "acts, speaks and cavorts like a stereotypical gay man" (Greven, 2004, p. 44).

From a psychological point of view, Samantha's sex drive may seem to be more typical of men than women, but we have to remember that despite average differences *between* the sexes, there are also significant variations *within* each sex (Gangestad & Simpson, 2000). Because of both biological and cultural factors, for most of our evolutionary history, concentrating on a few high-quality, long-term partnerships may have been a preferred option for women—and for the most part, it still is. However, modern evolutionary theory and research makes it very clear that for some women, in some circumstances, more opportunistic, short-term matings would have been advantageous. Firstly, there is unquestionable evidence that more equitable sociocultural norms "tend to attenuate sex differences" (Schmitt, 2005, p. 273). When women are socially permitted to have sex, they often do. In fact, a recent study found that in the United States, the vast majority of women have more sex partners than the vast majority of men; only 5% of most sexually active men have more sex partners than women do (Harper et al., 2017). And secondly, traits such as attachment styles and sociosexuality predict sexual behaviours "above and beyond the effects of gender" (Geher & Kaufman, 2013, p. 103). For instance, regardless of their sex, people with dismissive attachment style claim that they are comfortable without close emotional relationships. Also, women who score highly on sociosexuality measures (high SOI) have a different perception of the potential costs and benefits of casual sex. For example, they do not seem to be particularly worried about the risks of pregnancy or sexually transmitted disease. In her study of people who had one-night stands, Anne Campbell (2008) was surprised to discover that the levels of concern about such risks were almost the same for men and women, despite the fact that the consequences for women are much more serious. While most women prioritize male commitment, women with high sociosexuality see more benefits in "having a sexual partner who is willing to experiment sexually, experiencing orgasms with the sexual partner, becoming more aroused, being more sexually appreciated and delighting in the novelty of a new sex partner" (Greiling & Buss, 2000, p. 959). Such women are also more interested in perfecting their skills of seduction and put more emphasis on material benefits of short-term affairs, such as expensive gifts or career advancement (Greiling & Buss, 2000). They also *increase* their threshold of physical attractiveness for short-term mates, while men usually *lower* their standards of beauty for such partners (Buss & Schmitt, 2011, p. 773 and references within).

Samantha exhibits many traits typical of both the dismissive attachment style and high sociosexuality. For example, she has very high expectations about the physical attractiveness and sexual prowess of her partners. She also often dates very rich men and the opportunity to experience their lavish lifestyles as well as the expensive gifts she receives from them are just as welcome as the sexual pleasure.

"We are not monotonous, I mean monogamous types"[3]

Many chick lit heroines every now and then just want to have sex. Carrie Bradshaw wonders about brothels for women and calls Mr. Big her male prostitute (SATC, 5:7 "The Big Journey"), Miranda Hobbes is despondent about not having had sex for six months, Bridget Jones "[feels] like throwing [herself] after [Daniel Cleaver] shouting, 'Shag me! Shag me!'" (Fielding, 1996, p. 104), but Samantha is one of very few who simply want sex without a relationship. Samantha's approach prompts Carrie to wonder in one episode whether New Yorkers are in fact "evolving past relationships" (SATC, 2:11 "Evolution"). In this episode, Samantha plans to take revenge on her ex-boyfriend by rekindling his desire and then dumping him, but she is happy to discover that unlike many men she has met, she had not "evolved past having feelings" (SATC, 2:11). In other words, despite all her bravado, Samantha is not incapable of attachment. Indeed, as research shows, a woman's promiscuity does not have to be a life-long immutable characteristic (Scelza, 2013, p. 261), strong sexual appetite does not eliminate the desire for affiliation (Garcia & Fisher, 2015; Garcia & Reiber, 2008), and casual sex can initiate emotional attachment (Fisher, 2005, p. 195).

In the course of the series, Samantha has several relationships that go beyond just having sex. For example, at the end of Season 1, she surprises everyone by announcing that she is in love. In this case, her declaration is an ironic cliff-hanger and a narrative joke since the other three women are at that point in the story without partners. As Season 2 resumes, Samantha and James's relationship plays as a reversal of the usual heterosexual scenario: *He* drags *her* into couples therapy accusing her of problems with intimacy. The reason for the failure of this relationship is more in keeping with Samantha's character than the idea of her being in love: James's penis is too small to satisfy her sexual needs. In a comical contrast, the finale of Season 3 has Samantha dating a man whose penis is too big even for her. True to her "try-sexual" motto, Samantha also tries to have a lesbian relationship, and it is serious enough to span three episodes (SATC, 4:3–4:5). However, Samantha finds that it involves too much talking, and she soon gets tired of "the emotional chat-show" (SATC, 4:5 "Ghost Town")—another sign that Samantha does not have the typical feminine relationship expectations. It is worth noting that each of the other three characters has a storyline about non-heterosexual attractions (most notably Miranda in the sequel *And Just Like That*). Such "sexual fluidity" is not unusual for women (Diamond, 2008), but based on their experiences, the four women of *Sex and the City* conclude that they are "definitely heterosexual" (SATC, 1:3 "Bay of Married Pigs").

Two of Samantha's most significant and long-lasting relationships are with Richard Wright and Jerry "Smith" Jerrod. Both men meet her most important requirements: They are very good looking, and they match her sexual adventurousness. But in both cases, the expectation of sexual exclusivity, which is one of the defining characteristics of romantic love, becomes a stumbling block. The trajectory of these relationships is not really surprising in light of the recent research. Helen Fisher (2011) argues that, given the effects of sex on the brain chemistry, often stimulating feelings of attachment, even the most sexually adventurous people can fall in love when they find an exciting-enough partner. However, there is always a risk that their personalities and attachment styles will get in the way of a long-term commitment. And without strong social pressure to remain in a formal relationship—such as there would have been for Lydia Bennet—partners soon go their separate ways.

Richard Wright is a hotel magnate with his own private jet. When he first meets Samantha, he is arrogant and openly sexist and refuses to give her a PR job despite her impressive resume (SATC, 4:10 "Belles of the Balls"). But when Samantha does not give up in light of his double standards, he is impressed with her "balls" and hires her. The fact that she is not intimidated by him professionally also attracts him sexually. Richard is a typical cad, with an attitude "who needs a wife when you can have a life" (SATC, 4:12 "Just Say Yes"). Samantha readily agrees with this motto and is happy to participate in his extravagant lifestyle without expecting, or offering, any serious commitment. However, perhaps because of their remarkable similarities, soon they both start developing feelings for each other, which they both find difficult to admit to. Richard woos Samantha with expensive gifts and romantic gestures but avoids any definitive commitment. Samantha claims she only likes Richard because she finally found a man with "a perfect dick" (SATC, 4:13 "The Good Fight") and talks about monogamy as if it was an infectious disease (SATC, 4:15: Change of a Dress). However, to her initial horror, she realizes that she is not interested in having sex with other men. After a period of an emotional tug of war, Samantha and Richard declare love for each other and decide to give monogamy a go (SATC, 4:17 "A 'Vogue' Idea").

The situation makes Samantha feel very vulnerable, and almost immediately, she becomes obsessed with the idea that Richard must be cheating on her. Season 4 ends with the confirmation of Samantha's fears when she catches Richard with another woman (SATC, 4:18 "I Heart NY"). He claims that it is "just sex" and that he loves Samantha, but this time, she is not able to separate sex from her emotions. After his profuse apologies at the beginning of Season 5, she gives him another chance but realizes she is not able to trust him. The episode in which Samantha finally breaks up with Richard is set in Atlantic City and compares relationships to gambling. In keeping with the metaphor, Carrie narrates Samantha's decision by saying: "And there, high above the casino, Samantha pulled her highest bet, her heart, off the table" (SATC, 5:3 "Luck Be an Old Lady"). The whole story confirms to Samantha that love makes her weak and vulnerable and that men cannot be trusted.

Samantha's longest relationship is with the much younger Jerry "Smith" Jerrod whom she meets early in Season 6. As with Richard, it starts off as a purely sexual adventure, and even more than with Richard, Samantha resists any intimacy beyond the sexual. After several "dates" consisting of wild role-play sex, Smith suggests just being themselves and getting to know each other better. Samantha, who is not even sure what his name is, responds: "I'm afraid we want different things. You want to tell me all about you and I don't want you to tell me all about you. It spoils the fantasy" (SATC, 6:4). But, as with Richard, as the sexual relationship continues, she is experiencing conflicting emotions: She is equally uncomfortable when Smith calls her his girlfriend and when he says that she is "nobody special" (SATC, 6:7 "The Post-It Always Sticks Twice"). Several episodes later, Smith tries to hold Samantha's hand; she considers this gesture "perverse" and in a desperate attempt to avoid it, falls over and breaks her toe (SATC, 6:11 "The Domino Effect"). The scene is an ironic visual metaphor for falling in love. With her foot in plaster, Samantha is finally prepared to take Smith's hand as an admission that she needs him not only in bed.

Unlike Richard, Smith is much younger than Samantha (he is 28, while Samantha is 45) and is a struggling actor and part-time waiter. This reversal of roles illustrates the range of possibilities in gender relations: Power dynamics within heterosexual relationships are not pre-determined by sex but often depend on circumstances. This state of affairs initially suits Samantha. Early on, to emphasize the unemotional, impersonal nature of their connection, she even tries to pay Smith for sex, which he finds offensive (SATC, 6:3 "The Perfect Present"). The difference in age and status gives Samantha a convenient excuse to disguise her girlfriend position with the more comfortable, emotionally neutral role of a publicist.[4] She transforms his image, emphasizing the sexiness of his body, and even changes his name from the unfortunate Jerry Jerrod to Smith. With her help, he becomes an overnight success.

Samantha is initially attracted to Smith because he is extremely good looking, a motivation entirely consistent with what research tells us about female short-term mating. But as the relationship develops, the disparity in their social status troubles Samantha, and she starts to feel that he cannot match the appeal of more powerful, dominant men. When comparing Smith to Carrie's current boyfriend, Alexandr Petrovsky, a successful artist who used to be associated with the famous Studio 54, Samantha says: "You've got yourself a man, a real power player. Smith is hot but he's a baby" (SATC, 6:13 "Let There Be Light"). In the same episode, Samantha accompanies Smith to a party which happens to be hosted by Richard Wright, another power player. Samantha is clearly attracted to the idea of a partnership with a man like Richard, whom she considers her equal, and Richard once again lures her with emotionally charged declarations that he ruined "the best thing [he] ever had". Samantha leaves the party telling disappointed Smith, "You play with your friends, and I'll play with mine." But while having sex with Richard, she realizes that he is utterly self-absorbed, and she is not enjoying the encounter. She goes back to Smith who is still waiting for her downstairs.

In the next few episodes, Smith further demonstrates his commitment—the trait which has particular value for women in long-term relationships. When Samantha is diagnosed with breast cancer and has to undergo surgery and chemotherapy, Smith not only shaves his head in solidarity but also stays with Samantha when she considers herself unattractive and her libido is at an all-time low (SATC, 6:14 "The Ick Factor" and 6:15 "Catch-38"). Until then, Samantha has been convinced that men and women only want and need each other for sex, but Smith proves to her otherwise. Her happy ending within the original television series is her opening up to a possibility of a heterosexual relationship based not just on physical desire but on mutual trust and support.

Samantha's trajectory within the last three seasons of the series, including her relationships with Richard and Smith, has some surprising parallels with Marianne Dashwood's in *Sense and Sensibility*. A vivacious woman falls for an equally exuberant man but is betrayed by him and after a life-threatening illness finally appreciates the love of another, more devoted man. Like Marianne and Willoughby, Samantha and Richard are so alike that they seem designed for each other. But like Willoughby, Richard is too self-centred to have much consideration for Samantha's feelings. Even his regret for having ruined the relationship is motivated entirely by his ego—in which it resembles Willoughby's final confession. Smith does not initially seem like a suitable partner for Samantha. Their difference in age and social status is similar to that between Colonel Brandon and Marianne—although in *Sex and the City* it is the woman who is much older and more affluent. Like Colonel Brandon, Smith has successfully faced adversity in the past, and his overcoming of alcohol addiction is a sign of his strength of character and emotional maturity. Most importantly, like Colonel Brandon, Smith is willing to wait and forgive, even when Samantha leaves him to have sex with Richard. Her behaviour on that occasion is somewhat similar to Marianne's, who first mocks Brandon with Willoughby at Barton, and later in London leaves the room when Brandon arrives because he is *not* Willoughby. Like Brandon, Smith has to watch his chosen woman being attracted to another, less worthy man. Given men's tendency for sexual jealousy, this may be the most serious test of their commitment, and romantic heroes are often put through it: Mr. Darcy must witness Elizabeth's attraction to Wickham and Mr. Knightly must watch Emma flirt with Frank Churchill. Finally, both Brandon and Smith support the women they love through serious illness, and both Marianne and Samantha finally come to appreciate each man's loyalty.

Marianne's story ends with the then-obligatory marriage, but Samantha's continues past the happy ending of the television series into the *Sex and the City* film (2008), which requires a new development, a new crisis. When the first film picks up the story three years after the conclusion of the TV show, Samantha and Smith are still together, living in Los Angeles where she is managing his stellar career. And although they have been happy together, Samantha begins to realize that the professional arrangement which initially conveniently disguised her emotional investment has turned out to have unpleasant side effects for her self-image. She starts to resent the fact that Smith's career has taken over her life, that in the course of a normal day, she says his name more often than her own, and that her evenings are occupied by the endless waiting for him to return from a film set. It seems like she has turned into this dreaded figure—a housewife. Even more importantly, prompted by their very attractive and sexually active neighbour, she starts to miss the sexual freedom she used to have.

When Samantha finally decides to end the relationship with Smith, they have the following conversation:

SMITH: You don't love me anymore?
SAMANTHA: Yes, I love you. It's just…I'm just gonna say the thing you're not supposed to say. I love you, but I love me more. And I've been in a relationship with myself for 49 years and that's the one I need to work on. You're gonna find a wonderful woman who loves being in a relationship.
SMITH: What will you find?
SAMANTHA: I don't know. But that's a risk I'm willing to take.

When breaking up with Richard in Season 5, Samantha used the same argument: "I love you, but I love me more". The line is ultimately about Samantha's self-interest but resonates differently in each case. With Richard, it ends a relationship full of deception and emotional power struggles. Samantha cannot trust him and is not prepared to be hurt. Breaking up is about self-protection. With Smith, this line concludes an emotionally fulfilling relationship that has run its course—at least for Samantha. She does not trust *herself* to stay faithful to Smith and does not want to take the risk of hurting him. It is about protecting the trust they do have in each other. The two remain good friends, and in the second *Sex and the City* film (2010), Samantha accompanies Smith to the premiere of his new blockbuster. Nevertheless, in both cases, the relationships come to an end because of the irrepressible desire for sexual variety. In the first case, Richard cannot stay faithful to Samantha; in the second, she feels trapped by the loyalty she feels towards Smith and the expectation of monogamy that comes with it. Ultimately, she is more comfortable with, indeed is looking forward to, the unknowns of new relationships. To use Judith Saunder's words about another female character with a "restless sex drive", Samantha is "'faithful' to its gratification rather than to any individual partner" (2018, p. 185).

"Are we sluts?"[5]

Variety, novelty, sense of adventure—these are some of the main reasons the psychologists Cindy Meston and David Buss (2009) identified for why women have sex. Like Samantha, many women may like sexual variety but also realize potential consequences of sex. The seriousness of these consequences has changed with social attitudes and with the availability of reliable contraception, but the risks did not get eliminated altogether. The women of *Sex and the City* (and countless other modern romantic stories) enjoy the sexual freedom but also suffer some of the costs: Carrie worries about her late period, Samantha is scared she may have HIV, Miranda gets chlamydia, then she accidentally gets pregnant, and when this happens Carrie and Samantha admit to having had abortions. And from time to time, they all suffer from broken hearts.

In past stories, women who were sexually active outside of the socially sanctioned marital context faced some form of narrative punishment. Austen, despite her criticism of the sexual double standard, exiles Lydia to Newcastle and Maria Bertram abroad, and she allows Eliza Brandon to die off-stage. Even now, some critics interpret Samantha's breast cancer as a punishment for her licentiousness, but there is little narrative evidence for this interpretation. Firstly, the diagnosis is another opportunity to establish the importance of female friendships alongside heterosexual relationships, as Samantha delivers the news about her illness during Miranda's wedding reception. Secondly, the way she approaches her condition confirms Samantha's courage and irrepressible spirit, especially when she removes her wig during the speech at a cancer benefit dinner, inspiring other women at the dinner to do the same (SATC, 6:19 "An American Girl in Paris: Part Une"). And finally, Smith's commitment to her during the treatment despite her low libido shows her that there can be more to male-female relationships than just sex. His declaration of love during the time when she is not feeling at all sexual or attractive enables her happy ending within the TV show.

However, Samantha's promiscuity does occasionally create problems for female friendship and coalitions, and she is censored for her transgressions in that regard. For example, in one episode, her career and social position are threatened when she is ostracized by a powerful socialite whose husband she had slept with (SATC, 2:5 "Four Women and a Funeral"). As Buss points out, even in relatively permissive cultures, "women known as promiscuous suffer reputational damage", and it is often other women who enforce the rules of sexual conduct as a way of safeguarding their own position on the marriage market and eliminating potential competitors (2003, p. 92). In another episode, Samantha upsets Charlotte by sleeping with her brother who is going through an emotionally messy divorce (SATC, 2:15 "Shortcomings"). And the most serious disagreement she has with Carrie starts when Carrie walks in on Samantha giving a blow job to a delivery man in her office, even though she had been expecting Carrie (SATC, 5:4 "Cover Girl"). In both of these cases, Samantha's drive for self-gratification leads her to behave in a rather selfish, inconsiderate way. Indeed, one of the charges against her character is that the merits of her independence as a woman are often undermined by the fact that she is "inconsiderate and thoughtless" (Weisser, 2013, p. 121). But once again, such a reading does not have much textual support. Despite the few instances quoted above, Samantha is consistently shown as a caring and loyal friend, even if she is outspoken, impulsive, and often blunt—unlike Lydia who never seems to think about anyone but herself. In fact, while Samantha resists emotional intimacy with men, she enjoys and values it with her three female friends and is often the one who provides invaluable support in Carrie's darkest moments.

"Some love stories are short"[6]

Samantha is perhaps the most positive representation of "the desiring, sexually active, economically independent single woman" (Jermyn, 2009, p. 13) in popular culture, and this affirmation of unrestrained female sexuality is markedly different from Austen's. Austen disapproves of Lydia's mating strategy because of its selfishness and because in her cultural environment giving in to sexual impulse was extremely risky. Also, Lydia is very young, and her elopement is as much the result of her naivety as it is the result of her lack of self-control and poor character judgement. Samantha, on the other hand, has a wealth of life experience behind her. She is about a decade older than her three friends and is already facing with aplomb what Carrie and Miranda identify as their "scary age": mid-forties (SATC, 4:11 "Coulda, Woulda, Shoulda"). For Lydia, because of her youth and her culture, a marriage stands for increased freedom from family control and many social restrictions. For Samantha, who has financial and social independence available only to a small proportion of women even today, a relationship means constraint. Samantha's cultural environment allows her to express her high sociosexuality in a way that Lydia never could. But her desire for independence and variety is not new, as Lydia's story confirms.

Feminist evaluations of Samantha have been mixed. Her insistence on sexual pleasure and agency is consistent with the post-second-wave positions, but the kind of impersonal sex she usually practices has been heavily criticized by many feminists as typical of male pornography. At the same time, her relationship with Smith at the end of the TV show was received by critics not as a recognition of more feminine sexuality but as a renunciation of her independence. Samantha's conclusion within the first film attracted equally contradictory evaluations. Her objections to the marriage-like relationship with Smith are recognized as reminiscent of the feminist arguments but are apparently "never treated seriously as a point of view, because Sam is a broadly drawn comic character" (Weisser, 2013, p. 118). Meanwhile, her inability to remain committed to the handsome and loyal Smith is seen as a warning against being "too free spirited": "You end up with no emotional anchor, only empty sex. ... Sure enough, at the end of the movie, when all the rest are happy and have their men, Samantha is left with her dog" (Weisser, 2013, p. 119).

What is missing from these evaluations is the appreciation of Samantha's individuality and the particular way it makes her approach recurrent life choices between intimacy and commitment on the one hand and novelty and autonomy on the other. For Samantha, the latter are stronger, but even she falls in love a few times. And even though her love stories are short, she has very strong and stable emotional anchors in her female friends. That is the point of that last scene in the movie: Samantha is not excluded from the circle of happy couples and families, despite her different mating strategy.[7]

Other modern romantic heroines have casual sex but usually with a more-or-less explicit goal of finding a committed partner. Indeed, one of the best-documented benefits of casual sex is its potential to jump-start a long-term relationship, as the stories of Samantha's three friends, discussed in the next three chapters, demonstrate.

Notes

1 SATC, 3:4 "Boy, Girl, Boy, Girl".
2 SATC, 5:6 "Critical Condition".
3 SATC, 4:15 "Change of a Dress".
4 Stephanie Harzewski (2011) makes a similar point but draws a different conclusion.
5 SATC, 3:6 (title of the episode).
6 *Sex and the City* (2008).
7 Her absence from the sequel *And Just Like That* was due to Kim Cattrall's unavailability to reprise her role and the narrative explanation for it is unconvincing.

References

Austen, J. (1813/2003). *Pride and prejudice*. Penguin.
Buss, D. M. (2003). *The evolution of desire: Strategies of human mating* (Rev., Kindle ed.). Basic Books.
Buss, D. M., & Schmitt, D. P. (2011). Evolutionary psychology and feminism. *Sex Roles, 64*(9), 768–787. https://doi.org/10.1007/s11199-011-9987-3
Campbell, A. (2008). The morning after the night before. *Human Nature, 19*(2), 157–173.
Diamond, L. M. (2008). *Sexual fluidity: Understanding women's love and desire*. Harvard University Press.
Dye, T. (2015, Apr 20). 7 Things Samantha Jones from *Sex and the City* taught us about being confident & independent. *Bustle*. https://www.bustle.com/articles/77262-7-things-samantha-jones-from-sex-and-the-city-taught-us-about-being-confident-independent
Fielding, H. (1996). *Bridget Jones's diary: A novel*. Picador.
Fisher, H. E. (2005). *Why we love: The nature and chemistry of romantic love*. Henry Holt and Co.
Fisher, H. E. (2011). *Why him? Why her? How to find and keep lasting love*. Oneworld.
Gangestad, S. W., & Simpson, J. A. (2000). The evolution of human mating: Trade-offs and strategic pluralism. *Behavioral and Brain Sciences, 23*(04), 573–587. http://dx.doi.org/10.1017/S0140525X0000337X
Garcia, J. R., & Fisher, H. E. (2015). Why we hook up: Searching for sex or looking for love. In S. Tarrant (Ed.), *Gender, sex, and politics: In the streets and between the sheets in the 21st century* (pp. 238–250). Routledge.
Garcia, J. R., & Reiber, C. (2008). Hook-up behavior: A biopsychosocial perspective. *Evolutionary Behavioral Sciences, 2*(4), 192–208.
Geher, G., & Kaufman, S. B. (2013). *Mating intelligence unleashed: The role of the mind in sex, dating, and love* (Kindle ed.). Oxford University Press.
Greiling, H., & Buss, D. M. (2000). Women's sexual strategies: The hidden dimension of extra-pair mating. *Personality and Individual Differences, 28*(5), 929–963. https://doi.org/10.1016/S0191-8869(99)00151-8
Greven, D. (2004). The museum of unnatural history: Male freaks and *Sex and the City*. In K. Akass & J. McCabe (Eds.), *Reading Sex and the City* (pp. 33–47). I. B. Tauris.
Harper, C. R., Dittus, P. J., Leichliter, J. S., & Aral, S. O. (2017). Changes in the distribution of sex partners in the United States: 2002 to 2011–2013. *Sexually Transmitted Diseases, 44*(2), 96–100. https://doi.org/10.1097/olq.0000000000000554
Harzewski, S. (2011). *Chick lit and postfeminism*. University of Virginia Press.
Henry, A. (2004). Orgasms and empowerment: *Sex and the City* and the third-wave feminism. In K. Akass & J. McCabe (Eds.), *Reading Sex and the City* (pp. 65–82). I. B. Tauris.
Jermyn, D. (2009). *Sex and the City* (TV milestones series). Wayne State University Press.
Meston, C. M., & Buss, D. M. (2009). *Why women have sex: Understanding sexual motivations—from adventure to revenge (and everything in between)*. Times Books.
Ridley, J. (2003, July 1). Confessions of a suburban sexpot. *Mirror*. www.thefreelibrary.com
Rowe, K. (1995). *The unruly woman: Gender and the genres of laughter*. University of Texas Press.
Saunders, J. P. (2018). *American classics: Evolutionary perspectives*. Academic Studies Press. http://www.jstor.org/stable/10.2307/j.ctv4v3226
Scelza, B. A. (2013). Choosy but not chaste: Multiple mating in human females. *Evolutionary Anthropology: Issues, News, and Reviews, 22*(5), 259–269. https://doi.org/10.1002/evan.21373

Schmitt, D. P. (2005). Sociosexuality from Argentina to Zimbabwe: A 48-nation study of sex, culture, and strategies of human mating. *Behavioral and Brain Sciences, 28*(2), 247.

Sex and the city. (1998–2004). [Television series]. Star, D. (Creator), & King, M. P. (Producer and Director). HBO.

Sex and the city. (2008). [Motion picture]. King, M. P. (Director/Writer). New Line Cinema.

Sex and the city 2. (2010). [Motion picture]. King, M. P. (Director/Writer). New Line Cinema.

Stoller, D. (1999). Sex and the thinking girl. In M. Karp & D. Stoller (Eds.), *The Bust guide to the new girl order* (Kindle ed.). Penguin Books.

Varasteh, A. (2014, Nov 16). 12 Reasons why Samantha Jones is the best character on *Sex and the City*. *Her Campus at Boston University.* http://www.hercampus.com/school/bu/12-reasons-why-samantha-jones-best-character-sex-and-city

Weisser, S. O. (2013). *The glass slipper: Women and love stories.* Rutgers University Press.

Wolf, N. (1993). *Fire with fire: The new female power and how it will change the 21st century.* Chatto & Windus.

9
CHARLOTTE YORK

"You fantasize about a man with a Park Avenue apartment and a nice stock portfolio"[1]

Charlotte York is an optimistic art dealer from a traditional WASP background. Out of the four women of *Sex and the City*, she has the most idealistic approach to relationships, holds the most conservative views on sex, and is the only one who expressly aspires to being a wife, mother, and domestic goddess. For many critics, including her friend Miranda, she is the embodiment of the anti-feminist, regressive desire to return to the kind of feminine mystique criticized by Betty Friedan (1963/1997): motherhood and domesticity as the ultimate female fulfilment.

Despite her seemingly naïve romanticism, Charlotte has a very pragmatic, business-like approach to finding a husband. Samantha describes her romantic fantasy as "a man with a Park Avenue apartment and a nice stock portfolio" (SATC, 3:1 "Where There's Smoke"). Charlotte herself proclaims that "professional women [should] approach finding a mate with the same kind of dedication and organization they bring to their careers" (SATC, 3:7 "Drama Queens"). In fact, her mating strategy is very similar to that of Austen's Charlotte Lucas. In contrast to her fictional predecessor, Charlotte York longs for a fairy-tale romance, but she has an equally strong desire for "a townhouse in the city [and] a beach house in East Hampton" (SATC, 1:10 "The Baby Shower"). Unlike Charlotte Lucas, who arguably cannot afford to be romantic, this Charlotte does not have to worry too much about her financial future—she is well-educated and has a successful career as a manager of an art gallery—but she still puts great emphasis on the material and social position of her potential mates. In other words, she can afford to be romantic but still demands a "comfortable home".

Women's search for resources has been shown cross-culturally to be one of their main mate selection criteria (see Chapter 2), but it has been difficult to establish whether this is a conditional or constant strategy (Campbell, 2002, pp. 185–186; Eagly & Wood, 1999). Feminists see women's focus on resources as resulting entirely from cultural conditions, and research shows that "as women become more 'empowered' (as measured by nationwide statistics on women's earnings, representation in government and their participation in professional occupations), they place less importance on the value of a prospective partner's earnings" (Campbell, 2002, p. 185). Indeed, only 14% of Americans say they would

DOI: 10.4324/9781003320982-15

marry for financial stability (Fisher, 2016, p. 300). At the same time, women seem to be very sensitive to the local ecology: The more challenging local circumstances are, the more value women place on their partners' resources, regardless of their own (Geary et al., 2004, p. 38). One study comparing female mate preferences in different American cities found that women's emphasis on men's earning potential was greater in cities with a higher cost of living (McGraw, 2002). In many cultures, even women who have plenty of their own resources still put a high premium on the resources and status of a potential mate (Buss, 1989; Wiederman & Allgeier, 1992). The strategy appears to pay off: According to one study, women who marry resource-rich men not only have more children but also report greater marital satisfaction and are less likely to get divorced (Bereczkei & Csanaky, 1996); in another interesting study in China, partners' wealth even predicted the frequency of women's orgasms (Pollet & Nettle, 2009). Finally, when women leave their husbands, it is often because of inadequate resources (Betzig, 1989). Another very important reason is infertility which, perhaps not incidentally, is also very relevant to Charlotte's story.[2]

Is "closing the deal ... paramount"?[3]

Austen condemns mercenary fortune hunters like Lucy Stee or Isabella Thorpe, although she portrays Charlotte Lucas with a bit more sympathy. Many of her heroines reject men who do not offer much beyond money but end up marrying well anyway; even Captain Wentworth and Edward Ferrars must secure decent income before Anne Elliot and Elinor Dashwood can marry them. Similar narrative trends continue in chick lit despite significant socio-economic changes: The idea of marrying for money is usually disparaged or dismissed, but at the same time, most romantic heroes are well-off, if not fabulously rich, like Christian Grey (James, 2012). For example, in *Bridget Jones: The Edge of Reason* (Fielding, 1999), Rebecca, who competes with Bridget for Mark Darcy and who comes from a much wealthier family than Bridget, is presented as just as shallow and manipulative as Austen's Miss Bingley, and she ends up with the rather unattractive and emotionally unstable but wealthy Giles Benwick. Bridget, unlike Austen's heroines, does not have to consider a marriage of convenience—she is able to support herself. But this does not nullify the attraction of resources and status. Both men she is considering, Daniel and Mark, are better off financially and have a higher social position than Bridget herself.

In another notable example, the heroine of the bestselling *Confessions of a Shopaholic* (Kinsella, 2000/2007), Rebecca Bloomwood, has a very good reason to look for a rich husband: her mounting credit card bills. She briefly considers marrying her flatmate's cousin, Tarquin, who happens to be at number 15 on *Harper and Queen's* Hundred Richest Bachelors list, worth about 25 million pounds (p. 186). He is in love with her, would be able to pay off her debts, and would enable her to indulge in her shopping obsession. She is completely uninterested in him until she learns about his fortune, at which point she tries to talk herself into being attracted to him while fantasizing about a lavish wedding and "No more money troubles ever. *Ever*" (p. 193). But of course, she cannot go through with it because she does not love him. Instead, she falls in love with Luke Brandon, an exceptionally intelligent businessman. He is older, more confident, and more masculine than Tarquin, a typical romantic hero, and Rebecca is attracted to him right from the beginning of the book, even before she discovers that he too is very rich.

Sex and the City may open with the cynical statement that "self-protection and closing the deal are paramount" in Manhattan's dating scene (SATC, 1:1), but the rest of the show does not endorse this stance.[4] Nevertheless, it frequently explores the connection between money and relationships. One of the early episodes (SATC, 1:9 "The Turtle and the Hare") presents a rather critical perspective on those marrying primarily for financial reasons. The four protagonists attend a wedding of a friend, Brook, who marries more for money than love, and it is implied that she is not happy. In the same episode, Carrie briefly contemplates marrying her gay friend, Stanford, so that he can get his inheritance from his grandmother, but quickly dismisses the idea. In Season 2, Miranda meets the kind and funny Steve (SATC, 2:8 "The Man, the Myth, the Viagra"), whom she will eventually marry, but before that happens, they break up twice. The first time, it is specifically because of the difference in their financial situation: She is a successful lawyer, he a bartender who cannot afford to buy the kind of suit Miranda wants him to wear to accompany her to a work function. It is worth noting, however, that during this brief first relationship, it is Steve who feels more uncomfortable about relying on Miranda's earnings than Miranda is about sharing them with him (SATC, 2:10 "Caste System"). Later on, when he opens his own bar, she regrets that he did not show that kind of ambition and drive while they were together (SATC, 4:5 "Ghost Town"). So, while Steve has always been caring and fun to be with, it is the combination of his newly improved status, increased resources, and sense of responsibility that makes it possible for Miranda to reconsider their relationship once again (I analyse this relationship in much greater detail in the next chapter). All Carrie's serious relationships are with men whose resources are more substantial than hers. Mr. Big in particular follows the traditional pattern of a romantic hero who can impress with his wealth and success, but even the salt-of-the-earth Aidan is in a position to buy Carrie's apartment when she is not (SATC, 4:12 "Just Say Yes"). In fact, Aidan's marriage offer and Big's first proposal are both about securing a "comfortable home" for Carrie. At one point in her relationship with Aidan, she wonders "Is this a real estate merger? Am I a real estate bride?" (SATC, 4:12). And in the first movie, Carrie and Big decide to get married because "it makes sense" given that he is about to buy an expensive penthouse apartment for them.

The fact that romantic heroines take money into consideration is not as cynical as it may seem. Cross-cultural ethnographic research demonstrates that love and financial considerations are always intertwined, and that sharing resources is a concrete proof of the elusive emotion of love (Nelson & Jankowiak, 2021). However, for some women, resources seem to be the most important mate choice criterion, sometimes overriding other important considerations.

Trey: "A doctor from family money"[5]

In *Sex and the City*, the character whose mating strategy is most focused on resources is Charlotte York. Like Charlotte Lucas, this Charlotte is determined to get married, even though her socio-economic circumstances are far better. But unlike her literary predecessor, who was "plain" and just wanted "an establishment", the modern Charlotte perceives her own mate value as higher than Charlotte Lucas did hers, and consequently, she initially has much higher expectations regarding her potential mates. The man she is looking for must have the "Big Three: looks, manners, money" (SATC, 1:4 "Valley of the Twenty Something"). Unfortunately, not many men can meet her criteria, and during the first two seasons of the show, she rejects numerous candidates.

At the beginning of Season 3, Charlotte, tired of dating, vows to find a husband that year. When she meets Trey MacDougal, he ticks all the boxes: Not only is he handsome and sophisticated but he is also "a doctor from family money" (SATC, 3:8 "The Big Time"). He is exactly *the kind of man* Charlotte wants to be married to. She fits Trey's bill equally well: She is attractive and educated—and like Austen's Mr. Collins, Trey does not want to spend too much time looking and does not care much about the individuality of his future wife. He shares this attitude with his mother, Bunny: When Charlotte meets her, the only question we witness Bunny asking is whether her future daughter-in-law can play tennis, and having received a positive answer, she determines that Charlotte is well-qualified for the privileged, leisured lifestyle of the MacDougal family (SATC, 3:9 "Easy Come, Easy Go"). Incidentally, Bunny's role is not dissimilar to Lady Catherine's instructing Mr. Collins to find a wife to complete his image, and both women are equally arrogant and interfering.

Like Charlotte Lucas, Charlotte York gets engaged barely knowing her future husband and takes things into her own hands to bring her marriage about. She notices that Trey's mother is easily able to manipulate her son into doing what she wants by using subtle body language. Charlotte successfully copies Bunny's technique first by making Trey change his mind about his order in a restaurant, and a few minutes later, when Trey fails to propose at an appropriately romantic moment, she employs it again to suggest that they should get married (SATC, 3:9). Like Mr. Collins who is easily talked into changing the addressee of his proposal twice in as many days, Trey is just as easily manoeuvred into proposing to Charlotte as he is into ordering a salad. Although Charlotte is later upset about the fact that, in effect, she proposed to herself, she is also delighted with the result.

The next episode continues to consider the clash of Charlotte's romantic ideals and her financial ambitions. When Trey casually presents her with a prenuptial agreement, Charlotte is disappointed and uncomfortable (SATC, 3:10 "All or Nothing"). She does not want to talk about divorce before she even gets married; it does not fit into her fairy-tale dream. But she is even more disappointed to discover that the document puts her value as a wife at $500,000. Bunny informs Charlotte that this is a standard amount in the MacDougal family, which is a further confirmation of the fact that Charlotte is treated as a generic wife, rather than an individual in her own right—in the same way, she sees Trey as an appropriate candidate for a husband (and in the same way Charlotte Lucas and Mr. Collins thought of each other). When Charlotte asks her friends for advice, they tell her that prenuptial agreements are pretty standard these days, and that it really is all about how much she loves and wants to marry Trey. In the end, Charlotte's business-like approach to marriage comes to the fore once again and she decides to negotiate—not with Trey but with Bunny. What she disputes is not the need for a prenuptial agreement but her value, and when she manages to raise it to $1 million, she is happy to sign the contract.

Through all of this, Charlotte is trying hard to maintain the romantic fantasy. Perhaps the ultimate example of this is the fact that Charlotte refrains from having sex with Trey. Two weeks after meeting him, she announces, "I think he could really be the one", and she does not want to "ruin it by having sex too early" (SATC, 3:8). To match her idealized image of Trey, she assumes an equally idealized persona of a chaste, innocent ingénue, fantasizing about being able to "erase [her] sexual past and start again" with Trey (SATC, 3:8).

She even voices such ridiculous statements as "I read that if you don't have sex for a year, you can actually become re-virginized" (SATC, 3:8).

The storyline is as an ironic comment on the idea of the sexual primacy of the romantic hero often criticized by feminists. As Rosalind Gill and Elena Herdieckerhoff observed, regardless of how sexually liberated and experienced chick lit heroines are, when they finally meet their Mr Right, "their innocence is narratively restored", and they become "re-virginised" (2006, p. 494). Usually, they experience sex with the hero as much more comfortable and enjoyable than their previous experiences; sometimes they reach their first orgasm despite having been sexually active for years. In this way, "the specialness" of the first sexual encounter between the heroine and hero, as well as the suggestion that it is only the hero who can "make her into a real woman", is maintained, and consequently, "the codes of traditional romance are reinstated 'through the back door'" (Gill & Herdieckerhoff, 2006, p. 494).

However, Charlotte's behaviour leading up to her disappointing night, naïve as it may appear, and the broader romantic trends criticized by Gill and Herdieckerhoff can be explained in terms of our evolved psychology. Women are well aware of the male preference for sexual reticence in long-term partners, because it acts as an indication of future fidelity; hence, women often highlight it to prospective mates by delaying sex. And they are not alone: Men who have a strong long-term orientation do not rush into sex either. Carrie's boyfriend Aidan is a good case in point: His refusal to have sex after their first few dates is an early sign of his unequivocally long-term orientation. Furthermore, the more positive sexual experience of romantic heroines, including a higher likelihood of orgasm when they find their Mr. Right, is not just a fictional convention but one of the bio-psychological mechanisms of mate choice (see Chapter 2). And Charlotte's story highlights just how important such cues may be.

The night before the wedding, unable to maintain her idealized image, Charlotte turns up, quite drunk, at Trey's apartment. She is expecting passionate sex, but to her horror, she discovers that her "perfect" husband-to-be cannot get an erection (SATC, 3:12 "Don't Ask, Don't Tell"). Given the overall ethos of the programme, this should have been the ultimate deal breaker, but it does not stop Charlotte marrying her perfect-on-paper fiancé. Like Charlotte Lucas, Charlotte York is prepared to overlook serious deficiencies of her partner in order to achieve her ultimate goal of high social status and financial prosperity. But while Austen's Charlotte successfully adjusts to her new married life, the modern Charlotte is bitterly disappointed. Both she and her new husband claim that they love the other and, despite Trey's reluctance, try different ways to overcome his erectile problem, including couples therapy, but do not achieve much success (SATC, 3:15 "Hot Child in the City"). When the sexually frustrated Charlotte kisses a sexy gardener on the MacDougal country estate, unperturbed Bunny announces that she is a true member of the family now, and Trey does not even make a scene (SATC, 3:17 "What Goes Around Comes Around"). Instead, he is prepared to resign himself to the fact that he cannot meet some of Charlotte's needs and therefore will occasionally have to "look the other way". At that moment, Charlotte realizes that despite having a "perfect husband" with a "perfect tennis court", and a "perfect country house", what she longs for is "that perfect connection with an imperfect person" (SATC, 3:17). Unlike Charlotte Lucas, Charlotte York is not prepared to stay in an emotionally unfulfilling marriage and, importantly, is not socially obliged to—so Trey moves out. In the finale of Season 3, Trey admits that their marital problems were most likely caused by his mistaken motives for marrying. He agreed to the marriage because he thought "it was time", because at his age, "people expect you to get married", to which Charlotte replies: "That sounds familiar" (SATC, 3:18 "Cock-A-Doodle-Do"). The conversation reveals that the couple's motivation for marriage is somewhat similar to Mr. Collins's in terms of fulfilling cultural expectations with a *socially* suitable partner.

"The perfect catch"[6]

Charlotte and Trey reunite briefly in Season 4, but their marriage once again falls apart over their fertility issues and Trey's unwillingness to keep looking for a solution (I discuss this in Chapter 12). While divorcing Trey, Charlotte meets Harry Goldenblatt, her lawyer. He does not seem to be her type: bald, chubby, and somewhat uncouth. But Charlotte is moved by his "humour, compassion, and acceptance" (SATC, 6:1 "To Market, to Market"). She realizes that with him, she does not have to play any games. Unlike Trey, Harry is able to satisfy Charlotte sexually, and he wholeheartedly supports her desire for children. Charlotte's happy ending within the television series is a successful adoption of a little girl, and in the first movie, she gives birth to another daughter—for unlike Trey, Harry is able to father a child.

In her feminist analysis, Stephanie Harzewski (2011) connects Charlotte's (and other *Sex and the City* characters') apparent preoccupation with external appearances to a particular postfeminist social trend, which she calls "late heterosexuality". It is characterized by "the aesthetic imperative", or "compulsory style", which posits "aesthetic pleasure [as] increasingly likely to be among our top criteria" regardless of how important or how mundane the object (Harzewski, 2011, p. 203, n. 8). She argues that this attitude informs the modern Anglo-American concept of identity and interpersonal relationships. Indeed, Charlotte is preoccupied with appearances. In Season 1, she breaks up with a man who really wants to get married because they disagree on a pattern for a formal dining set: "It would never work. He was American Classic; she was French Country" (SATC, 1:3). But in choosing Harry, she lets go of such superficial expectations, suggesting that "the aesthetic imperative" is not a sufficient explanation for her final decision. Her love for Harry signals her emotional growth while at the same time satisfying the main criteria of her mating strategy: material resources and motherhood. Her initial requirements for "looks, manners, money" are more extensive than Charlotte Lucas's "desire for an establishment" but equally instrumental. Despite different economic circumstances and options, both women display a certain failure of emotional intelligence, and both end up in emotionally unfulfilling marriages. Charlotte York has a chance to recover, largely due to the possibility of divorce and ability to support herself (although she profits financially from her divorce as well).

The failure of her marriage to Trey makes Charlotte realize that her initial, exclusively external criteria were inadequate as the basis for a long-term relationship. She adjusts them when she chooses Harry for the traits of his character. Still, her main priority is unchanged. She compromises on Harry's looks and sophistication but not on his resources: The diamond in the engagement ring he gives her is larger than the one she received from Trey. This kind of trade-off is consistent with the findings of evolutionary psychologists: Women, especially those for whom material resources are important, most readily compromise on their long-term partner's physical attractiveness, while his kindness, intelligence, and loyalty are seen as much more necessary (Li et al., 2002). Charlotte's story also highlights the importance of reproduction in mate choice: Harry becomes an ideal partner for Charlotte because, unlike Trey, he is able to get her pregnant. Interestingly, Austen too connects the drive for resources with reproduction. Although we do not know anything about Charlotte Lucas's desire for children, she is the only young woman in the novel whom we see not only choosing her mate but also becoming a mother.

In romantic fiction, a man without sufficient resources and with a low social standing is unlikely to be an attractive marital prospect, but at the same time, resources in themselves are never a good enough reason to marry. The intricate interplay between these simultaneously competing and complementary factors and the question of how to best balance them is prominent in most popular stories for women, from Austen's novels to modern rom-coms. The heroines of these stories never face real destitution or starvation, so they are never really *forced* to marry for money. How they value their mate's resources reflects less social imperatives than their individual priorities.

Notes

1 SATC, 3:1 "Where There's Smoke".
2 Infertility is also one of the most common reasons for men to divorce their wives. Another reason especially important for men is the wife's infidelity (Betzig, 1989).
3 SATC, 1:1 "Sex and the City".
4 This attitude is much more characteristic of Bushnell's book of *Sex and the City* (1996), as well as her other fiction, for example *Trading Up* (2003).
5 SATC, 3:8 "The Big Time".
6 SATC, 6:8 "The Catch".

References

Bereczkei, T., & Csanaky, A. (1996). Mate choice, marital success, and reproduction in a modern society. *Ethology and Sociobiology*, 17(1), 17–35. https://doi.org/10.1016/0162-3095(95)00104-2
Betzig, L. (1989). Causes of conjugal dissolution: A cross-cultural study. *Current Anthropology*, 30(5), 654–676. https://doi.org/10.1086/203798
Bushnell, C. (1996). *Sex and the city*. Abacus.
Bushnell, C. (2003). *Trading up*. Abacus.
Buss, D. M. (1989). Sex differences in human mate preferences: Evolutionary hypotheses tested in 37 cultures. *Behavioral and Brain Sciences*, 12(01), 1–14. https://doi.org/10.1017/S0140525X00023992
Campbell, A. (2002). *A mind of her own: The evolutionary psychology of women*. Oxford University Press.
Eagly, A. H., & Wood, W. (1999). The origins of sex differences in human behavior: Evolved dispositions versus social roles. *American Psychologist*, 54(6), 408–423.
Fielding, H. (1999). *Bridget Jones: The edge of reason*. Picador.
Fisher, H. E. (2016). *Anatomy of love: A natural history of mating, marriage, and why we stray* (Rev., Kindle ed.). W. W. Norton & Company. (1992)
Friedan, B. (1963/1997). *The feminine mystique*. W.W. Norton.
Geary, D. C., Vigil, J., & Byrd-Craven, J. (2004). Evolution of human mate choice. *The Journal of Sex Research*, 41(1), 27–42. https://doi.org/10.1080/00224490409552211
Gill, R., & Herdieckerhoff, E. (2006). Rewriting the romance. *Feminist Media Studies*, 6(4), 487–504. https://doi.org/10.1080/14680770600989947
Harzewski, S. (2011). *Chick lit and postfeminism*. University of Virginia Press.
James, E. L. (2012). *Fifty shades trilogy: Fifty shades of Grey, Fifty shades darker, Fifty shades freed* (Kindle ed.). Random House.
Kinsella, S. (2000/2007). *Confessions of a shopaholic*. Dial Press Trade Paperbacks.

Li, N. P., Bailey, J. M., Kenrick, D. T., & Linsenmeier, J. A. W. (2002). The necessities and luxuries of mate preferences: Testing the tradeoffs. *Journal of Personality and Social Psychology, 82*(6), 947–955. https://doi.org/10.1037//0022-3514.82.6.947

McGraw, K. J. (2002). Environmental predictors of geographic variation in human mating preferences. *Ethology, 108*(4), 303–317. https://doi.org/10.1046/j.1439-0310.2002.00757.x

Nelson, A. J., & Jankowiak, W. (2021). Love's ethnographic record: Beyond the love/arranged marriage dichotomy and other false essentialisms. In C.-H. Mayer & E. Vanderheiden (Eds.), *International handbook of love: Transcultural and transdisciplinary perspectives* (pp. 41–57). Springer International Publishing. https://doi.org/10.1007/978-3-030-45996-3_3

Pollet, T. V., & Nettle, D. (2009). Partner wealth predicts self-reported orgasm frequency in a sample of Chinese women. *Evolution and Human Behavior, 30*(2), 146–151.

Sex and the city. (1998–2004). [Television series]. Star, D. (Creator), & King, M. P. (Producer and Director). HBO.

Wiederman, M. W., & Allgeier, E. R. (1992). Gender differences in mate selection criteria: Sociobiological or socioeconomic explanation? *Ethology and Sociobiology, 13*(2), 115–124.

10
MIRANDA HOBBES

"Soulmates only exist in the Hallmark aisle of Duane Reade Drugs"[1]

Miranda Hobbes is a successful and ambitious lawyer. Out of the four protagonists of *Sex and the City*, she is the most career-focused and working in the most male-dominated profession. She holds the strongest feminist views, and through her storylines, the series explores lingering social prejudices and institutional discrimination against single women (in the first few seasons) and working mothers (in the last two seasons and the feature films). Miranda has been described as "the most logical character on *Sex and the City*" and "the voice of reason" (Cunigan, 2016; Dye, 2015), but her rationality often turns into cynicism, especially when it comes to men. Most importantly, Miranda is very reluctant to show her true feelings and almost misses out on a devoted partner. In that respect, she resembles Austen's Jane Bennet. However, Miranda is not shy; instead, she is fiercely independent and very sceptical about men's ability to commit. Such *commitment scepticism* is an ancient emotional mechanism which evolved to protect women from costly mate-choice errors, and how to calibrate its level is a frequent concern of romantic fiction.

Miranda's commitment scepticism is exceptionally high. According to her, "soul mates only exist in the Hallmark aisle of Duane Reade Drugs" (SATC, 4:1 "The Agony and the 'Ex'-tasy"). This attitude is evident in her on-again and off-again relationship with Steve Brady, a bartender she meets in Season 2 of the series (2:8 "The Man, the Myth, the Viagra"). They have casual sex followed by a brief relationship but break up because of the mismatch in their financial positions (SATC, 2:10 "Caste System"). They date again in Season 3 and even move in together but soon break up again because of Miranda's commitment issues (SATC, 3:8 "The Big Time"). Later, Steve is diagnosed with testicular cancer, and Miranda supports him through the treatment (SATC, 4:9 "Sex and the Country"). During that time, they have one-off sex which unexpectedly results in Miranda's pregnancy (SATC, 4:10 "Belles of the Balls"). Steve embraces his paternal responsibilities and even proposes marriage, but Miranda declines (SATC, 4:12 "Just Say Yes"). Throughout Seasons 5 and 6, Steve continues to show his kindness and support, which eventually prompts Miranda to admit that she loves him and ask him to marry her (SATC, 6:14 "The Ick Factor").

DOI: 10.4324/9781003320982-16

Who needs a man?

Miranda's search for a partner is complicated by her dismissive, even resentful, attitude towards men. Unlike Samantha, who is equally independent but craves men's company for her own sexual pleasure, Miranda tries to do without men. In one of the early episodes when the four women are discussing why people get married, Miranda says: "What's the big deal? In 50 years, men are gonna be obsolete anyway. I mean, already you can't talk to them, you don't need them to have kids with, you don't even need them to have sex with anymore"; and she declares she is in love with her new vibrator (SATC, 1:9 "The Turtle and the Hare").

One of her main charges against men is that they are generally "self-centred and unappreciative" (SATC, 1:1 "Sex and the City"). In this attitude, she is very similar to the character of Sharon (aka Shazzer) in *Bridget Jones's Diary*, a caricature of a strident feminist, who opines that men are "stupid, smug, arrogant, manipulative, self-indulgent bastards [who] exist in a total Culture of Entitlement" (Fielding, 1996, p. 125). Like Miranda, Sharon believes that men's dominance is quickly coming to an end: "Men … are so catastrophically unevolved that soon they will just be kept by women as pets for sex" (p. 77). But while Sharon's militant feminism is usually expressed in hilarious, drunken rants and immediately undercut by Bridget or one of her friends swooning over some man, Miranda makes a much more credible effort of living up to the feminist ideal of an independent, career-focused woman (of which more later). Although she frequently dates, she disapproves of her friends' preoccupation with men. In one episode, she complains that despite being smart, they seem to talk only about boyfriends (SATC, 2:1 "Take Me Out to the Ballgame"). On several occasions and in relation to all three of Carrie's most serious partners, she criticizes Carrie for prioritizing their needs and interests over her own—a mistake she is determined not to make. She is equally critical of Charlotte's determination to find a rich husband as she is of Carrie's search for a soulmate. However, unlike Samantha, who can satisfy her need for meaningful relationships through her female friends and is entirely comfortable with separating sex from emotional connection, Miranda is more conflicted, showing the anxieties associated with being single.

The myth of a one-night stand

Despite all her reservations, Miranda has not completely given up on men and goes on almost as many dates as her three friends. She is, however, much more sceptical about men's ability to be emotionally sincere and about their willingness to commit (what Fielding's Sharon refers to as "emotional fuckwittage"). The way in which she meets her future husband, Steve Brady, is a good example. The episode is framed by the idea of "urban relationship myths", which according to Miranda and Samantha are "unbelievable fairy tales concocted by women to make their love lives seem less hopeless" but "make you feel even more hopeless, because this fabulous, magical relationship is never happening to you" (SATC, 2:8). The myth Miranda recalls is specifically about "the guy who couldn't commit":

> …and the woman broke up with him and moved to Kansas. One night, she comes walking home. In the rain! Always in the rain! He stands there in front of her door with an engagement ring. He says, "Marry me," and they live happily ever after. (SATC, 2:8)

In this episode, Miranda has particularly good reasons to be suspicious of other people's commitment. In the opening sequence, she is publicly humiliated when she is forced to answer her date's phone only to discover that it is his wife calling, after he assured her that he was divorced. And it is not just men who let Miranda down. Later in the episode, Carrie cancels her evening plans with Miranda because Big offered to cook her dinner at his place. Miranda accuses Carrie that she "just dropped [her] life and ran right on over to his" and that once again "it's all about him". Disappointed and hurt, Miranda ends up going back home with the bartender, Steve. After sex, Steve tells her that it was "really special" and wants to see her again, but Miranda responds, "Look… You don't have to do this. You don't have to make believe you're gonna call. Let's just call this what this was: a one-night stand". Steve's reaction is an early sign of his long-term orientation, as short-term oriented men usually emotionally disengage after sex and often find their partner less attractive than before sex (Haselton & Buss, 2001). Having said this, his reaction is more easily faked than Aidan's postponement of sex discussed in the next chapter, so Miranda's scepticism is justified in this situation.

But Steve does not give up. When he turns up a few days later at Miranda's flat repeating that he likes her and wants to take her out, she translates it to mean: "I think you're an easy lay and I'd like to have sex again". He is so persistent that she eventually allows him to join her and the other three women at a bar aptly called Denial but then makes fun of him in a way that makes even her best friends uncomfortable. Her behaviour leads to the following conversation:

STEVE: Why do you hate guys so much?
MIRANDA: Excuse me?
STEVE: We just met, so I know that it ain't all about me.
MIRANDA: What do you want?
STEVE: I just wanna get to know you better. Do me a favor. Can you, for one second, believe that maybe I'm not some "full-of-shit" guy? That maybe I do like you? That maybe the other night was special? Do you think maybe you can believe that?
MIRANDA: No. Maybe I've just slept with too many bartenders. (SATC, 2:8)

The fact that he correctly identifies Miranda's distrust is a testament to Steve's people reading skills, and the fact that he persists despite her cynicism is another strong sign of his willingness to commit to her. But what changes Miranda's mind on this occasion is the behaviour of another man, Carrie's elusive boyfriend, Mr. Big. That night, he was supposed to come to dinner with the four women to get to know Carrie's friends better, but at the last minute, he made an excuse to get out of the plan. Just as Carrie is about to tell her friends that her "happily ever after really was just a myth", Big arrives at the bar, which as Carrie's voiceover explains, "shook Miranda's lack of belief system to the very core" (SATC, 2:8). Miranda leaves Denial, literally and metaphorically, catches up with Steve, and kisses him as the voiceover concludes, "From that night on, promiscuous women everywhere would tell the tale of the one-night stand that turned into a relationship". The scene, unsurprisingly, takes place in the rain.

This "tale of the one-night stand that turned into a relationship" is an important idea, in fiction and in real life. Although Miranda is dismissive about the prospect of any relationship with Steve, many women who engage in casual sex do hope that it may lead to something more serious. Indeed, many evolutionary psychologists contend that "perhaps the best documented benefit of a woman's short-term mating is the acquisition of a long-term partner" (Shackelford et al., 2004, p. 407; see also Greiling & Buss, 2000).

Helen Fisher, one of the leading researchers of romantic love, emphasizes that "casual sex is *rarely* casual" (2011, p. 219, emphasis in the original): It stimulates the production of various neurochemicals, such as dopamine, norepinephrine, oxytocin, and vasopressin, all of which are associated with intense feelings of romantic love, exhilaration, and attachment. These neurobiological reactions apply to both men and women, but the sexual experience generally seems to have more serious emotional implications for women than it does for men. Whether in the context of a one-night stand or a budding relationship, intercourse produces in women (usually more than in men) feelings of vulnerability, bonding, and love (Haselton & Buss, 2001; Townsend et al., 1995). So, even though the immediate motivation for casual sex may be physical gratification, and this is equally true for both genders (Garcia & Reiber, 2008; Townsend, 1995), women are generally more willing to have sex when there is a chance of forming a long-term relationship and are less willing than men to continue a sexual relationship if the emotional component is missing (Shackelford et al., 2004; Townsend, 1995). In fact, many women, including those with permissive attitudes to sex, admit that they find it difficult not to get emotionally involved with their sexual partners, even if they do not want to have such involvement (Townsend, 1995, p. 189). Furthermore, whether or not they would like to see a man again, women are overwhelmingly more concerned about whether the partner cares about them, whether sex was all he was after, and whether he will contact them again (Townsend, 1995; Townsend et al., 1995). Women are also much more sensitive to both anticipated and actual signs of rejection after a sexual encounter, for example, when men do not contact them or act as if nothing had happened (Campbell, 2008). Apparently, women want their sexual partners to want to see them again regardless of whether the women themselves want to continue the relationship (Townsend et al., 1995). Clearly, such a wish on the part of the man acts as a confirmation of the woman's desirability; it shows her that she has options and grants her control over the course of the relationship.

Chick lit authors understand these concerns and often incorporate them into their storylines. For example, Bridget Jones captures these anxieties perfectly. When her sexy boss, Daniel Cleaver, asks for Bridget's number, she feels like an "irresistible Sex Goddess. Hurrah!" but soon despairs when he does not call: "Wasted two days glaring psychopathically at the phone … Why hasn't he rung? Why? What's wrong with me? Why ask for my phone number if he wasn't going to ring?" (Fielding, 1996, pp. 26–27). When they eventually go on a date, she storms out of his apartment when he suggests that the sex they are about to have is "just a bit of fun".[2] Later on, after she has had sex with Daniel, she goes from euphoria to anguish in the space of a few sentences within the same journal entry:

> 6 p.m. Oh joy. Have spent the day in a state I can only describe as shag-drunkenness, … It was so lovely. … But as the rosy clouds begin to disperse, I begin to feel alarm. What now? No plans were made. Suddenly I realize I am waiting for the phone again. How can it be that the situation between the sexes after a first night remains so agonizingly imbalanced? Feel as if I have just sat an exam and must wait for my results.

11 p.m. Oh God. Why hasn't Daniel rung? Are we going out now, or what? (p. 60)

For the next several days, Bridget continues to be confused and upset about Daniel's nonchalance: "I am so depressed. Daniel, though perfectly chatty, friendly, even flirty all week, has given me no hint as to what is going on between us, as though it is perfectly normal to sleep with one of your colleagues and just leave it at that" (p. 67).

Although Bridget's casual sex with Daniel jumps-starts a (somewhat one-sided) relationship, it soon transpires that Daniel really was just interested in "a bit of fun" rather than a serious commitment. The relationship ends quickly and painfully, at least for Bridget, with the arrival of Daniel's American fiancée. Bridget's disappointment is perfectly echoed in a statement made by one of the interviewees in a study about women's experiences of casual sex: "A lot of times I thought I was starting a relationship, the guy was only after sex" (Townsend et al., 1995, p. 38).

Commitment sceptic

While Bridget's story reflects women's desire to convert casual sex into a lasting relationship, Miranda's dismissive attitude after her night with Steve illustrates another long-standing feature of female mating psychology: commitment scepticism. Her behaviour could also be seen as an attempt to retain control over her interactions with men and a defence strategy pre-empting potential rejection. In narrative terms, Miranda's reaction after sex with Steve is a reversal of the common chick lit trope of the woman obsessing about whether a man likes her enough to call. In Miranda's case, the obstacle that needs to be overcome on the way to the happy ending is not *his* lack of interest but *hers*, a narrative pattern used by Austen for Emma Woodhouse and Mr. Knightley. And Miranda is not the only chick lit character adopting this stance. The heroine of Marian Keyes' bestselling novel, *Rachel's Holiday*, describes her morning after casual sex in similar terms:

> As I was leaving, Luke asked for my phone number. In silence I tore a page from my diary, neatly wrote my phone number on it, then, as he watched in astonishment, crumpled it up into a ball and threw it into the trash. 'There,' I said, with a dazzling smile, 'that's saved you the trouble'. (1997/2006, p. 108)

Just as Miranda is suspicious of Steve's declarations and thinks he is only interested in sex, many women do the same in real life. Research shows that women tend to doubt men's long-term intentions and overestimate male focus on sex (Geher & Kaufman, 2013; Haselton & Buss, 2000). This means that women's assessment of men's interest may often be incorrect, but this commitment scepticism may be a useful bias because it reduces "the likelihood of costly mate-choice errors" (Geher & Kaufman, 2013, p. 139). Given that women must necessarily carry more biological costs when sex results in pregnancy, female sexual psychology should be specifically designed to minimize mating mistakes, and a high level of scepticism "may well be an adaptive strategy in the long run—women using such a decision-making rule may be more likely to actually end up with honest, committed, and long-term-relationship-seeking males" (Geher & Kaufman, 2013, p. 139). And, as if to confirm this supposition, our two fictional commitment sceptics, Miranda and Rachel, both acquire loyal boyfriends, while those who optimistically assume that they are in a serious relationship too quickly—like Bridget Jones or Marianne Dashwood—end up with a broken heart.

But the fact that commitment scepticism is a species-typical proclivity in women does not explain why Miranda is so much more sceptical than her three friends, or other romantic heroines. Just as with any species-typical behaviour, there may be an optimum level of scepticism in a given environment, and there clearly is a whole range of individual differences in the level of distrust women display (Geher & Kaufman, 2013, p. 225). And according to Randolph Nesse (2001), the more suspicious people are of others' ability to commit, the more difficulty they will have forming relationships, which may in turn deprive them of the substantial fitness benefits that derive from interpersonal commitments.

Miranda's particularly high level of commitment scepticism goes hand in hand with her fearful attachment style, her negative self-concept, and her self-sufficient attitude. As already mentioned in my discussion of Lydia Bennet in Chapter 4, when talking about the way people form relationships, psychologists use the concept of attachment styles, which are based on the different ways we tend to think about ourselves and others: "Whether or not the self is judged to be the sort of person toward whom anyone, and the attachment figure in particular, is likely to respond in a helpful way" and "whether or not the attachment figure is judged to be the sort of person who in general responds to calls for support and protection" (Bowlby, 1973, p. 204). Individuals with a *secure* attachment style tend to think positively about both themselves and others; they have low levels of anxiety and low levels of avoidance. Those with various types of *insecure* attachment are negative about either themselves or others. Miranda exhibits characteristics of a *fearful* attachment style. Fearfully attached individuals tend to think negatively about both themselves and others. They tend to agree with the statement: "I am uncomfortable getting close to others. I want emotionally close relationships, but I find it difficult to trust others completely, or to depend on them. I worry that I will be hurt if I allow myself to become too close to others" (Bartholomew & Horowitz, 1991, p. 244).

As already mentioned, Miranda has a rather negative opinion of men (the would-be attachment figures), considering them egocentric and self-entitled. She also has a relatively low self-concept, especially when it comes to her attractiveness as a romantic or sexual partner. Within the *Sex and the City* narrative, it provides a strong contrast to Samantha's cockiness about her sex-appeal and to Charlotte's girly conviction that she will be a perfect wife. From the beginning of the series, we know that Miranda is smart and successful, but we also learn about her insecurities. In the episode "Three's a Crowd" (SATC, 1:8), Charlotte asks her friends' advice on an idea of a threesome suggested by her current boyfriend, and Miranda is offended to be the only one not considered as a potential partner. She then has recurring dreams about being rejected by her friends, which her therapist interprets as a sign of her low self-esteem and need for acceptance. In order to test her attractiveness, she answers a newspaper ad asking for a threesome partner, and when the young attractive couple accepts Miranda, her peace of mind is restored (even though she does not go through with the threesome). In another episode, when a guest at an engagement party asks Miranda if she is seeing "anyone special", Miranda responds: "Actually no but I am seeing a whole bunch of unspecial guys. That's one of the requirements to date me. ... I'm serious: Do any of you have a completely unremarkable friend or maybe a house plant I could go to dinner with on Saturday night?" (SATC, 4:1). The remark, while funny, is a great illustration of her frustration with men, her discomfort with her single status and her self-doubt. In the very next episode, Miranda is disbelieving when a man at the gym tells her she is sexy: "Sexy is the thing I try to get them to see me as *after* I win them over with my personality" (SATC, 4:2 "The Real Me"). In fact, she deliberately minimizes her feminine sex-appeal: She is the only one of the four characters with a short haircut and a masculine dress style, in contrast to Samantha's often revealing outfits, Charlotte's Stepford wife style, and Carrie's quirky but ultra-feminine wardrobe.

Miranda's high commitment scepticism and her insecure attachment style are strongly related to her desire for independence, which is a trait of her personality, reinforced by the feminist ideals of self-reliance. She is the first of the four women to buy her own apartment (SATC, 2:5 "Four Women and a Funeral"), which signifies both her financial and her emotional independence: She does not wait for her Prince Charming, or his money, to establish a home for herself. However, in a true *Sex and the City* fashion, the episode is not a straightforward celebration of Miranda's autonomy. It is also used to comment on lingering prejudices against single women and on the anxiety of being single. First, Miranda has to deal with the inherent sexism of the bureaucratic process and its officials, suspicious of her single woman status without the financial backing of a father or husband. Then, she also has to face her own fears when she learns that the flat she is buying used to belong to a woman who never married. When she died, it took a week to discover her body, and "rumour has it, the cat ate half her face" (SATC, 2:5). The rumour is clearly a comical nod to Bridget Jones's hysterical dread of "dying alone and being found three weeks later half-eaten by an Alsatian" (Fielding, 1996, p. 20) and is also repeated in another chick-lit bestseller *Good in Bed* (Weiner, 2001). But Miranda's fear becomes real when she accidentally almost chokes on her dinner.

Miranda's independent spirit is also linked to her characterization as a driven career woman, which is often used to explore the conflict between her professional ambitions and her personal happiness, a theme which is common in chick lit and in Hollywood films (e.g., *Fatal Attraction, 1987 or Working Girl,* 1988). In fact, both times she breaks up with Steve, it is connected with her professional success. The first break-up is precipitated by Steve's conviction that she should be with someone who is "more on her level"; she interprets it as "being punished for being successful" (SATC, 2:10). When they renew the relationship, the happiness does not last long either, because the somewhat up-tight and super-organized Miranda interprets Steve's care-free attitude as lack of maturity (SATC, 3:8). Her annoyance with Steve is exacerbated by the fact that she is working particularly hard at that time in order to earn a promotion. So, at the same time as she becomes a partner at her law firm, she loses her romantic partner.

Miranda insists on her self-sufficiency even in situations when it is quite obvious that she needs support, be it practical or emotional; for example, after her eye surgery (SATC, 3:1 "Where There's Smoke"), or when her mother dies (SATC, 4:8 "My Motherboard, Myself"). The situation that best illustrates Miranda's desire for self-sufficiency and her commitment scepticism is the way she deals with her pregnancy and motherhood. When she accidentally gets pregnant to her then ex-boyfriend, Steve, she does not think she is ready to have a child and arranges an abortion but after some consideration, does not go through with it. Steve offers to help and suggests marriage, but she tells him: "You don't have to do anything. I'll take care of the baby and support it, and you can visit whenever you want, but it's not going to be your problem. It's my decision, and it's just something I want to do for me" (SATC, 4:12). Steve, of course, sticks around. As in the previous two situations of surgery and bereavement, he is there for Miranda without being asked and regardless of the fact that he is not in a relationship with her at the time. His unwavering commitment is what wins her over in the end.

"That is love"[3]

Although Miranda eventually builds a happy marriage, her path to love is rather unromantic. During their on-again-off-again relationship, Miranda is most attracted to Steve when he is dating someone else. For example, when she and Carrie run into Steve and Aidan with their new girlfriends, they both wonder why it is that their ex-boyfriends suddenly look so much more attractive. After she has had her son, Brady, and once again rejected Steve, Miranda is obviously jealous about his current sexy-looking girlfriend. In light of what we know about female sexual psychology, this is not very surprising: Women (and females in other species) use other females' attraction to a male as a sign of his desirability, especially if those other females are attractive (Meston & Buss, 2009, p. 24). This tendency is reflected in other narratives, not only *Sex and the City*. In *Rachel's Holiday*, the heroine is ambivalent about her feelings for her one-night stand, Luke, until she spots him in a bar with another beautiful woman: "It was indeed Luke. However, he was accompanied by none other than the exquisite Anya, skinny, tanned, almond-eyed Anya. The first thought that jumped into my head was, *if he's good enough for Anya, he's good enough for me*" (Keyes, 1997/2006, p. 299, emphasis in the original). Austen's *Emma* also discovers her love for Mr. Knightley only after Harriet's attraction to him.

After a few false starts, Miranda realizes that Steve is the man for her, even though—or perhaps because—he is more like Colonel Brandon than Mr. Darcy. During their time together in Season 3, Miranda says that what she loves about Steve most is that he is predictable and comfortable (although, in a true *Sex and the City* style, her moment of blissful domesticity is undercut by the crude realities of living together when she is faced with Steve's dirty underwear; SATC, 3:7 "Drama Queens"). Her contentment at this point is contrasted with Carrie's anxiety about Aidan's homeliness, which Carrie soon rejects for more emotional drama with Big. Miranda, however, prioritizes Steve's stability.[4] In a later season, when the women discuss how many great loves one can have in a lifetime, Miranda says about Steve: "He's a friend, not a core shaker" (SATC, 5:1 "Anchors Away"), and when she is struggling to juggle motherhood and her demanding career, she jokes that she could marry Steve just to get some help (SATC, 5:6 "Critical Condition"). As Steve transforms himself from a bartender to a bar owner, Miranda appreciates his increased maturity and status—he certainly becomes closer to what he earlier called as "her level"—but it is Steve's continued kindness and support that convince her to give their relationship another chance. After a year of raising a child together, she finally recognizes and admits the strength of her feelings for Steve, and *she* asks *him* to marry her.

However, the wedding—very understated and performed in a community garden—is not Miranda's true happy ending within the series. While her marriage signals her willingness to believe in Steve's commitment and her readiness to rely on him, for her happy-ever-after to be complete, she must reconcile her desire for autonomy with her own commitment to the people in her life. After the birth of her son Brady, Miranda insists that she is still "the same person" and only gradually comes to accept that her social and professional lives will need to change because she is now "plus one" (SATC, 5:5 "Plus One Is the Loneliest Number"). She makes a symbolic acknowledgement of this by putting Brady's photo in front of her business card on her desk. In Season 6, she cuts down her working hours in order to spend more time with Brady. Naming her son Brady, which is Steve's family name, getting him christened in order to please Steve's mother, and getting formally married are other steps on her journey. Another big step is her decision to sell her Manhattan apartment and buy a townhouse in Brooklyn, a move which is not only geographical but which also signals a significant shift in Miranda's priorities: It acknowledges her family responsibilities and the importance of human connection. Finally, when Steve discovers that his mother is suffering early signs of dementia, Miranda invites her to live in their new family house and helps to look after her. Miranda's faithful housekeeper concludes, while watching Miranda carefully bathing her mother-in-law: "That is love. You love" (SATC, 6:20 "An American Girl in Paris: Part Deux").

In the first *Sex and the City* movie, Miranda's faith in Steve's commitment is once again severely tested when he cheats on her in a one-off encounter, a behaviour which is very out of character, but which is explained by the fact that Miranda again seems to be prioritizing her career over her personal commitments. Steve is genuinely sorry for his breach of trust and really wants to repair the relationship. Nevertheless, he is also concerned that even if they do get back together, Miranda might keep punishing him in the future. Miranda's refusal to forgive Steve, or even listen to his explanations, is paralleled with her own attempts to regain Carrie's friendship and trust after contributing to the failure of Carrie's wedding.[5] Both storylines require Miranda, once again, to overcome her unusually high reluctance to trust others, to acknowledge the importance of mutuality in interpersonal relationships, and to adjust the relative value of rational and emotional considerations. While Miranda tries to approach her marriage crisis in a purely logical way, by making a list of all the pros and cons of getting back with Steve, she finally makes her decision based on a strong feeling: A memory of a tender, happy moment together tips the balance in Steve's favour.

The two *Sex and the City* movies also continue to explore the recurrent conflict between Miranda's demanding career and her personal commitments. She does her best to emulate the feminist ideals of self-sufficiency and professional success, but after the arrival of her son and then the crisis in her marriage, this stance becomes untenable and does not bring personal happiness. She gradually accepts, and finds fulfilment, in her commitments to other people: as a mother, wife, and friend. As the final step in this process, she leaves her highly competitive law firm, where as a woman she is not appreciated, and joins a more female-friendly firm. Not surprisingly, such a narrative progression is seen in terms of an anti-feminist backlash (Weisser, 2013), a "weary acknowledgement that feminism would never succeed in socializing the workplace or in implicating men in childcare responsibilities as fully as women" (Whelehan, 2005, p. 195). But instead of being viewed as a sign of feminism's failure, Miranda's narrative conclusion, and many others similar to hers, should be seen as an affirmation of feminine values. Miranda does not relinquish her professional ambitions—just the impersonal, cut-throat ways of achieving them. She does abandon masculine corporate structures (so often criticized by feminists) only in order to contribute to alternative, more female-friendly ones. Instead of professional competitiveness and personal independence, Miranda and other chick lit heroines like her opt for cooperation and affiliation, which have been vital for women throughout our evolutionary history, both in sexual and social relations.

Notes

1 SATC, 4:1 "The Agony and the 'Ex'-tasy".
2 In the movie adaptation, Bridget does have sex with Daniel at the first opportunity, but Daniel does not make this unromantic proviso, allowing Bridget to believe even on that first night that by having sex they are starting a relationship. This change was most likely due to the time limits of a feature film.

3 SATC, 6:20 "An American Girl in Paris: Part Deux".
4 This kind of stability, despite rejection or obstacles, is also a crucial part of the attraction of Austen's Colonel Brandon, Captain Wentworth, and Edward Ferrars.
5 During Carrie and Big's pre-wedding dinner, Miranda, in a moment of anger and disappointment, tells Big that getting married "ruins everything". Although it is not clear how much this statement affected Big, both women think it contributed to his last-minute doubts.

References

Bartholomew, K., & Horowitz, L. M. (1991). Attachment styles among young adults: A test of a four-category model. *Journal of Personality and Social Psychology, 61*(2), 226–244.

Bowlby, J. (1973). *Attachment and loss: Vol. 2. Separation.* Basic Books.

Campbell, A. (2008). The morning after the night before. *Human Nature, 19*(2), 157–173.

Cunigan, M. (2016, May 4). 11 lessons from *Sex and the City*'s career driven feminist Miranda Hobbes. *The Odyssey Online.* https://www.theodysseyonline.com/11-lessons-from-sex-and-the-citys-career-driven-feminist-miranda-hobbes

Dye, T. (2015, April 18). 8 life lessons from Miranda Hobbes, the most logical character on *Sex and the City*. *Bustle.* https://www.bustle.com/articles/77145-8-life-lessons-from-miranda-hobbes-the-most-logical-character-on-sex-and-the-city

Fielding, H. (1996). *Bridget Jones's diary: A novel.* Picador.

Fisher, H. E. (2011). *Why him? Why her? How to find and keep lasting love.* Oneworld.

Garcia, J. R., & Reiber, C. (2008). Hook-up behavior: A biopsychosocial perspective. *Evolutionary Behavioral Sciences, 2*(4), 192–208.

Geher, G., & Kaufman, S. B. (2013). *Mating intelligence unleashed: The role of the mind in sex, dating, and love* (Kindle ed.). Oxford University Press.

Greiling, H., & Buss, D. M. (2000). Women's sexual strategies: The hidden dimension of extra-pair mating. *Personality and Individual Differences, 28*(5), 929–963. https://doi.org/10.1016/S0191-8869(99)00151-8

Haselton, M. G., & Buss, D. M. (2000). Error management theory: A new perspective on biases in cross-sex mind reading. *Journal of Personality and Social Psychology, 78*, 81–91. https://doi.org/10.1037/0022-3514.78.1.81

Haselton, M. G., & Buss, D. M. (2001). The affective shift hypothesis: The functions of emotional changes following sexual intercourse. *Personal Relationships, 8*(4), 357–369. https://doi.org/10.1111/j.1475-6811.2001.tb00045.x

Keyes, M. (1997/2006). *Rachel's holiday.* Harper Collins.

Meston, C. M., & Buss, D. M. (2009). *Why women have sex: Understanding sexual motivations—from adventure to revenge (and everything in between).* Times Books.

Nesse, R. M. (2001). Natural selection and the capacity for subjective commitment. In R. M. Nesse (Ed.), *Evolution and the capacity for commitment* (pp. 1–44). Russell Sage Foundation.

Sex and the city. (1998–2004). [Television series]. Star, D. (Creator), & King, M. P. (Producer and Director). HBO.

Sex and the city. (2008). [Motion picture]. King, M. P. (Director/Writer). New Line Cinema.

Shackelford, T., Goetz, A., LaMunyon, C., Quintus, B., & Weekes-Shackelford, V. (2004). Sex differences in sexual psychology produce sex-similar preferences for a short-term mate. *Archives of Sexual Behavior, 33*(4), 405–412. https://doi.org/10.1023/B:ASEB.0000028893.49140.b6

Townsend, J. M. (1995). Sex without emotional involvement: An evolutionary interpretation of sex differences. *Archives of Sexual Behavior, 24*(2), 173–206. https://doi.org/10.1007/bf01541580

Townsend, J. M., Kline, J., & Wasserman, T. H. (1995). Low-investment copulation: Sex differences in motivations and emotional reactions. *Ethology and Sociobiology, 16*(1), 25–51.

Weiner, J. (2001). *Good in bed: A novel* (Kindle ed.). Pocket Books.

Weisser, S. O. (2013). *The glass slipper: Women and love stories.* Rutgers University Press.

Whelehan, I. (2005). *The feminist bestseller: From Sex and the Single Girl to Sex and the City.* Palgrave Macmillan.

11
CARRIE BRADSHAW

"Tell me I'm the one"[1]

Carrie, the protagonist and narrator of *Sex and the City*, is the embodiment of the traditional romantic quest. Like Bridget Jones and Ally McBeal, she has been declared "not quite the daughter feminists were hoping for" (Vincent, 1998, p. 49), and what disqualifies her most, apart from her passion for such feminine frivolities as fashion and shoes, is her determined search for love. Feminist critique of Austen and popular romances often focuses on the idea of marriage (or a promise of a long-term, marriage-like relationship in more recent texts) as narrative closure. This narrative strategy is said to posit female sexuality as "something that needs to be contained, controlled, and eventually concentrated upon only one man" (Smith, 2008, p. 80). In the case of *Sex and the City* and other chick lit, there is some disagreement about whether this criticism is still valid. Supporters of chick lit texts contend that while the search for Mr. Right undoubtedly remains an important feature of these narratives, it has been considerably transformed in many ways, and the status of the romantic hero has been diminished (Harzewski, 2011). The perfect man, although still dreamt of, "is certainly no longer the sole guarantor of women's happiness and emotional health" (Hermes, 2006, p. 80). Fans of chick texts often interpret their heroines as strong, independent women who "don't need a man" to be fulfilled (Robinson, 2011, p. 117). Scholars also note the presence of female characters who are not defined primarily by their relationship to a man but more through their relationships with each other, as in *Sex and the City* (Gerhard, 2005; Gill, 2007; Mabry, 2006), or through their work, in the case of *Ally McBeal* (Moseley & Read, 2002). However, many others ascertain that although chick lit heroines have independent incomes and tight circles of friends, they still need to be validated by a man (Gill & Herdieckerhoff, 2006). Imelda Whelehan concludes that modern heroines "do not enter full maturity until their future with The One is sealed" (2005, p. 216). Stephanie Harzewski makes this point about Bridget Jones, saying that her "self-esteem is fragilely dependent on her status as somebody's girlfriend" (2011, p. 68).

Indeed, these female characters, while supporting feminist ideals, openly admit that they long for a heterosexual relationship. Bridget Jones, in her typical self-deprecating style, resolves that she will not "sulk about having no boyfriend, but develop inner poise

DOI: 10.4324/9781003320982-17

and authority and sense of self as woman of substance, complete without boyfriend, as best way to obtain boyfriend" (Fielding, 1996, p. 2). Ally McBeal also declares "I plan to change [society]. I just want to get married first" (*Ally McBeal*, 1:11 "Silver Bells"). My contention, however, is that these fictional women are, as Deborah Jermyn put it, "discerningly single, rather than single and desperate" (2009, p. 53). Unlike Austen heroines, they have many options available to them, but a mutually fulfilling relationship with a man who combines evolutionarily important traits—intelligence, kindness, commitment, social power, and masculine appearance—is still the most appealing. And such desire is not anti-feminist.

Carrie's mating strategy, as well as her final choice, are very similar to Elizabeth Bennet's, and many points made in relation to *Pride and Prejudice* apply to the main romantic plot in *Sex and the City*. These numerous parallels could be seen as due to generic conventions, and that is partly true, but evolutionary and cognitive studies of fiction strongly suggest that generic conventions have likely been shaped by human psychology and emotional repertoire (Carroll, 2022; Carroll et al., 2012; Grodal, 2009, 2017; Hogan, 2011). Regardless of the changes in socio-economic circumstances, Carrie faces the long-standing dilemmas of mate choice. Like Samantha, Carrie is attracted to handsome men but does not find casual sex fulfilling. Like Charlotte, she often worries about her financial future but refuses to be a "real estate bride" (SATC, 4:12 "Just Say Yes"). And like Miranda, she expects full commitment from her partner but is prepared to show emotional vulnerability before he does. Like Elizabeth Bennet, Carrie wants a man who will meet her high standards and appreciate her individuality. She considers three serious candidates (plus a number of other short-term boyfriends). She falls in love with the handsome and successful Mr. Big, but he is not ready to commit to her. She gets engaged to Aidan Shaw, a very family-oriented, down-to-earth kind of guy, but he is intent on "improving" Carrie. She moves to Paris with Aleksandr Petrovsky who is flamboyantly romantic but turns out to be utterly self-absorbed. Luckily, after a few false starts, both Carrie and Mr. Big realize the value of a committed relationship with each other.

Discerningly single

The notion of female choices is Carrie's particular concern throughout the narrative. In one episode, she muses, inviting the viewer to do the same: "I thought about choices. Since birth modern women have been told that we can do and be anything we want, be an astronaut, the head of an internet company, a stay-at-home mom. There aren't any rules any more. Choices are endless" (SATC, 3:10 "All or Nothing"). But having options means that choosing becomes more, not less, difficult. Especially when the stakes, and the expectations, are high, and the reasons for settling on one option are not as urgent or compelling as they used to be. Carrie continues:

> But is it possible that we've gotten so spoiled by choices that we've become unable to make one? That part of us knows that once you choose something, one man, one great apartment, one amazing job, another option goes away? Are we a generation of women who can't choose just 'one from column A'? Did we all have too much to handle, or … Can we have it all? (SATC, 3:10)

This seeming reluctance to "choose just one" has been a recurrent theme in the criticism of the show (Greven, 2004), but it may be a fair reflection of female sexual psychology. Females of most sexually reproducing species, from insects to primates, are very picky about their partners, and human females are probably the pickiest of all, especially when environmental conditions are relatively female-friendly. The psychologist Bruce Ellis argues that "women's sexual tastes become more, rather than less, discriminatory as their wealth, power and social status increase" (1995, p. 273), and others note that a "tendency to think that there just might be someone better out there during the mate-search process" is a typical female psychological bias (Geher & Kaufman, 2013, p. 134). The economist Paul Seabright suggests that the problem is exacerbated by modern communication technologies:

> The more easily Prince Charming can find his Cinderella, the more likely it is that instead of blushing winningly at him, she will reply: 'I'll see if I can fit you into my schedule … The very technologies that help us to find our ideal partners, whether in our professional or our romantic lives, crowd the attention of those partners and raise the stakes in the contest to find ways to stand out from the crowd, requiring ever more elaborate and unpredictable ways of staking a claim to their attention. (2012, p. 152)

The journalist Stella Smith summarized the dilemma of a "single bright female" by saying:

> I'm an attractive, 40-something divorcee. I've got my own house, a degree, and a career. I have a brain too. But it seems to be impossible to meet a man who comes anywhere near my level. Why? Are they out there? … Are we too fussy? … I refuse to settle for Mr Wrong. (2016, p. 13)

Carrie, like her three friends, and other chick-lit heroines, also refuses to settle for Mr. OK, or Mr. Second-Best. But how do you find Mr. Right in the crowded New York City? As I explain in Chapter 2, the process of mate selection involves not only assessing the qualities of potential partners, but also making a choice to commit to one through love.

"Cupid has flown the co-op"[2]

The first episode of the series, like the opening of Bushnell's book which inspired it, announces "the end of love in Manhattan": "Welcome to the Age of Un-Innocence. … No one has breakfast at Tiffany's, and no one has affairs to remember. … Cupid has flown the co-op" (SATC, 1:1). This is soon followed by Samantha's assertion that "this is the first time in the history of Manhattan that women have had as much money and power as men, plus the equal luxury of treating men like sex objects". Carrie wonders whether women really have given up on love in order to "throttle on power". She decides to test Samantha's claims and have sex, "like a man", without any commitment or concern for mutuality. She feels "empowered and incredibly alive" after the experience but soon questions whether this unemotional sex is really all that she wants. And that is when she meets Mr. Big.

From the first encounter, their relationship is positioned between the temptation of short-term sex and the possibility of a long-term commitment. Big knows that Carrie is not opposed to casual sex—he sees her personal supply of condoms spill out of her handbag when they accidentally bump into each other on the street. Later in the episode, when Carrie is waiting for a taxi late at night, Mr. Big stops to give her a ride; he picks her up on the street corner, like a prostitute. Indeed, when Carrie tells Big she is "a kind of sexual anthropologist", he asks, "you mean like a hooker?". He diagnoses her sexual bravado as: "You've never been in love"; and when Carrie asks if *he* has ever been in love, he responds with his now iconic line: "Abso-fucking-lutely".

The pilot episode explicitly invokes feminist arguments about love as disempowering for women and asserts women's right to sexual freedom and pleasure. At the same time, it raises questions about the need for connection, mutuality, and emotional intimacy, often highlighted in feminist concerns about women's sexual liberation. The differential appeal of casual sex and long-term attachment for women and men has also been an important question for evolutionary psychologists, revealing some striking gender similarities as well as differences.

In Justin Garcia and Chris Reiber's study (2008), when asked about their motivation for engaging in hook-ups, men and women equally identified sexual pleasure as the main reason (90% of both sexes), but they were also equally interested in emotional fulfilment (54% of both sexes) and equally open to the possibility that the hook-up may lead to a relationship (50% of both sexes). In fact, 505 out of 507 participants stated that they would like to be in a traditional romantic relationship at some point. But the responses differed significantly (and in the predicted direction) when participants were asked about "an ideal outcome" of their one-night stand. For men, a traditional romantic relationship and further hook-ups were almost equally appealing, with 32% preferring the former and 29% opting for the latter. In contrast, women showed a much stronger preference for committed relationships, with 43% choosing this option compared to only 17% who favored additional hook-ups.

Anne Campbell questions the idea that women view short-term relationships "as a prelude to more desirable long-term relationships" (2008, p. 164) because her study of attitudes to casual sex found that women were only *slightly* more disappointed than men when their one-night stands did not continue. However, the slightness of this difference is significant for exactly the opposite reason. Female participants in her study judged their one-night stand experiences overwhelmingly more negatively than men did—and yet were still only slightly more disappointed that these encounters did not develop into long-term relationships. Rather than a lack of interest in long-term partnerships, these findings suggest that many women want them so much that they are willing to overlook the negative aspects of casual sex in the hope that it may lead to serious commitment.

Throughout her narrative, Carrie is open to having sex with newly met men, but she usually treats these encounters as potential springboards for what she ultimately wants: a relationship that is both passionate *and* committed. She tests Samantha's proposition about turning men into sex objects but soon realizes that this simple reversal of power is not satisfying enough for her; especially not when faced with the possibility that a man like Mr. Big—rich, powerful, handsome, and sexy—*can* fall in love.

Mr. Big: "The Big journey"[3]

Unlike Elizabeth and Darcy, who start off prejudiced against each other, Carrie and Big are instantly drawn to each other. But, like Elizabeth, Carrie misinterprets some of Big's early behaviour. For example, she thinks he does not treat their relationship seriously and perhaps is even ashamed of her because on their first date, he takes her to a small, rather obscure Chinese restaurant; on another occasion, he does not introduce her to an acquaintance they accidentally meet; and finally, he opts out of meeting her friends one afternoon (SATC, 1:6 "Secret Sex"). In all instances, however, Carrie's interpretation of Big's actions is a result of the *fundamental attribution error* (as it was for Elizabeth): They do not reflect Big's lack of feelings for Carrie but are due to other causes. Big considers that small restaurant to have the best Chinese food in New York; he cannot remember the name of the friend they bump into; and when Carrie invites him to meet her friends, he already has court-side tickets to a basketball game of his favourite team.

Like Darcy, Big has high expectations about women's beauty, and although he never suggests that Carrie is not attractive enough for him, the knowledge of the fact that he often dates models makes Carrie feel insecure. She thinks she is "out of his league" and feels "invisible" (SATC, 1:2 "Models and Mortals"). Carrie's anxieties about appearance are common for modern chick lit heroines, who like Austen's heroines, are rarely the most beautiful in the room. Samantha is the only one who declares herself free of such worries, in the same way that she claims to be free from the delusions about romantic love. The issue of female beauty is not only a recurrent theme in romantic fiction but is also an area repeatedly analysed by both feminist and evolutionary scholars. Feminists have identified "the beauty myth" as one of the biggest sources of oppression for modern women (Wolf, 1991). Evolutionary psychologists studying sex differences in mate selection often emphasize the male requirement for female physical attractiveness but also admit that modern culture may lead to maladaptive overvaluation of physical beauty (Buss & Schmitt, 2011).

As I have argued in relation to Jane and Elizabeth Bennet, Austen repeatedly questions the assumption that beauty is the basis of female power and relationship success, and modern romantic fiction takes a similar stance. For example, Bridget Jones is a bit heavier than she would like to be and her struggles with beauty regimes, such as make-up, hair removal, or figure-enhancing underwear, are a constant source of comedy. The women she competes with for either Daniel Cleaver or Mark Darcy are slimmer and more obviously attractive but are also soulless, cruel, and mercenary. In the end, despite Bridget's seeming inability to meet conventional beauty standards, and despite her rivals' better compliance with them, both the caddish Daniel and the perfect boyfriend Mark recognize her superiority to other women. And as I explained in Chapter 6, such re-evaluation of a person's attractiveness as we learn more about their personality and values is not just a romantic fantasy but a well-documented human psychological tendency.

Just as Darcy gradually interprets Elizabeth's physical features in light of her intelligence and honesty, Big assures Carrie that he is attracted to her not just because of her appearance. After a lacklustre date with yet another model, Big traces Carrie down and explains: "There's so many gorgeous women out there but in the end you want to be with the one who makes you laugh" (SATC, 1:2). In Season 2, he unexpectedly marries the tall, slim, and beautiful Natasha, whom Carrie describes as "a stick figure with no soul" (SATC, 2:18 "Ex and the City"), but the marriage soon breaks down because Big cannot deny his attraction to the much more complex Carrie.[4] On the whole, the series aligns its conclusions with what we know from empirical research: Men do prioritize beauty in short-term sexual encounters, but when it comes to long-term relationships, they are equally, or more, interested in the woman's intelligence and kindness (Buss, 1989).

Like Darcy, Mr. Big has money, status, good looks, but starts off as seemingly arrogant and aloof. On a few occasions, Carrie admits that his confidence and sense of superiority may have been attractive at first, but in the long run, they are not conducive to a healthy relationship. Just as Elizabeth makes Darcy confront his faults, so Carrie forces Big to reevaluate his detachment and arrogance. Like Darcy, Big has to admit that he did not do Carrie justice, and in fact, really hurt her *several* times (SATC, 5:7 "The Big Journey"). But the first major stumbling block in their relationship is Big's reluctance to fully commit to Carrie. In the finale of the first season, he wants Carrie to come on holiday with him but refuses to introduce her to his mother, arguing that she does not need to meet yet another of his girlfriends. But Carrie does not want to be just another girlfriend.

Aidan: "Just say yes"[5]

After breaking up with Big, Carrie dates several other men and almost gets married to Aidan Shaw, who is the antithesis of Big. Aidan is "warm, masculine, and classic American" (SATC, 3:5 "No Ifs, Ands or Butts'). He designs and hand-makes wooden furniture and is consistently associated with nature, nurturance, and domesticity: He has a dog, a cabin in the woods, and when he first moves in with Carrie, she is shocked about the fact that he brings a pot plant.

The prominent psychologist of love, Helen Fisher, identifies four main personality types related to different ways people form and maintain relationships, and Aidan perfectly fits the "Builder" type (2011, pp. 130–133). As Fisher explains, builders "generally aren't interested in casual sex"; what they look for is

> a stable and predictable team player, someone who shares their fidelity to family and tradition ... And when they find 'the one,' Builders nest—and take on all the responsibilities of a true partnership. They plan to be sexually faithful. And they strive to be the 'good husband' or the 'devoted wife.' Indeed, Builders are willing to do time-consuming drudgery, going far beyond what is expected of them, to maintain their vows. (Fisher, 2011, p. 133)

Aidan's attitude to Carrie illustrates many of the points mentioned by Fisher. It also provides a strong contrast to Mr. Big. When Carrie and Aidan start dating, she is ready to have sex within the first couple of weeks, but Aidan wants to "take it slowly". He is down-to-earth, caring, and keen to connect with Carrie's friends: He makes a special piece of furniture for Charlotte's wedding present; he helps Miranda when she has an accident at home and Carrie is unable to come; he and Steve go to Miranda's mother's funeral (even though at that time neither of them is in a relationship with Carrie or Miranda). He also wants Carrie to meet his parents when they are visiting in New York. And not long after Aidan and Carrie break off their engagement, he marries another woman and becomes a father.

On the face of it, Aidan is a perfect boyfriend. The critics identify him as the ideal of postfeminist masculinity, "the new sensitive man" (di Mattia, 2004, p. 24), and some fans of the show are still upset that Carrie first cheats on him and then refuses to marry him. But Carrie has good reasons: Right from the beginning, Aidan cannot accept Carrie as she is and tries to improve her. When they first meet, he tells Carrie he cannot date a smoker.

He does later admit that she is more than a smoker, and that perhaps he will have to learn to live with her smoking, but since she promises to quit in order to please him and repeatedly fails, it remains a contentious issue between them. When Aidan first sees Carrie's apartment, he notices cracks in the ceiling and scuffed floorboards, and offers to renovate it for her (SATC, 3:9 "Easy Come, Easy Go"). Initially, Carrie interprets it as a sign of his caring attitude, but it causes major disruption to her work and an uncomfortable feeling that she has lost control over her life. It is while Aidan is polishing her floors, and she is forced to work at a hotel, that she cheats on him with Big for the first time and smokes her first cigarette after promising to quit. In contrast, when Big sees Carrie's apartment for the first time, he announces, "I like it"; she realizes that it is a bit shabbier than his place and says she wants to change a lot of things, but he replies, "I like it the way it is" (SATC, 1:11 "The Drought"). At one point, Aidan also tells Carrie that he loves her, including her flaws, that "flaws are the best part" (SATC, 3:12 "Don't Ask, Don't Tell"). However, his proposal and his rush to get married are mainly motivated not by his acceptance of Carrie but by the fact that he still does not trust her after her infidelity. The engagement ring he gives her is his way of staking his territory, making a claim on her. It is an act of possession, not love and acceptance—and Carrie tries to minimize its force by wearing the ring on a chain around her neck, not on her finger. Despite all his sensitivity and nurturance, when it comes to living with Carrie and then proposing to her, like Mr. Collins and Mr. Darcy, Aidan prioritizes his own feelings and does not give enough consideration to the woman's feelings. In other words, the relationship between Aidan and Carrie lacks some of the elements that make love such a powerful mechanism of choice: mutual trust and appreciation of each other's individuality (see Chapter 2).

Petrovsky: "Not a boyfriend; lover"[6]

Aidan's down-to-earth homeliness is contrasted with the theatrical glamour of Carrie's partner in the final season of the show, Aleksandr Petrovsky, a famous Russian artist, played by an equally famous Russian ballet dancer, Mikhail Baryshnikov. He is as suave as Big and as needy of Carrie's devotion as Aidan. He is also very romantic, wooing Carrie with grand gestures. But his romanticism is often over the top, so much so that in one episode, it literally sweeps Carrie off her feet and makes her faint (SATC, 6:14 "The Ick Factor").

Petrovsky also used to be the ultimate cad; he had a nickname Aleksandr the Great because of all his sexual conquests. When he meets Carrie, he apparently has his womanizing days behind him. In fact, he wants to continue the relationship with Carrie so much that he insists she moves with him to Paris. The move promises the ultimate romantic fairy-tale ending, but it also requires the ultimate sacrifice from Carrie: leaving behind her friends, her work, and her home. Unfortunately, after the move, Carrie discovers that although she does not need to compete for Petrovsky with other women, she still has to compete for his attention—with his art and his own narcissism. Although he repeatedly claims that he needs Carrie, in the last episode of the series, he symbolically lets go of her hand as soon as he perceives that his new exhibition at a Paris gallery is going to be a success. When Carrie complains about feeling abandoned, he says: "I thought I was clear all along about who I am" to which Carrie responds: "Well, maybe it's time to be clear about who I am. I am someone who is looking for love. Real love. ... And I don't think that love is here in this expensive suite, in this lovely hotel, in Paris" (SATC, 6:20 "An American Girl in Paris: Part Deux").

"You're the one"[7]

It is after Carrie realizes that she will not find love with Petrovsky in Paris that Big finds her and finally tells her that she is "the one". This declaration is often derided as a sentimental cliché, but it expresses an important psychological principle identified by cross-cultural research as one of the defining characteristics of romantic love: the recognition of the beloved's uniqueness (see Chapters 1 and 2). Such recognition is crucial for long-term commitment: It signals that the man cares enough about one particular woman to forego other mating opportunities. It is what every romantic heroine, from Elizabeth Bennet and Jane Eyre to Bridget Jones and Anastasia Steele from *Fifty Shades of Grey* wants: to be recognized as a unique individual; not just an object of desire, or a fertile womb, or a socially acceptable wife but an autonomous consciousness not easily replaced by or substituted for another.

Moreover, Big's "rescue", although spectacularly sentimental, is not just about the *romantic* happy ending, but it reunites Carrie with the job and the city she loves, and most importantly, her friends. It also signals Big's ability to embrace Carrie's social circle and acknowledge their importance in her life (just as Darcy must accept Elizabeth's family): Before he goes to Paris, Big consults Miranda, Samantha, and Charlotte receiving their permission and encouragement to try to get Carrie back. As in many romantic narratives, the recognition of female bonds *alongside* heterosexual romance is a recurrent element of *Sex and the City*. The three weddings during the TV series (Charlotte's wedding to Trey and then to Harry, and Miranda's wedding to Steve) are all followed by the assurance that they do not replace or undermine the friendship between the women. The episodes in which the weddings take place celebrate the marriages but conclude with the focus on the four friends and the support they offer to each other in one case in the wake of Carrie's break-up from Aidan and in another in light of Samantha's breast cancer diagnosis. This emphasis on female friendships satisfies the feminist call for sisterhood but also highlights the importance of female alliances throughout our evolutionary history (Campbell, 2013; Taylor et al., 2000). In Austen's world, such alliances were usually formed between biological sisters, but in the modern urban environments, where people are often separated from their relatives, close bonds with genetic kin are increasingly replaced by equally close friendships which provide both emotional and practical support and are especially important for women (Ackerman et al., 2007). In fact, such substitution of kin for non-kin is not a new phenomenon as it often happens in tribal bands (Boehm, 2012, pp. 57-58). Its significance to women is most likely due to female exogamy (or ancestral patrilocality): Since women often left their relatives to live with their husband's communities, they regularly needed to forge bonds with genetically unrelated individuals (Campbell, 2013).

"Still in love"

The first *Sex and the City* movie finds Carrie and Big three years later "still in love" and makes them face the pragmatic side of a long-term relationship. Big wants to buy a fabulous penthouse apartment for them, and a discussion about its legal ownership prompts a decision to get married, simply because it "makes sense" in their circumstances. Big wants a small private ceremony, but Carrie's wedding plans keep growing and growing. On the day, Big gets cold feet, and the rest of the movie is about Carrie dealing with the heartbreak and Big trying to get her back.

Feminist critics claim that Carrie and Big's marriage plans fail because Big's fist proposal lacks romantic rhetoric (Harzewski, 2011, p. 116; Weisser, 2013, p. 118). But the issue is more in substance than in style: It is not about indulging in romantic clichés but about establishing a suitable basis for a long-term interpersonal commitment. Like Mr. Collins's proposal to Elizabeth Bennet, Big's suggestion of marriage is all about preserving the woman's right to property. There was a similar problem with Aidan's proposal which was prompted by the fact that Carrie could not afford to buy out her apartment, but he could. If the evolutionary research discussed in Chapter 2 is right about the crucial role of emotions in long-term commitments, a marriage needs to be based on more than just what "makes sense" at a given moment.

Just as it was in the TV series, the appreciation of each other's subjectivity is also at stake in the film, but this time, both Big and Carrie are equally at fault. Yes, he humiliates her by his last-minute doubts, but they are prompted by the fact that she completely neglects *his* feelings about their wedding. In the TV series, Carrie complained that Aidan's marriage plans were proceeding without her, but in the film, *she* does the same thing to Big. His anxiety is not about marrying Carrie, but about the pageantry of the ceremony she gets sucked into. As he puts it in the film, he needs to know that behind the symbolic veil Carrie is wearing, it is still her.

The happy ending of the film once again emphasizes Big's understanding of who Carrie is. He makes his second proposal using a Manolo Blahnik shoe in the massive walk-in closet he built for her. The scene attracted a lot of feminist criticism not only for mimicking a supposedly regressive Cinderella moment but also for apparently focusing on the banal and glorifying the consumerist aspects of the programme: Carrie not only surrenders in marriage but does it because of a designer shoe. But such a reading does not sufficiently consider the underlying recurrent symbolism of the show. The fashion, and particularly designer footwear, stands for all the feminine interests so often dismissed in patriarchal culture as insignificant. Recall, for example, Virginia Woolf's pointed comments about the sexist hierarchy of values in fiction: "Speaking crudely, football and sport are 'important'; the worship of fashion, the buying of clothes 'trivial'" (1928/2004, pp. 85–86). The fashion of *Sex and the City* is for many fans one of its most attractive aspects, and while for "serious" critics its symbolism may seem frivolous, the points made through it are not. Carrie's clothes and shoes are more than an expression of her individuality (as clothes usually are even for those who do not want to admit it). When Aidan moves in with Carrie, she signals that she is ready for their relationship by making room for his things in her closet, but instead of appreciating the gesture, Aidan "mocks" her clothes (SATC, 4:13 "The Good Fight") and completely cannot relate to Carrie's distress when his dog chews up her favourite Manolo sandal. On a few other occasions, the loss of Carrie's shoes symbolizes either a violation or devaluation of her selfhood (e.g., SATC, 3:17 "What Goes Around Comes Around", 6:9 "A Woman's Right to Shoes"). Hence, the luxurious closet and the designer shoe (consumerist as they admittedly are) signal that Big truly understands and values Carrie in the totality of the person that she is. Furthermore, like the finale of the TV show, the conclusion of the first film also underscores the importance of Carrie's female friendships. She is finally prepared to listen to Big's apologies after she learns that he helped Charlotte get to hospital for the birth of her baby. And their small civil wedding is validated by the presence of her three best friends.

Most feminist analyses, including those that find evidence of progressive ideas within *Sex and the City* and other chick lit texts, ultimately bemoan the fact that the feminine identity offered by these narratives is still defined by monogamous heterosexuality (Gerhard, 2005; Gill & Herdieckerhoff, 2006; Hermes, 2006; Mabry, 2006; Rowntree et al., 2012; Whelehan, 2005). However, there are some who recognize that the feminist value of *Sex and the City* should be measured by its attempts to redefine rather than abolish heterosexual relationships (Henry, 2004) and by its insistence that strong female bonds "could coexist with the search for heterosexual sex and romance rather than [serve] as a radical alternative to it" (Jermyn, 2009, p. 56). My analysis demonstrates that both of these elements are not just feminist wishful thinking but are deeply ingrained in the evolutionary architecture of female psychology. Carrie and other romantic heroines actively select men whose physical, psychological, and social traits have been advantageous for female reproductive success, as well as conducive to personally fulfilling and socially beneficial relationships.

Notes

1 SATC, 1:12 "Oh Come All Ye Faithful".
2 SATC, 1:1 "Sex and the City".
3 SATC, 5:7 (title of the episode).
4 Carrie's comment is a classic example of competitor derogation, one of the most frequent strategies employed by women when they compete for desirable man (see Grant, 2020).
5 SATC, 4:12 (title of the episode).
6 SATC, 6:13 "Let There Be Light".
7 SATC, 6:20.

References

Ackerman, J. M., Kenrick, D. T., & Schaller, M. (2007). Is friendship akin to kinship? *Evolution and Human Behavior*, *28*(5), 365–374. https://doi.org/10.1016/j.evolhumbehav.2007.04.004
Ally McBeal. (1997–2002). [Television series]. Kelley, D. E. (Creator). Fox Network.
Boehm, C. (2012). *Moral origins: The evolution of virtue, altruism, and shame* (Kindle ed.). Basic Books.
Buss, D. M. (1989). Sex differences in human mate preferences: Evolutionary hypotheses tested in 37 cultures. *Behavioral and Brain Sciences*, *12*(01), 1–14. https://doi.org/10.1017/S0140525X00023992
Buss, D. M., & Schmitt, D. P. (2011). Evolutionary psychology and feminism. *Sex Roles*, *64*(9), 768–787. https://doi.org/10.1007/s11199-011-9987-3
Campbell, A. (2008). The morning after the night before. *Human Nature*, *19*(2), 157–173.
Campbell, A. (2013). *A mind of her own: The evolutionary psychology of women* (2nd ed.). Oxford University Press.
Carroll, J. (2022). Evolution: How evolved emotions work in literary meaning. In P. C. Hogan, B. J. Irish, & L. P. Hogan (Eds.), *The Routledge companion to literature and emotion* (pp. 85–97). Routledge.
Carroll, J., Gottschall, J., Johnson, J. A., & Kruger, D. J. (2012). *Graphing Jane Austen: The evolutionary basis of literary meaning*. Palgrave Macmillan.
di Mattia, J. (2004). "What's the harm in believing?": Mr. Big, Mr. Perfect, and the romantic quest for *Sex and the City*'s Mr. Righ". In K. Akass & J. McCabe (Eds.), *Reading Sex and the City* (pp. 17–32). I. B. Tauris.
Ellis, B. J. (1995). The evolution of sexual attraction: Evaluative mechanisms in women. In J. H. Barkow, L. Cosmides, & J. Tooby (Eds.), *The adapted mind: Evolutionary psychology and the generation of culture* (pp. 267–288). Oxford University Press
Fielding, H. (1996). *Bridget Jones's diary: A novel*. Picador.
Fisher, H. E. (2011). *Why him? Why her? How to find and keep lasting love*. Oneworld.
Garcia, J. R., & Reiber, C. (2008). Hook-up behavior: A biopsychosocial perspective. *Evolutionary Behavioral Sciences*, *2*(4), 192–208.
Geher, G., & Kaufman, S. B. (2013). *Mating intelligence unleashed: The role of the mind in sex, dating, and love* (Kindle ed.). Oxford University Press.

Gerhard, J. (2005). *Sex and the City*: Carrie Bradshaw's queer postfeminism. *Feminist Media Studies*, 5(1), 37–49. https://doi.org/10.1080/14680770500058173

Gill, R. (2007). *Gender and the media*. Polity Press.

Gill, R., & Herdieckerhoff, E. (2006). Rewriting the romance. *Feminist Media Studies*, 6(4), 487–504. https://doi.org/10.1080/14680770600989947

Grant, A. (2020). "Sneering civility": Female intrasexual competition for mates in Jane Austen's novels. *EvoS Journal: The Journal of the Evolutionary Studies Consortium*, 11(1), 15–33. https://doi.org/10.59077/QSHP9625

Greven, D. (2004). The museum of unnatural history: Male freaks and *Sex and the City*. In K. Akass & J. McCabe (Eds.), *Reading Sex and the City* (pp. 33–47). I. B. Tauris.

Grodal, T. (2009). *Embodied visions: Evolution, emotion, culture, and film*. Oxford University Press.

Grodal, T. (2017). How film genres are a product of biology, evolution and culture—an embodied approach. *Palgrave Communications*, 3(1), 17079. https://doi.org/10.1057/palcomms.2017.79

Harzewski, S. (2011). *Chick lit and postfeminism*. University of Virginia Press.

Henry, A. (2004). Orgasms and empowerment: *Sex and the City* and the third-wave feminism. In K. Akass & J. McCabe (Eds.), *Reading Sex and the City* (pp. 65–82). I. B. Tauris.

Hermes, J. (2006). *Ally McBeal*, *Sex and the City* and the tragic success of feminism. In J. Hollows & R. Moseley (Eds.), *Feminism in popular culture* (pp. 79–95). Berg.

Hogan, P. C. (2011). *Affective narratology: The emotional structure of stories*. UNP. https://doi.org/10.2307/j.ctt1df4gnk

Jermyn, D. (2009). *Sex and the City* (TV milestones series). Wayne State University Press.

Mabry, A. R. (2006). About a girl: Female subjectivity and sexuality in contemporary 'chick' culture. In S. Ferriss & M. Young (Eds.), *Chick lit: The new woman's fiction* (pp. 191–206). Routledge.

Moseley, R., & Read, J. (2002). "Having it Ally": Popular television (post-)feminism. *Feminist Media Studies*, 2(2), 231–249. https://doi.org/10.1080/14680770220150881

Robinson, P. (2011). Mobilizing postfeminism: Young Australian women discuss *Sex and the City* and *Desperate Housewives*. *Continuum*, 25(1), 111–124. https://doi.org/10.1080/10304312.2011.538469

Rowntree, M., Moulding, N., & Bryant, L. (2012). Feminine sexualities in chick lit. *Australian Feminist Studies*, 27(72), 121–137. https://doi.org/10.1080/08164649.2012.648259

Seabright, P. (2012). *The war of the sexes: How conflict and cooperation have shaped men and women from prehistory to the present* (Kindle ed.). Princeton University Press.

Sex and the city. (1998–2004). [Television series]. Star, D. (Creator), & King, M. P. (Producer and Director). HBO.

Sex and the city. (2008). [Motion picture]. King, M. P. (Director/Writer). New Line Cinema.

Smith, C. J. (2008). *Cosmopolitan culture and consumerism in chick lit*. Routledge.

Smith, S. (2016, July 17). Single bright female. *New Zealand Herald Sunday Magazine*, 11–13.

Taylor, S. E., Klein, L. C., Lewis, B. P., Gruenewald, T. L., Gurung, R. A. R., & Updegraff, J. A. (2000). Biobehavioral responses to stress in females: Tend-and-befriend, not fight-or-flight. *Psychological Review*, 107(3), pg. 411–429.

Vincent, N. (1998). I am woman, hear me whine [Book Review]. *National Review*, 50(14), 49–50.

Weisser, S. O. (2013). *The glass slipper: Women and love stories*. Rutgers University Press.

Whelehan, I. (2005). *The feminist bestseller: From Sex and the Single Girl to Sex and the City*. Palgrave Macmillan.

Wolf, N. (1991). *The Beauty myth: How images of beauty are used against women*. Vintage.

Woolf, V. (1928/2004). *A room of one's own*. Penguin Books.

12
MOTHERS AND OTHERS

Throughout this book, I have argued that romantic fiction reflects female mating psychology shaped by the reproductive realities of the human species. In cultural terms, too, motherhood has always been an important part of female social and individual identity. Why then, some might ask, has romantic fiction, and literature in general, been so much more focused on courtship than on raising children? Commenting on this state of affairs, Brian Boyd explains:

> Stories ... tend to thrive on the conflict of wills, on the tension between cooperation and competition that lies at the heart of social life. In love, the initially (and sometimes subsequently) imperfect alignment of the wills of lovers during the testing phases of courtship, or their relation to others—rivals or disapproving parents or jealous partners—offers big-stakes drama. After potential couples sort out their differences or overcome their obstacles, reproduction tends to follow; but gestation and childbirth, for all their strain and danger, *lack the elements of conflict and choice* that most often drive stories (2014, p. 269, emphasis added).

This is certainly true of Austen's fiction: Her stories focus on how the heroines find the right husbands but leave them before they become mothers, and children are not mentioned in the denouements of the novels. This is likely due, at least in part, to the generic conventions Austen was operating under.[1] But the idea of motherhood is present in Austen's works by default, because in her time, it was a more-or-less inevitable consequence of sex (barring fertility issues, of course). Most of her married women have children, and Charlotte Lucas and Mrs. Weston in *Emma* become pregnant shortly after their weddings.

On the one hand, the picture of motherhood Austen paints in her fiction is often not very positive. Many mothers are either dead or separated from their daughters for most of their stories (this is the case for Emma Woodhouse, Anne Elliot, Fanny Price, and Catherine Morland). Those that are present, are immature (Mrs. Bennet and Mrs. Dashwood) or indolent (Lady Bertram). This means that the heroines have to rely mostly on their own moral, intellectual, and emotional resources. Doting mothers and their preoccupation with their children, usually to the exclusion of any other concerns, are also subject to Austen's irony, for example in the portrayals of Isabella Knightley in *Emma* or Lady Middleton in *Sense and Sensibility*.

Austen's ambivalence about motherhood is hardly surprising. She was well aware of the physical toll of frequent pregnancies and childbirth among her relatives acquaintances. For example, her sister-in-law, Elizabeth Knight, died at 34 after giving birth to her eleventh child. In her letters, Austen bemoans other women who have many children: "poor Woman! how can she be honestly breeding again?" (to Cassandra, 1 October 1808; Le Faye, 1995, p. 140); and "poor Animal, she will be worn out before she is thirty" (to Fanny Knight, 23 March 1817; Le Faye, 1995, p. 336). She also advises her niece not to be in a rush to have children: "By not beginning the business of Mothering quite so early in life, you will be young in Constitution, spirits, figure & countenance, while Mrs. Wm Hammond is growing old by confinements & nursing" (to Fanny Knight, 13 March 1817; Le Faye, 1995, p. 332). Her two most exuberant heroines do not show much interest in mothering for the most part of their stories: Elizabeth Bennet goes on a trip with her uncle and aunt Gardiner, leaving Jane to look after their children, and Emma Woodhouse is confident that, since she does not plan to marry, her nephews and nieces will provide enough compensation.

At the same time, Austen is very clear about the importance of good parenting, and many of her heroines clearly show motherly potential. For example, Jane Bennet is the favourite aunt of the Gardiners' children; Lady Russell thinks Anne Elliot is particularly fit for domestic life, which Anne demonstrates by being a more affectionate and considerate carer for her sister Mary Musgrove's children than Mary is herself (see also Chapter 6). The emotional and moral maturity demonstrated by other heroines gives us a strong clue about the kind of mothers they would be if their stories were to continue. Once married, Elizabeth becomes a positive role model for Darcy's younger sister Georgiana and for her own sister Kitty, even though she did not have much influence on her in their family home dominated by the silliness of their mother and the detachment of their father. Elizabeth's energy and stamina also signal that she is physically much better prepared for the challenges of pregnancy and motherhood than the weak and sickly Anne de Bourgh (as already noted in Chapter 7). After her marriage, Fanny Price devotes herself to educating her younger sister and improving her temper (and also keeps to her regime of daily exercise). Elinor Dashwood is eventually recognized by her sister Marianne as a model to emulate. The heroes, too, must show their caring side by guiding and protecting their younger siblings (as is the case for Mr. Darcy and Henry Tilney) or other young women in vulnerable positions (as Mr. Knightley does for Harriet, Edmund Bertram for Fanny, and Colonel Brandon for Eliza Brandon). This demonstrates their potential to be not only sensitive husbands but also affectionate fathers. And they are usually presented as physically strong, healthy, and energetic—with the exception of Colonel Brandon who likes "the constitutional safeguard of a flannel waistcoat" (SS, p. 352) but is far from being as senile and infirm as Marianne initially perceives him to be.

"Coulda, woulda, shoulda"[2]

In most chick lit texts, the focus remains firmly on the romantic quest, but that quest is very often complicated by the question of motherhood. This question has become so much more salient precisely because for many modern women, it is a conscious and deliberate choice which can and often needs to be tackled separately from the issues of sex, love, and marriage. And the ability to make a choice has inevitably heightened the possibility of conflict in this decision: The conflict between lovers when one of them wants children and the other does not, the conflict between a woman's professional and personal goals, and finally the conflict between a woman's desire for independence and her desire for love—maternal, as well as romantic. This is not to say that these conflicts did not exist until now, but without access to reliable contraception and safe abortion, and with vastly different social norms and expectations, women had significantly less control over reproduction.

Different facets of the modern motherhood dilemma, from the trivial to the really serious, are well captured by Bridget Jones's comical reaction to the idea that she might be unexpectedly pregnant by her new unreliable boyfriend Daniel Cleaver:

> Although it was only 12.45 I thought a vodka and orange wouldn't do any harm since it was a genuine emergency, but then I remembered that baby wasn't supposed to have vodka. I waited, feeling like a weird sort of hermaphrodite or Push-me-pull-you experiencing the most violently opposed baby sentiments of a man and a woman both at the same time. On the one hand I was all nesty and gooey about Daniel, smug about being a real woman—so irrepressibly fecund!—and imagining fluffy pink baby skin, a tiny creature to love, and darling little Ralph Lauren baby outfits. On the other I was thinking, oh my God, life is over, Daniel is a mad alcoholic and will kill me then chuck me when he finds out. No more nights out with the girls, shopping, flirting, sex, bottles of wine and fags. Instead I am going to turn into a hideous grow-bag-cum-milk-dispensing-machine which no one will fancy and which will not fit into any of my trousers, particularly my brand new acid-green Agnés B jeans. This confusion, I guess, is the price I must pay for becoming a modern woman instead of following the course nature intended by marrying ... when I was eighteen. (Fielding, 1996, p. 119)

In this case, the pregnancy issue quickly goes away when it turns out that Bridget misread the result of the test, but Fielding (like Austen) provides glimpses of what motherhood may be like through Bridget's close friend Magda, especially in the sequel, *Bridget Jones: The Edge of Reason* (1999). Fielding mostly shows the chaotic, messy side, like toilet training or noisy kids' parties, and puts Bridget in situations involving children she cannot handle, and from which she is repeatedly "rescued" by Mark Darcy. Unlike Austen, Fielding does show us her protagonist as a mother but not until the third instalment of the diary (Fielding, 2013), in which Bridget is Mark Darcy's widow raising two children and trying to find a new partner. She chooses a schoolteacher with two sons of his own, a much more fatherly figure than any of the other candidates. The third movie in the franchise, *Bridget Jones's Baby* (2016), also written by Fielding (but based on the renewed column for the *Independent*, rather than the third novel) tackles a different aspect of motherhood. It shows Bridget unexpectedly pregnant and unsure who the father is: her old flame Mark Darcy or the new heartthrob, billionaire Jack Qwant.[3]

While Fielding focuses more on the realities of having children, *Sex and the City* presents an extensive treatment of the question of whether, when, and how to be a mother, and through its four characters provides a range of responses. Not surprisingly, Samantha openly states that "babies are not [her] scene" (SATC, 5:6 "Critical Condition"), and after attending a baby shower, she throws an "I'm not having a baby party" to celebrate her childlessness (SATC, 1:10 "The Baby Shower"). She is also completely unperturbed by the fact she had two abortions. Samantha's attitude in this matter is in line with her short-term mating strategy which often entails prioritizing mating effort over parenting effort. For the other three characters, however, reproduction is a crucial factor in their decisions about sexual and romantic partners.

Charlotte is on the opposite end of the spectrum from Samantha: Children are essential part of her feminine, domestic fantasy. As soon as she and Trey decide to have children, Charlotte quits her job to devote herself completely to the baby project. Her friends, especially Miranda, disapprove of this decision, but Charlotte emphatically responds: "I choose my choice!" (SATC, 4:7 "Time and Punishment"). Both Miranda and Charlotte invoke their different understandings of feminist principles to support their arguments, and the episode has been cited in almost every piece of writing discussing the series' ideological credentials. Charlotte's stance is usually denounced as an example of the backlash logic which uses the hard-won post-feminist freedoms to reinstate regressive, pre-feminist ideals. But some argue that the focus on the personal rather than the systemic dimension of such decisions is not without merit (Lotz, 2006, p. 114)—and it clearly holds much appeal for the audience.

Moreover, Charlotte's dream is not uncritically endorsed by the narrative but used to explore its challenging aspects. Regardless of her determination, Charlotte's motherly ambitions, like her first marriage, are repeatedly marred by problems. First, her seemingly perfect husband, Trey, has erectile problems, and later, Charlotte discovers that she also has fertility issues. Couples therapy and IVF do not help, and Charlotte's plan of international adoption meets with strong opposition from Trey's mother who, like Austen's Lady Catherine de Bourgh, wants to maintain the purity of the family bloodline. Eventually, Charlotte divorces Trey, mainly because he does not share her enthusiasm and determination for having children. With her second husband, Harry, not only does she have "unbelievable" sex (SATC, 5:7 "The Big Journey"), but also manages to adopt one girl (SATC, 6:20 "An American Girl in Paris: Part Deux"), and eventually gives birth to another in the first *Sex and the City* film (2008). The adoption is Charlotte's happy ending within the television series, and the birth of her daughter initiates the reconciliation between Carrie and Big in the first movie. But being a mother does not turn out as idyllic as Charlotte had imagined either. She struggles so much, in fact, that in the second movie (*Sex and the City 2,* 2010), she ends up using Carrie's empty apartment as her occasional refuge. In the sequel *And Just Like That*, the challenges of raising young teenage girls remain the main focus of Charrlotte's storylines.

Carrie is ambivalent about having children and on several occasions ponders the impact it would have on her identity and her relationships. In one early episode, her gay friend, Stanford, suggests that they should get married so that he could receive his inheritance (SATC, 1:9 "The Turtle and the Hare"). Carrie briefly considers this idea but quickly comes to the realization that it would not work because at some point in the future, she would like to have a family. In the very next episode, Carrie and the girls visit a friend who recently married, moved to the suburbs, and is expecting a baby (SATC, 1:10). This makes Carrie face her anxieties about her life not following the socially expected course but also her fears of what she perceives as a stifling suburban existence. At the same time, Carrie's period is late, and she is not sure how she feels about it. Her uncertainty reflects the state of her relationship with Big at that stage. More importantly, however, it reflects her concern about her ability to fulfil the role of a mother while maintaining her sense of self: "Could I do this? Would I be any good? Would I somehow manage to stay me?" (SATC, 1:10).

In Season 3, a similar concern makes Carrie end the relationship with the marriage-obsessed Aidan; his family orientation is confirmed when he becomes a father soon after this break-up (SATC, 6:1 "To Market, to Market") and in the Season 2 of *And Just Like That* chooses his children over a renewed relationship with Carrie. In the final season of *Sex and the City*, Carrie emphatically asserts that her life as a childless woman who spends her money on designer shoes is just as valid as the lives of her married friends who constantly expect her to spend money on wedding and baby gifts to celebrate their life choices (SATC, 6:9 "A Woman's Right to Shoes"). But a few episodes later, while looking after Miranda's son, she wonders whether she can continue the relationship with Petrovsky after he announces he had a vasectomy and does not want any more children (SATC, 6:15 "Catch-38"). The situation makes Carrie ponder the extent of social pressure and individual desires:

> Did we want babies and perfect honeymoons, or did we think we should have babies and perfect honeymoons? How do we separate what we could do and what we should do? And here's an alarming thought: It's not just peer pressure, it seems to be coming from within. Why are we should-ing all over ourselves?

It also makes her question the force of romantic and maternal love when she wonders if Petrovsky would love her enough "to make up for the fact that [she] didn't have a baby" (SATC, 6:15). When she eventually finds her true love with Big, they decide that it is going to be "just the two of us, no children" (*Sex and the City 2*, 2010). This decision is only possible because of modern contraceptive technology and does not invalidate my evolutionary argument but highlights the difference between *ultimate* and *proximate* goals mentioned in Chapter 1: A desire for romantic relationships is a proximate mechanism that facilitates the ultimate goal of reproduction, whether or not that goal is actually achieved or even consciously registered.

Miranda's position changes over time. In the first season, she is convinced that "marriage and baby equals death" and compares mothers to members of "a cult": "They all think the same, dress the same and sacrifice themselves to the same cause—babies … I've lost two sisters to the motherhood. I know what I'm talking about" (SATC, 1:10).[4] In Season 2, when she learns that she has "a lazy ovary" which may cause fertility issues, Miranda considers freezing her eggs to preserve her options (SATC, 2:11 "Evolution"). When she accidentally gets pregnant to her on-and-off boyfriend Steve in Season 4, her first reaction is that she is not ready to have a baby and she arranges an abortion but changes her mind at the last minute (SATC, 4:11). At first, she cannot get excited about the pregnancy, but in the end, motherhood becomes a catalyst for her romantic happy ending and her personal transformation.[5]

Miranda's decision to have a baby is contrasted with Carrie coming to the conclusion that the abortion she had years earlier was the right choice, given her own immaturity and the unsuitability of the father. More importantly, it is paralleled with Charlotte's desperate and unsuccessful attempts to start a family. Charlotte is initially upset at Miranda's news, and even more so, at the prospect of the abortion, but when Miranda decides against it, Charlotte joyfully exclaims: "We're having a baby!" (SATC, 4:11). Charlotte's reaction is an expression of the four women's friendship and solidarity. In a broader sense, it alludes to the fact that for most of human history having children has been a communal concern. This sentiment expressed by the traditional African proverb, "It takes a village to raise a child", and often invoked by second-wave feminists as an expression of female solidarity, is also highlighted in evolutionary explanations of the exceptionally cooperative human reproductive behaviour (Hrdy, 1999, 2009, 2024). Although in true Miranda fashion, she is determined to go it alone, she soon discovers that she is not able to, and her storylines in Seasons 5 and 6 revolve around her struggles as a single working mother (see also Chapter 10). Her financial position allows her to hire help—with some mixed results: The nurse, although competent, is emotionally detached, but the housekeeper, Magda, gradually becomes a surrogate grandmother (SATC, 5:3 "Luck Be an Old Lady"). Miranda's friends help when they can: Carrie and Charlotte look after Brady when Miranda and Steve go on their short honeymoon (SATC, 6:15), and even Samantha reluctantly babysits once (SATC, 5:6), but the realities of modern urban living and their busy careers mean that they cannot provide sufficient assistance. Miranda's neighbour, also a mother, says that if her friends do not have children, they will not understand her situation.

Miranda struggles so much that at one point, she confesses she could marry Steve just to get some help (SATC, 5:6), and despite her initial reluctance, she comes to realize that he is the person she can most rely on. He is by no means perfect. The first time Miranda asks him to look after their son while she goes away, Steve panics, and Magda has to step in. He is occasionally late picking Brady up and puts his condoms in the nappy bag. Nevertheless, he is the person who most consistently provides emotional and moral support during Miranda's pregnancy and after Brady's birth. From an evolutionary point of view, this is understandable: As a father, he has big genetic investment in the child, and Miranda's family is not close by. His unwavering commitment to her and her son prompts Miranda to reconsider their relationship, but it takes most of Season 6 before she is able to admit her feelings to Steve. Finally, it is during Brady's first birthday party that she proposes to Steve (SATC, 6:14 "The Ick Factor").

"Husbands are ... negotiable"[6]

Miranda's marital conclusion is preceded by and predicated on her experience of motherhood. When she is marrying Steve, they already have a son together, she is struggling to look after him alone, and Steve has shown plenty of evidence for his paternal investment. The unconventional path leading up to the mum-plus-dad-plus-baby solution suggests that the story aims for more than just a not-so-subtle reaffirmation of the nuclear family ideal, as many critics have suggested. In fact, Miranda only opts for it once she has unsuccessfully tested other options. Furthermore, both *Sex and the City* and other chick lit texts offer a range of other solutions.

In the movie *Bridget Jones's Baby* (2016), Bridget's accidental pregnancy and the birth of her son also reunite her with the boy's father, Mark Darcy, who has shown plenty of commitment and father-potential in all the different instalments of the story. But the happy ending has an unusual twist: The other father-candidate, having supported Bridget through the pregnancy, also stays in the picture, holding the baby during Mark and Bridget's wedding and playing with him afterwards. Jennifer Weiner's bestseller *Good in Bed* (2001) has another heroine, Cannie, who accidentally becomes pregnant to her ex-boyfriend, Bruce. Although she was the one who broke up with him, when faced with the prospect of having a baby,

Cannie hopes that Bruce might come back to her, or at least show interest in the child, but he does not. His rejection echoes the actions of Cannie's father who abandoned his family and was very critical of Cannie as a child. It thus reinforces Cannie's negative view of men's commitment, and of herself as not worthy of men's love and loyalty. Weiner's solution is to surround Cannie with women: her sister, her mother and her lesbian partner, Bruce's mother, and two close friends—although she also provides Cannie with a potential male partner, the caring doctor who has supported her through the pregnancy and postnatal depression. In evolutionary terms, he does not have a genetic interest in the baby but has identified Cannie as a high value mate and an attractive life companion.

All these fictional family arrangements may seem thoroughly modern and only possible because of liberal Western social norms. However, they all have precedents in other cultures and historical periods, and are in fact a testament to what the anthropologist Sarah Blaffer Hrdy considers the most important feature of the human breeding system: flexibility. As she explains: "Care is a fungible commodity, and humans have always been unusually flexible and opportunistic not just in eliciting care but also in providing it, relocating, adjusting, juggling, and compensating in strategic ways" (2009, p. 164). In some conditions, especially when the environment is particularly harsh or dangerous, having a male protector and provider is so crucial to children's survival that certain cultures developed the idea of partible paternity—they believe that a child can be fathered by more than one man, which in practice creates back-up fathers (Hrdy, 2009, pp. 153–156). In other circumstances, the absence of a father does not make much difference, but only as long as the mother can count on other sources of help, such as relatives (Hrdy, 2009, pp. 151–152).[7]

We find evidence of such flexibility in Austen's novels, too. Fanny Price, Jane Fairfax, Frank Churchill, Mary and Henry Crawford, and Emma Watson are all brought up by various relatives, a practice not uncommon at that time. In several novels, aunts, an old family friend, or a governess become mother figures—for various reasons and with mixed results. Some men, like Mr. Darcy and Colonel Brandon, assume fatherly duties, and Harriet Smith is anonymously provided for by her biological father.

Miranda Hobbes's path to marriage and motherhood (as well as other stories referenced in this chapter) highlights two things. On the one hand, it emphasizes that for many women in Western societies, reproduction has become a considered and purposeful decision, not an inevitable consequence of sex. This, of course, is liberating, but it also carries the burden of choice. At the same time, it shows that despite some very sophisticated reproductive technologies, we are still not—and perhaps never will be—fully in control of our reproductive capacities, just as we are not fully in control of our sexual desire. It is not inconceivable that as technology develops, we might gain more control over reproduction, and that if such conditions persist for long enough, our psychology will adjust. For example, an analysis of women's sperm donor choices shows that some of the preferences are strategically (although not always consciously) adjusted to the specific, and from an evolutionary point of view, novel circumstances (Whyte et al., 2016). While women usually prioritize a man's resources over his youth, the opposite is true when they are choosing an anonymous sperm donor, most likely because neither the woman nor her baby will benefit from the man's resources, but his young age is a sign of the viability of his sperm. However, cues of the donor's kindness, intelligence, and reliability remain firmly at the top of the wish list, a sign of their continuing importance in female sexual psychology.

It is also important to note that in all the chick lit texts discussed above, even when the heroines' pregnancies are unplanned, they result from consensual sex with men with whom the women have strong and positive emotional connections—this, of course, is worryingly often not the case in real life. Also, the heroines are financially secure (although Cannie's income as a newspaper reporter is rather modest, soon after she discovers the pregnancy, she manages to sell a film screenplay which makes her rich). Finally, the option of abortion is genuinely available to most of them. So, like the romantic happy endings, these motherhood stories are somewhat idealized scenarios: The emphasis is not on the constraints that women might be facing but rather on their ability to mobilize various support networks and, most importantly, to make a relatively free choice about their futures. Nevertheless, the dilemmas faced by the heroines and the narrative solutions are easily recognizable and consequently appealing to large audiences.

Despite the narrative insistence on choice and the appreciation of female agency, many critics continue to measure the feminism of texts like *Sex and the City* by the degree to which its characters manage to live *outside* of heterosexual and familial bonds. Given our continued reliance on sexual reproduction, this criterion is unlikely to be met. What I have tried to emphasize is the degree to which the mate choices of the female protagonists lead to emotionally fulfilling relationships, create positive meanings in their lives, and satisfy one of the basic human needs: the need for affiliation.

Notes

1 The tendency to prognosticate about future generations emerged in the Victorian era.
2 SATC, 4:11.
3 The independence of the print and screen media allows Fielding to use the same readily recognizable and much liked characters to explore different storyline options. But while this gives her more creative freedom in some ways, it is not without limitations. For example, the character of Jack Qwant (played by Patrick Dempsey) replaced Daniel Cleaver, because Hugh Grant who played Cleaver in the first two movies apparently was not available to reprise his role—a classic case of how external, non-narrative factors can affect the shape of a screen narrative.
4 Bridget Jones also assigns mothers somewhat hostile and irrational traits: "Heart was sinking at thought of being ... surrounded by ex-career-girl mothers and their Competitive Child Rearing. Magda, once a commodity broker, lies about Harry's age, now, to make him seem more advanced than he is. Even the conception was cut-throat, with Magda trying to take eight times as much folic acid and minerals as anyone else" (Fielding, 1996).
5 The series' greater focus on and more sympathetic treatment of motherhood in later seasons could be linked to Sarah Jessica Parker's engagement as the executive producer and her own struggles to become a mother, which have been well documented by women's magazines. Season 5 of the series was cut short because of the star's pregnancy.
6 Weiner, 2001, p. 248.
7 Other cooperatively breeding animals (e.g., marmosets and tamarins) also have the ability to adjust parental care, depending on "their current physical condition, breeding prospects, and the availability, willingness, and competence of the assistance on hand" (Hrdy, 2009).

References

And just like that. (2021–2023). [Television series]. Star, D. & King, M. P. (Creators). HBO Max.
Austen, J. (1811/2003). *Sense and sensibility*. Penguin.
Boyd, B. (2014). Life history into story. *Philosophy and Literature, 38*(1A), A267–A278

Bridget Jones's baby. (2016). [Motion picture]. Maguire, S. (Director). UK: Miramax Films.
Fielding, H. (1996). *Bridget Jones's diary: A novel*. Picador.
Fielding, H. (1999). *Bridget Jones: The edge of reason*. Picador.
Fielding, H. (2013). *Bridget Jones: Mad about the boy*. Jonathan Cape.
Hrdy, S. B. (1999). *Mother nature: A history of mothers, infants, and natural selection*. Pantheon Books.
Hrdy, S. B. (2009). *Mothers and others: The evolutionary origins of mutual understanding*. Belknap Press of Harvard University Press.
Hrdy, S. B. (2024). *Father time: A natural history of men and babies*. Princeton University Press.
Le Faye, D. (Ed.). (1995). *Jane Austen's letters* (3rd ed.). Oxford University Press.
Lotz, A. D. (2006). *Redesigning women: Television after the network era*. University of Illinois Press.
Sex and the city. (1998–2004). [Television series]. Star, D. (Creator), & King, M. P. (Producer and Director). HBO.
Sex and the city. (2008). [Motion picture]. King, M. P. (Director/Writer). New Line Cinema.
Sex and the city 2. (2010). [Motion picture]. King, M. P. (Director/Writer). New Line Cinema.
Weiner, J. (2001). *Good in bed: A novel* (Kindle ed.). Pocket Books.
Whyte, S., Torgler, B., & Harrison, K. L. (2016). What women want in their sperm donor: A study of more than 1000 women's sperm donor selections. *Economics & Human Biology, 23*, 1–9.

CONCLUSION

Concluding her study of Austen's novels, Ashley Tauchert writes: "Reading feminine romance through feminist epistemology, there appears a body of knowledge so consistent with itself that one only has to pause for a moment to be hit by the oddness of arguments that credit the dream of romance as false consciousness" (2005, p. 168). She then asks us to consider "what difference it would make to favour the tropes of romantic comedy for making sense of the world and our place within it" (p. 169). Similarly, Eva Illouz claims that romantic love is not "a form of false thinking" but a utopia which makes us "dream about a better world, about alternative arrangements", and even if those dreams do not come true, they generate hope and "inspire change" (2006, p. 44). My analysis of *Pride and Prejudice* and *Sex and the City*, two extremely popular romantic narratives, was prompted by my uneasiness about the false consciousness claims. Throughout this book, I have tried to demonstrate that these texts do not undermine but promote feminist ideals of female autonomy, gender equality, and social harmony, and that they do it by highlighting the importance of love in male-female relationships.

In most feminist interpretations, romantic love, in life and in fiction, is seen as an oppressive ideology which justifies male dominance and idealizes female passivity. Some scholars have put forward various arguments to defend romantic love and romantic fiction, but even most of those accounts still treat love as a cultural invention specific to Western modernity. Undoubtedly, cultural contexts shape our ideas about and experiences of love, but its importance in real life and its hold on our imaginations cannot be fully explained without recognizing that our sociality and culture are contingent on our evolutionary make-up. In line with current evolutionary theory and research, I argue that romantic love and long-term pair-bonding is a key feature of human reproduction and social organization. This does not mean that everyone must fall in love, that this love must be heterosexual, or that life without love is meaningless. But love is one of the fundamental human drives, and like other emotions, it is "the engine of our behaviour and the actively chosen motivation of meaningful action" (Solomon, 2003, p. 204). Consequently, fiction is saturated with ideas relevant to love and sex—and the social norms that we have applied to them.

DOI: 10.4324/9781003320982-19

My reading of romantic fiction challenges the assumed passivity of its heroines by emphasizing the notion of female mate choice. Within the bio-cultural framework, real women and their fictive counterparts are strategizing creatures who carefully analyse and actively contribute to their socio-sexual environments. By highlighting how different constellations of personality traits, attachment styles, and environmental influences combine to produce unique individual strategies, I demonstrate that a biologically informed account is neither reductive nor prescriptive. Both *Pride and Prejudice* and *Sex and the City* examine the complexities of female mate choice and present a range of female socio-sexual strategies which may be viable to different degrees and may provide different levels of satisfaction depending on individual and environmental circumstances. Lydia Bennet and Samantha Jones prioritize sexual desire and physical attractiveness of their partners, although the risks of such a strategy are different due to their ages and social contexts. Charlotte Lucas and Charlotte York prioritize material resources and social respectability, although their levels of attractiveness to and dependence on men are different. Jane Bennet and Miranda Hobbes are both emotionally guarded and very circumspect about men's commitment, although their personalities differ significantly. Finally, Elizabeth Bennet and Carrie Bradshaw have different opportunities for self-realization but similarly high expectations for a romantic relationship, and both select socially powerful men. Rather than denying Elizabeth's and Carrie's authority or suppressing their subjectivity, as suggested by many feminist critics, both stories encourage their heroine's moral growth and self-knowledge and demand that the heroes recognize and appreciate their individuality. Rather than justifying Mr. Darcy's and Mr. Big's arrogance, both stories require them to temper it in order to establish a loving bond. Both Mr. Darcy and Mr. Big start off as detached and domineering, with enough physical strength, social power, and natural self-confidence to impose their will on others. Like many other romantic heroes, they have the means to be sexual and social bullies but, like many other romantic heroines, Elizabeth and Carrie refuse to be bullied into submission. Instead, they prompt these powerful men to learn the value of empathy, respect, and affiliation, not only in relation to their chosen women but in relation to the women's kin and social networks. And it is these values that ultimately make Mr. Darcy and Mr. Big most attractive as long-term partners.

Romantic happy endings, with their promise of marital bliss made possible by the seemingly improbable transformation of the hero from an aloof, arrogant loner to a caring lover, are usually seen as naïve, escapist fantasies—not only by many feminists but also by some evolutionary critics. Feminists claim that the happy resolution is only possible because the heroine "turns rape into lovemaking" (Snitow, 1979, p. 153), abandons her own subjectivity, and submits to the masterful male. On the other hand, romance writers and evolutionary scholars alike, while admitting the importance of love in literature and in life, propose that the romantic conclusion requires masculinity to be diminished or compromised (Krentz, 1992; Salmon & Symons, 2001). These objections are based on the assumption that men are—either because of cultural conditioning (in the feminist accounts) or because of their biological heritage (in the evolutionary accounts)—invariably and inevitably more interested in promiscuous sex and aggressive dominance than in loving commitment and cooperation. The myopic emphasis on sex differences may indeed make romantic love seem like an unattainable fantasy. But Bridget Jones was not far from the truth when she made "the ground-breaking" discovery that "maybe [men] are not the unattainable strategic adversary aliens after all, but just like us" (Fielding, 1999, p. 281).

Indeed, a pioneering study of nineteenth-century literature found that male and female protagonists are very similar to each other in terms of personality and motivation, despite their sex differences (and the same applies to antagonists; Carroll et al., 2012, p. 9). Moreover, feminine romances are not the only stories advocating love and marriage as the conclusion of the protagonist's journey. Analyses of folk tales from different cultures show that the goal of love and marriage is equally important for male and female characters (Gottschall et al., 2004), and the quest for romantic union is a universal and the most common literary theme (Hogan, 2003). In many stories, a powerful man falls in love with and devotes himself to one special woman, often foregoing other sexual opportunities. For example, in *The Odyssey*, one of the most enduring stories of Western civilization, the hero rejects "the male fantasy" of sex with goddesses and virgin princesses in favour of an enduring marriage (Boyd, 2009, pp. 225–226).

Empirical research discussed in Chapters 1 and 2 suggests that such stories are not just pro-monogamy propaganda promoting ideological myths that have nothing to do with our real emotional and physical needs. Although it is true that men are, on average, more positive about unencumbered sex with multiple partners, the overwhelming majority of men state that they do want long-term committed relationships (Garcia & Reiber, 2008; Pedersen et al., 2002). A whole range of physiological, psychological, and social adaptations make such relationships not only possible but personally fulfilling, socially beneficial, and conducive to reproductive success (Buss, 2018; Fletcher et al., 2015; Hrdy, 2024). And it is well established by now that when it comes to choosing long-term partners, men's and women's most important criteria are remarkably similar: Both sexes prioritize intelligence and kindness and look for mates with whom they can develop compatible and cooperative partnerships (Buss et al., 1990; Buss & Schmitt, 1993; Li et al., 2002).

This is a crucial point because most feminists argue that romantic fiction is fundamentally structured around gender conflict, and the marriage at the end is a sign of the heroine's defeat in the war of the sexes. But research suggests that the main antagonism in many novels is not between male and female characters but between selfish opportunists and prosocial cooperators regardless of their sex (Carroll et al., 2012). Indeed, both *Pride and Prejudice* and *Sex and the City* reward kindness and prosociality in the male characters and reject antagonistic or exploitative sexual tactics often marked by undue dominance. Also, contrary to feminist objections that romance places the heterosexual couple as "the highest good" (Snitow, 1979, p. 148), the "be all and end all" of a woman's life (Ferguson, 2013, p. 251), both Mr. Darcy and Mr. Big acknowledge the importance of other people in the lives of Elizabeth and Carrie, respectively, and extend their generosity and respect to their partners' social circles. By coming together, both hero couples do not isolate themselves but become the nexus of extended and more intertwined social networks. In this way, these narratives promote more cooperative and equitable interpersonal relations both within and beyond the heterosexual couple.

Romantic fiction does not ignore or deny sex differences and the resulting conflicts. Within male-female relationships, there certainly is potential for coercion, exploitation, and violence; and competition between, and within, sexes form a significant part of our biological heritage. But evolution is just as much about identifying and capitalizing on opportunities for cooperation. Our species' capacity for cooperation and commitment is a significant feature of our breeding system and our social organization, and clearly has given us substantial fitness advantages (Frank, 1988; Hrdy, 2009; Nesse, 2001; Seabright, 2012; Wilson & Wilson, 2007). Marriage, with all its social, economic, and reproductive consequences, is one of the most significant cooperative ventures involving high levels of trust and commitment. Being able to use such commitments successfully is particularly important for women given that their biologically necessary investment in reproduction is substantially higher than men's. Romantic love is the emotional mechanism evolved to help humans, both men and women, identify partners with whom such a venture may be possible. And romantic fiction simulates this important decision-making process.

Romantic fiction imaginatively rehearses different options and opportunities for intimate relationships, weighs up different combinations of internal and external factors that influence people's mating decisions, and considers the most likely consequences of these choices. In doing so, it provides a training ground for audience's cognitive and emotional skills—Theory of Mind, empathy, calculation of risks and rewards—which are involved in strategizing about interpersonal commitments. Romantic fiction also imagines a world in which men and women recognize and respect each other's differences and use them not as the source of conflict but as the basis for mutually enriching cooperation. This, as many readers claim, provides inspiration and energy to pursue such a vision in real life.

Romantic happy endings may be idealized, but for as long as humans reproduce sexually, they provide more realistic and more productive solutions than the radical feminist calls for women to abandon heterosexual relationships. Women cannot thrive or even feel safe by rejecting all men; they need to find men who share the view that cooperation, mutual love, and respect are the best solutions to the eternal challenges of reproduction and survival. And there are many men who do share this view, not least because it is in *their* own best interest: Such an attitude builds communities with less intense male competition, reducing aggression and violence, and increasing the chances that their children will prosper.

Perhaps most importantly, by focusing on the power of female mate choice, romantic fiction illuminates the evolutionary process through which a further transformation of gender relations is possible. If female mate choice influences the development and prevalence of different physical and psychological traits in males, then women—through the collective force of their individual sexual and romantic choices—can reduce male aggression, violence, dominance, and increase nurturance, empathy, and cooperation. Within this framework, romantic love emerges not as a tool of oppression perpetuating the status quo but as an instrument of selection in a long-running attempt to effect change.

The true triumph of romantic love is not in sweeping the woman off her feet nor in bringing a man to his knees but in enabling the man and the woman to stand together, holding hands. It is a utopian vision unlikely to be achieved in every relationship, not least because evolution maintains individual differences. And yet, as a species, we have been living it: We are the most social and cooperative species on earth, and (unlike in other ultrasocial or cooperatively breeding species) the foundation of human cooperation lies in the intimate dyads of male and female.

References

Boyd, B. (2009). *On the origin of stories: Evolution, cognition, and fiction*. Belknap Press of Harvard University Press.

Buss, D. M. (2018). The evolution of love in humans. In K. Sternberg & R. J. Sternberg (Eds.), *The new psychology of love* (2 ed., pp. 42–63). Cambridge University Press. https://doi.org/10.1017/9781108658225.004

Buss, D. M., Abbott, M., Angleitner, A., Asherian, A., Biaggio, A., Blanco-Villasenor, A., Bruchon-Schweitzer, M., Ch'U, H.-Y., Czapinski, J., Deraad, B., Ekehammar, B., Lohamy, N., Fioravanti, M., Georgas, J., Gjerde, P., Guttman, R., Hazan, F., Iwawaki, S., Janakiramaiah, N., ... Yang, K.-S. (1990). International preferences in selecting mates: A study of 37 cultures. *Journal of Cross-Cultural Psychology, 21*(1), 5–47.

Buss, D. M., & Schmitt, D. P. (1993). Sexual strategies theory: An evolutionary perspective on human mating. *Psychological Review, 100*(2), 204–232.

Carroll, J., Gottschall, J., Johnson, J. A., & Kruger, D. J. (2012). *Graphing Jane Austen: The evolutionary basis of literary meaning*. Palgrave Macmillan.

Ferguson, A. (2013). Feminist love politics: Romance, care, and solidarity. In A. G. Jónasdóttir & A. Ferguson (Eds.), *Love: A question for feminism in the twenty-first century* (pp. 250–264). Routledge.

Fielding, H. (1999). *Bridget Jones: The edge of reason*. Picador.

Fletcher, G. J. O., Simpson, J. A., Campbell, L., & Overall, N. C. (2015). Pair-bonding, romantic love, and evolution. *Perspectives on Psychological Science, 10*(1), 20–36. https://doi.org/10.1177/1745691614561683

Frank, R. H. (1988). *Passions within reason: The strategic role of the emotions*. Norton.

Garcia, J. R., & Reiber, C. (2008). Hook-up behavior: A biopsychosocial perspective. *Evolutionary Behavioral Sciences, 2*(4), 192–208.

Gottschall, J., Martin, J., Quish, H., & Rea, J. (2004). Sex differences in mate choice criteria are reflected in folktales from around the world and in historical European literature. *Evolution and Human Behavior, 25*(2), 102–112.

Hogan, P. C. (2003). *The mind and its stories: Narrative universals and human emotion*. Cambridge University Press.

Hrdy, S. B. (2009). *Mothers and others: The evolutionary origins of mutual understanding*. Belknap Press of Harvard University Press.

Hrdy, S. B. (2024). *Father time: A natural history of men and babies*. Princeton University Press.

Illouz, E. (2006). Romantic love. In S. Seidman, N. Fischer, & C. Meeks (Eds.), *Handbook of the new sexuality studies* (pp. 40–48). Routledge.

Krentz, J. A. (Ed.). (1992). *Dangerous men and adventurous women: Romance writers on the appeal of the romance (Kindle ed.)*. University of Pennsylvania Press.

Li, N. P., Bailey, J. M., Kenrick, D. T., & Linsenmeier, J. A. W. (2002). The necessities and luxuries of mate preferences: Testing the tradeoffs. *Journal of Personality and Social Psychology, 82*(6), 947–955. https://doi.org/10.1037//0022-3514.82.6.947

Nesse, R. M. (2001). Natural selection and the capacity for subjective commitment. In R. M. Nesse (Ed.), *Evolution and the capacity for commitment* (pp. 1–44). Russell Sage Foundation.

Pedersen, W. C., Miller, L. C., Putcha-Bhagavatula, A. D., & Yang, Y. (2002). Evolved sex differences in the number of partners desired? The long and the short of it. *Psychological Science, 13*(2), 157–161. https://doi.org/10.1111/1467-9280.00428

Salmon, C., & Symons, D. (2001). *Warrior lovers: Erotic fiction, evolution and female sexuality*. Weidenfeld & Nicolson.

Seabright, P. (2012). *The war of the sexes: How conflict and cooperation have shaped men and women from prehistory to the present* (Kindle ed.). Princeton University Press.

Snitow, A. B. (1979). Mass market romance: Pornography for women is different. *Radical History Review, 1979*(20), 141–161. https://doi.org/10.1215/01636545-1979-20-141

Solomon, R. C. (2003). *Not passion's slave: Emotions and choice*. Oxford University Press.

Tauchert, A. (2005). *Romancing Jane Austen: Narrative, realism, and the possibility of a happy ending*. Palgrave Macmillan.

Wilson, D. S., & Wilson, E. O. (2007). Evolution: Survival of the selfless. *New Scientist, 196*(2628), 42–46. https://doi.org/10.1016/S0262-4079(07)62792-4

INDEX

abortion 141, 159, 176, 178, 181
affiliation (connection) 10, 11, 100, 137, 161, 181, 184
agency 2, 5, 6, 27, 33, 34–35, 43, 53, 56, 69, 73, 85–86, 181; women not being passive 99, 103, 120–123, 131, 184; *see also* autonomy; passivity
Agreeableness 70, 97, 100, 104, 105, 106–107, 114, 117
Ally McBeal (1997–2002) 131, 135, 163, 164
alpha male 11, 40, 55, 107, 111
And Just Like That (2021–2025) 8, 130, 177, 178
androcentric bias 3, 5, 33
antagonists 77–79, 98, 101, 113; and protagonists 55, 57, 114
appearance, beauty 5, 40, 78, 86, 88, 91, 95n9, 99–100, 111–113, 122, 136, 148, 167
Atkinson, Ti-Grace 19
attachment 21–22, 76–77, 79, 137
attachment styles 76–77, 136, 158
Auerbach, Nina 68, 118
Austen, Jane: letters 73, 83n4, 83n12, 93, 107n3, 110, 175; life 73, 75, 87, 92–93, 94, 98, 175
autonomy 3, 6, 10, 19, 20, 25, 28, 34, 37, 53, 99, 123, 142, 159, 160, 183; constraints on 10, 34–35, 85, 129; *see also* agency
Ayesha at Last (Jalaluddin) 8

Bainbridge, Beryl 49
Bateman's principle 36
beauty *see* appearance
birds 22, 35, 36–37
Boehm, Christopher 55, 113
Boyd, Brian 51, 58, 174

Bride and Prejudice (2004) 8
Bridget Jones's Diary (Fielding) 8–9, 154, 159; Jones, Bridget 130, 135, 146, 156–157, 158, 159, 163–164, 167, 170, 176, 184–185
Bridget Jones: The Edge of Reason (Fielding) 146, 176
Bridget Jones's Baby (2016) 176, 179
Brontë, Charlotte 55, 67, 112; *Jane Eyre* 55, 56, 112, 115, 170; Rochester, Mr. 55, 56, 115
Brown, Lloyd W. 98–99, 101–102
Buss, David 21, 24, 26, 39, 40, 41, 141
Butler, Marilyn 92, 98, 100, 106

cads 77–79, 80, 101, 119, 138, 169; and dads 38–39, 73
Campbell, Anne 136, 145, 166
career, women's work and professional ambitions 93, 137–138, 139, 140, 145, 153, 159, 160–161, 163, 169, 176, 177, 179
Carroll, Joseph 51, 54–55, 95, 120, 122, 185
change, transformation: in gender and social relations 3, 4, 5, 6, 11, 20–21, 27–28, 34–35, 43, 49, 54, 57–59, 123, 186; in one's priorities 21, 23, 56, 120, 160–161
chastity 36–37, 73, 74, 98, 148–149
chick lit 1, 2, 8–9, 49, 50, 55, 57, 129–132, 146, 149, 156, 157, 159, 163–164, 171–172, 175–176, 181
choice: individual choice 6, 34–35, 164–165; as prerequisite for change 6, 35; *see also* mate choice
Chwe, Michael Suk-Young 88, 89

commitment: as component of love xi, 6, 20–22, 23, 48, 52, 107; as mate choice criterion 3, 10, 41, 53, 69, 97, 100, 104, 116, 120, 139–140, 153, 164, 166, 184, 186; importance for men 38, 185
commitment scepticism 10, 39, 153, 154–159; circumspection 11, 58, 103, 184; *see also* trust
compatibility 40–41, 87–88, 91; *see also* homogamy; similarities between the sexes
competence: and social status 40, 114; and warmth 108n11
competition, competitiveness: female 4, 5, 36, 69, 111, 141, 161, 167, 169, 172n4; male 28, 35, 38, 39; vs. cooperation 174, 186
Confessions of a Shopaholic (Kinsella) 146
conflict: and cooperation 57, 105; between the sexes 4, 6, 20, 54–55, 56, 185–186; in stories 174
Conscientiousness 107n5, 114
consumerism 35, 171
context: cultural or environmental 4, 5, 9, 22, 24, 39, 69, 82, 132, 145–146; individual circumstances 106, 138; *see also* niche (environmental, evolutionary)
contraception 10, 105, 134, 141, 176, 178
contrast of characters in fiction 11, 69, 73, 74, 77, 82, 85, 86, 93, 97, 101, 110, 158, 164, 168
Coontz, Stephanie 25, 29n8, 29n10
cooperation: between genders xi, 3, 6, 20–21, 43, 59, 97, 100, 185–186; social 79, 93, 123, 161, 174; and marriage 26–27, 29n10; and reproduction 2, 20–21, 105; vs. domination 40, 55, 111, 114–115, 184; *see also* prosociality; ultra-sociality
cooperative breeding 21, 37, 105, 178–179, 180, 181n7
copulation, copulate 36, 37; face-to-face copulation 22
Crusie, Jennifer 8
culture: as a crucial force in human evolution 3–5, 24; cultural variations in love 20, 23, 24–25, 27; cultural variations in marriage 26

Daly, Meg 135
Damasio, Antonio 33, 42, 94
damsel in distress 50, 98, 120
Dark Triad personality 77–78
Darwin, Charles 5, 33, 35
de Beauvoir, Simone 19
deception 79, 102, 140; *see also* honesty
Deresiewicz, William 73
desire, sex drive 10, 19, 21, 22, 37, 90, 136, 140, 184; female 3, 53, 72–74, 75, 81–82, 99, 130–131; *see also* love, as passion, intimacy, commitment
differences between the sexes *see* individual differences; sex differences
disgust 57, 81; sexual 90–91
divorce 10, 22, 26–27, 37, 73, 146, 150
dominance 1, 19, 115, 119, 184, 185, 186; vs. prestige 39–40, 55, 113–114; male control of women 4, 6, 20, 25, 34, 40, 50, 73

Easterlin, Nancy 55, 115
education (for women) 10, 72–73, 108n14
Eliot, George 49, 67, 95n9
Ellis, Bruce 165
elopement 26, 72, 73, 74, 79, 81, 82, 95n10, 120
Emma (Austen): Churchill, Frank 74, 78, 79, 102, 106, 116, 140, 180; Elton, Mrs. 101; Fairfax, Jane 57, 79, 93, 102, 103, 180; Knightley, Isabella 175; Knightley, Mr. 99, 102, 123, 140, 157, 160, 175; Martin, Mr. 99; Smith, Harriet 99, 103, 160, 175, 180; Weston, Mrs. 57, 174; Woodhouse, Emma 57, 69, 74, 78, 79, 81, 93, 99, 102, 106, 123, 140, 157, 160, 174, 175
emotions, feelings 33, 41–42, 94, 171, 183; control of 80–81, 111, 119; and fiction 51–52, 164; lack of 88, 93; as (not) socially constructed 1, 48
emotional closeness, intimacy 22, 26, 132, 142,
emotional guardedness 10, 102–103, 132, 184
emotional intelligence *see* intelligence, emotional
emotional maturity, stability 41, 54, 69, 101, 139
emotional needs (vs physical) 2, 10, 117
emotional well-being: and marriage 20, 27; and romantic fiction 3, 57–58
empathy 11, 21, 97, 100–101, 117, 184
environment *see* context
equality in gender relations 3, 27–28, 34, 49, 51, 123, 135, 183
Evans, Mary 28
Extraversion, extravert 75, 100, 107n5, 118, 119

family, kin, relatives 9, 21, 24–25, 26, 56, 100, 105; flexible family arrangements 180; loyalty to 116–117; nuclear family 24, 179; substitution for friends 170
fatherhood *see* paternal investment
Fausto-Sterling, Anne 5
Fear of Flying (Jong) 131
feelings *see* emotions
female choice *see* choice
feminism: backlash against 50, 129, 145, 161, 177; second wave 19, 22, 27, 34, 43, 67,

110, 130–131, 135, 179; third wave 34, 130, 135
feminist goals, ideals 3, 5, 34, 68, 154, 159, 161, 183
feminist scholarship: on Austen 9, 67–68, 72, 85, 90, 92, 97, 98, 106, 110, 119, 120–121, 122, 123; on biology 3–4; on choice 6, 34–35, 50; on empathy 100–101; on heterosexuality 1, 6, 19, 34; on love x, 1, 6, 19–20, 22, 23, 25, 27, 52, 56, 93, 166, 183; on marriage 6, 19, 25, 26, 68; on romantic fiction x, 1–2, 7, 48, 49, 50–51, 53, 54, 57, 58, 183, 184, 185; on sex 34, 90, 130–131; on *Sex and the City* and chick lit 9, 129, 142, 145, 149, 150, 163–164, 170, 171–172
fertility 36, 37, 129, 177, 178
fiction, storytelling: biocultural analysis of x, 48, 51, 52, 53, 54, 68–69, 97, 112; as cognitive and emotional simulation 2, 11, 51, 53, 57–58, 186; effects of 3, 6, 7, 11, 49, 57–59, 130–131, 186
Fifty Shades of Grey (James) 56, 146, 170
Firestone, Shulamith 19, 27
first impressions 78, 104, 111–113
Fisher, Helen 21–22, 25, 27, 137, 156, 168
fitness interdependence 21, 28n4; inclusive fitness 29n5, 44n2, 94
fitness indicator 36, 78, 112,
Flesch, William 79, 117
flexibility in human biology, reproduction 4–5, 37, 38, 53, 180
flirting 44n4, 74–75
Foucault, Michel 90
Friedan, Betty 145
Fraiman, Susan 110, 123
Frank, Robert 33, 41, 42, 80, 94
Freudian psychoanalysis 3, 57, 90
friendship between women 9, 19, 56–57, 59, 68, 93, 102, 141–142, 170, 171–172, 178–179; *see also* tend-and-befriend strategy
Fordyce, James 49, 98
fundamental attribution error 118, 167

Garcia, Justin and Chris Reiber 166
Geher, Glenn and Scott Barry Kaufman 78, 79, 112
Gemmel, Nikki 135
generosity 101, 104, 105, 107, 115, 185; *see also* kindness
genes 4, 20, 28, 36, 94; genetic diversity 37, 41; genetic investment 21, 179; genetic mutations 35, 40, 78
genre, generic conventions 49, 50, 52, 68, 164, 174; conventions of sentimental fiction 72, 74, 82

Gerhard, Jane 131
Gilbert, Sandra and Susan Gubar (*The Madwoman in the Attic*) 67, 68, 72, 98, 102, 110
Gill, Rosalind 131
Gill, Rosalind and Elena Herdieckerhoff 149
Gilligan, Carol 28, 58
Gigerenzer, Gerd 115
Goleman, Daniel 33, 42, 58, 80, 93,
Good in Bed (Weiner) 159, 179–180
Greer, Germaine 43, 54
Grosz, Elizabeth 4, 5–6, 33, 59

happiness, fulfilment 2, 7, 10, 20, 27, 52, 70, 74, 81, 82, 87, 89, 97, 106–107, 123, 142, 163, 172,
happy ending xi, 8, 11, 52, 68, 119, 129, 139, 150, 160, 170, 171, 181, 184, 186
Hardy, J. P. 121, 123
Harzewski, Stephanie 150, 163
Hoagland, Sarah 35
Hogan, Patrick Colm 52, 69
Hollway, Wendy 27, 34
homogamy 41, 69; *see also* compatibility; similarities between the sexes
homosexuality, homosexual relationships, 23–24, 27, 28n3, 40, 137; lesbian existence (Hoagland) 44n1; rainbow community xi; Samantha Jones as a gay man 136
honesty 10, 97, 101–102; honest/dishonest signalling 79, 117–118; *see also* deception
hooks, bell 27, 28
hormones 21–22; testosterone 21, 22, 28; oxytocin and vasopressin 22, 156; dopamine 21, 22, 156
Hrdy, Sarah Blaffer 21, 33, 36, 37, 179, 180

Illouz, Eva 28, 183
individual differences/variations xi, 2–3, 4, 5, 6, 10, 22, 33, 34, 35, 41, 43, 52, 69, 72, 91, 132, 136, 158, 184; more important than cultural differences 25
individualism 6, 35; vs. collectivism 25
individuality, subjectivity 54, 56, 88, 116, 121, 123, 142, 148, 164, 169, 171, 184; *see also* uniqueness
infatuation 74, 82, 99
infertility 27, 146
infidelity 22, 27, 41, 168, 169; adultery 36, 37, 73, 74; affairs 26, 37; cheating 138, 161
intelligence 3, 41, 94, 111, 114, 122, 167, 185; emotional 42, 73, 81, 119, 122, 150; mating 79, 81, 117
intercourse 19, 77, 90, 156; *see also* copulation
introversion, introverted 97, 102, 118, 119

Jackson, Stevi 34
Jane Eyre see Brontë, Charlotte
Jankowiak, William and Edward Fisher 22–23
Jeffreys, Sheila 25
Jermyn, Deborah 164
Johnson, Claudia 67–68, 72, 73, 82, 92

kin *see* family
kindness 3, 11, 41, 94, 106–107, 111, 114, 117, 119–120, 132, 151, 153, 164, 180, 185; *see also* generosity; prosociality
Krentz, Jayne Ann 54, 57; *The Vanishing* 56

Lady Susan (Austen): Susan, Lady 74, 98, 100, 101–102, 103; Vernon, Frederica 93, 98, 99, 103
Lessing, Doris 49
love 19–28, 41–43; and cooperation 6, 20–21, 185–186; falling in love 41, 43, 73, 74, 99, 117, 137, 138, 142, 166; homosexual love 23–24, 27, 28n3; love at first sight 74, 82; and marriage 25–27, 93; as mechanism of mate choice 2, 7, 20–21, 34, 41–43, 169, 186; in non-Western cultures 22–25, 52; as passion, intimacy, commitment xi, 6, 21, 23, 28n3, 52, 107; as recent patriarchal myth x, 1, 6, 19, 22, 48, 183; and reproduction 2, 20–21, 28, 183; as transformative 6, 20, 21, 23, 27–28, 43, 110, 185–186; as universal human drive 2, 6, 20–24, 28, 183; *see also* feminist scholarship, on love; pair-bonding
Love and Friendship (Austen) 74

mammals 4, 21, 22, 25, 36; *see also* primates
Mansfield Park (Austen): Bertram, Edmund 101, 175; Bertram, Maria 73, 74, 77, 79, 80, 81, 82, 100, 101, 141; Bertram, Julia 73, 74; Bertram, Lady 174; Bertram, Sir Thomas 103; Crawford, Henry 56, 74, 77, 78, 79, 81, 93, 104, 106, 117, 180; Crawford, Mary 69, 77, 100, 101, 104, 180; Price, Fanny 56, 69, 73, 79, 93, 98, 99, 100, 101, 103, 104, 106, 107n5, 117, 121, 174, 175, 180; Rushworth, Mr. 77
marriage, matrimony 1, 6, 19–20, 25–27, 28, 29, 81, 85, 91, 106, 142, 160, 170–171, 185–186; arranged marriage 26; benefits of 25, 27; as a goal in stories 9, 48, 50, 52, 54, 68, 69–70, 120–121, 123, 163, 185; and love 25–27; and reproduction 26, 27, 94, 160, 171, 177, 178–180; and resources 26, 39, 85–88, 92–93, 146–147, 151–151; *see also* feminist scholarship, on marriage
mate choice 21, 26, 33–43, 78, 110; constraints, restrictions on 39, 42, 54, 67, 93; female choice 2, 6, 9, 33, 35–36, 48–49, 53–54, 69, 184; individual preferences and priorities in 39–41, 69, 82, 85–86, 88, 90, 91, 151, 180, 184; the power of 2, 33, 35–36, 59, 186; recurrent dilemmas and trade-offs in 2–3, 10, 53–54, 129, 142, 159, 164, 176; *see also* sexual selection; strategy
mate value 41, 86, 113, 147
mating strategy *see* strategy
Mazzeno, Lawrence 67, 92
McMaster, Juliet 73
McNay, Lois 34
Millet, Kate 19, 27–28
modesty 73, 98–99
Modleski, Tania 50, 55, 57
monogamy 1, 9, 20, 26, 28, 112, 136–140; life–long vs. serial 26, 27, 37; desire for exclusivity 21, 26
morality, moral principles 35, 42, 54, 57, 81, 82, 92, 93; moral growth 68, 69, 74, 81–82, 123, 150, 184; moral integrity 9, 73, 79, 92, 95, 97, 100, 106, 111, 116, 119, 175
Morris, Ivor 67
motherhood 101, 130, 145, 150, 160, 174–181

Nesse, Randolph 158
Newton, Judith Lowder 68, 121, 123
Nettle, Daniel 74, 100, 101
niche (environmental, evolutionary) 4, 101, 105; *see also* context
Northanger Abbey (Austen) 49, 67; Morland, Catherine 56, 57, 67, 69, 72, 99, 174; Thorpe, Isabella 72, 74, 79, 82, 92, 98, 100, 102, 104, 117, 146; Thorpe, John 56; Tilney, Captain 74, 78, 79; Tilney, Henry 67, 69, 99, 117, 175

The Odyssey 185
orgasm 37, 57, 136, 146, 149
ovulation, oestrus 37
ovum, egg 37–38, female gamete 53

pair-bonding 2, 21, 25, 28, 183; *see also* love
parental control (of mate choice, marriage partners) 26, 42, 67, 105
parental investment 36, 76
parental love 21; maternal love 176, 178
passivity, submission (of women) 1, 2, 5, 19, 33, 34, 36–38, 50, 53, 54, 58, 68, 74, 97, 98–99, 102, 103, 106, 110, 120–121, 123, 131, 135, 183, 184; *see also* agency
paternal investment 36, 38, 76, 112; fatherhood 22; male care, nurturance, provisioning 21, 25, 28, 168, 175
paternity certainty 36; paternity confusion 37
patience 79, 80–81, 104
Perry, Ruth 90

personality 10, 11, 38, 69, 74, 77–78, 118, 135, 168; *see also* Agreeableness, Conscientiousness, Extraversion, introversion, Openness to Experience
Persuasion (Austen): Benwick, Captain 74; Clay, Mrs. 79; the Crofts 74; Elliot, Anne 52, 57, 69, 79, 87, 98, 100, 101, 117, 121, 146, 174, 175; Elliot, Elizabeth 100; Elliot, Mr. 78, 79; Musgrove, Louisa 69, 74, 101; Musgrove, Mary 175; Wentworth, Captain 52, 69, 74, 101, 146, 162n4
pleasure: aesthetic 36, 150; in evolutionary theory 36, 57–58, 80–81; literary 57–58; sexual 34, 37, 73, 130, 131, 134, 135, 142, 166
Polhemus, Robert 75
polygamy, polyamory 26, 38
Poovey, Mary 50, 57, 67, 68
poverty, being poor, lack of resources 87, 92, 93, 110–111, 115, 116, 117; *see also* resources
pregnancy 105, 151, 153, 157, 159, 176, 178, 179, 181
pride: hubristic vs. authentic 114, 119
Pride and Prejudice (Austen) 2, 7–9, 43, 49, 68, 164, 183, 184, 185; Bennet, Elizabeth x, 7, 10, 11, 53–54, 56, 57, 69, 73, 74, 75, 76, 77, 78, 80, 81, 87, 88, 89, 91, 92, 93, 94, 95, 97, 98, 99, 101, 103, 106, 107, 110–123, 130, 132, 140, 164, 166, 167, 168, 170, 171, 175, 184, 185; Bennet, Jane 10–11, 56, 69, 70, 73, 77, 81, 87, 88, 93, 97–107, 110, 111, 112, 115, 118, 132, 153, 167, 175, 184; Bennet, Kitty 76, 101, 175; Bennet, Lydia 10, 57, 69, 70, 72–82, 93, 94, 95n10, 97, 98, 101, 103, 107, 110, 111, 120, 122, 132, 134–135, 137, 141, 142, 184; Bennet, Mary 73, 76, 77, 82, 88, 101; Bennet, Mr. 75, 76, 99, 101, 107, 115; Bennet, Mrs. 76, 88, 99, 101, 105, 106, 107, 111, 114, 121, 174; Bingley, Caroline 69, 81, 92, 94, 97, 100, 101, 102, 105, 107, 111, 114, 115, 116, 117, 118, 119, 121, 122, 123, 146; Bingley, Charles 57, 69, 81, 87, 97–98, 99, 101, 102, 103, 104–107, 110, 111, 113, 114, 115, 116, 118, 119, 121, 122; Collins, Mr. 49, 53, 56, 69, 82, 85, 86, 87, 88, 89, 90–91, 92, 93, 94, 95n10, 110, 111, 116–117, 148, 150, 169, 171; Darcy, Fitzwilliam x, 7, 11, 54, 55, 56, 57, 69, 72, 78, 79, 81, 89, 92, 93, 94, 97, 98, 99, 102, 103, 104, 105, 106, 107, 111–123, 140, 160, 166, 167, 168, 169, 170, 175, 180, 184, 185; Darcy, Georgiana 69, 73, 74, 77, 79, 80, 81, 105, 106, 115, 120, 122, 175; de Bourgh, Anne 69, 97, 103, 107, 121, 122, 124n14, 175; de Bourgh, Lady Catherine, 73, 88, 89, 93, 94, 101, 105, 106, 114, 119, 121, 123, 148, 177; Fitzwilliam, Colonel 54, 89, 110, 115, 116, 117, 119; Gardiner, Mrs. (aunt) 80, 113, 117, 118, 120, 175; Lucas, Charlotte 10, 69, 70, 73, 85–95, 97, 102, 103, 107, 110, 111, 112, 114, 117, 118, 132, 145, 146, 147, 148, 149, 150, 151, 174, 184; Lucas, Sir William 88, 94, 111; Pemberley 57, 81, 93, 94, 95, 117; Wickham, George 54, 57, 69, 72, 73, 74, 77–79, 80, 81, 82, 91, 92, 95n8, 102, 103, 104, 106, 107, 110, 111, 113, 114, 115, 116, 117, 119, 120, 122, 140
Pride and Prejudice (1995) 8–9
Pride and Prejudice (1940) 82
Pride and Prejudice and Zombies (Grahame-Smith) 54
primates 4, 21, 25, 28, 36, 37, 111, 165
principle of least interest 79
promiscuity 36, 38, 41, 73, 76, 137, 141; *see also* strategy, short-term, sex, casual
proposal (of marriage) 56, 86, 87, 88, 91, 93, 116, 123, 147, 148, 169, 170
prosociality 40, 100, 114, 120, 185; *see also* cooperation, ultra-sociality
punishment, being punished 50, 72, 79, 81, 94, 97, 114, 141, 159

Rachel's Holiday (Keyes) 157, 160
Radway, Janice 49, 50, 57, 58
rape 19, 50, 55–56, 59n6, 68, 124n8; rapist mentality 55–56, 95n5
reason, rationality 33, 41–42, 111, 153, 161; bounded 42, 94; social 115, 120
Regis, Pamela 8
reproduction, having children 2, 6, 20, 26, 28, 33, 35, 39, 42, 43, 85–86, 94, 150–151, 174, 177–178, 180, 181, 183; reproductive technologies 180
reproductive success 2, 11, 20–21, 29n5, 35, 36, 38, 86, 94, 100, 107, 172, 185
reputation 72, 74, 79, 141
resources, wealth 3, 9–10, 39, 85–95, 112–114, 116, 117–118, 136, 145–151, 180, 184; fortune hunting 39, 92, 146; and love 24, 39, 93, 147
Rich, Adrienne 34
Richardson, Samuel 8, 55, 98–99; *Pamela* 8, 55
Roach, Catherine 51, 57
romance novels, mass-produced, Harlequin, Mills and Boon 8, 49, 50, 53
romantic love *see* love
Run, Catch, Kiss (Sohn) 131

Salmon, Catherine 53, 54, 57, 118
Saunders, Judith 95n9, 140
Schmitt, David 132
Seabright, Paul 105, 165
seduction 73, 74, 81–82
Segal, Lynne 34
self-awareness 54; self-knowledge 119, 184
self-control 75, 80–81, 141
selfishness 73, 79, 81, 82, 141, 142
Sense and Sensibility (Austen): Brandon, Colonel 77, 139–140, 160, 162n4, 175, 180; Brandon, Eliza 74, 77, 141, 175; Dashwood, Elinor 56, 69, 87, 93, 98, 100, 101, 107n5, 121, 130, 146, 175; Dashwood, Marianne 56, 69, 74, 77, 79, 80, 82, 87, 98, 99, 101, 119, 130, 139–140, 158, 175; Dashwood, Mrs. 77, 174; Ferrars, Edward 93, 102, 106, 117, 146, 162n4; Middleton, Lady 175; Palmer, Mr. 99; Steele, Lucy 69, 92, 98, 101, 102, 104, 117, 119, 146; Willoughby, John 74, 77, 78, 79, 106, 116, 139
Sex and the City (Bushnell) 7–8, 9, 131, 151n4, 165
Sex and the City (1998–2004) x, 2, 7–10, 34, 43, 56, 58, 129–132, 183, 184, 185; Big, Mr. x, 11, 56, 129, 130, 136, 147, 155, 160, 164, 165–168, 169, 170–171, 178, 184, 185; Bradshaw, Carrie x, 7, 8, 10, 11, 56, 129, 130, 131, 132, 135, 136, 137, 138, 139, 141, 142, 147, 154, 155, 159, 160, 161, 163–172, 177–178, 179, 184, 185; Brady, Steve 147, 153, 154–157, 159, 160–161, 168, 178–179; Goldenblatt, Harry 150–151, 177; Hobbes, Miranda 7, 10–11, 129, 130, 132, 136, 137, 141, 142, 145, 147, 153–161, 164, 168, 170, 177, 178–179, 180, 184; Jerrod, Jerry "Smith" 137–140, 141, 142; Jones, Samantha 7, 10, 78, 129, 130, 132, 134–142, 145, 154, 158, 159, 164, 165, 166, 167, 170, 176, 177, 179, 184; MacDougal, Trey 147–150, 151, 170, 177; MacDougal, Bunny 148–149, 177; Petrovsky, Alexandr 139, 164, 169–170, 178; Shaw, Aidan 130, 147, 149, 155, 160, 164, 168–169, 170, 171, 178; Wright, Richard 137–140; York, Charlotte 7, 10, 129, 130, 132, 141, 145–151, 154, 158, 159, 164, 168, 170, 171, 177, 178, 179, 184; *see also And Just Like That*
Sex and the City: The Movie (2008) 7, 140, 142, 147, 150, 161, 170, 177
Sex and the City 2 (2010) 7, 177
sex: casual, without love 38, 77, 131–132, 134–136, 138, 142, 154–157, 165–166; empowerment through sex, sexual liberation 9, 34, 50, 130–132, 135–136; and love 22, 156; and reproduction 37
sex differences 24, 38, 39, 40, 136, 166; *see also* individual differences; similarities between the sexes
sexual double standard 72, 82, 90
sexual selection 5, 6, 11, 26, 35–36, 43; *see also* mate choice
sexuality, female 34, 38, 49, 58, 73–74, 130–132, 134–136, 142, 163
shame 57, 81
The Sheik (Hull) 54, 55–56
similarities between the sexes 23–24, 27, 37, 40, 69, 80, 87–89, 91, 111, 166, 185; *see also* sex differences
Singer, Irving 26
single, being single 27, 92, 93, 100, 130, 135, 142, 153, 154, 158, 159, 164–165; old maid 86; spinsterhood 85,
Smith, Stella 165
Smuts, Barbara 4, 55
social constructivism 1, 3, 22, 24, 48, 49, 90
social status 39–40, 88, 105, 112–117, 139–140
Solomon, Robert 42–43, 119, 183
sperm 37–38, 53; sperm donor 180
Stasio, Michael and Katryn Duncan 85, 92, 94, 120
Steinem, Gloria 34–34
Stoller, Debbie 135
strategy: long-term, restricted 25, 28, 36, 38, 39, 41, 54, 57, 111–112, 149, 155, 168–169, 185; sexual, mating, reproductive 2, 11n2, 33, 22, 83n2, 130, 184; short-term, unrestricted 10, 44n4, 72–82, 134–142; short-term vs. long-term strategy 36–37, 38–39, 40, 80–81, 132, 156, 166
strength: physical male 53, 55, 57, 175, 184; female stamina, physical energy 121, 124n14, 175
Symons, Donald 36

Tauchert, Ashley 183
tend-and-befriend strategy 56–57, 100; *see also* friendship between women
Theory of Mind (ToM) 51, 68, 100, 107n6, 186
Thompson, Denise 35
Thurston, Carol 51, 58
Todd, Janet 9
Todd, Peter and Geoffrey Miller 41–42, 94
trade-offs 91, 150; cost-benefit, risk-reward 2, 36–37, 38–39, 58, 74, 80–81, 85, 97, 136, 141, 186

trust 11, 28, 42, 102, 138–140, 161, 169, 186; *see also* commitment scepticism

ultimate and proximate evolutionary goals 20, 28n2, 35, 178
ultra-sociality 2, 51, 101, 105, 186; *see also* cooperation; prosociality
uniqueness, individuality of the beloved 21, 41, 43, 50, 170–171, 184
upbringing 75–77, 87

Vance, Carol 34
variations *see* individual differences

Watsons, The (Austen) 87; Watson, Emma 87, 92, 180
wealth *see* resources
Wharton, Edith 95n9
Whelehan, Imelda 131, 161, 163
Wolf, Naomi 8, 34, 135, 167
Wollstonecraft, Mary 29n11, 67, 98–99, 101, 108n14
Woolf, Virginia 49, 67, 171

Zunshine, Lisa 119